AF531010

GOD THE SELF AND NOTHINGNESS

Reflections Eastern And Western

GOD
THE SELF
AND NOTHINGNESS

Reflections Eastern And Western

Edited by Robert E. Carter

A New ERA Book

PARAGON HOUSE
New York

Published in the United States by

International Religious Foundation
481 Eighth Avenue
New York, New York 10001

Distributed by

Paragon House Publishers
90 Fifth Avenue
New York, New York 10011

A New Ecumenical Research Association Book

Library of Congress Cataloging-in-Publication Data

God, the self, and nothingness: reflections eastern and western /
edited by Robert E. Carter. – 1st ed.
p. 331 cm.
"A New ERA book."
ISBN 0-89226-072-6 : $29.95
ISBN 0-89226-073-4 (pbk.) : $14.95
1. God—Comparative studies. 2. Self. 3. Nothingness (Philosophy) 4. Philosophy, Comparative. I. Carter, Robert Edgar, 1937– . II. International Religious Foundation.
BL205.G64 1990
291.2–dc20 89-77138
CIP

Acknowledgments

SEVERAL PEOPLE HAVE ASSISTED with the initial editing of this volume. Marjorie Haugan, Real Fillion, and Pal Singh Dosaj have been of invaluable help in shaping certain sections, as well as individual sentences which needed editorial "first aid." I offer my heartfelt thanks to them for taking the time to make this book better than it would otherwise have been.

Ann Robertson and Marg Tully were ever willing to type and re-type chapters, as said chapters made their way to my office from so many parts of the world. I am grateful for their patience and care.

To each of the authors I extend my thanks for getting material to me quickly, and in remarkably finished form. The cooperative nature of this project required just the kind of insight and vision which they displayed in the quality of the material itself, and in the honing of it for publication.

Grateful acknowledgment is made for permission to reprint Huston Smith's "Philosophy, Theology, and the Primordial Claim," which appeared in *Cross Currents*, Vol. XXXVIII, no. 3, pp. 276–288 and Sōiku Shigematsu's, "Ralph Waldo Emerson's Zen Universalism," which appeared in *Dialogue & Alliance*, Vol. 2 - No. 1, pp. 95–101.

To all of the above, and to those at New World Foundation Publishing and Paragon House who have helped in bringing this volume to completion, I express my appreciation for your assistance and good will, and my pleasure at the overall ease and fruitfulness of the endeavor.

Table of Contents

Eastern Reflections

Foreword

SOMETIMES VOLUMES DRAWN FROM CONFERENCES lack punch and coherence. This is not at all so with these papers first sketched out and discussed at a trio of conferences and skillfully put together by Robert E. Carter. They focus on the convergence and tensions between Eastern and Western conceptions of the ultimate. The East here means Hindu and Buddhist contributions, ranging from India and Sri Lanka to Japan. The West includes both Jewish and Christian reflections. Within the traditions there is variety of emphasis, as illustrated in the case of Judaism by the contributions of Zwi Werblowsky and Manfred Vogel. Within Christianity we range from Cusanus to Kierkegaard. In Buddhism there is emphasis both on Mahayana and the Theravada, and Hindu multiplicity is always there beneath the surface. Yet there remain some unities, despite the manifest divergences of thought, language, and practice. Nothingness, love, and personhood are three vital themes. I think there is a lot to learn from this volume.

The papers here are not conceived as being at the level of inter-religious dialogue (important an industry as that enterprise may now be), but at thinking through the wonderful ideas supplied by different great civilizations now come together within the contemporary global network. It is a truism that we are living in the global culture, but often we have not learned the real lesson of this: in the West, Confucius, the Buddha, Sankara, and Dogen are as much our intellectual and spiritual ancestors as are Moses, Jesus, Muhammad, Shakespeare and Jefferson ancestors of the East. If I here neglect the South it is merely because the present volume is conceived, not as covering everything, but as selecting for treatment some major figures of the northern hemisphere. This means that philosophy and religious reflection have from now on to be conducted on a world basis. Thinking through the issues is hard, but the effort is rewarding, as will be discovered from the lively but tough-minded articles in this volume.

The 1960s had their pains, but they opened the way in the West to a much more widespread appreciation of cross-cultural living. The results were sometimes crude: now, twenty-five years later, we are reaping the reward of all that creative turbulence. This volume explores the symbolisms of both Being and Nothingness. Between them there may be no gap once we realize that Nothing is not nothing, nor is Being something.

Ninian Smart
University of California Santa Barbara

Introduction

CROSS-CULTURAL EXPLORATION is no longer a luxury to be engaged in by a few intellectual adventurers with a taste for the exotic, intensified by a boredom resulting from the perception that their own traditions have shriveled in importance and insight. Ours is an age of the reading and the re-reading of *texts*. The assumption that a tradition has lost its power to provide meaning is now regularly laid to rest by new and variant readings—of *Job*, the Greek classics, and even a controversial film interpretation of the life of Jesus.

To the extent that Hans-Georg Gadamer's claim that texts do not have a literal meaning has filtered down from the academy to the literate generally, ours has become an age of interpretive plurality. It is an interpretive plurality which applies even to the most sacred and seemingly least interpretively variable of texts. All texts are understandable only from the context of the tradition, i.e., from the context of one's cultural inheritance as a perspectival gestalt from which, and by means of which, one comes to understand anything at all. To read is to read from a perspective, and to read from a perspective is to "translate" otherwise dead and strictly foreign marks on paper into one's own language of understanding.[1] Yet if so much is up for grabs, then it is important to seek out perspectival variations—as part of one's growing and changing horizon of understanding—as a means of continuously checking out the worth and power of one's translational habits.

It is no easy task to indicate how one can alter one's perspective and translational habits, however, for the material of potential change must be looked at through the very lenses and habits that one is supposedly examining. Gadamer suggests that such change and temporary advance is the result of the courage to put one's context-of-understanding at risk. Socrates had also argued that the humility to expose one's assumptions to the questioning of others, together with the wisdom to know that one did not know, would make genuine transformation possible.[2] J.Z. Young insightfully suggests that the suppleness of mind and perspective sought can be encouraged by seeking out new circumstances, new contexts, new translations. Young, a noted brain physiologist, reminds us that "the cortex of the new-born baby has perhaps few innate traits; it is in the main a blank sheet of possibilities. But the very fact that it becomes organized minute by minute, day by day, throughout the years, reduces progressively the number of alternative ways of action."[3] There is hope, however, for "we may forget, or learn new ways of speaking about the world. Some people manage to go on learning new ways much longer than others. Probably a part of their secret is that they constantly seek new circumstances."[4] He continues by remarking that the temptation to stick to the old rules of understanding is very strong indeed, but adds provocatively, "a really useful and interesting brain is always starting off on new ways."[5] The fact that our cultural unity is at a low ebb (and this seems to apply wherever one lives), that cultural, racial, religious and linguistic pluralism is everywhere evident, and that the challenges from the academy of hermeneutics, deconstruction, and post-modernism generally, all lead to a global re-thinking of assumptions and positions that reaches all the way to hopeless relativism. Still we continue to live, to act, to worship or not as before, and we do so in a world-context where, for instance, Japanese management practices and economics meet their American counterparts. If we did not bother to put our cultural assumptions at risk on purely intellectual grounds, we have now begun to do so on economic grounds. The West has awakened to the cultures of the East, *because* the East has begun to make its mark economically, and with a vengeance! Such success, and the increasing industrial success of Korea, China, and India has forced us to ask, "by means of what cultural, religious and philosophical differences have Japan and Korea made their way so quickly to the economic and industrial forefront of contemporary society?"

The present volume is a varied attempt to reconsider religious traditions both from within a tradition and by comparison with other traditions. Either way, these original re-interpretations break new ground as the authors attempt to make sense of texts and practices from the vantage points of dialogue among scholars and practitioners of varying traditions, from many parts of the world. The essays are the result of three conferences: two sponsored by the New Ecumenical Research Association, in Coronado, California (Dec. 29, 1986–Jan. 3, 1987), and Key West, Florida (April 15–22, 1988), and The Sixteenth International Conference on the Unity of the Sciences, Atlanta, Georgia (Nov. 16–19, 1987). The present volume is a selection of some of the best essays from those conferences, grouped according to the theme "God, the Self and Nothingness."

God, the Self, and Nothingness

Nishida Kitarō, who is considered to be Japan's foremost modern philosopher, and who was equally at home in the major Western and Eastern philosophic traditions, characterized the West as having taken "being as the ground of reality," and the East as having "taken nothingness as its ground. I will call them reality as form and reality as formless, respectively."[6] The attempts to explicate the meaning of "God," of "Nothingness," and the relationship of the human individual to either or both of these conceptions constitutes the subject matter of this volume.

Huston Smith's provocative essay examines the primordialists' claim that (1) there is "a Reality that is everywhere and always the same," and (2) "that human beings always and everywhere have access to it." The importance of this claim is introduced in the first half of his essay by reviewing in extremely readable detail the recent history of philosophy, which leaves the modern reader in a "philosophical way-station" where truth and understanding are but current socio-cultural preferences. Smith worries that we are left with a hopeless relativism based on consensus alone. Nevertheless, he is not hostile to the cleansing effect of the deconstructionists who have brought us to the brink of re-thinking our traditions, in order to find a place to stand, and from which to look out at the "pure white light" of reality.

It is interesting that Smith identifies the primordial claim with *tradition*, and that he presumes that there is a privileged reading of the world's traditional religious texts which passes beyond, or beneath, the literal and more orthodox readings of the various traditions. He accepts the charge of elitism for such privileged reading, observes that literal relativism is logically unlivable, insofar as there would be nothing constant on which to stand in order to decide anything, and warns that the term "God" is not, for his purposes, as suitable a term as the "Absolute."

"God" is historically tied to the person, whereas "Absolute" "widens the screen." The personal dimensions of the Absolute are real, but do not exhaust "the abysmal infinity of the Godhead which our rational minds can no more fathom than a two-dimensional mind could fathom the nature of a sphere." Yet we can plumb something of the infinite depth of the Absolute by that faculty within us which "lies deeper in us than reason; it is something like the tropism of plants that orients them towards light." In any case, it is by means of this natural leaning towards the Absolute that we can come to grasp the primordial commonality which renders the various colors of the diverse traditions of religiosity a single pure white light. Thus, Smith holds that there is an interpretative perspective which sheds light on, and even summarizes the differences between traditions, while yet at the same time respecting their colorful doctrinal uniqueness.

R.J. Zwi Werblowsky explores further the mystical claim that there is a capacity within us which is deeper than reason. His exploration of the mysticism of Jewish Kabbalism reveals in a crisp and forthright way the importance to Judaism, including the mystical Kabbalistic tradition, of deciding what is the ultimate relationship of the God of Judaism to the human individual self, and of God to nothingness. He rehearses the usual assumption that mysticality necessitates that the self, in becoming one with the divine, loses its own separate identity, and is ultimately submerged in the Beloved. Werblowsky, following the suggestion of G. Scholem, writes that "the mystic transformation of Judaism had as its highest contemplative value the experience of *communion* as distinct from *union*." The very conception of communion implies God's otherness, else there would be nothing with which to commune. Werblowsky calls it a "new and amazing conception of the Deity," one which appeared to jeopardize the sacred monotheism of Judaism. The oneness of God had become not triune, but *ten-fold*. The divine totality, or *pleroma* was held to be complex, "consisting of ten potencies or foci." These ten "manifestations" of the deity's self-revelation, the ten *sefiroth*, were taken to be ten aspects of a single and unified deity. Nevertheless, the ten "became more and more personified."

Equally amazing is the emphasis on *nothing* that Werblowsky finds in this paradigmatically Western tradition. Mystics "really experience God as the great 'nothing,' as something so utterly hidden that not even existence as such can be predicated of it." *En Sof* ("literally 'Infinite'") is the divine which is completely hidden, and which is not to be found even in Scripture. The first *sefiroth*, *Kether*, is the nothing out of which all else arises, even the other nine *sefiroth' Kether* is the as yet undifferentiated, and yet from it erupts the divine "being" as the remaining nine *sefiroth*. The divine is both being and nothing, as unity. Nothing is an aspect of God himself. It is the "primordial ground" (Boehme's *Urgund*) of all things, including whatever of the divine is, or can be manifest to us.

A very different perspective – again within Judaism – is taken by Manfred Vogel, who carefully unpacks the logical implications of the God of monotheism, or more specifically, the God of "biblical faith." Vogel contends that the issue is only superficially one of monotheism vs. polytheism, a purely arithmetical issue. What is actually affirmed by the biblical "divine," however, is that the divine is the *ultimate* and as such, implies oneness. Surely an accurate system of understanding can have but one ultimate, and it should come as but a small surprise that many polytheistic religions have an ultimate power underlying and unifying their specific pantheon of gods. Thus, the many are actually penultimate, not ultimate. The salient issue, then, is not the one vs. the many, but the *kind* of being the ultimate being is. Biblical monotheism *necessarily* holds that the divine is "a person, i.e., a being-of-consciousness, a Thou," whereas non-monotheistic religions affirm "a non-conscious being, a blind being-of-power, an It." Herein lies the real difference between monotheism and polytheism. By its very essence a Thou is non-quantifiable, and is indivisible, a *one* "that has no parts." Such an interpretation is quite unlike the Kabbalistic ten-fold *pleroma* of the divine. Indeed the tendency towards pantheism which Werblowsky recounts would be exactly what Vogel would predict for a position which did not affirm the unity-of-person of biblical monotheism. Little wonder the tension within Judaism between the possibly heretical Kabbalistic mystics who wrote of a nothing within God, and of a God of various parts, however allegedly unified.

If God is a Thou, then the divine person is separated by a "gap," an "over-againstness," from the world and from other (created) persons. By contrast, non-monotheistic traditions are pantheistic in removing the "gap." They affirm that selves, and the world generally are one and the same with God, i.e., they are "non-other." Monotheism requires that God be an *other*; non-monotheistic pantheism that God is the same. Vogel stresses that the very structure of (personal) consciousness implies that consciousness has its object (the now famous doctrine of intentionality). A conscious subject has as a necessary object of consciousness an overagainstness, and hence there is a necessary "gap" between knower and known. A *thou* can arise only if there is an *other*: "it takes two not only to tango but to constitute a personal being, a Thou." Kabbalistic thought by contrast, as we have seen, sought to attribute *both* oneness and manyness, person and non-person (prior to differentiation), otherness and sameness to the divine. As will be seen, Western mystics like Eckhart, and most Eastern traditions, similarly attempt to include these evidently contradictory characteristics within the divine nature. Clearly the battle of interpretation of the divine nature is joined and seemingly has already been so from the beginnings of philosophy and theology.

Ewert Cousins explores the wider range of mysticism within Christianity, by comparing and contrasting the mystical thought of Augustine and Eckhart. Remarking that the self has been strongly affirmed in Christian thought, he attributes to Augustine the codification of the Christian understanding of the self as in the image of God. Hence, "because the self has its own ontological status, it is not identical with God nor absorbed into God." The self is clearly and distinctly other, and the first part of Cousins' paper is an analysis of the classical Augustinian account of the implications of this doctrine. This "common doctrine" was challenged in the fourteenth century by the German Christian mystic, Meister Eckhart, who spoke of a "not-self." Cousins' definition of mysticism is both broad enough and crisp enough to use as a touchstone of understanding for this volume:

> I am taking mysticism to refer to that kind of human experience in which one has an immediate and intuitive consciousness of transcendence or the transpersonal, whether this be in the context of nature, the self, the divine, or what has been called emptiness or the void.

The reader will wish to study the methodology for the study of mysticism which Cousins' provides in some detail. For the present, however, it is enough to glean from his conclusions something of the resultant contrast in this preliminary typology of Christian mysticism. The inner life of God the Father is "imaged" in the human self as awareness of eternity, truth, and goodness for the trinitarian Augustine. Even in the midst of the mystical experience, the intentionality of such consciousness maintains a distinction between the self as immersed in contemplation of God and the differentiated self reaching up to a higher glimpse of the divine.

The contrast is evident in that "while Augustine's mystical experience retains the self, Eckhart's seems to lose the self. In so doing, Eckhart presents the most striking example within the Christian tradition of a doctrine of the not-self." Evidently heavily influenced by the Augustinian tradition, Eckhart accents God's nature as stripped of all of the positive attributes which Augustine made focal in his analysis of the meaning of "the image of God." The Godhead is above the God of positive characteristics, and the paradigmatic "poor man" of Christianity is to be stripped of not only material and egotistical possessions, but "even of God!" The self is thereby "emptied," even of the pretense of knowledge of God. The Eckhartian intentionality of consciousness is "the emptiness of the Godhead," including God's triune nature. There remains but the "divine abyss." The self penetrates the divine itself as abyss, and the resultant "divine emptiness" appears to wipe away the self (as "image") as well. What is awakened, Cousins contends, is an intentional awareness of "the desert of the Godhead" from which the soul now "finds itself undifferentiated." This is the "not-self."

Cousins reaches the provocative conclusion that Augustine provides a bridge "to those traditions which affirm a position similar to the traditional Christian understanding of the self as image of God, and Eckhart may provide a bridge to those which hold a doctrine of the not-self."

Emilie Zum Brunn's treatment of Eckhart and Nicholas of Cusa continues the exploration begun by Cousins, but with a twist: she finds, particularly in Eckhart, an ecumenism manifested in his openness to discovering equally valid strategies for union with the divine in "the pagan masters, i.e., the Greek philosophers." Zum Brunn shows that Eckhart's emphasis on the "deification" of the self is common to much Greek and Oriental thought, as well as to Eckhart's brand of Christianity. Thus, "some may be surprised that Eckhart's fundamental aim should be 'to become God in God' by returning, thanks to the virtue of detachment, to our original being in the Deity." This accommodating ecumenism is possible for Eckhart because of his belief in the "universality of truth," a belief which "follows from the nature of God: *unus*, the One, and from that of man: *universus*, turned towards the One...." Through detachment, one apparently loses one's self, yet thereby one regains one's "original nature," *viz* one's "kinship with God."

In the century preceding the fourteenth-century Eckhart, a French mystic named Marguerite Porete composed a book which Zum Brunn terms "an important pre-Eckhartian witness." Tried by the authorities of the Inquisition, found guilty of "heresy and relapse," she was burned alive in 1310. Her book, *The Mirror of Annihilated Souls*, spread "all over Europe during the Middle Ages and up to the Renaissance." Zum Brunn finds Marguerite Porete a significant mystic no doubt because of the purity of her spirit, but also because she exposed a spirituality which united the mysticism of love with the mysticism of being. Porete uses the term "self" (*soi*) to describe the ordinary, separate, created self, and "without herself" (*sans elle*) to pinpoint the state of detachment from the ordinary self, and thereby making possible union with the divine. Once again the issue is that of annihilation of self in God, and while Porete writes of annihilation and deification, what is in fact lost is the old, selfish being, and what is gained is "a state of being incomparably higher." Does this constitute true and complete selflessness? She tells us that we can "become God," and says of this that "she need no longer long for Him as if He were separate from her."

At the end of her essay, Zum Brunn resolves the issue by explicitly showing that Porete's description of the divine nature maintains a dimension of the Ultimate that is both ineffable and transcendent. The knowable aspects of the divine being are his being, his love, and his triune nature. Beyond this, "however high our knowledge of God may be in contemplation, something of him remains and will ever remain inaccessible to our grasp." God is inevitably "more than what he communicates of himself to us." Yet it is precisely this that is somehow glimpsed, for in Porete's words, "He is neither known, nor loved, nor praised... and this is the sum of all their love and the last stage on their way." It is this "ineffable transcendence," this something more which is beyond human access,which saves Porete from the charge of pantheism, of the self as being the *same* as God, of the nondifferentiation of self and God. Still, God could be more, and yet the lesser individuals could still be swallowed up in him, like drops of water annihilated in an ocean of waves. That this is not the case is evident in Zum Brunn's poetic account of Porete's highest visions. "This identification...makes the soul which obtains it all the more conscious, and happily conscious of the *Ultimate's ineffable* transcendence."

Mysticism may be said to take love as its theory of knowledge. The standing outside of oneself of mystical ecstasy is achieved by forgetting the ordinary self and identifying with the object/subject of one's love. The resultant loving union is often compared with real human life, where bride and bridegroom unite in sexual ecstasy, yet remain separate and distinct persons. With Eckhart, the Godhead beyond God seems to imply a total loss of self, and, as Marguerite Porete urged, a complete loss of God as knowable. Yet, as Brian Gaybba recounts, love has also played a significant role in the development of non-mystical or academic theology. As he writes in his conclusion, "there is a long and strong tradition within Christian thought that love enables...the understanding of divine truth to take place." His analysis of what there is about love which makes possible the knowing of the divine is that love makes the lover more like the beloved: "The basis of that ability is found in love's power to conform the believer to God." In Augustine's theology, love purifies the soul's "eye," focusing it on God, and at the same time transforms the soul's nature such that it is more "in the image of God." God is love, and to love, both God and one's neighbor, is to transform oneself by bringing out one's godly characteristics. The lover "conforms" to the beloved, and thereby "love deepens our knowledge of what is loved."

Within monastic life, the goal was union with God, i.e., to become like God. Put more strongly still, Gaybba argues that "it would be unthinkable for a thirteenth-century theologian that one could savor divine realities without being united with them through love." Little changed until the middle of the thirteenth century, when Aristotelian epistemology began to override the epistemology of love. Aristotle emphasized logic, not love; reason, not ecstasy. "There was no need to appeal to a divine illumination, no need to appeal to love." Love moved to the background of theology, and with Aquinas the Aristotelian emphasis is given "full force." Love has but a motivational role to play, and "wisdom" is now taken to refer to the knowledge of reason, rather than the knowledge of love-as-conformation. Nevertheless, Aquinas continued to speak of the importance of "love as bringing about an affinity with the divine that enabled a more accurate judgment of divine realities to occur." Furthermore, the principles of theology themselves are still held to come from divine revelation, and hence the basis of the "science" of theology, in Chenu's words "is precisely that which makes it mystical." Perhaps the mystical claim is stretching things a bit, but at least it is clear that love and the non-rational have a place in Thomistic theology. In this sense, love legitimates the insights of theology.

Increasingly, love is pushed further into the theological background, and ceased to play a significant epistemological role in academic theology. Instead, "it remained alive mainly in the mystical movement, one that became antagonistic to academic theology." Gaybba contends, nevertheless, that we would do well to focus on the notion of *insight* and the personal relationships which serve as the assumptions to be investigated within the sociology of knowledge, for these play something of the role that was played by the earlier epistemology of love. The concrete example given is that of contemporary liberation theology, wherein "one must do what is right in order to know what is right." One must live "the Gospel" in order to understand it.

In sharp contrast with the mystical and even the rational academic theologizing of the Middle Ages is Kierkegaard's treatment of God and the self. Nona Bolin traces the appearance of the self in Kierkegaard's by now well-known theory of three stages. The lowest stage, the aesthetic, is not yet constitutive of personal identity, for the aesthete is unable to "express the universal in his love for another." The aesthete is unable to form a genuine commitment, for his thirst for conquest—one lover after another, endlessly without satiation—places his nature inevitably "outside himself." Bolin stresses that "without the commitment to the universal, the aesthete has no inner self. He is simply a shell, a shadowgraph [*symparanekromenoi*] and for him time is circumstantial." The aesthete is outside himself, living the image of Don Juan, ever in search of yet another conquest, never resting within a relationship, or within himself.

The ethical individual of the second stage, finds in conjugal love, and the daily repetition of loving the same person, the "divine...by reason of its occurrence everyday. Conjugal love...is the imperishable nature of a quiet spirit." Authentic conjugal love is an inner movement of the heart, and one spontaneously accepts the duties and obligations of conjugal love as a result. The ethical requirements of duty, loyalty, steadfastness, etc., are universal, and not situational or temporary. This is what makes them ethical. And their validity as universals is the context within which the self "chooses himself absolutely." The self arises absolutely, now, as a self absolutely for he/she has chosen absolutely. Such choice is freely taken, and as such intended. This opens one's interiority, one's self-nature as inner as distinct from the aesthete's self which has no inner nature, and hence cannot truly love, as inner to inner self.

The ethical stage is a comfortable one, and one sinks into it as a Christian sinks into his/her comfortable old couch of churchgoing and ritual. The "fear and trembling" of genuine religiosity has gone out of it. A quiescent unity is created, and "the absolute difference between God and man is obliterated." Faith becomes doctrine, and is passed on "like real estate." Ethics is a rational activity, and it is a necessary step in becoming truly religious to realize that ethics, as the criterion of the right, is in question, as is the power of reason itself. Kierkegaard always shocks, and the shock is at full effect in *Either/Or* where he writes, "There is only one way of supporting the claim that you are in the right...learning that you are in the wrong." The ethical is the lifeline which must be abandoned, jettisoned, if one is to make the turn to religion. This is infinite resignation, and it requires the "teleological suspension of the ethical." The required step is not a rational step, nor is the infinite turn to God rational, yet the turn opens the "gap" between the individual and God. God has to be encountered as "absolute otherness," and "cannot be understood in any traditional way, *not even in terms of the mystical* tradition." God is unknowable. Even the incarnation does not resolve this otherness. Rather, Jesus communicates this very otherness of God to us. What we have revealed to us is our finitude, our difference from God. Part of our selfhood is the recognition within ourselves of what we are not. The *deification* of Eckhart and Porete, and even the "made in the image of God" metaphor, is now left behind. In Bolin's words, "The I confronts its own delimitation such that it is what it is only through the experience of what it is not." Faith now takes the place which the mystics gave to *love*: it is unconditional! But for Kierkegaard it includes the acceptance of the paradoxicality of believing in an unknown God, with no help whatsoever from reason or theology of the usual sort, and requires the relinquishing of oneself to the otherness of God. Whereas the usual hope is that by losing the self one finds a better one, for Kierkegaard, to lose the self is genuinely to lose it. Only a leap of faith remains to take one over the abyss of annihilation without reward, and that is without guarantee.

East-West Transition

Most of the themes discussed in the first half of this volume will be taken up again in the second half, which is Eastern in its focus. Ninian Smart's essay serves as a profound bridge between East and West, and it does so by utilizing a central Christian notion—the Trinity—to understand Indian philosophy and doctrine. Smart proposes a thought experiment, and while it is not his point to say so, it is a thoroughly unKierkegaardian one. Imagine that *we are divine*, he suggests! A strength of Christianity is that God is thought of as having created the sort of world that he would willingly enter into himself. Jesus as the incarnate son is obviously the key image, but throughout the Judeo-Christian tradition God repeatedly acts within human history in this world. Hinduism is replete with divine *avatars*, incarnations of Brahman in this world, and similarly insistent that underneath all the surface noise of egoistic longing and materialist clinging to the fragile social creations of this world, we are all actually divine. The more extreme mystical assertions of Eckhart and Porete within the Christian tradition are both commonplace and accepted in Hinduism: *we are divine*, but we remain ignorant of this very divinity, for the most part.

Hinduism has its *avatars*, and Buddhism has its *bodhisattva* model. Smart notes that whereas not all the *avatars* of Hinduism carry an overt moral message, the Buddhist *bodhisattva* image is essentially a moral one. The *bodhisattva*, like the Buddha himself, is compassionate, benevolent, and loving. What drives this compassion is no simple allegiance to a code of ethical behavior, but a transformation of the notion of *self*. The self, as an individual, discrete, created-at-one-time eternal substance, is a delusion. In place of the self, Buddhists speak of the not-self, *anatta*. This doctrine breaks down the walls of isolation between myself and others. As a not-self, I am a continuously changing field of causal factors, and as such I am what I am in part because of what others are. The totality of circumstances which affect me causally constitute me as I am: a non-discrete intersection or focus of influences, shifting like the "clouds," the image which Smart employs to capture the point. The result of this widening of the boundaries of self, to include whatever influences my focus-as-consciousness, is that I "see that my sole difference from my neighbor is that I affect 'my' future events more than but only more than I affect my neighbor's." In a sense that is more than just metaphorical, I am my neighbor, and she me. Smart remarks provocatively, "I merge with my environment, and overlap with other people." The self is now intrinsically an ecological self, or better, a cosmic-ecological self. Given this new not-self understanding, the aware person now sees "that a self-less person ought to take her wider role in diminishing" the suffering in this world. The result is a view of the not-self as benevolent and compassionate.

Added to the *avatar-Bodhisattva* images, is one taken from Ramanuja: the analogy of the cosmos itself as the *body* of *God*. Smart himself raises the issue of pantheism head on, and puts it to rest as a valid accusation against this perspective by pointing out that while the universe may be thought of as being God's body, this need not be taken to imply that God *is* (only) the cosmos. God/Brahman may be conceived as both within (immanent in) the cosmos, and without (transcendent of) it. But insofar as we are part of the cosmos, and insofar as the cosmos is God's body, then we are divine. Smart then inquires, "So how does the Lord stand in relation to souls? As he stands in relation to the material cosmos." He is the "supersoul," the soul of souls, the "inner controller or *antaryamin*." God/Brahman is both "beyond" us, and yet "embedded" in the depths of each person's soul. The metaphor of "in the image of God" has taken on new meaning. The moral Smart draws from *antaryamin* as secretly, quietly guiding conscious creatures from within (the *Holy Spirit*, the third aspect of the Trinity) is that "the individual can by exploring her own consciousness penetrate to the divine within—which is where in experience the person meets, so to speak, the Spirit."

The concealed, secret operation of the divine within is in line with Smart's perception of divine revelation as "opaque," or obscure: "It is obscure because creatures need a screen, so to speak, between themselves and the Divine Power if they are to have freedom. So Brahman is concealed behind the world, or buried deep within it." This is a challenging gloss on the relationship between God and human freedom.

Smart's assumption—a powerful one for this volume in particular—is "that truth is to be found in the traditions far beyond the Christian." Christians, or others can benefit mightily by enlarging or redirecting their own understanding of the conceptions of their own tradition, by encountering the interpretations of a relevant and similar sort in other traditions. Smart emphasizes that one must be careful not to reduce the distinctness of other traditions to conform to one's own orthodoxy, for the encounter must be genuinely *dialectical*. It must be mutual. In Gadamer's terms, one must put one's own tradition at risk, but not because one is willing to lose it, but only because one will allow its enrichment. Thus, while "it is not realistic to look on the diverse traditions and subtraditions as simply pointing to some single truth," it is equally unrealistic in this pluralistic world to assume that other traditions have nothing to say to us about our own religiosity. "It is better to see the differing traditions as having lessons for one another, and as presenting visions which may help to correct one another." The resultant humility recognizes the "opacity of truth" and seeks a model of the *complementarity* of traditions, rather than an either-or model of faith, tradition, and human understanding. In a final affirmation of this vision, Smart warns that "no faith, whether secular or religious, will in the foreseeable future come to dominate our globe. It will long remain plural."

Finally, and in seeming anticipation of part two of this volume, Smart indicates that the threefold divine Being also transcends the Trinity itself. Speaking of God/Brahman/the Divine as feminine, he writes:

> The threefold Divine Being has three centers of consciousness, one being the *Isvara* [the Father who enters the world], another the *atavara* [the Son] and the third the *antaryamin* [the Holy Spirit]. Of course God transcends these forms.... Beyond the way we relate to her, God is unspeakable: She is the Brahman which is without form. She is the Void, emptiness. She is Suchness, *tathata*. She is that at which the finger points, the dark side of the moon.

She is, as Huston Smith indicated in the opening essay, light in itself, and a "pure white light that summarizes all the wave-lengths" of tradition, future cross-cultural encounters of understanding, and the *hidden* within all of these.

Eastern Encounters

The emphasis on religious experience, as contrasted with religious knowledge, is stressed in S.P. Banerjee's analysis of Hinduism. Hindu spirituality "starts from and returns to an experiential basis." The experience of God/Brahman is pluralistic in that the human mind struggles to grasp the divine nature in a manner easily intelligible to it. Hence, the multiplicity of god forms. The result is not polytheism, however, but henotheism. Henotheism is the "adoring and worshipping of the ultimate Godhead in different forms and locations." What is not so easily dismissed, however, is the distinction "found in some trends of [Hindu] thought...between the God with attributes [*Isvara*] and the attributeless Absolute or the Ultimate [Brahman]." Banerjee discusses the issue of Creation in Hindu thought by providing three models of God as creator: the *potter*, the *spider*, and these two Hindu models are contrasted with Christian creation *ex nihilo* which he terms the *magician*. Whichever of the two Hindu views is considered, an "unbridgeable gulf" between creator and created, God and creatures, is avoided. He quotes Sri Aurobindo approvingly, who writes that "the error is to make an unbridgeable gulf between God and man, Brahman and the world."

Nevertheless, Advaita Vedanta views the *many* of creation to be, in some sense, unreal or illusory, and only the Creator, the *One* is real. In this system Isvara and Brahman are not identical. Even Isvara/God is negated along with worldly multiplicity. For the Advaita Vedantist, "after liberation (*moksa*) the liberated soul and the Ultimate Reality become identical, shorn of any form of distinction." Banerjee warns that such a view is not acceptable to a theist, for the crucial distinction between worshipper and worshipped is eliminated. For the Hindu theist, *bhakti*, the practice of the worship or love of God, may be given a value and place even higher than *moksa*/liberation.

What results is a difference within Hinduism which is irreconcilable: Advaita theory contends that any of the so-called divine attributes (such as omniscience, omnipotence, mercifulness, etc.) apply only to the *penultimate* divinity, *Isvara*, who is not the Ultimate, while for theistic systems God is the Ultimate, and the divine attributes *do* apply.

Appropriately, Banerjee ends his survey of Hindu traditions with a mention of the concept of "nothing." First, and in contrast with some Buddhist traditions, the term "void" is not used. Advaitists do employ the *via negativa* in arriving at the "non-dual Brahman," the Ultimate beyond divine names and qualities. Other uses are noted, but the conclusion reached is that "nothing" is used methodologically, or "relativistically," i.e., as a means to grasping the ultimateness of the Ultimate.

Krishna Sivaraman's analysis of Hindu Vedanta, and Mahāyāna Buddhism begins with the recognition that theistic and non- or trans-theistic versions of the Ultimate or Absolute "criss-cross the frontiers of the two traditions influencing each other conceptually and semantically." Sivaraman's focus is on the notion of "nothing" as a "category of religious meaning, and as a significant description of the divine." He counsels that there are three perspectives on the Ultimate in Buddhist and Hindu thought: the theistic, the non-theistic, and the trans-theistic.

Picking up the thread of spirituality as experience based, Sivaraman holds that "nothing" is a term which refers, within Buddhism, to "confrontation with nullity that is intrinsic to existence itself," namely human suffering. Yet even within Hinduism, the origin is experiential, namely that of error or delusion. What makes it difficult for one to elucidate the precise logical sense of "nothing" is that it is, in a sense, pre-logical: talk and analysis of "nothing" "presupposes a pre-logical encounter with 'nullity' (*tuccha*), an experience where we find ourselves at the very boundary of existence and strike against what in some sense may be called the transcendent or absolute dimension." Perhaps it ought to be indicated here that from the foregoing it is not yet clear whether there is an actual experience of nullity itself—whatever that might mean—or whether what is experienced is the inadequacy of all conception, and the encountering of the boundary, beyond which is the divine, transcendent, absolute dimension.

The sense of nothing applies as well to the self as permanent and implies a renunciation of all values previously assumed and cherished. There is a transvaluation of values resultant, and a transformation of one's perspective on self and world, which now never are (static), but are forever changing. Positively, the whole world of things (*saṃsāra*) is given new value and meaning, for each and every thing is seen afresh, with new eyes, "against the abyss of nothing," *śūnyatā*. Sunya refers not only to nothing in the negative sense of unreality, but positively to that reality which "cannot be expressed through conceptualization, affirmative or negative." To deal with this twofoldness, there are "two kinds of utterances" within Buddhism. Those which, because they can be understood conceptually, ought not to be taken literally, and those which lead beyond such conceptualization and are recognizable as such only by those who can see beyond them.

Hindu Vedanta refers to the Ultimate within the language of being, but only by qualifying the language through use of its negative form: the Ultimate is not that which is not, is preferable to saying that he/she *is*. The Ultimate is that which makes being possible and therefore is not to be identified with being, or beings. The Ultimate is the necessary and sufficient condition of all that is, but is not itself another one of them. It is akin to light, which makes possible the seeing of objects in a room, and yet is not itself one of the objects, nor is it, in any simple sense, itself seen.

Sivaraman resolves the earlier unanswered question about whether one has an experience of nullity, or only an experience of the emptiness of the world of things, including one's own self at the end-wall of conceptual comprehension, for he writes that "it is a revelatory situation," and culminates in a "confrontation with Being which Hindu theology calls 'God,' the 'Ultimate,' and Buddhism would rest content to label as 'nothing.'" On the other hand, the tension is maintained, nonetheless, for he quotes Nāgārjuna approvingly in maintaining that nothing is not actually some*thing* but signifies only "the absence of being as itself a view," or a thing. The empty silence with which one is left may be taken to point to a transcendent and ineffable Ultimate beyond words, or to a denial of all such *signifiers*, except for the flow of this world. *Nirvana* may be *saṃsāra* and *saṃsāra* alone.

P.D. Premasiri approaches Buddhism from the perspective of the spiritual *transformation* of the self. He urges that Buddhism is a non-theistic religion, yet unabashedly argues that it is a religion which is just as concerned with spiritual perfection and salvation as is any theistic tradition. In plain words, "Buddhism speaks of no creator God, of no creation, of no theological plan and above all of no substantial entity called an individual self or soul awaiting to be redeemed by the grace of God." The goal of ***nirvana*** (*Nibbana*) means "peace," or "calm," and is release from the characteristic suffering of this world. Suffering itself is an unsuitable result of wrong thinking, and the *Middle Way* of the Buddha walks between two common but delusory ways of conceiving of reality, *viz.*, *eternalism* and *annihilationism*.

The former posits enduring substance, a substantial reality behind change of whatever sort, and causes one to grasp after such ontological assurance, usually ultimately grounded in enduring "entities such as God, Brahman," etc. Annihilationism holds that existence is discontinuous, and hence that the self does not survive after death, and that long-term spiritual endeavour is futile. The middle way between the two extremes is the Buddhist doctrine of dependent (or interdependent) origination, in which there is no first cause or creator, and all existence is relative or impermanent. Instead, the self is but an intersection of multiple causes, and a changing intersection of varying causes at that. The self is a non-self, a dynamic complex of influences. "'I' in our linguistic usage does not refer to an enduring entity but to a changing psychophysical process." The psychic process (as opposed to the merely physical ones) can continue on, influencing and being influenced, after the death of the body. For this reason, suffering continues beyond the limits of a lifetime, and until the driving conditions of "ignorance and craving" are dissipated. Greed, hatred, and delusion constitute the chains of evil which hold us firmly to lives of suffering.

Enlightenment is the breaking of these chains. The main break is the elimination of the delusory conception of the self as permanent. Craving results from a conception of the self as separate and distinct from the not-self, which one craves because of the delusory separation. Attachment to the self is the cause of that selfishness which considers the desires of the self even "at the expense of everything else conceived as the not–self." It is the *ego* which is the delusory, yet all too real, chief cause of evil and suffering.

The overcoming of suffering requires the dissolving of the notion of the self. Nirvana is the state achieved when the suffering self is eliminated. It is a bliss which Premasiri contends is not a later state of achievement, "but immediately here and now." Such a one no longer creates and sustains suffering for her/himself, or for others.

As to what happens to such a one after death, the Buddha's reply "was that he becomes like the flame of a lamp which is blown out." To probe beyond this, and to inquire about immortality in any other sense, is both irrelevant and unanswerable. Early Buddhism makes no such metaphysical claims, whether concerning the continued existence of the self, or a primary ground of being, a Heaven. There is only release from suffering here and now, and the resultant blissful peace and calm of such release.

David Kalupahana's way into the issues surrounding the self and not-self is to examine the wrong-headed assumption that there is such a thing as "ultimate objectivity," a "view from nowhere" which avoids the coloring subjectivities of culture, ego, time and place. The Buddhist begins his reorientation of perspective by avoiding "the search for ultimate objectivity regarding the subject." Buddha's doctrine of non-self (*anatta*) "is intended to get rid of the 'ghost in the machine' without, at the same time, abandoning any part of the machine." Kalupahana identifies the "dispositions" as being much overlooked yet key ingredients in the makeup of the self, for they unify and integrate the various bundles of awareness (*khandha*) which characterize the self. It is the dispositions which unify and thereby individuate "the subjective stream of consciousness."

Not only is there no objective knowing separate from the dispositions, the bundles, and the stream of conscious dynamism, but there is no object in the same sense as there is no subject (self): "Just as much as stepping outside of ourself will enable one to understand and appreciate the truth about the individual subject, a similar stepping out of the subject will be conducive to the better understanding and appreciation of the object itself." Both self *and* object are "de-mystified and de-solidified." After pointing out numerous similarities between this approach, and the philosophically idealist stance of Bishop Berkeley, Kalupahana deftly contrasts the positions, and the difference is crucial:

> This Buddhist approach, however, differs from that of Berkeley in that the elimination of a mysterious substance to account for the identity and the reidentification of the object is not followed by the introduction of an equally mysterious conception of God. The identity as well as the continuity of the object is explained in terms of the principle of dependence (*patriccasamuppada*) to which we shall return soon.

For this moment, it is important to emphasize that one must be "tough-minded" to attend simply to what is before one, without the slightest addition, accepting the things of perception "as they have come to be."

The great second-century Buddhist Nāgārjuna steadfastly maintained that "dependent arising" (also sometimes called dependent origination, interdependent origination, and even the declaration of interdependence) is a key conceptual tool in the ridding both of substantialist interpretations of both subject and object. Elimination of such substantialist interpretations is called "emptying," and the resultant "emptiness" is *sunyata*. To prepare the ground for an account of dependent organization, Kalupahana suggests that the Buddha himself advocated a three-value logic, in place of standard Western true/false two-value logic. The third value is "the confused," which "allows the possible" to be discussed (in addition to what is the case, and what is impossible). Even the notion of truth, however, takes on a special Buddhist flavor, for truth refers to what is available to us, and decidable on the basis of the experiential evidence of the present *context*. Kalupahana then applies this *contextualist* theory of truth to *ethics*.

The good is that which produces good consequences, "and such consequences are dependently arisen, i.e., depend upon various factors operating within each context." The moral good is contextually determined, and hence "the moral ideal (*dharma*) was never looked upon as an Absolute." Like the image of the raft in Buddhist literature, any effective notion of "good" is appropriate to get across a conceptual river; and, when it has served its purpose, it ought to be abandoned and not carried along one's way: "apart from the context, the raft has no meaning, and it is not possessed of absolute value." Varying contextual possibilities lie ahead, and such possibilities from-the-present counterfactual contexts help to "empty" the hold of the present, keeping open "the reality of new and varying contextual situations...that continue to unfold before humanity as a result of dependent arising and which need to be accounted for."

This analysis affords an insightful re-interpretation of a statement made by the Buddha which has often been taken as evidence of the scandal of immorality within Buddhism. The Buddha's admonition to "abandon the good" is not to be thought of as a skeptic's abandoning of each and all conceptions of the good, but as a warning against holding absolute moral laws as that which is normatively sought. Instead, moral laws are based on concrete moral situations and are thereby changeable. The Buddha "favored the modification of the ideal when it comes into conflict with the concrete," and, hence, was flexibly open to new possible contexts for decision-making. Still, the ultimate law remains, even though in constant need of revised interpretation to fit the ever-changing circumstances of this fluctuating world in which we live: the correct (middle) path must be benevolent, compassionate, loving, and must "contribute to the welfare of oneself as well as of others." How to do this is *dependent* on an analysis of the contextual factors involved.

It is emptying the situation, including those involved in it, of the rigidities and fixities of conception that allows one—as though for the first time—to see things as they actually present themselves, and then to set about to act compassionately accordingly.

John Mayer contributes the first of two essays on the contemporary Japanese philosopher, Nishitani Keiji. Nishitani's recently translated book, *Religion and Nothingness* ends with an exploration of the notion of the absolute or the ultimate as understood from the perspectives of time and history, and it is these themes which Mayer seeks to shed light on as well. The background both to Mayer's essay, and to Nishitani's book is a contrast between a cyclical, seasonal, or natural sense of time—found in India, the Far East, and Greece—and the linear, "once-and-for-all" sense of time of Biblical cultures. After pointing out that even recorded history accepts that the Greeks had significant contact with Eastern ideas, Mayer offers that the individual human being in ancient Greece envisioned himself as taking his place *in the cosmos* and the cosmos is understood as seasonally cyclical ("birth-life-death-rebirth").

By contrast, Jewish culture is based on the "environing whole of history," and not primarily on a sense of the cosmos: "in fact, there is not much Biblical evidence of the awareness of cosmos and the seasonal cycles. Of course it is not the case that the ancient Jew was unaware of these, but rather that he did not attribute much significance to it." The Greeks did not, by and large, emphasize historical continuity and telic unfolding, but simply recorded the coming and going of events. Indian thought, too, speaks of longer cycles of events, with no absolute beginning or end.

Leaving the background aside, Nishitani's foreground concern is that the negativity which emerges in modern times in the West (nihilism) is the direct outcome of "Western religious traditions." The central point that emerges is that Western nihilism has produced an undermining despair, fear, and spiritual paralysis, whereas the East has avoided such creeping despair and negativity "not so much by rebutting it, or avoiding it, but by taking it even more seriously than the European nihilists and secularists do, and arriving at a more spiritually sustaining doctrine of *sunyata* or *zettai mu*—absolute nothingness. This, of course, is the notion of nothingness that we have been stalking for many pages now, in this volume. It is a notion which is made supple and rich enough to "become its very opposite; fullness, life, being, *Tathata* suchness."

Nishitani amplifies the negative nothingness as a doctrine of positive fullness by adopting a Japanese term, whose dialectical force was made a modern Japanese philosophic landmark by Nishitani's teacher and colleague, Nishida Kitarō. The word is "*sive*," and its English approximation has the meaning "is exemplified by," "such as," or "namely." The dialectical usage turns out to be a linguistic formula for calling attention to the paradoxicality of living by dying (i.e., each day is a day closer to some hopefully, distant and yet that very activity *is* living itself), nothingness as fullness, part-whole, one-many, individual-group, personal-impersonal, etc.

While admitting that one sense of time is the stretching back and forward of a linear time in which events occur once, and once only, asymmetrically and irreversibly, he denies that it is either the only sense, or the most spiritual conception. But rather than a momentary, flashing-past sand running out of a glass timer model, the cyclical image can imply an "eternal present," a wholly thereness of the now, full-bodied and robust. The past is the no-longer from the present point, and the future is the not-yet. The linear line-of-time is not only not real, it is swallowed up in the rich fullness of the *momentary sive eternal* present, for the present has, for us, always been, and always will be. Yet it is also but an eternity in an instant, and as such a fragile and contingent emptiness. Here is the root of the positive turn: "this is not a threatening nihility, or better still, it is not merely a threatening nihility, it is a reassuring nihility that can fulfill itself with the transient content of the very-present present. Nothing, in particular, empties itself of its own nothingness to be momentarily disclosed as a this and a now." And while it remains true that suffering, life as death, etc., are not avoided on this fleeting-moment-of-eternity view, the abyss of threatening meaningless and this-worldly paralysis is avoided by a typically Eastern *de-emphasis* of the individual self's importance.

The self is to be overcome, "emptied of its self and personhood." When one lets go of the suffering of the center-focus ego, one's momentariness is merged "into the thusness-as-emptiness of Buddha-nature." The *whole* is now what there is, and the whole self-empties as individuals and as the ten-thousand things of this world. The formula we now know by heart, for the whole *sive* individual is the individual *sive* whole. The solution, salvation (nirvana) is not "yonder," on the other side of historical time, but "right now," close at hand, already here. "The Westerner situates transcendence in the wrong place." The cyclical view, with the Zen Buddhist special emphasis on the eternal now of the-moment-as-alone-real, does not put off redemption to another, later time, in another distant world. The present is the eternal, it is heaven (or can become so), for "the present is shot through with the eternal." The eternal and the present are always already simultaneous.

The issue of compassion is the culminating theme of Mayer's essay, and he links it with "co-dependent coorigination," a term we have already explored and which Nishitani calls "circuminsessional interpenetration." Individual and whole, birth and death are but aspects of the same reality, and the one is inextricably connected with the other because each is the other. Each interpenetrates each and is in turn interpenetrated. I care about the other because I am essentially connected with the other in the profound sense that I am the other! I care about another as I care about myself because I am, in fact, the other. The result is clearly a *cosmic compassion*, although these words are mine and not Mayer's or Nishitani's.

Anticipating my own concluding essay in this volume, Daniel Charles begins his account of Nishitani by emphasizing that the Ultimate, according to Zen Buddhism, can not only never be objectified, but is also "deep enough to encompass even God." More striking still is Nishitani's assertion that "God himself emerged from this nothingness. No doubt this is why most Christian mystics still speak of God as 'Him,'" whereas Zen thinkers more commonly speak of nothingness or emptiness. Admitting the easy assumption that an immanence of unified nothingness may indicate a pantheistic view, Nishitani remarks that the "existential" encounter of the omnipresence of God/Nothingness is not simply impersonal *or* pantheistic. Applying the logic of *soku-hi* which we have already encountered as *sive*, our relationship with the Ultimate whole is personal-*sive*-impersonal. What is behind the "mask" of individual personhood is "nothing at all." This complete nothingness behind persons, which is at the same time our connection-of-identity with the ultimate whole of things, is "the absolute negation of person," hence person-*sive*-impersonal. More precisely, even this "nothing standing behind" must be *emptied*, leaving the shocking Zen Buddhist insight and claim that "there is nothing that is nothingness, and this is *absolute* nothingness." Nothingness is not yet another thing, but that which can be acknowledged only as the negation of things (individuals, particularities). And, of course, against this background of seeming negativity, the world of individual things now stands out, foregrounded in a backlighted sea of nondifferentiation, and against which each and every thing is now seen as though for the first time. As in the famous ten oxherding paintings, after the blank "Zero" or empty circle of the eighth depiction, the ninth frame presents full-flowered blossoms, and a luxuriant landscape seemingly Eden-like in freshness and newness.[7]

Turning to Nishitani's view of history, Charles confirms that the background of nothingness ensures "a sense of history that realizes the absoluteness and incomparability of each moment." In each moment the whole, the eternal, is present insofar as all particular things are co-interdependently the same-as-nothingness beneath their particularity. A is A, and B is B, "*yet* at the same time A and B penetrate each other." Rather than being seen as a contradiction, what results is recognition of the "two sides of the same coin." Therefore, the self both *is* the self, and *is not* the self." The Zen Buddhist understanding of the true self is recognition of the self as arising as a particularity out of nothingness "at the root-source of history." Such a history of the point before and at the origin of the history (of individuals) itself, is a "suprahistorical history."

Yet we can find this seemingly distant and vague beginning of beginnings "in the home-ground of each man, underfoot and right at hand." In this sense we are both inside and yet (*sive*) outside of history, inside and yet outside of time. From the horizon of emptiness or nothingness, all time, and even the before time, enters into each moment. Again, the instant is eternity and, therefore, each particular time is also every other time. We are thereby delivered from the bondage of craving for progress, of historical inevitability, of getting somewhere in particular. Time simply continues to unfold, to manifest. Similarly, we are delivered from the bondage of the self-centeredness of the self, for the self is also a not-self. At our depths—our bottomless depth—ego is not ego.

Daniel Charles provides an interaction between Buddhist and Christian thought by comparing and contrasting the notions of God and absolute nothingness. Absolute nothingness is itself "the hall of ultimate reality," and not just the gate or portal leading to it. Absolute nothingness is not "nothing" in the negative and typically Western sense of denial or negation. Rather, it is what remains after both relative being and relative non-being (nothing) are themselves negated and overcome. Absolute nothingness is itself "beyond" both being and non-being, and yet the source of both, i.e., ontologically prior to both and out of which they arise. Positivity and negativity must both be overcome, and, by so doing, dualistic thinking itself is left behind. Charles agrees with Abe Masao that "the ultimate which is beyond the opposition between positive and negative is realized in the East in terms of negativity and in the West in terms of positivity." What Charles demonstrates here, as earlier essays in this volume have echoed as well, is that the West has also glimpsed the ultimate as that which can only be expressed in negative terms reminiscent of Eastern nothingness.

Pseudo-Dionysius the Areopagite wrote of God as the Godhead: "undefinable, unnameable, and unknowable, beyond dark and light, true and untrue, affirmation and negation." Yet, as Abe points out, Pseudo-Dionysius refers to the ultimate as "Him," and other Christian mystics of the same period called God "Thou." Charles emphasizes that the most recent study of the works of Pseudo-Dionysius argues that previous translations have added a hermeneutic overlay to the texts, straying from the "*non-metaphysical*" stance of the original. As the cause of all that exists, the divinity is both the same as, and different from, the beings created. Negatively, the divine is beyond being, while positively, it is the being of beings.

Religiously, there is the possibility of going beyond both affirmative and negative theology and to "plunge into a darkness of unknowing; such an unknowing is the requisite for an immediate experiencing of divinity as pure nothingness." But *negative mystical theology* requires the denying of the dualistically oriented claims of the sameness and difference between the divine and the things of the world. Quoting Pseudo-Dionysius, we read that from the vantage point of unknowing, "no unity or trinity or numbers, or oneness, or anything among beings, or anything known among being ... beyond all beyond logos and intellect...." It is the denial of every intellectual and ordinary linguistic standpoint. The God of Pseudo-Dionysius is even beyond the God of unity, from which multiplicity arises, of Plotinus, God is beyond both unity and multiplicity, both trinity and unity, and even beyond whatever is or might be "conceived by us or any other being." Charles deftly "corrects" interpretations of Plotinus as well, pointing out that there is ample evidence that he too pushes beyond language, beyond the conceptuality of the intellect, to the silence of the unspeakable and the unknowable.

The Eastern description of absolute nothingness is, thus, fully and exactly echoed by both Plotinus and Pseudo-Dionysius in the West. The same can be said of Meister Eckhart, as well. Charles asks, however, whether the Christian preference for speaking of the divine as "Him" does not remain as a significant difference between East and West on the ultimate. Wisely, he searches out an answer to this question by turning eastward, to the writings of Nishitani, who makes clear and distinct that the God of mystical negativity "is not impersonal in the usual sense of the word." Instead, our relationship with/to the divine is, in Nishitani's words, an "*im-personally* personal relationship, or a *personally* impersonal relationship." The mask of God-as-person has behind it nothing, but it is this very nothing which brings the mask ("person" comes from *persona*, meaning "mask"), the person, to *be*. The person emerges from nothingness, as an articulation of it, as Jesus himself within the Christian tradition "emerges from nothingness."

The resultant God-inspired ecstasy both deifies the human, and, through the relational, humanizes the divine. It is only through, in Mantzaridis' words, "the descending ecstasy of God and the transcendent ecstasy of man [that] their mystical meeting and union is achieved." Charles' evident Christian standpoint takes Christ as the profound revelation of the possibility of the deification of human beings. Nevertheless, he comes to understand this by means of the clear critique of Christian theology by an Eastern thinker and with the help of the re-discovery of the mystical tradition in Christianity so frequently occasioned by Eastern thinkers such as D.T. Suzuki, Nishida Kitarō, and Nishitani Keiji. In this way, his essay is truly reciprocal and comparative. Of course, the Buddhist is not likely to adopt the Christocentric realization provided, for a re-translation would no doubt stress that all humans are already divine, possessed of Buddha-nature and need only peel off the blinders of ignorance to see this. Zen Buddhist *satori* or enlightenment is more a seeing into one's own nature (*kensho*) and less an ontological transformation made possible by Christ entering the world, or an encounter with a God-becoming-human. Buddhism does not claim ontological transformation, but *recognition* of the always already. Still, Charles, too, ends by observing that "we live *already* in the realm of 'realized eschatology,'" and if the past/present/future/eternity distinctions are also overcome, the Buddhist-Christian differences may be considerably less than heretofore imagined.

Others have noticed that American Transcendentalism shares much in common with Eastern thought, but it is unusual to find a Zen Buddhist priest and noted scholar whose main intellectual concentration is the forging of links between East and West. Shigematsu Sōiku specializes in the study of the writings of Ralph Waldo Emerson. Just as Emerson remarked that "whatever we do, self is the sole subject we study and learn," the thirteenth century Zen Master Dōgen taught that "to learn the Buddhist way is to learn oneself." How does one study the self?

The image of inward-directed centripetal mental energy is applied to both Emerson and Zen. Whether we are scientists, ship navigators, architects, or members of any other profession, "the great business of life is to learn ourselves." Self-denial is a requirement for the turn inward, states Emerson, and God is to be found by so looking inward. Similarly, Shigematsu quotes the Chinese Zen Master Lin-chi I-hsuan who taught, "Don't seek any truth outside yourself!" and that "innocence" and "absolute submission" are necessary in order to meet God within. In Buddhist terms, it is essential that "one empty oneself as if to pour out a bowl with old dirty water and wait ... until we touch our original identity."

Emerson described this transformation of awareness revealing the original identity by means of his infamous "transparent eyeball" metaphor. All egotism eradicated, Emerson pictured himself as a transparent eyeball: "I am nothing; I see all; the currents of the Universal Being circulate through me; I am part or parcel of God."

Shigematsu includes a drawing of the transparent eyeball by a contemporary critic of Emerson. The critic missed the point, however, for to be truly transparent, it would have to have been without form, invisible, without color, size or weight. It would be "nothing at all" from the point of view of the external sense organs. As in the case with the famous Zen oxherding pictures, this nothingness could only be hinted at as an empty circle bounded by a fading brushstroke (picture number eight). Indeed, it is precisely Shigematsu's point that had Emerson "known the methodology of Zen practice, he could have expressed his thought more consistently."

As an alternative image, one might think of Zen as "a ball of Universal-Individual-Vital-ism." Imagine this sphere rolling along, and alternately showing these three "colors" or faces as it turns. Completing Dōgen's condensed teaching about the study of the self, we read that to learn about the self is to forget the self, and this in turn is confirmed by all of existence enlightening us, resulting in the casting off of one's body and mind. Thus, the self that we come to forget is the ego. This we must learn first. The result of this forgetting is that "we become 'nothing' and deep within ourselves, we are 'to perceive'" ourselves as confirmed. We then see things as though at a distance, and the distorting surface ripple and glitter is stilled. We are able to look at the world, the universe, apart from local change and coloration. "Human egotism is the very cause of distorted perception and biased vision. When it is gone, our existence returns to the original Nothing, which forms the basis of each and every thing." In Zen terms, this is the ***unborn*** mind, without form or appearance. The world of ten thousand things exists only conditionally, impermanently, interdependently, "and has no substance." Beneath or behind such impermanence lies nothing, the prevailing emptiness out of which everything with form arises. The ten thousand formed things are articulations of the formless, the so-called void. When one is likewise as though nothing, one sees all, i.e., one is confirmed and enlightened by all things. One is a transparent (nothing) eyeball (seeing everything).

Picture number nine of the oxherding sequence depicts a world renewed, radiant with beauty and seen as though for the first time by one who has just returned from the brink of the annihilation of death. The Buddha awakens from his meditative state, and the single star in the heavens is now indistinguishable from his own nature. At the depths of self, the awareness of cosmic interdependence makes all things one. The Buddha could say "I'm shining." Emerson, too, reporting an experience of ecstasy, exclaimed that he "felt the centipede" in him; "cayman, carp, eagle, and fox. I am moved by strange sympathies." Nothing is everything, and everything is nothing: ***nirvana*** is ***samsāra*** and ***samsāra*** is *nirvana*. Against the background of nothingness, everything is the foreground of everyday particularity and form is highlighted, stands out, is backlighted so to speak. The distinctions between bell, listener, and the ringing sound of the bell all merge into *ringing*. The "I" vanishes, and the bell becomes ringing only. Dualistic experience yields to non-dualistic pure experiences of the eternal now—right now, for there is no other time, ever, except right now. Emerson, too, indicates that his transparent eyeball experiences are akin: "A crow's voice filled all the miles of air with sound. A bird's voice, even a piping frog enlivens a solitude and makes world enough for us."

Body and mind have fallen off in that we now apprehend the world "without any human coloring and defilement by egotism." To see the world in this way is to be *transparent* to it, to let the world appear in its "suchness." The transparency of Zen can be taken as the analogue for Emerson's transparent eyeball. Not only this, but Emerson's God is "no other than the 'transparent eyeball,'" for "God in us worships God." It is God who sees the landscape, who is the landscape, and who is behind, or the background of the landscape itself. Emerson's God is Zen Buddhism's nothingness.

The final essay is my own, and much of what I have already said in this *Introduction* has touched on issues raised therein. Nevertheless, a few comments are needed to place the essay in context. The central figure of the essay is Nishida Kitarō, generally considered to be Japan's most famous and brilliant modern philosopher. The founding spirit of the Kyoto School, Nishida was succeeded in his chair at Kyoto University by Nishitani. It was Nishida and his boyhood friend, D.T. Suzuki, who revived both respect for and interest in Eastern thought and in particular Zen Buddhist thought. It is no less a struggle in our time than it was just a few decades ago in Suzuki's prime to hold fast to the ideals of earlier times, while recognizing the fact that it is Western ways of thinking which will bring prosperity, equality, and strength. The temptation was either to hide from Western new-think, and to become reactionary and out of touch, or to jettison the older ways altogether, and to dress and think like a Westerner.

It was Nishida who learned Greek, German, French, and English, at least to the extent to which he could work with Western philosophical sources, in order to use the state-of-the-philosophic-art to reveal the wisdom of Eastern thought, and, in particular, the Eastern pre-occupation with nothingness. As such, he is a *bridge par excellence* between East and West, for he struggled over a long lifetime to use Western philosophic techniques and concepts to unravel the meaning and significance of the most complex and difficult Eastern notions.

My way into Nishida's thought is via Heraclitus and William James. It was James who first used the term "pure experience," and this term catapulted Nishida to write his first book, *A Study of Good*. The account of the flow of pure experience leads to a rather intense analysis of the logic of *soku hi* "the absolute identification of the is, and the is not. A is A; A is not-A; therefore A is A. I see the mountains. I see that there are no mountains. Therefore, I see the mountains again, but as transformed." This resultant transformation is the seeing that the mountains both are (separate and particular mountains), and that they are not. They are empty, they co-exist with all else, and so penetrate and are penetrated by all else. The result is stereoscopic vision; the seeing of the part and the whole, the particular and the emptiness, the thingly-ness and the emptiness at one and the same time. Thus, in Nishida's own words, "One becomes the many, and the many becomes One.... The Absolute is what embraces both of these opposite directions as the Self-identity of contradiction." Nishida's at first cryptic depiction of things as self-contradictory identities now begins to make sense and to explain what heretofore was but disorienting. The world is simultaneously being and nothingness. All things are what they are, and yet, at the same time, are "lined" with nothingness, as a good kimono is lined with the most precious of silk. Ironically, the lining is unseen, hidden, at the inner depths of the kimono. Yet it can be recognized in the "hang" of the garment. It is the double aperture, the stereoscopic vision of which Nishida speaks that allows us to see beneath the surface hang of things, to their co-origination, their interpenetration, and to their classically Buddhist emptiness.

If nothing else, Nishida brings us, and language, to a more faithful representation of the richness of immediate experience, of lived experience, than was heretofore possible. As a gloss of hope for East/West understanding, Nishida wrote that, so far as he could see, "Reality is both being and non-being, it is being–*qua*–non-being and non–being–*qua*–being. It is both subjective and objective, both *noema* and *noesis*. Subjectivity and objectivity are absolutely opposed, but reality is the unity of subjectivity and objectivity, i.e., the self-identity of this absolute opposition."[8]

It would be too simple to suppose that the *Yang* orientations of the West, and the *Yin* orientations of the East could simply be taken to be two perfect halves of an ultimate whole. There is too much to be considered in the many traditions that will not fit and likely will not blend without force and compromise. Nevertheless, it would be an even greater mistake to suppose that the highest religious and philosophical achievements of East and West are necessarily in opposition, making the clashes to come inevitable. Instead, it would be wiser to struggle to see whether, as Nishida suggests, the greatest insights about the most important matters come from a joining of perspectives, Eastern and Western, in an attempt to glimpse whatever can be glimpsed of the infinite and inexpressible. Being and nothingness may *together* add up to a total which yields a more complete, though still only a partial, understanding of the "shadow of the Eternal." God, Godhead, Nothingness, the Ultimate, are ways of speaking about, if not the same reality, then about genuine aspects of, and stages along, the experiential "way" of human spirituality.

NOTES

1. Hans-Georg Gadamer, *Truth and Method*, ed. Garrett Barden and John Cumming (New York: Seabury Press, 1975), 349.
2. For a discussion of Socratic humility and education, see ch. 1 of R. E. Carter, *Dimensions of Moral Education* (Toronto: University of Toronto Press, 1984).
3. J. Z. Young, *Doubt and Certainty in Science: A Biologist's Reflections on the Brain* (Oxford: Oxford University Press, Galaxy 1960), 70.
4. *Ibid.*, 106.
5. *Ibid.*
6. Nishida Kitarō, *Fundamental Problems of Philosophy: The World of Action and the Dialectical World*. tr. with an introduction by David A. Dilworth (Tokyo: Sophia University, 1970), 237.
7. The ten classic drawings are by Kuo-an, while the original text dates from the twelfth century. One translation is by M. H. Trevor, *The Ox and His Herdsman* (Tokyo: The Hokuseido Press, 1969). A fine contemporary depiction is by Tomio Nitto, in my own *The Nothingness Beyond God: An Introduction to the Philosophy of Nishida Kitarō* (New York: Paragon Press, 1989).
8. Nishida, *Fundamental Problems of Philosophy*. 246.

Western Reflections

1

PHILOSOPHY, THEOLOGY, AND THE PRIMORDIAL CLAIM

Huston Smith

PRIMORDIAL MEANS "no matter where or when" and the primordial claim is that there is, first, a Reality that is everywhere and always the same; and second, that human beings always and everywhere have access to it. Not equal access if it is conscious access we are thinking of, for there is no reason to suppose that minds that differ in every other respect—mathematical talent, musical genius, problem-solving ability—flatten out when they turn to reality; some people scarcely think about reality at all. But there is no reason to suppose that people in the aggregate—societies, civilizations, and cultures—differ in metaphysical talent. Eliade tells us that for archaic societies "*the world exists because it was created by the gods*, and that the existence of the world itself 'means' something, 'wants to say' something, that the world is neither mute nor opaque, that it is not an inert thing without purpose or significance."[1] One can quibble about the plurality in the word "gods" in that statement—it would *be* a quibble, for the alternative to monotheism is not polytheism but dualism—but is there anything in the entire history of theology that supercedes, let alone retires, that initial, may we say primordial, discernment?

Not everyone will be persuaded by the primordial claim, which takes us back to the individual differences just alluded to. Logically speaking, the primordial is inescapable, being simply the *yang* side of the yang/yin, one/many polarity that governs thought throughout. (When we apply that logic to things, for example, it is at once evident that everything both resembles and differs from everything else: resembles it in that both exist, differs or there would not be two things but one.) But though it is impossible to dispense with the primordial, it can easily be downplayed, the obvious way being to grant it conceptual status only; it is an important tool for thought, but there is nothing in the objective world that corresponds to it. Nominalism versus realism, the abstract versus the concrete, monism versus pluralism, the one and the many—the alternatives have been debated a thousand times and will never be balanced to everyone's satisfaction because (providentially, may we assume, to the end that both poles receive their just due?) some minds, as the saying goes, are temperamentally "lumpers" while others are "splitters." This essay argues for the integrating, primordial term as not only indispensable but privileged; if we are to weigh the two poles (and if we are to be thorough we cannot avoid doing so), what endures is more important than what passes, what pervades is more important than what is local. Wholes are more important than their parts, for the sufficient reason that they include their parts. Earth exists, but "only heaven is great" (Chinese maxim).

One gets little inkling of all this from the current winds that are blowing in philosophy and religion, so it is with those winds that I shall begin. I could ignore them and simply *present* the Primordial Claim, but that would be to acquiesce to the current fate of that claim which is to be, not rebutted, but ignored. So if the mountains will not come to Muhammad, let Muhammad go to the mountains. Elsewhere I have presented the Primordial Claim in its own right, in both book and essay length.[2] Here the emphasis will be on its resources for helping philosophy and theology over shoals they are now traversing.

I begin with philosophy, using as my entree the plenary address Richard Rorty delivered at the Inter-American Congress of Philosophy which convened in Mexico City in 1985.

Philosophy

If nineteenth-century philosophy began with Romantic Idealism and ended by worshipping the positive sciences, Rorty points out, twentieth-century philosophy began by revolting against a narrowly empiricist positivism and is ending by returning:

> to something reminiscent of Hegel's sense of humanity as an essentially historical being, one whose activities in all spheres are to be judged not by its relation to non-human reality but by comparison and contrast with its earlier achievements and with utopian futures. This return will be seen as having been brought about by philosophers as various as Heidegger, Wittgenstein, Quine, Gadamer, Derrida, Putnam and Davidson.[3]

That says a lot in small compass, so let me repeat it while inserting a few particulars. The nineteenth century began with a reaction against the scientism of the Enlightenment, protesting its claim that mathematical demonstration provides the model for inquiry and positive science the model for culture. It ended, though, by swinging back to Enlightenment predilections and shunting off into literature the counter-Enlightenment sentiments that had given rise to the Romantic Movement and German Idealism. So philosophy entered the twentieth century allied to science. Experimental science being outside its province, this meant following Husserl and Russell into mathematics and logic. Husserl soon deviated from that program to found a brand-new approach to philosophy—phenomenology—which would replicate science's apodicticity without using its logic. Heidegger's *Being and Time* subverted that move and thenceforth continental philosophy renounced both apodicticity and deduction. In English-speaking countries, though, Russell's slogan that "logic is the essence of philosophy" persisted, and ability to follow completeness proofs for formal systems replaced foreign languages as a professional requirement.

Even the Anglo-American attempt to 'do philosophy' via logic eventually abandoned apodicticity, though, for non-Euclidian geometries showed logic to be flexible; since it works equally well with whatever primitives we begin with, it produces nothing that is unequivocal. In their *Principia Mathematica*, Whitehead and Russell spelled this out by developing a "logic of relations" to replace the logic of things, and Cassirer and C.I. Lewis went on to relativize Kant whose *Critique* had dominated modern epistemology. The human mind is not programmed to see the world in a single way. It sees it in different ways as times and cultures decree.

This drive towards pluralism didn't stop with epistemology; it pressed on into ontology. Having satisfied themselves that our minds require nothing of us, philosophers proceeded to argue that the world doesn't require anything of us either. Their way of doing this was to go after Plato's essences and Aristotle's substance, for if these exist they could draw the mind up short and thinking would not be indefinitely malleable. Again it is important to see this second rejection—the rejection of the fixity of things to accompany the rejection of the fixity of logic—as motivated by the same determination to stem the tide of the Enlightenment Project in its twentieth-century positivistic version, for, if there is a way things *are*, it was pretty clear that the twentieth century would take it to be the way the sciences collectively report; the Vienna Circle with its "unification of science movement" was championing just this denouement. Rorty brings these two rejections together and shows how central they have been to our century's philosophy:

> I do not think it far-fetched to see such different books as Carnap's *Logische Aufbau der Welt*, Cassirer's *Philosophy of Symbolic Forms*, Whitehead's *Process and Reality*, C.I. Lewis' *Mind and the World Order*, Langer's *Philosophy in a New Key*, Hartshorne's *The Divine Relativity*, Quine's *Word and Object*, Nelson Goodman's *Ways of Worldmaking*, Putnam's *Reason, Truth and History*, and Davidson's *Essay on Truth and Interpretation* as developments of the anti-Aristotelian and anti-substantialist, anti-essentialist implications common to *Principia Mathematica* and to the development of non-Euclidian geometries (*ibid*).

Again, we should not lose sight of the motivation in all this. Seeing no way in which (in the face of the scientistic temper of our century) it could register a view of reality that could compete with the scientistic one that was gaining ground, philosophy took the next best step. It went after the notion of a single world view *period*: the notion that there is one unequivocal, comprehensive way that things actually are, or if there is, that human minds can have any knowledge of what that way is. This meant renouncing what historically had been philosophy's central citadel, metaphysics. Better no metaphysics at all than the one that was threatening to take over.

But if the "post-Nietzschean deconstruction of metaphysics" excused philosophers from thinking about the world, what should they be thinking about? We saw that during the early, positivistic decades of our century when philosophers thought science was the royal road to truth,[4] they latched onto logic as the slice of science that they could service: let the empirical scientists discover synthetic truths; philosophers would monitor the analytic truths that were also needed. In 1951, though, Quine demolished the analytic/synthetic, fact/meaning distinction with his "Two Dogmas of Empiricism." With the analytic rug thus pulled out from under them, philosophers retreated to ordinary language for a preserve of meaning that didn't depend on logic yet needed attention.

Now, though, the wall around that refuge is being dismantled by Donald Davidson's critique of the distinction between the "formal" or "structural" features of discourse and its "material" ones. The correct theory of meaning, Davidson argues, is one that dispenses with entities called "meanings" altogether; instead of asking "What is the meaning of an expression?" it asks, "How does this expression function in this particular linguistic move?" With this total de-logicizing and naturalizing of language, the division between it and the rest of life disappears. Instead of a "structure" or body of rules that philosophers can isolate, study, and help others to understand—or even the multiple structures and rules that Lewis and Cassier talked about—language now looks like simply another human way of coping with the world.

This helps us to understand why philosophers in appreciable numbers seem to be moving towards closing down their discipline, for if logic isn't philosophy's essence (Quine) and language isn't either (Davidson), what remains? Wittgenstein came to see its only function as therapy—undoing the mental knots philosophy itself creates. Heidegger announced the end of metaphysics to which Rorty has added "the end of epistemology." And now James Edwards and Bernard Williams are turning down the lights on philosophical ethics with their *Ethics without Philosophy* and *Ethics and the Limits of Philosophy* respectively. What remains after these closures seems to be "conversation" and "play," to which neither Rorty nor Derrida see philosophy as having anything distinctive to contribute.

Philosophy is obviously in crisis, and I think we can see the reason why. It is coming to recognize that autonomous reason—reason without infusions that both power and vector it—is helpless. By itself, it can deliver nothing apodictic. Working (as it necessarily must) with variables, variables are all it can come up with. The Enlightenment's "natural light of reason" turns out to have been a myth. Reason is not itself a light. It is more like a transformer that does useful things, but on condition that it is hitched to a generator.

We have already watched Rorty point out that for the bulk of this century it was science's premises that powered Anglo-American philosophy, whereas continental philosophy turned to literature. He ends his address by noting that politics provides a third possible generator for philosophy, but he advises against it since "to assume that it is our task to be the avant-garde of political movements" would reduce philosophy to propaganda.

There is a fourth possible 'primer' for philosophy though, which Rorty doesn't mention, perhaps because he is himself powered by it to the point where he simply takes it for granted. This fourth generator is social science and the rising importance of names like Habermas and Gadamer suggest that the sciences of man are displacing the natural sciences in providing philosophers with their premises and problems. If science shouldn't monitor our thinking because it countenances only half of reality, and metaphysics (which tries to work from reality's whole) is pretense and delusion, let societies—"forms of life," or cultural-linguistic wholes—be the final arbiters of meaning, reality, and truth. It's as George Will says: "the magic word of modernity [is] 'society.'"[5]

The concept that points philosophy in society's direction is holism. Even while science powered philosophy, mounting evidence for the mind's propensity to gestalt its experience led Hanson to argue that "all facts are theory-laden" and Thomas Kuhn to write *The Structure of Scientific Revolutions*, for twenty-five years the most-cited book on college campuses and the one that turned "paradigm" into a household word. Heidegger and Wittgenstein had already pushed matters past theoretical into practical holism, though.[6] Because thinking invariably proceeds in social contexts and against a backdrop of social practices, meaning derives from—roots down into and draws its life from—those backgrounds and contexts. This means that in considering an idea, not only must we take into account the conceptual gestalt of which it is a part; we must also consider the social "forms of life" (Wittgenstein) whose "micro-practices" (Foucault) give gestalts their final meaning. "Agreement in judgment means agreement in what people *do* and *say*, not what they *believe*," Wittgenstein insists.[7]

This move to work in concert with the sciences of man signals more vitality than the proposal to abandon ship, but it seems unlikely that philosophers will content themselves indefinitely with deadening their questions in forms of life. For social wholes are self-enclosed; unrelieved, a form-of-life is a kind of collective "egocentric predicament," if not solipsism. Those predicaments can seem invincible if one accepts their premises, but philosophy has never entirely surrendered to them.

The two boundaries that social holism acquiesces to are, first, ones that separate such wholes from one another and, second, the one that isolates configurations of phenomenal experience as such from the nominal world that transcends them. Admittedly, both walls are difficult to breech. Two decades of trying to figure out how tribes that speak different languages could communicate have made us conscious of how difficult it is to transcend cultural-linguistic horizons, while phenomenology's *epoche* all but gives up the effort to transcend the phenomenal world; David Pears calls Wittgenstein's conclusion that "there is no conceivable way of getting between language and the world and finding out whether there is a general fit between them" the central thesis of his later years.[8]

When all is said and done, however—when we have made every concession we can think of to the difficulty (verging on impossibility) of climbing out of our skins, out of our languages, out of our cultures, out of our times—the fact remains: of all life forms on earth, we and we alone, possess the ability to view the world with detachment, which is to say to some degree trans-perspectively and objectively. This is the important point in Thomas Nagel's *The View from Nowhere*: that we can think about the world in terms that transcend our own experience and interests—and, yes, our times and cultures too, the primordialist claims—considering those from a vantage point which, being not entirely perspectival save as it is humanly so, is "nowhere in particular."

The first place where the limitations of cultural-linguistic holism are beginning to show up is in the difficulties it is having with the problem of relativism. If the issues of philosophy lead to (and deadend in) a plurality of collective, phenomenal configurations of experience leaving us no more than social functionaries, there appears to be no court of appeal for adjudicating between these collective experiences. If forms of life are the bottom line, what recourse is there for affirming that one such form is better than another? Is there any way we can take seriously the possibility that our own cultural-linguistic epoch, say, may have taken a wrong turn; and again, if so, by what criterion? Pragmatic outcomes seem to be the only court of appeal, but though useful for provisional purposes, pragmatic criteria never tell the whole story, for if cockroaches are to inherit the earth, that would not induce us to consider them our superiors. Cultural-linguistic holism stammers answers to relativism;[9] it can counter "vulgar relativism" by appealing to currents of consensus that underlie superficial differences. But this no more saves the day than the structural sturdiness of a house redeems it if it is about to slide off its mountain perch.

A second besetting problem for holism concerns truth, for which it can provide no basis other than consensus. It seems strained, for example, and in the end indefensible to argue (as Wittgenstein per Kripke argues[10]) that even the rules of arithmetic have no validity beyond the social consensus that supports them.

These difficulties are enough in themselves to suggest that social holism is at best a way-station in philosophy's journey. If we try to anticipate where it might go next, the primordialist suggests that, riding its current insistence that thinking is invariably "situated," philosophy take another look at the possibility that reason's basic situation is the generic human condition. The roots of thinking don't stop with collectivities; they extend deeper, into soil that human collectivities share in common.

What that soil might be, we shall come to in a moment, but first a brief transitional section on theology.

Theology

The section can be brief because mainline theology has lost its independent standing. The major theological seminaries have gravitated toward major universities and bought into their midst secular styles of thought.[11] The minds of mainstream theologians are now vectored more by the modern Western mind-set than by traditional doctrine. It is more important to those theologians that their philosophical colleagues validate their work as being, if not true, then at least meaningful, than that their ecclesiastical colleagues validate it as being orthodox.

The harm this does to faith—Bultmann vectored by Heidegger, Teilhard by Darwin, Process Theology by a philosopher who admitted to having read but a single book of theology in his life: Whitehead—passes largely unnoticed, but it relates to our topic in two ways, one sociological and the other substantive. Viewed from the sociology of knowledge, the most striking fact about the perennial philosophy in its twentieth-century revival is that it has occurred (through Guenon, Coomaraswamy, Schuon, and popularizers such as Aldous Huxley) outside the university and its seminary satellites while deriving its force partly from that extramural base.[12] As for the substantive point—the way academic styles of thought in fact compromise robust theological ones—the fact that the perennialists typically use the word "traditionalist" as their term of self-references shows that they all but define themselves in opposition to the modernist drift, but there is room here for only a single example of the drift itself. Let it be an immediate one.

There is a move afoot to replace what George Lindbeck calls the "experiential-expressive" approach in religious studies with the "cultural-linguistic" approach.[13] Whereas experiential-expresssivism sees religions as expressions or objectifications of inner, preconceptual experience of God, self and world, the cultural-linguistic approach insists that experience is shaped by its social context from the start. "Inner experiences are not prior to their linguistic exteriorization; rather, the symbol system is the pre-condition of the experiences—a sort of cultural, public a priori for the very possibility of 'private' experience."[14]

The overture here to philosophy's notion of cultural holism is obvious, and of course if that holism is accepted without question the jig is up for any sort of universalism, for we have already watched holism deaden in cultural pluralism. But it's not just universalism that's at stake. Ultimately the issue concerns man's position respecting his source and matrix —whether he is alienated from it or confirmed by it—and the issue provides as good an entry as any to the concluding section of our paper.

The Primordial Claim

Ontologically, the primordialist claims that we are bound to the ultimate so completely that in the end it is difficult if not impossible to differentiate us from it. Epistemologically, he claims that we can know our divine identity. Historically, he claims that the first two claims constitute the core of the Revelation that has spawned and powered the world's enduring religions. As we are living in a time when epistemology has upstaged ontology, it is best that we begin with it.

The Intellect. We can return to the dialectics with which this paper began. Do we know, or don't we?—are our lives infused with knowledge or nescience? Obviously both, but which side do we come down on? Current philosophy opts for ignorance: "virtually every contemporary...methodology takes as its starting-point how well we know how little we know," James Cutsigner writes.[15] Tradition (a word which from here on will be used as synonymous with "the primordial claim") champions the alternative. Even to be aware of our ignorance is to know, but the point lies deeper. In the traditional view we are theomorphic beings. Whether we are God (Atman *is* Brahman) or are made in the image of God (*Imago Dei*), the point is the same. Because God knows, we who derive from Him/Her/It know as well.

That needs to be said first, but once it has been said the obvious qualifications can follow. If we are God, *samsara* obscures that fact, while if we are created in the image of God that image has been tarnished by the Fall. So we are confused, bedazed, and temporarily lost—condemned to live a good part of our lives in considerable darkness. Even so, our gyroscope continues to function, and the needle of our compass still points north.

The orienting faculty that gyroscope and compass token here is not reason; *intellectus* is not *ratio* any more than *buddhi* is *manas*. The faculty that intellect and buddhi name lies deeper in us than reason; it is something like the tropism of plants that orients them towards light. An entire essay would be needed to account for the faculty systematically; the most we can do here is note a place or two where Western philosophy has moved up to the notion. Plato hinted at it when he spoke of "the eye of the soul." Medieval philosophers forged from his hints the concept of intellect as distinct from reason. Even Hume was on its track when, italicizing his words for emphasis, he noted that "*belief is more properly an act of the sensitive than of the cogitative part of our natures*."[16]

If (with small time for history) we look around us today we find allusions to an extra-rational component of knowing at every turn; it is implicit rather than explicit, but invariably present. Polanyi called it tacit knowing; in common parlance the word "intuition" is invoked. Cognitive psychologists look in its direction when they say that knowing, feeling, and action cannot be separated. We "*perfink*," Jerome Bruner tells us; which is to say, we perceive, feel and think at once. "To separate the three is like studying the planes of a crystal separately, losing sight of the crystal that gives them being."[17] Computer programers can make their machines do wonders, but one human capacity they cannot match: the power of a human being to summarize unconsciously his entire past—all that he has experienced and done—and let that summary affect his moves and decisions. Programmers cannot instruct their machines to do this because no one has the slightest idea how we do it ourselves.[18]

But back to epistemology per se. Consider an animal in the wilds. If we try to connect it to its environment by the physiology of perception we encounter so many inexplicable gaps that rationally (in Hume's sense of reason) we would have to conclude that the animal doesn't perceive its world at all. Yet all the while it behaves as if it perceives it; it proceeds toward food and shelter almost unerringly. With J.J. Gibson's ecological theory of perception pointing the way,[19] animal psychologists are coming to see that they have lost sight of this incontrovertible fact. Trying to account for knowledge as inference from noetic bits hasn't worked. We must begin the other way around, with the recognition that there is a world out there (realism), and that the animals are oriented to it. Noetic bits must assume their place within those givens instead of being asked to try to produce them.[20]

The Traditional notion of the intellect is in line with these developments in psychology; it applauds Gibson's realism. To object that our knowledge is imperfect in both extent and exactitude, and that our representations of the world are colored to some extent by the human noetic equipment[21] is to raise red herrings; no one contends otherwise as long as we do not allow the caveats to obscure the truths we have been speaking of.

As for philosophy, the constructive points in its practical holism are likewise to be applauded; knowing *is* a gestalt affair, and it does ride on micro-practices. But when cultural-linguistic holism turns negative, erecting fences around cultures that are said to be impregnable, the Traditionalist, wearing now his primordialist hat, is unpersuaded. There are ways in which every human being is almost exactly like every other human being that has ever lived: in his feelings of fear and insecurity, of inadequacy and aggression, of lust and loneliness.[22] What does the cultural-linguistic-holist say to this? That it isn't so? That we cannot sense such affinities across cultural barriers? That the affinities are unimportant? In the context of current discussions, primordialism can be seen as the attempt to pick up on a neglected point, a most important one: the extent to which, differences notwithstanding, we are all more human than otherwise. Yet similarity is not its final object; the goal is Reality. The commonality that occupies the primordialist most is the generic human capacity to encounter the Absolute. *Of course* human knowing is always situated. But beyond the childhood traumas in which Freud situates it, the classes in which Marx situates it, and the historical times in which Nietzsche situates it, it is situated in the generic human condition. Finally important in this condition is man's capacity to know God.

The Absolute. Because in the West the word God tends to be tied to his/her/its personal aspects, it is perhaps better to speak of the Absolute, to widen the screen. The personal dimensions of the divine are not unreal, but they are not inclusive. They are caught up and assume their place in the abysmal infinity of the Godhead which our rational minds can no more fathom than a two-dimensional mind could fathom the nature of a sphere. The trans-rational depths of the divine are accessible, but by reason only abstractly and with anomalous residues; kataphatic theology inevitably produces paradoxes analogous to the ones that turn up on two-dimensional maps of our three-dimensional earth. Only in the inclusive light of intellective discernment can these paradoxes be resolved. Such intellective knowing requires more than thought. It requires that the subject be adequated to its object according to the dictum that "only like can know like."

The Absolute solves the problem of relativism. Without it, relativism can be deferred—possibly to the point where some, unburdened by the long look, can live by the "provisional absolutes" the deferral allows. But short of the Absolute no final resolution of relativism is possible.

In the strict sense of the word, the Absolute is eternal: it is beyond time. As the rise of Process Theology suggests, the modern world's absolutizing of time has made God's eternity the greatest stumbling block of traditional theology; Whitehead and Hartshorne concede timelessness to God's abstract outlines, but not to the concreteness those outlines contain. This absolutizing of time seems out of step with the growing suspicion in science that time is derivative and dependent—Einstein called "the distinction between past, present and future...a stubbornly persistent illusion"[23]—but we can let that pass. Process theologians argue that if God is eternal, his foreknowledge precludes human freedom, and his immutability rules out love for his creatures. There are paradoxes here to be sure, but the Traditionalist sees even reason as able to resolve them to an appreciable degree if eternity is clearly distinguished from ever lastingness.

Translated to the phenomenal plane, the absolutizing of time produces historicism. The Traditionalist does not dispute the obvious fact that we are historical beings, or even that we are radically such. The question is whether we are totally such, which is to say historical without remainder. Anselm once said that St. Paul understood Moses far better than he and his contemporaries could. In so saying he acknowledged time's toll; he admitted that it had disadvantaged his generation in comparison with Paul's on the point in question. What in return does historicism concede to Anselm by way of his capacity to transcend his times enough to recognize that Paul's times allowed things his own did not while the age of Moses allowed even more? Unrelieved historicism is unrelieved relativism in its temporal mode, and as Hilary Putnam has stated outright, relativism is unlivable.

The infinite aspect of the Absolute provides the solution to the problem of evil. That finitude exists is beyond question, for here we are as witnesses. The infinite must include the finite—include it paradoxically, of course, as the Prajnaparamita eloquently testifies—or there would be something outside the infinite which by definition is impossible. So ontological gradations are required, that between the finite and the infinite being the one that is most important. When these gradations are considered in the mode of value or worth, they produce distinctions between better and worse and vistas open onto the primitive view of evil. *Esse qua esse bonum est*; being qua being is good; evil is the relative absence of good in the way shadow is the relative absence of light. The issue is subtle, but a sentence by St. Augustine points to the direction in which the traditional argument proceeds: "I no longer desired a better world, because I was thinking of creation as a whole: and in the light of this more balanced discernment, I had come to see that higher things are better than the lower, but that the sum of all creation is better than the higher things alone" (*Confessions*, VII, xiii, 19). Not to affirm that point is to complain about the admittedly-inferior-while-essentially-noble condition that is ours. How noble it can come to be seen is life's open-ended question.

The Transcendent Unity of Religions. The day's mail brings this note from a professor in a leading American seminary: "For many years I have studied thoroughly the normative texts of Islam and Christianity. There appears to be no evidence in the texts for...esoteric ecumenism." Such ecumenism, the writer goes on to say, is a curtain that primordialists drape over historical religions to veil their distinctive identities.

What is crucial here is to see that the primordialist agrees with the above assessment as long as one stays with the exoteric, relatively literal, reading of the texts in question. Moreover, there is nothing wrong with such reading. If one stays with it one must forfeit the possibility that the world's enduring religions are equal revelations from, and of, the one true God, but nothing turns on believing that they are thus equal. It is infinitely more important to believe—genuinely, existentially believe—that the teachings of one's tradition are true in their literal formulations, facing forthrightly the charge of exclusivism if it then arises, than it is to believe that ecumenism is so important that it justifies compromising theological convictions. Togetherness is nice, but it has no rights over truth.

The charge that the primordialist must face is elitism. Is there a reading of sacred texts which, without bypassing their literal meanings, presses beyond those meanings to deeper ones that inform their exoteric expressions without depending on them? Obviously it is a rhetorical question; the Traditionalist believes that there is such a reading and that he is trying to exercise it. Blue is not red, but both are light. Exoterics can be likened to people who hold that light isn't truly such, or at least that it is not light in its purest form, unless it is of a given hue. Meanwhile academicians have become so fearful that a hue will be overlooked or that some that are known will be victimized—marginalized is the going word—that they deny the existence of light itself. Here is nothing that hues instance and embody; nothing, in deconstructionist language, that texts signify. All that exists is an endless stream of signifiers.

The primordialist believes there is such a thing as light in itself—pure white light that summarizes all the wave-lengths—and that it is the Light of the World.

NOTES

1. *The Sacred and the Profane* (San Diego: Harcourt Brace Jovanovich, 1959), 165.
2. Booklength in *Forgotten Truth* and compressed to essay length in "Perennial Philosophy, Primordial Tradition" in my *Beyond the Post-Modern Mind*.
3. *Proceedings of the American Philosophical Association*, Vol. 59, (July 1986), 748.
4. As late as 1960 Quine was still contending in *Word and Object* that physics "limns the true and ultimate structure of reality."
5. George Will, *Statecraft as Soulcraft* (New York: Simon & Schuster, 1983), 34.
6. For the clearest statement of the difference between theoretical and practical holism, see Hubert Dreyfus, "Holism and Hermeneutics," in Robert Hollinger (ed.), *Hermeneutics and Praxis*, (Notre Dame: University of Notre Dame Press, 1985).
7. Hubert Dreyfus' paraphrase of Wittgenstein in *ibid.*, 235.
8. *The New Republic*, May 19, 1986, p. 39.
9. As in Richard Bernstein's *Beyond Objectivism and Relativism* (Philadelphia: University of Pennsylvania Press, 1985).
10. See Saul A. Kripke, *Wittgenstein on Rules and Private Language* (Cambridge: Harvard University Press, 1983). For a critique of Wittgenstein's position on this point see Ernest Gellner, "Gospel According to Ludwig," *The American Scholar*, Spring, 1984.
11. If this is true, we should not be surprised by the consequence. The theological consequence of secularism is atheism, and in the January 30, 1985 issue of *The Christian Century* Stanley Hauerwas and William Willimon write: "The central problem for our church, its theology and its ethics is that it is simply atheistic."
12. On the matter of that force, one thinks of Jacob Needleman's Foreword to the collection of Traditionalist essays which he edited under the title *The Sword of Gnosis*. "On close reading," he writes, "I felt an extraordinary intellectual force radiating through their intricate prose. These men were out for the kill. For them, the study of spiritual traditions was a sword with which to destroy the illusions of contemporary man" (p. 9).
13. *The Nature of Doctrine* (Philadelphia: Westminster Press, 1984).
14. Timothy Jackson, reviewing John Lindbeck's *The Nature of Doctrine*, in *Religious Studies Review*, Vol. 11, No. 3/July 1985, 236.
15. "Toward a Method of Knowing Spirit," *Sciences Religieuses/Studies in Religion*, 14/2 (Spring 1985), 152.
16. *A Treatise on Human Nature*, 183. Hume's famous point about causality is that it is impossible to make a "philosophical"—read rational—case for it, but without our "natural" belief in the "necessary connection" of cause and effect, we could never think beyond the sensory present because we would have no basis on which to reason forward to future events, backward through memory (which relies on causality as well) or even to contemporary unperceived cases.
17. Jerome Bruner, *Actual Minds, Possible Worlds* (Cambridge: Harvard University Press, 1986).
18. A striking example: Japanese chicken sexers are able to decide with 99 percent accuracy the sex of a chick, even though the female and male genitalia of young chicks are ostensibly indistinguishable. No consciously driven sexing effort could ever approach such accuracy. Aspiring chicken sexers learn only by looking over

the shoulders of experienced workers, who themselves cannot explain how they do it.

The most thorough discussion of this point appears in Hubert and Stuart Dreyfus, *Mind over Machine* (New York: The Free Press/Macmillan, 1986).

19. *The Ecological Approach to Visual Perception*, 1979.
20. See Marjorie Grene, "Perception, Interpretation, and the Sciences," in D. Depaw & B. Weber, *Evolution at a Crossroads* (Cambridge: M.I.T. Press, 1985).
21. Such coloring in no wise justifies the current attack on representational thinking per se. If Foucault is right in reporting that "representational thinking is everywhere at an end," that is a sign that something important has been lost sight of.
22. "Einstein's discovery of relativity taught us that the division of space-time into past, present and future is an illusion. The past and the future are not remote from us. The people of six hundred years back and of six hundred years ahead are people like ourselves. They are our neighbors in this universe. Technology has caused, and will cause, profound changes in the style of life and thought, separating us from our neighbors. All the more precious, then, are the bonds of kinship that tie us together" (Freeman Dyson, *Disturbing the Universe*, p. 193).
23. From a letter he wrote on the death of his closest friend to the friend's widow and son. The full statement reads: "Now he has departed from this strange world a little ahead of me. That means nothing. People like us, who believe in physics, know that the distinction between past, present, and future is only a stubbornly persistent illusion."

2

SOME PSYCHOLOGICAL ASPECTS OF THE KABBALAH

R.J. Zwi Werblowsky

A PROSPECTIVE WRITER on the psychology of the Kabbalah finds himself in an almost unique position. The usual requisites of scholarly writing, such as wide learning, complete mastery of the sources, sound judgment etc., not only do not help him here but, on the contrary, would actually deter him from broaching the subject at all. In fact, the only qualification a writer on the subject must possess is a certain carefree rashness.

The study of the Kabbalah is still in its beginnings and, since even Hebrew or rabbinic scholars need special training to master kabbalistic texts, it is not surprising that most publications on Jewish mysticism are confused mixtures of sheer humbug, occultism, Rosicrucianism, exotic theosophy and a general infatuation with 'secret lore.' Only very few authors, like A. E. Waite, could redeem their ignorance in philological and historical matters by a genuine, intuitive insight into the mystical motives and doctrines. The pioneer work of the late Professor G. Scholem has revolutionized this deplorable situation by putting the study of Jewish mysticism on a sound scientific basis. Though most of his writings are in Hebrew and pre-suppose first-hand acquaintance with the sources, his great work *Major Trends in Jewish Mysticism*[1] has placed an authoritative and reliable account of the subject in the hands of non-Hebraists. With so much basic spade-work still to be done, and while the philological, historical, and interpretative foundations are still being laid, it is certainly presumptuous and premature to build psychological castles in the air. Nonetheless, it is the privilege of fools to rush in where scholars fear to tread, and our attempt, even if unsuccessful, may not be without some use.

Kabbalah is, of course, not the same as Jewish mysticism, of which it is merely one phase. In spite of the devout kabbalistic belief that its esoteric teachings go back to Moses or even earlier,[2] it seems beyond reasonable doubt that Kabbalism in its specific sense developed in Provence and Spain during the 12th and 13th centuries. Its crystallization into a fully developed system and in major literary works (of which the *Zohar* has become the kabbalistic Bible) took place in Spain towards the end of the 13th century.

The student of the movement soon finds that on every step he is beset by innumerable problems. What, for example, is the relation of Judaism to mysticism? How can two such fundamentally different types of religion as the 'prophetic' and 'mystical'[3] combine? "Normative" Judaism seems, superficially at least, to be thoroughly extrovert; its relation to God is an objective I-Thou relationship; its main expressions are Law and Ritual; its major value is obedience to the divine will.

On the other hand, mysticism is usually held to be turned inward. The mystic withdraws into his soul; he tends to be indifferent to ritual; his aim is not obedience but union with the divine. Is the typical *unio mystica* at all conceivable in a traditional Jewish (Biblical-Rabbinic) framework? Can a Jew possibly echo Rumi's desire 'that all I's and Thou's might become one soul and at last be submerged in the Beloved'? Professor Scholem has argued[4] that the mystic transformation of Judaism had as its highest contemplative value the experience of *communion* as distinct from *union*. Communion or *debhekuth* means a turning to God, an awareness of his otherness, a loving clinging or adhering to him which implies no loss of identity.

There are other equally fundamental problems. The mythical element is extraordinarily strong in the Kabbalah.[5] How can one explain the resurgence of myth in the midst of what is usually considered to be the mortal enemy of mythical religion? By what channels or mechanisms did mythical and gnostic symbols re-assert themselves in medieval Jewry? What were the historical connections (if any) between the old, Oriental gnosticism and the almost explosive re-appearance of similar ideas in the kabbalistic systems of the 13th century and again later in the 16th century? There are as many problems of kabbalism as there are aspects of it.

For our present purpose we shall leave aside the earlier phases of Jewish mysticism, even that fascinating and psychologically interesting movement known as *merkabah*-mysticism. We shall concentrate on one aspect of the classical Kabbalah as it evolved in Spain in the 13th century. This is its new and amazing conception of the deity.

Reference has just been made to the mythological invasion of Judaism which the Kabbalah really constitutes. Perhaps it is worth pointing out that the emergence of the Kabbalah was preceded by a most radical 'demythologizing' of religion. The biblical God, in spite of the emphasis on his otherness, transcendence and eternity, was yet intensely personal and anthropomorphic. In fact he was all too human for the philosophical theologians who began systematically to explain away anything even remotely offensive to their philosophic susceptibilities. If the anthropomorphisms of the Bible were often disturbing, those contained in later rabbinic writings, particularly of the popular sort, were even worse. Following in the footsteps of the Islamic thinkers, the Jewish philosophers finally denied the possibility of attributing to God any positive qualities or attributes such as goodness, omnipotence and the like. But religious consciousness lives on the potent richness of images and symbols, and this 'purified' or rather sterilized concept of God may well have left it in a state of symbol-starvation. Even so, the philosophical tradition contributed very decisively to the formation of classical Kabbalah.

The new, kabbalistic image of the deity was of such complexity that, understandably enough, it seemed to many orthodox minds to jeopardize the essentials of Jewish monotheism. This monotheism had, in medieval philosophy, become almost monolithic and hence static. God was so much 'one' that nothing could be said about him. If, according to Aristotelian logic, attributes (i.e. adventitious characteristics added to an *ens*) suggested something more than strict unity, then the attributes had to go overboard. But now the kabbalists came with something worse than attributes: an image of the divine totality or *pleroma* as a complex organism consisting of ten potencies or foci. These potencies are not ten gods but ten aspects, stages or manifestations of the deity revealing itself. They are the well known ten *sefiroth*. The dynamic interrelations of the *sefiroth* make up the intensely dramatic inner life of the godhead which, in spite of its complexity, is essentially one. The kabbalists could not or would not use such categories as 'substance' and 'persons' when wrestling with the conceptual difficulties of their symbols; still, one cannot but sympathize with their orthodox critics who complained that they were substituting a tenfold God for the threefold one of the Christians. In fact, the emphasis on the essential unity of this divine *pleroma* grew more insistent as by the sheer inherent power of the kabbalistic symbolism the various *sefiroth* became more and more personified.

The word *pleroma* has been used advisedly in the preceding account. For the kabbalistic system immediately reminds us of the great gnostic systems of earlier centuries. But whereas the gnostic 'fullness' or realm of the divine consisted of hundreds and thousands of divine *aeons*, the kabbalistic *pleroma* is reduced to a manageable ten. Moreover, the gnostic *aeons* are rather chaotic and disorderly. They ascend and descend in almost anarchic freedom whereas the kabbalistic *sefiroth* are ordered in a strict hierarchy. This is one example of the aforementioned influence of the philosophic tradition. The notion of the cosmos as a series of descending emanations from a divine source is a familiar neoplatonic motif. And since medieval Arabic philosophy, including medieval Aristotelianism, was strongly neoplatonic, these notions were more or less commonplace. There is, in fact, definite evidence of specific neoplatonic influences on the early Spanish kabbalists. The classical doctrine of *sefiroth* is therefore an intriguing combination of gnostic and neoplatonic motifs. The cosmos as a hierarchical structure of successive emanations—this is neoplatonic.

But the idea that this cosmos is divine or, to be more exact, constitutes the fullness of the divine realm, and that the entities that make it up are divine forces, is thoroughly gnostic. The neoplatonic, emanatist scheme would picture the ten *sefiroth* as a straight, descending line; the first *sefirah* produces the second, the second the third and so forth down to the tenth. What happens then is a different matter. There may be further emanations which finally produce our material universe. In that case there would be no break at all but a gradual, imperceptible descent into the material world.

As against this radical neoplatonism the biblical idea of creation as a discontinuous act might be salvaged by letting the process of emanation stop with the tenth *sefirah*. God, i.e., this complex system of *sefiroth*, then proceeds to create a universe *ex nihilo*. However, we are not concerned here with kabbalistic theories of the world and creation, but with the idea of God. And in this connection it is important to realize that the descending line of successive emanations gives us only the order of 'procession,' the genetic line, as it were. The order of being, that is the dynamics of the *sefiroth*, is far more complicated and fascinating. (See Figure 2-1.)

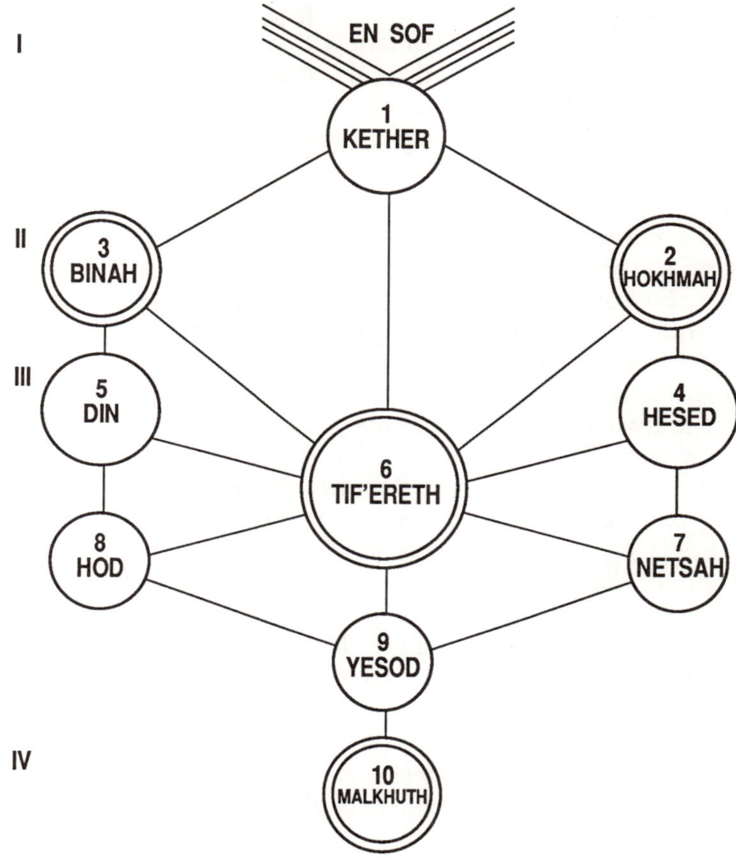

Figure 2-1 The Sephirotic "Tree."

1. the 'supreme crown' of God
2. the 'wisdom' or primordial idea of God; also 'father'
3. the 'intelligence' of God; also 'mother'
4. the 'love' or mercy of God
5. the 'power' of God (chiefly mainfested as stern judgment and punishment)
6. the 'compassion' of God (also 'glory'); male principle, sun, king, etc.
7. the 'lasting endurance' of God
8. the 'majesty' of God
9. the 'basis' or 'foundation' (of all active forces in God)
10. the 'kingdon' of God; also the mystical archetype of Israel, ***shekhinah***, bride, queen, soul, moon, etc.

cf. *1 Chronicles* 29:11 Thine,O Lord, is the greatness and the power, and the glory, and the victory, and the majesty; for all that is in the heaven and in the earth is thine; thine is the kingdom, O Lord, and thou art exalted as head above all.

We cannot consider here how the two patterns are reconciled by the kabbalistic writers but must be content with a superficial understanding of the 'sefirotic tree' itself. Incidentally, the image of the tree for the sefirotic system already occurs in the first kabbalistic text, the 12th, century book *Bahir*. It is certainly a suggestive symbol of the organic and growing unity of the divine totality.

Before looking closer at the 'tree,' we must, however, note another feature of the doctrine of *sefiroth*. For in addition to the surprising conception of the deity as the fullness and interrelation of ten distinct aspects or potencies, it also teaches a radical dualism between the hidden and unknowable *deus absconditus* on the one hand, and the manifest, self-revealing, accessible God of religious experience on the other. The former concept is clearly related to current philosophic ideas about the impossibility of knowing God, of predicating attributes of him or of saying anything meaningful about him except in negations. In fact, the very terminology employed to refer to this *deus absconditus* ('Cause of Causes' or *En Sof*, i.e., literally 'Infinite') openly betrays its philosophic lineage.

But the kabbalists had a knack of borrowing terms belonging to philosophic or rabbinic tradition and investing them with a new and original significance by giving them a peculiar kabbalistic twist. From the negative theology of the philosophers it is but one step to that of the mystics. They really experience God as the great 'Nothing,' as something so utterly hidden that not even existence as such can be predicated of it. It is this paradoxical fullness of the divine Nothing which Jakob Boehme called the *Ungrund,* (as distinct from the more familiar *Urgrund*) and the kabbalists called *En Sof.* An early kabbalistic text[6] describes it in these terms:

> Know that the *En Sof* which we have mentioned is not even hinted at in the *Torah* nor in the Prophets nor in the Hagiograph nor in the words of our Sages, but the mystics have received a slight hint concerning it .... And because this matter is mysterious and secret and hidden and very subtle, therefore our teacher Moses did not even hint at it. He taught us thereby that human thinking must not approach it at all .... From the hiddenness of *En Sof* which we have set forth, we can now understand and consider the exalted position of the First Emanation[7] which is near to it like the flame to the coal .... And because of its exceedingly exalted and subtle nature they referred to it by the word 'nothing' and the word 'thought' .... Even Moses did not hint at it or at the whole subject in any way that would clearly indicate it; but the mystics have a tradition that Moses did hint at it with the word 'By the Beginning' (*Gen.* 1:1).[8] This is to say that He[9] created God[10] by means of the 'Beginning.' The meaning is that there is a something which created, by means of the Beginning, God. The word 'God' here refers to the third emanation, and the word 'created' must be understood as 'emanated.'

Some of the obscurities of this text will become clearer as we proceed. But we do know at least that *En Sof* is so hidden that it is not even hinted at in scripture. However, an existing God means a manifested, revealed, and related God. The process of manifestation, revelation, or developing relatedness is identical with the process by which the Divine Nothing, as it were, comes into "Being." In the depth of the divine hiddenness, all turned in upon itself, there occurs a primordial, initial wrench by which it begins to turn outward, to unfold, to exist. Here existence is literally an *ex-stare* a process of extroversion in the introverted *En Sof.* That initial movement is described in a highly mystical passage in the *Zohar* as the concentration or crystallization of energy in one luminous point (or rather a point 'dark with luminosity') which bursts the closed confines of *En Sof.* The process of emanation has started.

However, this luminous point or spark, although termed the first *sefirah* or first emanation, is still too near to the *En Sof* to be 'real.' As our text puts it, it is near to the *En Sof* 'like the flame to the coal,' it is remote, inaccessible, 'nothing.' But it produces another potency, a second emanation called *Hokhmah*, the divine 'Wisdom.' This is the infinitesimal point from which development and existence really begin. In fact, it is at this point only that the deity enters a stage of manifestation of which existence can be predicated. *Hokhmah* is the real 'Beginning' and, as our kabbalistic text shows, was identified with the 'Beginning' of *Gen.* 1:1. In this the kabbalists simply took up an older identification of the Beginning of *Gen.* 1:1 with Divine Wisdom or *Sophia*.

But by another of their curious twists they also apply to *Hokhmah*, the first reality that 'is,' the old theologumenon of a *creatio ex nihilo*. The Hebrew phrase literally means 'something out of nothing'; for the kabbalist this is a symbolic way of saying 'Hokhmah out of *Kether*' or 'the first something out of the mystical nothing.' Like the divine Wisdom of earlier systems, *Hokhmah* contains within itself, ideally and prefigured, all that is to arise out of it. It is the Father of all.

We may note here in passing the male or patriarchal character of the whole system. There is no Great Mother at the beginning of things, and *Hokhmah-Sophia* is actually divested of her original female character in order to become a Father. Like Adam, whose wife is his own offspring and thus, in a way, his daughter, *Hokhmah* too emanates his consort, the Great Mother *Binah*. They are the primordial parents who between them generate the remaining seven *sefiroth* represented in kabbalistic literature by all available 'sevens,' but particularly by the 'seven days of creation' of *Gen.* 1. The first two of these seven, that is the fourth and fifth sefirah, are called 'love' or 'mercy' and 'strength' or 'judgment' respectively. They are really the two divine attributes of mercy and stern justice which play so important a role in earlier rabbinic literature, but they are transformed by their absorption in the kabbalistic *sefiroth*-system.

The sefirah *Din* or 'judgment' is of special interest because it is the origin or source of those powers which, under certain conditions, can become evil. Of course the kabbalists would not explicitly attribute evil to God, and in spite of their definite tendency towards a dualism of the Iranian or gnostic type, there is obviously a limit beyond which they would not go. Their compromise solution is that although there is no evil in the deity, there is something in it which, if left to itself and untempered by its opposite neutralizing potency, somehow produces evil. Evil is therefore a kind of hypertrophy of *Din*.

It is interesting to note how the kabbalists fully work out a notion vaguely implicit in earlier rabbinic literature and already adumbrated in the Old Testament itself.[11] This is the idea that the source of evil and of the demonic, destructive forces is none other than God himself in his aspect of righteous judge! It is essential, therefore, that the forces of mercy and judgment be harmonized and balanced. This is precisely the function of the central sefirah *Tif'ereth* which somehow acts as the hub and pivot of the whole system. In the dynamic flow and give-and-take of the sefiroth, *Tif'ereth* receives the power or influence of the higher potencies and, harmonizing them, passes them on to the lower ones.

Of these, *Netsah* and *Hod* (nos. 7 and 8) are a rather indistinguishable pair of twins while no. 9, *Yesod* is again of paramount importance. Standing at the end of the sefiroth-cluster, it is in a way the terminus of the divine flow of life. To be more exact: nothing can flow on to the tenth sefirah that does not go through *Yesod*. A glance at our diagram will confirm this and also show that for that same reason the tenth sefirah is rather isolated. Its connection with the remaining sefiroth is mediated by *Yesod* on which it depends for its life and sustenance. As it has also acquired a very distinct character of its own, it somehow comes to stand over against the other nine. As the end of the sefirotic tree it is the real terminus of the inner-divine life that unfolds in the ten *sefiroth*.

Throughout kabbalistic literature *Tif'ereth* and *Malkhuth* appear as the most important and interesting of the sefiroth. Probably by far the largest part of the *Zohar* is devoted to the relation between these two. This is very largely due to the fact that whereas *Tif'ereth* the central sefirah and the representative of the whole group of nine,[12] is conceived exclusively in male symbols (king, sun, bridegroom), *Malkhuth*, the last of the divine manifestations, is represented as female. Standing at the lowest, receiving end of the system, it is the receptive womb, the Moon, Bride, and Queen. It is only in relation to the nether worlds that *Malkhuth*, as that part of the deity which is nearest to them, acquires active, directing, or even ruling characteristics. Then the 'royal' aspect of her queenship is emphasized and the Bride is also Mother.

Still, it is essentially in her relationships with *Tif'ereth* that the erotic symbolism of the *Zohar* flourishes in lavish and exotic luxuriance, much to the dismay of many high-minded students of Jewish mysticism. The supreme and central mystery of the Kabbalah is the Holy Union or *hieros gamos* between these two *sefiroth*; but what it really amounts to is the unification of all the ten *sefiroth*; in fact, the unification of God. The greatest catastrophe that can happen is the destruction of the unity within the godhead, that is the separation of the *Shekhinah*[13] (as the 10th sefirah is also called) from her husband. This was precisely the sin of Adam. It is really the fate of God that is at issue, and man's efforts, both in good works and in mystical contemplation, should be directed to the one end of promoting the union of male and female within God. The gravity of sin is due to man's capacity to disrupt the divine union. *How* exactly man can operate these results cannot be considered here, but it is relevant to our purpose to understand *why* he can do it. The reason is to be sought in certain common medieval ideas about the correspondence or analogy of microcosm and macrocosm. The biblical phrase of man as the image of God is kabbalistically reinterpreted in this context to mean that the human frame reveals the same structure as the divine 'frame' of ten *sefiroth*. This again links up with pre-kabbalistic notions of a divine *anthropos*, the *adam kadmon*.

The result of all this is a kind of mystical anatomy that often went to grotesque lengths. The kabbalists themselves liked to quote *Job* 19:26, 'in my flesh shall I see God,' in support of their anatomic symbolism. The gist of it is the correlation of the body and the sefiroth; e.g., *Kether*—the head, *Tif'ereth* (the 'center' or 'middle column')—the spine or trunk, *Netsah* and *Hod*—the legs or testicles, *Yesod*—the phallus etc.

This anatomy explains why *Tif'ereth* and *Yesod* are not always clearly distinguished in kabbalistic symbolism. In fact they are often identified because *Yesod* is simply seen as an appendix or extension of *Tif'ereth*, or as the instrument of its male function. The significant feature of all this is that the sefirotic system really corresponds to two bodies: nine sefiroth constitute the male body, while *Malkhuth-Shekhijah* is the female womb or quite simply woman. As in the case of man himself,[14] the image of God, i.e., totality, is only achieved by the union of male and female. Here we have another example of how the kabbalists added a new, mystical layer to the traditional Jewish doctrine that perfection was only possible in the married state. To my knowledge Kabbalah is the first system in Western religions to develop a mystical metaphysics of the sexual act.

Before suggesting a few psychological possibilities of interpretation it may be useful to analyze the symbolic 'lay-out' of this amazing kabbalistic doctrine somewhat more closely. There is, in the first place, the number 10. But this 10 is essentially 9 + 1, from whatever side we look at it. Going downwards, it is made up of the 'nothingness' of *Kether* plus the nine 'existing' sefiroth from *Hokhmah* onwards. Inversely, there is the compact cluster of the nine higher sefiroth, in regard to which *Malkhuth* is basically different and isolated. *Malkhuth* is the last stage in the self-revelation of the Divine, but she is also the first stage of the Divine when approached from the human perspective. She is that aspect of God which the mystic encounters first in his contemplative ascent.

Ten is also 7 + 3, inasmuch as the first three sefiroth form a group apart. They are still too near to the *En Sof* to be real and relevant in the sense that the lower seven are. The latter are consequently termed the 'building' and are equated with the seven days of creation.[15] It will be remembered how our kabbalistic text,[16] in fact discovered an allusion to the first three sefiroth in the first verse of *Genesis* that is in a passage held to describe a state prior to the sevenfold act of creation. Continuing further in our mystic ascent, we leave the seven-day-world and the 'building' behind and approach the higher world in *Binah*, the mystical 8 or 7 + 1. As the *mediatrix* between the higher world and the lower seven, she is also the Great Mother who gives birth and nourishment to the cosmos of creation (i.e., the lower seven) and to whom all will in the end return. For that reason she is also called the 'Jubilee Year,' that is the beginning and end of the Great Cycle, and 'Paradise,' that is the *uterus-nirvanah*.

Another striking feature is the triadic arrangement. There are, to begin with, three lines: the male, right and therefore good line *Hokhmah-Hesed-Netsah*; the female, left and therefore 'sinister' and dangerous line *Binah-Din-Hod*, and the central column reaching from *Kether* to *Malkhuth* with *Tifereth-Yesod* in the middle. But even apart from these three lines the triadic pattern is apparent. The first nine sefiroth quite naturally fall into a pattern of three triads. The first triad, which represents the aforementioned 'higher world,' has its apex pointing upward, whereas the other two point downward. The *Shekhinah* stands outside these triangular arrangements as befits her role as the female + 1 added to the male configuration. The quaternity pattern of 3 + 1 is not only apparent in the general sefiroth scheme where *Malkhuth* is the complement to the other 9 (= 3 x 3),[17] but comes out even more explicitly in another form. The kabbalistic writers often reduce the ten sefiroth to a more basic pattern or 'grid' of four only. There is a very interesting passage in the *Zohar* which leaves no doubt that this quaternity is conceived as 3 + 1, that is *Hokhmah*, *Binah*, *Tif'ereth*, with *Malkhuth* added to them.

Nevertheless the reader will immediately notice that the 3 + 1 definition is not yet the whole story. For the last mentioned four sefiroth exhibit the typical quaternity pattern of two pairs of opposites, each representing one aspect of the male-female polarity. We thus have:

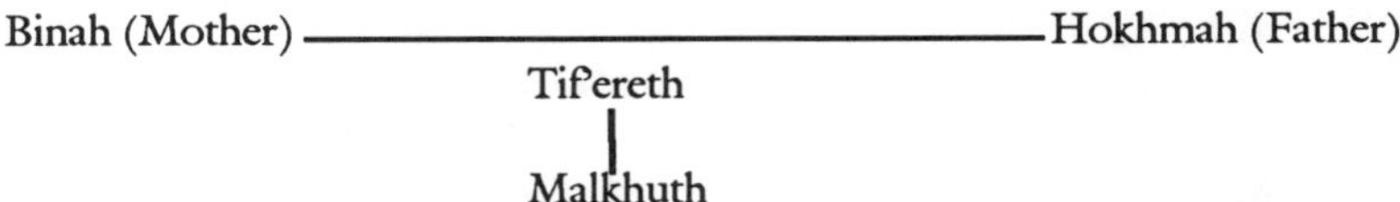

The two lines do not intersect, but the pattern is there. This quaternity symbol appears as a rule when the doctrine of *sefiroth* is combined with mystical interpretations of the tetragrammaton or Holy Name (YHVH). The first letter is merely a dot in Hebrew and therefore easily represents the 'primordial point,' *Hokhmah*. The second and fourth letters are identical and refer to the female (i.e., identical or at least similar) potencies. In fact *Binah* and *Malkhuth* are often described as the Higher and Lower Mother respectively. The third letter is a straight, vertical line and thus an obvious symbol of the trunk, spine or phallus (i.e., *Tif'ereth*).

There is a characteristic difference between these two pairs of opposites that deserves attention. 'Father' and 'Mother' are described in words and images that have indeed a remotely sexual connotation, but no erotic interest whatsoever attaches to them. The whole vocabulary is 'metaphorical,' as it were. *Hokhmah* and *Binah* are thought of as in eternal union; no crisis or danger ruffles the perpetual calm of their fertile embrace. In the relations of the lower pair, however, sexual imagery is to be taken almost literally, and erotic dynamism is real and alive. Here danger also lurks and 'separation' threatens to upset the economy of the inner-divine household. The relations of *Tif'ereth* and *Malkhuth* are intensely dramatic. Union, love, separation, yearning, exile—all these and much more go into the complex intensity of this relation with its ups and downs. Since the tenth sefirah is also called *Kenesseth Yisrael* ('the *ekklesia* of Israel') and represents, as it were, the celestial archetype of the historic Israel within the divine *pleroma*, even Israel's vicissitudes in exile are merely the reflection in the historic sphere of an essentially inner-divine drama.

But there is more at issue than mere anguish of separation or destruction of unity when the *Shekhinah* is torn from her partner. The tenth *sefirah* although situated on the central line of conciliation, yet has an intrinsic affinity to the sinister, left side. This is, of course, connected with her feminine nature. She is specifically related to the fifth sefirah 'stern judgment' and is often called the lower or lesser *Din*. This means that like the higher or major *Din* she is somehow related to the demonic powers. But whereas *Din* may be the remote source of the forces of evil, *Shekhinah* does not produce them but is already surrounded and threatened by them like a 'rose among the thorns.' This is the *Zohar's* own mystical allegory of the image in the *Song of Songs*. The moment *Shekhinah* is separated from her partner and thus automatically cut off from the beneficent, male and good influence of the right side, she is in danger of losing herself to the demonic side. Here again the historic fact of Israel's exile and suffering among the nations becomes a symbol for an essentially divine tragedy.

The almost ambivalent character of the tenth *sefirah*, her uneasy proximity to the demonic, may, perhaps, help us on the way towards a solution of a rather odd puzzle. The correlation male-right and female-left is a well known commonplace. What seems to be unique in the Kabbalah is the attribution to the male side of qualities that we should normally consider to be female. How are we to understand a symbolic system in which love, mercy, forgiveness etc., are male, but strength and stern, punitive judgment are female qualities? Perhaps the answer should be sought in some specific patterns of the Jewish psyche. The antifeminine tendency of the Kabbalah on which Professor Scholem has commented[18] is actually anticipated in the Bible. Not only is the biblical God exclusively and aggressively patriarchal, in conscious and intended contrast to the Mother Goddesses of surrounding cultures, but the primacy of the male is also assured by the order of creation. Eve proceeds from Adam, not man from a mother. The psychological background of this repression of the female side, namely the fear of and revolt against the Great Mother, need not be stressed here. Eve is the serpent's instrument in undoing Adam, and Job's wife is the unwitting accomplice of Satan when she counsels her husband to 'curse God and die.'

There is only one possible explanation for all this: the 'demonization' of the feminine aspect. It reflects a state of insecurity in the male psyche, a mortal fear of being overpowered by the fatal attraction of the irrational powers of the deep. Protection is found in the usual mechanisms of overcompensation. The male world is characterized by order, clarity and light, by freedom from irrational fears. It is a reliable world, without threats of sudden abysmal dangers, and thence a world of love, mercy and life.

The female world is full of dangers; for the male psyche it is the source of the unexpected, the incalculable, of that which can always upset its order. It is potentially destructive either by producing evil or by falling prey to it. Of necessity its existence is bound up with certain protective reflexes such as strict law, limitation, suppression, discipline and the necessity of judgment. To administer judgment and punishment is, of course, nothing but releasing in a more or less controlled way precisely those destructive forces that one has dreaded so much and on account of which the patriarchal law was introduced. Here the profound ambivalence of law and judgment becomes apparent. The law is one of death, and judgment spells destruction, as St. Paul well knew. But they are necessitated by the maternal world and by man's attempt to fight free of it. The ambivalence and potential destructiveness of *Din* is therefore no isolated phenomenon. It is closely related to that of the feminine symbol.

The supremacy of male values is borne out by another aspect of kabbalistic symbolism. It is true that compared with the exclusively patriarchal, masculine tradition of Jewish theology the kabbalistic development testifies to a considerable widening of the horizon. The feminine element is now considered to be an essential, indispensable part of the total divine personality. It is admitted into the divine *pleroma* and, in fact, the *hieros gamos* within the deity is the supreme aim and purpose of the pleromatic life. Still, it is hardly possible to speak of a balance between the two forces. We may allow that the three-line pattern exhibits a well-balanced parallelism of a male, female and middle line. We even have a *Magna Mater* symbol fairly high up in the sefirotic hierarchy. The fact remains nevertheless that in the dense and central symbolism of the union of *Shekhinah* and *Tif'ereth* the whole complex of nine sefiroth is virtually uniting with the tenth. In this perspective the whole sefirotic system except *Malkhuth* is conceived *sub specie masculinitatis*. Psychologically this would mean that the female side is accepted and recognized, but is not yet differentiated, let alone considered as equal. Her 'monadic' character contrasts sharply with the differentiated structure of the male partner.

One further point deserves to be mentioned in this connection as it has had far-reaching consequences for Jewish mysticism. Our examination of the male-female relation within the divine should now enable us to grasp more fully Professor Scholem's point about mystical *communion* v. mystical *union*. It will be fairly obvious by now why there cannot be any question of union with the divine. The whole problem of union or unification has been located by the kabbalists in the heart of the divine itself and not in the relation between man and God. If we want to find anything like a mystic divinization of the self, then we must look for it along the lines of the doctrine of man as the image of God. As we have seen, this theosophical *analogia entis* has led to a mystico-magical conception of the theurgic significance of human acts. The interdependence of the higher and lower worlds, i.e., of the divine *pleroma* and the human sphere, is such that 'union' and 'separation' of the divine potencies largely depend on man's parallel efforts. And since self-realization, contemplative ascent to the world of the *sefiroth* and divine self-realization (if so it may be called) coincide for the kabbalist, *unio mystica* can only mean that by performing a sort of mystical union within his own self (which is, after all, a theomorphic *sefiroth*-structure too), the kabbalist parallels the divine union in his contemplative effort and thereby actually brings it about or, at least, promotes it.

I do not pretend to have covered anything like the whole doctrine of *sefiroth* as it appears in 13th-century Spanish kabbalism. But enough has been said, perhaps, to suggest some tentative psychological hints.[19] In fact, a few psychological viewpoints were already smuggled in fairly obviously when attention was drawn to the projection of the whole *unio*-problem on the divine personality, to the greater differentiation of the male as compared with the female, and to the male 'demonization' of the feminine symbol. The implicit suggestion was that the kabbalistic image of the divine is a numinous and complex projection of the unconscious psyche in its totality. For readers familiar with the basic ideas of C. G. Jung's psychology, this point hardly needs any laboring and a few brief hints will suffice to indicate the general trend of such an interpretation.

One methodological *caveat* should, however, be entered at this juncture. I do not believe that it is possible in this type of work to arrive at a completely watertight and satisfactory explanation which would account for every single detail. The historian of religion differs from the practicing psychologist in that he cannot insist on wresting significant meaning from every detail of a complex phenomenon by amplifying it beyond recognition. The method may have its uses in the highly individual analytic situation where intuition plays a legitimate part and where first-hand associations are available. Scholarly research has no such facilities and must be content, so far as psychological viewpoints are concerned, with a fairly probable over-all interpretation of the phenomenon. This methodological principle was already maintained by medieval philosophers with regard to the philosophical interpretation of theological matters.[20] The historian of religion who wants to make use of psychological categories can only endorse it.

The 'unconscious,' we should remember, is a *Grenzbegriff*; as a term or concept it denotes a limit. However far we push our psychological analyses, this limit is always there. Not only is there that mysterious point at which consciousness once began, but with all our knowledge of unconscious factors, mechanisms, processes, images and functions we are still surrounded by that vast ocean of 'nothingness' or unconscious non-existence out of which our conscious being rises like a luminous little island. And if we conceive of consciousness as evolving or growing in spite of its complex structure, then we must also remember that the *sefiroth*, in spite of their complex spatial arrangement, are emanations, that is successive stages in the unfolding or self-revelation of the divine personality. They not only describe the dynamics of the divine *pleroma* but actually constitute a theogony. On the one hand is *En Sof*, the fullness of inert, undifferentiated, depth or non-being. On the other hand we have its manifestation in the functional system of the *sefiroth*. Between them intervenes the dawn of consciousness and being. A hidden movement within the *En Sof*, a mysterious wrench, an energy-charged point that breaks through—and the process of unfolding and differentiation is initiated. Then centers of energy are produced, poles of opposites crystallize, fields of forces and tension-systems establish themselves. We have seen how the first stage of this process, the as-yet undifferentiated Nothingness of *Kether* is followed by the primordial point of Wisdom, the seed that fathers all that is to come.

Only then follows the mother, *Binah*. Still remote and part of the 'higher' world of original, intangible, and unfathomable beginnings, she is the womb in which all exists in embryonic prefiguration. She gives birth to everything, and everything returns to her at the end of the Great Cycle. The next stage epitomizes the principle of antagonistic opposites. *Hesed* and *Din* not only stand for the attributes of mercy and stern judgment but for a fundamental polarity which is the source of all those tensions which make up the fabric of being. Negatively, these tensions can develop to such degree that their hypertrophy destroys the 'building.' The structure as a whole is thus conceived as a delicately balanced field of forces which exists by virtue of its dynamic equilibrium. If this equilibrium is upset and the centrifugal tendencies of individual potencies towards independence, that is towards autonomous function, are satisfied, then these functions can turn into demonic powers, i.e., negative complexes. We have seen how this danger is associated particularly with the left or female side. Finally, at the very end of the system, comes the great feminine symbol *Malkhuth-Shekhinah*.

There is no way to the mystery of the godhead but through *Malkhuth*. The tenth sefirah in the process of emanation is also the first stage on the mystic's reverse road of ascent back to the origins. The first divine potency which he encounters is *Malkhuth*, called garden, sea, earth, house, temple and gate. The last term is particularly relevant for our immediate purpose. According to the kabbalistic exegesis of *Gen.* 28:17,

Malkhuth is the House of God and the Gate of Heaven, *porta coelis*. Heaven, in this context, obviously refers to *Tif'ereth*, but there is no means of ascent unless by this gate. One cannot help being reminded of the function of the anima figure as the first image encountered by man on his 'descent' in which he attempts to grope along the trunk of the tree of life to the point where it plunges its roots in the depth of nothingness. The empirically attested relation of the anima with the 'shadow' offers some intriguing analogies to the association of *Malkhuth* with the demonic forces and with the 'left side of *Din*.'

A priori one would expect the tenth sefirah to represent not so much the anima as rather the ego, and perhaps something of the sort is indicated by the description of *Malkhuth's* function with regard to the 'lower,' non-pleromatic world. *Malkhuth* or 'kingdom' is the potency by which the whole external cosmos is ordered and ruled; it exercises government and maintains the proper administration of life-forces. The existence of law and order, i.e., of *kosmos*, depends on its influence, and we may therefore have some grounds for attributing to it characteristics of the conscious function. Nevertheless, we must not ignore its essentially feminine character and the overwhelming amount of anima-symbolism connected with it. For aught we know, *Malkhuth* may stand for either anima or ego, for both or for neither. We must be careful not to confound our doubtful conjectures with valid interpretations. To qualify for the latter class, our suggestions would need to be supplemented by a careful analysis of the vast range of kabbalistic symbolism and by more textual and philological work. Until then our thoughts on the subject are, at their best, merely stimulating suggestions; they cannot hope to be more.

One such suggestion has been more or less explicitly the guiding principle of our reflections. The kabbalistic doctrine of sefiroth has been interpreted here as a grandiose system of projection by which the kabbalist finds the structure of his own psyche, its functions and individuation drives, in the numinous sphere of the godhead. The path is cleared for this projection by the biblical teaching of man as the image of God and by the medieval microcosm-macrocosm theories. That the medieval *homo religiosus* looks upward where the modern *homo psychologicus* looks downward need not detain us here. The kabbalist too has his tree of life whose crown is the *Shekhinah* and whose roots are sunk in a mysterious abyss. Only the roots are on high, and the tree grows downwards. The tenth sefirah is therefore the point where the projective *pleroma* contacts human consciousness (*in casu*: the contemplative mystic's mind). In view of this we may, perhaps, define the *sefiroth*-tree more precisely as a mirror–projection. This would agree with the fact that, as in a mirror, the right and left sides of the sefiroth system are facing the right and left of the beholder (i.e., literally the contemplating mystic). They do not correspond to what should be the right and the left side of the *sefiroth*-tree in its own right.

The unreflected naivete of this representation of right and left is all the more remarkable as Jewish tradition was not at all naive on the subject. On the contrary, it repeatedly had occasion to point out that when facing another person or object right and left were reversed.[21] For example, the rubrics are explicit in their instructions that when bowing at the end of prayer one should bow to the left first 'which is the right hand side of the *Shekhinah*'[22] and then to the right 'which is the left of the *Shekhinah*.'

It was a commonplace among medieval philosophers that in order to know God man had to know himself first. The kabbalists, in their projected and god-centered world, plumped straight for God. What they encountered was their own soul in disguise. For aught we know their oblique self-knowledge, dressed up as mystical knowledge of God, was perhaps nearer the truth than the more direct, rational self-knowledge of the philosophers. An age which does not yet possess the proper tools for adequate psychological analysis can probably do more justice to the realities of the psyche when it has a sphere in which it can project unhampered its mythical truth. Projecting 'upwards' at least guarantees that the numinous quality of this reality is not lost. An honest, philosophical psychology could hardly achieve this result in the Aristotelian climate of the Middle Ages nor, for that matter, in the climate of later ages. The task of withdrawing our projections while respecting the numinous realities of the soul seems as impossible as squaring the circle. But, as is well-known, the two operations are more or less the same; and, if they are really imposed on modern man, then he can hardly hope to neglect them with impunity.

NOTES

This paper is based on a talk given originally to the Analytical Psychology Club, London, on February 25, 1954, and published in their journal *Harvest* no. 3, 1956.

1. Jerusalem 1941, New York 1946, London 1955. References are to the 2nd edition. Of particular relevance to our present theme are chapters 1, 5 and 6.
2. A belief held by the Jewish Kabbalists no less fervently than by Pico della Mirandola and his contemporaries, Robert Fludd and the 17th-century English neoplatonists and some modern theosophists.
3. Using this typological antithesis in the sense in which it is used by Heiler (*Das*

Gebat) and other phenomenologists of religion.

4. *Op. cit.*, 123 and in his article "*Devekuth* or Communion with God," *Review of Religion*, Jan. 1950, 115 f.
5. Cf. Scholem, "Kabbalah und Mythus," *Eranos-Jahrbuch*, XVI, 1949 (Zürich 1950).
6. *Ma'arekheth ha'Elohuth*, ch. VII.
7. I.e., *Kether*.
8. The Hebrew particle usually translated 'in' ("In the beginning") can also be rendered 'by' or 'by means of.'
9. Or rather 'it,' i.e., the unnamed because unnameable subject of the sentence. From the point of view of Kabbalistic grammar, the subject is thus 'non-existent.'
10. 'God' is therefore the object of the sentence. As our text goes on to explain, 'God' is here synonymous with the third sefirah *Binah*.
11. *Zachariah*, 3:1f. Cf. also Riwkah Schaerf, "Die Gestalt des Satan im Alten Testament," in C.G. Jung, *Symbolik des Geistes*, Zürich, 1948.
12. Or at least of the central group of six from *Hesed* to *Yesod*. This is in fact the whole *sefiroth*-system minus the higher realm of the first three and the final sefirah *Malkhuth*.
13. Cf. Scholem, "Zur Entwicklungsgeschichte der Kabbalistischen Konzeption der Schechinah," *Eranos-Jahrbuch* XVIII, 1952 (Zürich 1953).
14. Cf. *Gen.* 1:27; 2:18, 24 and the many comments in Talmudic and Midrashic literature.
15. The tenth sefirah thus corresponds to the Sabbath.
16. Supra p.
17. If we consider only the lower group of seven sefiroth, then Malkhuth is number six (= 2 x 3) plus one.
18. *Major Trends*, 37–8. Misogynic tendencies can be detected in the symbolism of almost all religions.
19. The psychological interpretations put forward here are similar to those advanced by S. Hurwitz, "Archetypische Motive in der Chassidischen Mystik," in *Zeitlose Dokumente der Seele*, vol. III of the "Studien aus dem C.G. Jung Institut," Zürich 1952. Hurwitz seems to be the pioneer of the psychological study of Kabbalah and his essay is a very useful introduction to kabbalistic mysticism from a psychological angle.
20. Cf. Maimonides, *Guide of the Perplexed*, III. 26.
21. Cf. also Jacob's crossing of hands *Gen.* 48: 13–14 or the Talmudic passage b. *Menahoth* 34b which is partly responsible for kabbalistic customs in connection with the wearing of phylacteries.
22. I.e., God, whom the worshipper faces in prayer.

3

GOD AS 'NOTHING' IN KABBALAH

R.J. Zwi Werblowsky

THE PROFESSIONAL SCHOLAR tends to shy away from subjects that are in fashion and which serve as a free-for-all of academic journalism. "Divine Nothingness" is one of these popular bandwagons and, to make things worse, everybody who feels the calling to contribute to the Christian-Buddhist dialogue has a field day with Buddhist nothing, or emptiness, or void, and with the apophatic "nothing" of Christian mystical theology, and waxes lyrical over Being, Non-Being, Meister Eckhart, Nāgārjuna etc.

The author, having been duly frightened away from this theological journalism, will confine his essay to one technical subject and examine one particular expression of the Occidental tradition, to wit the early kabbalistic doctrine of divine being and nothingness as it developed in the 12th and 13th centuries, and culminated in the *Zohar* (northern Spain, second half of the 13th century). This kabbalistic doctrine forms part, as will be seen, of the larger Occidental heritage, the neoplatonic roots of which bore their medieval fruit not in their original Greek form but (and this applies also to Western Christianity) as mediated by Scotus Erigena's translations of Greek neoplatonic traditions. It is important to remember that neither Eckhart and the Rhineland mystics, nor the analogous English phenomena (e.g., *The Cloud of Unknowing*) would be thinkable without the influence of the prior Latin translations of Erigena and their dissemination.

There is, of course, a kind of immanent logic which pushes in the direction of allegorical interpretation of scriptures or, of more immediate significance for our subject, in the direction of *theologia negative*—especially when there are powerful outside stimuli such as, e.g., the philosophical critique of religious anthropomorphism. Classical rabbinic discourse (still a far cry from "systematic theology") did not shrink from the most massive anthropomorphic imagery, probably because original anthropomorphism had already been overcome and hence no defence mechanisms were required any more.

But the "gnosticizing" texts of early Jewish mysticisms (*Merkabah, Hekhaloth, Shi'ur Qomah*) go much further. They project a superdimensional image of God, possibly prompted by the desire to provoke, by the sheer overwhelming power of the astronomical numbers, a numinous tremor in face of the *rex tremendae majestatis*. Over against this mode of expression, we have the anti-anthropomorphic tendency of the early Aramaic translations of the Bible (the *Targum*), even more pronounced in the philosophical-allegorical exegesis of Philo, and reaching its climax in medieval philosophy. Maimonides' doctrine of attributes, i.e., his denial of the possibility of positive attributes of God, undoubtedly represents the acme of this philosophical development. But then the next step becomes unavoidable: what is the status of the concept of "being" or "existence"? Lack of time prevents me from broadening the question and raising the wider issue of the transformation of philosophical problems into mystical experience and the related phenomenon of the transformation of philosophical technical terms (e.g., Being and Non-being) into mystical symbols. As an illustration we might give Aristotle's *steresis* which was used by some authors in the sense of mystical Nothingness.

The Hebrew term *middoth* ("qualities"), in theological parlance divine qualities such as Mercy, Justice, etc., and subsequently in the usage of the Hebrew translators of Arabic philosophical texts, "attributes" in the technical sense, was taken over by the kabbalists but given a mystical-theosophical twist and identified with the inner-divine potencies of the kabbalistic doctrine of sefiroth. Since the divine *pleroma* of the sefirotic world is, in spite of its apparent internal multiplicity, also the world of the mystical unity of the Godhead—the divine Nothing is not even One, it is "Above One"—there occurred, to give but one of any number of possible examples, another terminological shift. Medieval philosophy described the sphere beyond matter (e.g., the world of the angels) as the world of separation from matter, in contrast to the material, sub-lunar world. Hence angels were also called "separate intelligences" (Hebrew *sekhalim nifradim*) inhabiting the *mundus separatus*.

The interest of the kabbalists went in the opposite direction: not from the sublunar world upwards but from the heights of the divine downward. The sefirotic realm of divine, perfect mystical unity is followed by a sphere of being that is separate from the divine *pleroma* of absolute Oneness. The angels too are separate from this sphere of absolute unity and hence are called *intelligentiae separatae*! The *mundus separatus* viz. *mundus sparationis* is thus "separate" not so much from the sublunar and material world as from the divine-sefirotic *mundus unitatis*.

I shall not try to summarize here the basic teachings of the Kabbalah. The reader is probably familiar with the writings of G. Scholem on the subject. Hence I shall not discuss the doctrine of the *sefiroth* as such but rather deal briefly with the apparent dualism between the Godhead as manifest (viz. manifesting and revealing itself) in the *sefiroth*, i.e., the God of Creation, Revelation, Salvation—in short, the God of religion on the one hand, and the *En Sof*, the Godhead *in nihilo suo absconditus*. The analogy with the gnostic dualism of the *agnostos theos* and the *pleroma* is more apparent than real and is, in fact, misleading. The divine "Being" issues, or rather erupts, from the divine "Nothing." When referring to this process most texts, borrowing from the neoplatonic tradition, use the term "emanation." Already Gregory of Nyssa explicitly interpreted the notion of *creatio ex nihilo* in the sense of emanation out of the divine *nihil*. Nevertheless, the kabbalistic doctrine of the sefirotic emanation should not be (mis)understood as a form of pantheism. The divine emanation, i.e., the sefirotic *pleroma* is the deity manifesting itself in its dynamism. The underlying problem is similar to that of the Christian Trinity. The sefirotic *pleroma* is both the subject of religion and the object of mystical contemplation. The striving beyond it to the sphere of the divine Nothing is taboo to the kabbalist. God is immanent in his *sefiroth* though not necessarily in his created world. But, as I pointed out elsewhere, the mystical goal of, e.g., Angelus Silesius

> Was man von Gott gesagt, das g'nuget mir noch nicht,
> Die über-Gottheit ist mein Leben und mein Licht....
> Wo soll ich dann nun hin?
> Ich muss noch über Gott in eine Wüste ziehn

is alien to the kabbalist, although in his reading of the first sentence of the book of *Genesis*, the sentence is construed in such a way that it has no subject. The whole sentence is grammatically object, because its missing subject is not just absent; it is literally non-existent because it is the Divine Nothing! On the other hand the kabbalistic texts never tire to repeat over and over again what appears to them to be an essential point: the unity of the divine in both its modalities of Nothingness and of manifest Being. Thus not only the ten sefiroth are "one" (cf. once again the Trinity), but also the *sefiroth* and the Nothingness from which they issued. And in the divine *superesse* these two modalities coincide. "For Being is the Nothing according to the manner of Nothing, and the Nothing is Being in the manner (i.e., in the modality) of Being," according to Rabbi Azriel, one of the most eminent pre-Zoharic kabbalists.

We must forego here a closer examination of the relationship of philosophical-mystical discourse to the experience underlying them, and the extent to which this relationship is determined by its cultural context. Instead, we shall concentrate here on the background of the Occidental (including the kabbalistic) experience of the Divine Nothing.

The notion that God surpasses all human understanding is good biblical tradition. That distinctions made by the human intellect do not necessarily apply to the divine Being is a philosophical commonplace. It matters little for our present purpose whether we use, for this state of affairs, the symbols *hyperesse* or *superesse*, Darkness and Night, "pure thinking" (i.e., that which cannot be grasped by ordinary thought), the complete "indifference in unity," or "perfect inseparateness." This "pure thinking," i.e., that which cannot be grasped by ordinary thought, is precisely the Greek *akatalepton*, translated by Scotus Erigena as *incomprehensibilis* which, in its turn, is the Nothing from which all creation issues. Already Gregory of Nyssa spoke of God as Nothing in the sense of the negation of everything thinkable and utterable. Hence he also identified creation *ek tou me ontis* (i.e., *creatio ex nihilo*) with *ek tou theou*. The early kabbalistic texts used by the author of the *Zohar* make use of formulations which appear to be exact Hebrew translations of these definitions. Being issues not from "a" nothing but from "the Nothing" that is God Himself (Scotus Erigena). In G. Scholem's pregnant definition: "Nothingness is not 'the nothing': it is *His* Nothing."

As has already been noted, Nothingness and Being thus become modalities of the one inseparable, indistinct and equal *superesse*. The latter term occurs, in Hebrew translation, among the early kabbalists. This divine Nothing is *indistinctio* viz. *indifferentia*. The corresponding kabbalistic term sounds, according to Scholem, like a literal translation of Thierry of Chartres' (first half of the 12th century) *Aequalitatis Unitatis*. If we were to render the kabbalistic definition of *En Sof* into Latin, it would probably be something like *aequalitas perfecta in unitate perfecta*—which would bring us into close proximity to Meister Eckhart for whom "in Gott sind alle Dinge glich und sind Gott selber." It should be added that in Eckhart's usage also, Latin *similis* does not mean "similar" but *glich* ("equal").

Of considerable interest is the definition of *En Sof* as given by the German Renaissance humanist and Hebrew scholar Johannes Reuchlin in his *de arte cabbalistica* (1517):

> nominatur *En Soph* id est infinitudo, quae est summa quaedam res secundum se incomprehensibilis et ineffabilis, in remotissimo suae divinitatis retrocessu et in fontani luminis inaccessibili abysso se retrahens et contegens, ut sic nihil intelligatur ex ea procedere, quasi absolutissime deitas per ocium omnimoda sui in se ipsa clausione immanens, nuda sine veste ac absque ullo circumstantiarum amictu nec sui profusa, nec splendoris sui dilatata bonitatis *indiscriminatim ens et non ens*, et omnia quae rationi nostrae videntur inter se contradictoria, ut segregata et libera unitas simplicissime implicans.

Here we have *indistinctio* as well as *coincidentia oppositorum.* Reuchlin was aware that this mystical conception had also been "bequeathed to posterity by a certain highly philosophical German arch-priest some fifty-two years ago as his definite opinion." Indeed, this highly philosophical German archpriest, none other than the Cardinal Nicolas of Cusa, died in 1464, i.e., exactly 52 years before Reuchlin penned this paragraph. The kabbalistic doctrine expounded by Reuchlin can be found in very similar wording in the "theses" of Count Pico della Mirandola, whence Reuchlin probably took it. The striking analogy of the kabbalistic definition with the doctrine of Nicolas Cusanus would have surprised Reuchlin much less had he been aware of their common source—none other than Scotus Erigena (*de divisione naturae* i.72).

A detailed analysis of the Zoharic doctrine of *En Sof* is beyond the scope of the present essay, especially as my main purpose here is the relation of the kabbalistic doctrines to the Western philosophico-mystical tradition. We shall, therefore, dispense with an account of the "sefirotic tree," the emanation of the ten *sefiroth* from *En Sof* and the relation of the sefirotic *pleroma* to the lower spheres of being. Nevertheless, a few words should be said about the initial stages of this process.

The most "mysterious" stage in this process of emanation is the emergence of the first sefirah called *Kether*. *Kether* is the mysterious point of irruption at which the unfolding fullness of the self-revealing, self-manifesting, "being" Godhead issues from its hidden *Ungrund* in the Divine Nothing. It is probably unnecessary to remind readers that the term *Ungrund* was coined only much later by the German theosophist/mystic Jacob Boehme, who in a staggeringly profound pun substituted for *Urgrund* (primordial ground) the word *Ungrund* (non-ground). The complexity of this process which defies all imagination (the *Zohar* speaks of the bursting forth of a "dark flame") is evident also from the terminological fact that *Kether* is called, in the early kabbalistic texts, *'ayin* ("Nothing"). The first sefirah of the divine self-manifestation is thus still called *nihil*. This, of course, complicates our understanding of the relation of *Kether* (=*'ayin, nihil*) to *En Sof*, the divine non-being.

In fact, the early kabbalists still argue the question whether *Kether—'ayin*, being too close to *En Sof*, could properly be considered as a first sefirah at all. If not, i.e., if *Kether* is still considered as assimilated to *En Sof*, there would only be nine instead of ten *sefiroth*—a kabbalistic heresy!—and at some other point an additional sefirah would have to be introduced to complete the number ten. The latter alternative is rejected by most kabbalists, but this does not solve the problem of the first sefirah. As a matter of fact only the second sefirah (called *Hokhmah* "Wisdom," i.e., a kind of male *sophia*) is considered as the beginning of all "being." *Hokhmah* emanates from "nothing" (i.e., from the first sefirah *Kether*) and is the primordial point from which the divine Being (=the sefirotic *pleroma*) unfolds.

The identification of *Hokhmah* as the "primordial point" is of interest because mystical symbolism often uses mathematical symbolism. (Cf. for instance the well-known definition of God as a circle, the center of which is everywhere and the periphery nowhere; cf. on this subject D. Mahnke, *Jnendliche Sphare und Allmittelpunkt*, 1937). A surface is an infinite number of lines, much as a line is an infinite number of points. A point has no dimension at all. Even the tiniest point made by us with the thinnest possible tip of a pencil is already, strictly speaking, a two-dimensional surface. There is thus no better symbol for the transition from nothing to being than precisely this mysterious case of the "point." Only with the third sefirah does that realm of the divine being begin that is accessible to mystical meditation.

The passage from Reuchlin quoted above (which, as we have seen, renders the doctrine of R. Azriel), as well as our reference to the probable source of this doctrine, again raise the problem of pantheism. Scotus Erigena's teaching was indeed adopted with a definitely pantheist interpretation by R. Azriel's older contemporary David of Dinant who, not surprisingly, was condemned by the Church as a heretic. The *Zohar* unquestionably displays pantheistic tendencies, but I would not make bold to call its doctrine pantheistic without careful qualifications. The author's main problem is the relationship, or rather identity, of the hidden deity, the divine *nihil*, on the one hand, and its "living garment," i.e., its active, dynamic "being" as manifest in the *sefiroth*. The *sefiroth* are not simply emanations of the Plotinian kind; they are very Godhead in which (under the modalities of "being" and "nothing") all things are—to quote Eckhart again—*glich*. The implications of this doctrine are rather unusual and surprising. Unlike many other contemplative systems, the Kabbalah prohibits contemplation of the three highest sefiroth, not to speak of the divine Nothing, *'ayin*, or *En Sof.* Only the meditation on the seven lower sefiroth, i.e., the mystical communion with the living deity in its manifest "being" is regarded as possible and as permissible.

Almost 30 years lie between the composition of the first and the second paper here.* Kabbalistic research has seen immense, at some points even revolutionary progress, during this period, but I preferred not to make any changes or additions. The juxtaposition of these two papers is meant to illustrate the argument that there is more than one method of studying a religious phenomenon. In our case: the one is psychological, the other philosophico-theological. A variety of approaches is never contradictory; it is complementary.

---

*This paper was originally presented in German at a colloquium of the *Oratio Dominica* Foundation in September 1983 on the subject of *Sein und Nichts in der abendländischen Mystik*. The revised English version was presented at a New Era Conference on "God: The Contemporary Discussion," in the Section "God, Nothing, and the Ultimate" held December 29, 1986–January 3, 1987 in Coronado, California.

4

THE ONE, THE MANY, THE OTHER, THE DIVINE

M.H. Vogel

OUR AIM IN THIS PAPER is quite straightforward. It is simply to try and explicate the meaning of the three terms which appear in the title, i.e., the terms of "the one," "the many," and "the other." But by saying that the task is straightforward and even simple we in no way mean to imply further that it is unimportant, insignificant, or peripheral. Not at all. Indeed, if anything, we view this task to be of utmost significance promising to yield to us very fundamental insights into the nature and structure of the religious phenomenon. For these three terms delineate and characterize in an essential way the fourth term appearing in the title, i.e., the term of the divine, which is after all the very cornerstone term in the religious discourse. Thus, by explicating what the terms of "the One," "the Many," and "the Other" really signify, we should gain a much deeper understanding of what the notion of the divine means and this cannot but give us a much clearer understanding and appreciation of the structure of the religious phenomenon.

Even more specifically, the explication of these terms should greatly help us understand and appreciate the most major and most fundamental bifurcation that characterizes the religious phenomenon, namely the bifurcation between biblical religions and pagan religions (or, to follow the terminology of Dialectical Theology, the bifurcation between biblical *faiths* and pagan *religions*). For clearly, the distinction between the one and the many leads us directly to the bifurcation between monotheism and polytheism, and the distinction between the other and the non-other leads us just as directly to the bifurcation between theism and pantheism, and this means that we are led to two characterizations which go to the very core of the bifurcation between biblical faiths and the pagan religions. Thus, our approach to the task of this paper would proceed through the clarification of the bifurcation between biblical faiths and pagan religions and in doing so hope to clarify the very structure of the religious phenomenon.

The distinction between biblical faiths and pagan religions has often been depicted in terms of the distinction between monotheism and polytheism. Namely, the essence of biblical faiths is seen to lie in their monotheistic formulation while the essence of pagan religions is seen to lie in their polytheistic formulation. Biblical faiths are monotheistic while pagan religions are polytheistic and so the fundamental bifurcation within the religious phenomenon is the bifurcation between monotheism and polytheism.

Now, usually the significations of the notion of monotheism and that of polytheism are formulated in terms of their literal meaning, that is to say, the notion of monotheism is taken to signify a world-view formulation in terms of one god while the notion of polytheism is taken to signify a world-view formulation in terms of many gods. The bifurcation is between one god and many gods—a bifurcation between the one and the many, in short, a bifurcation that is purely *arithmetical*.

The fact, however, that the bifurcation is purely arithmetical did in no way deter people from seeing the bifurcation as most fundamental and significant. Indeed, many people (and not just the vast majority of common people but also many sophisticated philosophers and theologians) see in this purely arithmetical transition a transition which signifies a momentous change, a radical advance and breakthrough in the spiritual and intellectual history of mankind. For after all, so runs their argument, in moving from the many to the one we assert the principle of unification, the principle that ultimately all of reality is unified, that ultimately it has but one cause, one source. Thus, monotheism, in contrast to polytheism, signifies the great achievement of mankind in realizing the ultimate unification of all reality. Monotheism formulates, albeit in the religious domain, the ideal and goal which has come to define and guide the whole of the scientific enterprise, and in this sense it assumes all the value and significance which we have come to recognize in the scientific enterprise.

As said, there can be no denying that this view is widely held. However, whether this view, in the last analysis, is valid is a different matter. Indeed, as we have tried to argue on a different occasion, this view is ultimately invalid. Let us attempt to briefly recapitulate our argument.[1] In the main, we have tried to show two things: first, that the very nature of the religious phenomenon implicates a notion of the divine which precludes its being many and, second, that indeed, appearances to the contrary notwithstanding, there are no concrete historical instances where the divine (when the notion is properly grasped) is many.

Namely, we have tried to argue first, that the notion of the divine, ought, by its very essence, to implicate at least one thing and that is that it is ultimate; that whatever else it may or may not signify, it ought to signify the ultimate—it is the ultimate principle in terms of which the structures of faith of the religious phenomenon (which, as said, is itself, in the last analysis, but the articulation of a world-view) are constituted.[2] But if this is so then the notion of the divine must by its very definition signify oneness. For clearly, in any one system, in any one context, one cannot have more than one ultimate. And second, we have tried to argue that although there can be no denying that a polytheistic faith was confessed by many historical religions, indeed, by the vast, preponderant majority of all historical religions, this does not mean that all these religions do in fact confess that the divine (using the notion in the signification delineated above) is many; indeed, in truth, they too, if anything, really confess that the divine is one. For, we would submit that without exception all the gods involved in the various polytheistic formulations, i.e., all the gods of the various pantheons, fall short of being ultimate—they are all always and without fail penultimate but never ultimate. We do not have a single case where we can confront in the gods of the pantheon a god in the sense in which we are using the notion here, i.e., in the sense of it being an ultimate being. Indeed, given our preceding argument, this should not in the least surprise us—it could not have possibly been otherwise seeing that we cannot have an entity be ultimate when there are more than one of its kind.

Clearly what we have here is a confusion which the imprecision of language and the looseness of its usage sometimes bring about. Namely, we have here an instance where the same word, i.e., the word "god," is allowed to apply to two kinds of entities, an ultimate and a penultimate entity. Thus, the minute the confusion is cleared and we become precise in our language, insisting that the notion of God apply exclusively to a being that is exclusively ultimate, we readily can see that "the many" asserted by polytheism does not refer to the notion of God—the gods of the pantheon who are indeed many are not truly god.

We have an assertion of "the many" in polytheism but not with respect to the divine but rather with respect to some other being. Indeed, in most of these polytheistic formulations, there is a reference to yet another being beyond the many gods of the pantheon, be it called Moira, Fatum, Dike, Ma'at, or whatever else and it is this being which seems to constitute for these formulations the ultimate being. But this being (as we would expect) is unfailingly one and never many. Namely, it is not that in polytheistic formulations, i.e., in pagan religions there is no reference to an ultimate being, to a God. Such reference does indeed exist (if it did not, they could not be legitimately perceived as manifestations of the phenomenon of religion) except that it is not constituted by the gods of the pantheon, but rather by a certain power, a certain fate, a certain necessity, a certain law lying beyond these gods and (what should be most interesting and telling in view of the point we are trying to make here) this ultimate being—this power, necessity, fate, law—is indeed without exception always one and never many.

Thus, the dividing issue between monotheism and polytheism, between biblical and pagan religions, is not really arithmetical. "The one" versus "the many" really expresses some other factor, some other dimension, by which the division is brought about.

Indeed, we have suggested that the division lies in the ***kind*** of being the ultimate being is, namely, that the division between biblical and pagan religions (the former being associated generally with the monotheistic formulation, while the latter is generally associated with the polytheistic formulation) does not lie in the claim that the former has only one God (i.e., only one ultimate being) while the latter has many Gods (i.e., many ultimate beings), but rather that although, in the last analysis, both have one God (i.e., one ultimate being) they differ in that in the former this God, this ultimate being, is by its very essence a person, i.e., a being-of-consciousness, a Thou, while in the latter it is by its very essence a non-conscious being, a blind being-of-power, an It. This (and not the arithmetical consideration) constitutes the real division, the real difference, between biblical and pagan religions, between monotheism and polytheism.[3]

Indeed, if we penetrate more deeply into this matter we will see that the contrast between "the one" and "the many" can indeed carry precisely this signification of the personal versus the impersonal, in addition to the purely arithmetical signification. Namely, we will see that it can signify not only a contrast between a single entity and a plurality of entities but also a contrast between a personal entity and an impersonal entity. For a personal being, i.e., a being-of-consciousness, a Thou, is by its very essence non-quantifiable. This is so because consciousness, i.e., the "stuff" for which it is but the expression, is by its very essence non-quantifiable. Consciousness, like pregnancy, presents us with an either-or rather than a more or less calculus—one is either conscious or not. As such, a personal being, a being-of-consciousness, a Thou, is neither divisible nor multipliable. In this sense it must be one, it cannot be anything else but one.

In other words, it must be constituted of what some medieval theologians would refer to as a simple nature, a nature that has no parts. As against this, a non-personal being, i.e., a being-of-power, an It, is by its very essence quantifiable. And again this is so because power, i.e., what in this case constitutes the "stuff" for which the being is but the expression, is by its very essence quantifiable. Power by its very essence constitutes a continuum and thus always lends itself to a more or less. It can always be divided or multiplied. In this sense it is always "a many" and not "a one."

But clearly, the signification of the notion of "the one" and of "the many" which we introduced in the preceding discussion is quite different from the purely arithmetical signification which these notions also possess. Namely, in the arithmetical signification we are referred to the number of exemplars of the entity—single or plurality; as against this, in the signification introduced in the preceding discussion we are referred to the substance of the entity, to the kind of entity it is, to how it is constituted—as a simple, undifferentiated and, therefore, indivisible entity or as a compounded, differentiated and, therefore, divisible entity.

Thus, there is no denying that two distinct and quite different significations are implicated in our discussion. Still, granting this, there is also no denying that both significations are feasible and legitimate and, indeed, were widely utilized in the past. And all that we are saying here is that in terms of the latter signification, i.e. that in terms of the non-arithmetical signification, a meaningful, telling, and valid distinction can be introduced by the contrast of "the one" versus "the many." Indeed, what is being introduced is nothing less than the fundamental and pregnant (in implications) distinction between the divine *qua* ultimate being constituted as a personal being, a Thou, and it being constituted as an impersonal being, an It.

Thus, according to this when we say that god is one we would be saying that the ultimate being is, by its very essence, constituted as a personal being, as a Thou, and when we say that God is many we would be saying that the ultimate being is, by its very essence constituted as an impersonal being, as an It. This is a distinction that in the context of the phenomenology of religion is both meaningful and applicable; it is a distinction that can throw a great deal of light on the phenomenon of religion. As such, it is a distinction that is not only acceptable but, indeed, necessary.[4]

Now, in this context, i.e., in the context where "the one" and "the many" no longer signify a mere quantitative contrast between arithmetical numbers but rather a qualitative contrast between the personal and the impersonal, consciousness and power, the Thou-being and the It-being, the signification of the third notion included in our topic, i.e., the signification of the notion of "the other," receives an importance that is fundamental to our attempt to, so to speak, unpackage the signification of the notion of the divine. Perhaps, in order to gain greater clarity and comprehensiveness, we ought to add the contrary notion of "the non-other" and thus constitute a contrast between "the other" and "the non-other" (indeed, in a way parallel to the contrast between "the one" and "the many" which we constituted above). Certainly, we should be in a much better position to explicate more fully and clearly the notion before us and show its importance if we can undertake the explication in terms of a contrast, i.e., in terms of two opposed alternatives, rather than in terms of a single, self-sufficient notion. So let us proceed to examine the notion of "the other" in contrast to the opposite notion which it inescapably implicates, namely, in contrast to the notion of the "non-other" or, in other words, to the notion of "the same."

In essence what is involved in the contrast between "the other" and the not-other is the question of whether or not an "over-againstness" characterizes the relation to the object. Namely, the question is whether the object is separated from the subject in the sense of constituting a distinct, different entity, an other, or whether the object, in the last analysis, is not really separated from the subject but rather is joined to it within an all-encompassing oneness, thus constituting, in the last analysis, an all-pervading sameness encompassing subject and object. In other words, the question is whether there is a "gap" between subject and object or whether subject and object are embedded in an underlying all-pervading continuum—is reality constituted—as a multiplicity of distinct entities separated from each other by a "gap" or is it constituted as a one continuum where the so-called different entities are but abstracted different points on a single line? Clearly, an authentic other is feasible only in the former alternative but not in the latter one.

Now, in light of this, when we attribute the aspect of otherness to the divine, i.e., when we constitute the divine as an other, we mean to say that the divine is over-against the world (rather than at one with it), that a "gap" separates the divine from the world (rather than a continuum in which both are embedded). But this is really tantamount to saying that what we have here is a theistic and not a pantheistic formulation. For this is, we would submit, precisely what respectively the theistic and pantheistic formulations intend to signify. Namely, both formulations impinge upon the kind of relation that subsists between God and the world.[5] They differ, however, in the kind of relation which they delineate. Thus, theism delineates a relation in which God and the world are over-against each other while pantheism delineates a relation where, in the last analysis, God and the world are one and the same. Or, to use the terminology of this paper, in theism God is an other with respect to the world while in pantheism He is one and the same with the world, a non-other. Thus, by saying that God is an other we are saying that we are dealing with a theistic God, i.e., a God who relates to the world theistically while by saying that God is a non-other we are saying that we are dealing with a pantheistic God, i.e., a God who relates to the world pantheistically.

We should be clear, however, that the degree of separateness, of distancing, i.e., the extent of the "gap" that exists, is a secondary and different issue that is in no way to be confused with the theistic-pantheistic contrast. For obviously the question of the degree of separateness, of distancing, falls completely within the theistic alternative. It merely further articulates the theistic alternative by spelling it out more precisely—is it a big or a small "gap"? But as long as there is a "gap," no matter how small, we clearly remain within the theistic alternative. Thus, we should not confuse the theistic-pantheistic contrast with another contrast that also has wide applicability in the study of the religious phenomenon, namely the contrast between immanence and transcendence, i.e., between the immanent God and the transcendent God. For this contrast addresses itself precisely to the issue of the *extent* of the "gap" that exists between God and the world—an immanent God being a God who is close at hand, who enters the world, and who, therefore, can be encountered fairly frequently and at close quarters; while a transcendent God, is a God who is very remote, who removes himself from the world, and who, therefore, can only rarely, if at all, be encountered and then only in a very nebulous and fleeting way.

But, as such, the immanent-transcendent contrast remains as said, within the theistic alternative—it merely spells out, so to speak, how theistic the alternative is to be, i.e., how far over-against each other the parties are to be from each other. But the immanent God, even the very immanent God, is still a theistic God, for as long as an over-againstness, a "gap," exists, no matter how minimal or minuscule it may be, we are having a theistic and not a pantheistic God. Thus, although the two contrasts are often used interchangeably, it is not really valid.[6]

But to return to our main concern in this paper, namely, to return to the task of explicating the three attributes which the title of this paper assigns to the divine, (the attributes of "the one," "the many," and "the other"), let us now attempt to see what linkage, if any, can be constituted between the three. Well, we have already established that "the one" and "the many" are linked as the mutually exclusive poles of a contrast. The question then before us is really with respect to the third attribute, i.e., with respect to the attribute of "the other." Can we establish any connections, any linkage, between it and "the other" two attributes?

It would seem to us that we can; indeed, it would seem to us that we can establish a linkage not only with regard to the attribute of "the other" but also with regard to its alternative, contrasting attribute, i.e., with regard to the attribute of "the non-other" or, in other words, with regard to the attribute of "the same."[7] In other words, what we are claiming is that there is a linkage between the two contrasting sets, between "the one" versus "the many" contrast and "the other" versus "the same" contrast; more specifically, we are claiming that, on "the one" hand, a linkage can be established between the attribute of "the other" (from the latter contrast) and the attribute of "the one" (from the former contrast) and that, on "the other" hand, a further linkage can be likewise established between the attribute of "the same" (from the latter contrast) and the attribute of "the many" (from the former contrast).

And, of course, what we mean here by linkage is that the attribute from the former contrast would implicate in a necessary and inescapable manner the corresponding attribute from the latter contrast. Thus, what we claim is that, on the one hand, the attribute of "the one" necessarily and inescapably implicates the attribute of "the other" and that, on the other hand, the attribute of "the many" necessarily and inescapably implicates the attribute of "the same." And, of course, it should be quite clear that if our claim is valid it would clearly imply that the attributes of "the other" and of sameness are not just peripheral, accidental characterizations of the divine; but that they are very fundamental and essential characterizations. For after all they are necessarily implicated by that which constitutes the very being of the divine.

But is our claim valid? Can we really substantiate it? Well, at first sight it certainly would not seem so. Indeed, if anything, our claim would appear to be outrightly self-contradictory. For how is it possible to link "the one" with "the other"? Does not "the other" necessarily implicate a twosomeness—a subject and an object (or two subjects) at any rate, not just one being but a second one over-against it? In other words, far from implicating "the one," does not "the other" necessarily implicate "the many"? And by the same token how is it possible to link "the many" with "the non-other," with "sameness"? Does not "the many" necessarily suggest differentiation and, therefore, the lack of "sameness," namely, "an other" rather than "a non-other"? Indeed, if anything, it would appear as if the valid claim is constituted exactly by the very opposite of what we have suggested; namely, that "the one" should be linked to "the non-other" and "the many" to "the other." In other words, it would appear that in order to get things right, i.e., in order to establish the valid claim, we have to put our suggestion on its head.

But if we think a little bit more carefully about this matter we will readily see that this is really not so. For our claim runs into self-contradiction only because "the one" and "the many" have been implicated in terms of their arithmetical signification. Namely, it is only when "the one" signifies a single entity, and "the many" signifies a plurality of entities and nothing else that linking the former to "the other" and the latter to "the non-other" runs us into insoluble contradictions. But it was precisely the very thrust of the argument that the essential signification, of "the one" and of "the many" is not to be found in the arithmetical signification. The notions of "the one" and of "the many" may indeed carry the arithmetical signification, but it is not their essential signification when they are taken in the context of the religious discourse. Rather, in the context of the religious discourse, they signify the kind of being which characterizes the ultimate. Namely, in this context "the one" signifies essentially a "being-of-consciousness," a personal being, a Thou and "the many" signifies essentially a being-of-power, an impersonal being, an It.

But now, with respect to this latter signification, all the difficulties and contradictions associated with the arithmetical signification evaporate. With respect to "the one" signifying a being-of-consciousness, a personal being, a Thou and "the many" signifying a being-of-power, an impersonal being, an It, there is no problem, no contradiction whatsoever, in linking the former with the notion of "the other" and the latter with the notion of "the non-other" of "sameness." Indeed, not only is there no contradiction, no difficulty with such a linkage, but a very good case can be made that it is necessary and inescapable. Namely, a very good case can be made that the notion of "the one," when signifying a being-of-consciousness, implicates by its very inner logic (thus implicating necessarily and inescapably) the notion of "the other," while the notion of "the many" when signifying a being-of-power implicates by its very inner logic the notion of "sameness."

Briefly stated, the underlying argument would run as follows: consciousness is by its very essence constituted in terms of over-againstness. There can be no such thing as consciousness period; consciousness can arise only as consciousness *of* something or someone. Thus, it can arise only in terms of a something or a someone that is over-against it. Take the over-againstness, the "gap," and consciousness per force must collapse and disappear. And from this it clearly follows that a conscious being, a personal being, a Thou, can arise only if there is "an other," i.e., if there is an other conscious being, an other personal being, an other Thou. Consciousness, personhood, Thouness, can arise only in the context of a twosome—it takes two not only to tango but to constitute a personal being, a Thou. In this way "the one" when signifying a personal being, a Thou, necessarily implicates by its very inner logic "the other," i.e., an other personal being, an other Thou. On "the other" hand power is by its very essence constituted in terms of a continuum; it abhors a vacuum, a break, a "gap," in its flow. The very expression of power is movement and movement is by its very essence constituted as a flow, a change, that is continuous. Indeed, any distinctiveness, any separation, that may arise in the context of power can thus arise only through abstraction. Only through abstraction can separation (and thus multiplicity) be established; in concrete reality there is only a continuous, uninterrupted, flow. As such, indeed, we can see that a divine being who is constituted as a personal being, i.e., a God who is constituted as a Thou-God, will of necessity implicate an other, a theistic view and a divine being who is constituted as an impersonal being, i.e., a God who is constituted as an It-God, will of necessity implicate sameness, a pantheistic view.[8]

Thus, the notion of a Thou-God will necessarily implicate a theistic view, while the notion of an It-God will necessarily implicate a pantheistic view. In this sense, the notions of "the one," "the many," "the other" (and "the non-other") are intimately connected and are notions which provide the very fundamental delineation of the divine.

NOTES

1. The full argument is presented in our essay "monotheism" appearing in the *Encyclopedia Judaica*.
2. It is because of this understanding of the religious phenomenon and the notion of the divine that it makes sense to view secular ideologies (such as, for example, communism) as pseudo-religious and that one can talk of concrete, earthly things such as money, power, or career as someone's "god." Indeed, it is precisely because of this understanding (whereby the notion of the divine is to signify by its very essence ultimacy) that the notion of idolatry as that which takes a non-ultimate being to be "god" can arise.
3. Indeed, in fairness we should say that in some quarters of scholarship it was sensed that the purely arithmetical aspect is problematic and, even more tellingly, that the really divisive aspect lies in the distinction between a personal and an impersonal ultimate being. We do not say that it was clearly and consciously known but only that it was sensed. That it was sensed as can be seen in the fact that some scholars felt constrained to qualify the monotheistic alternative by the adjective ethical; namely they felt constrained to speak not of the monotheistic dimension pure and simple but of ethical monotheism. For in introducing the notion of the ethical, we would want to argue, one inevitably implicates that the concerned party—which in our case is clearly the divine being, i.e., that being which is the ultimate being in the discourse—is personal and not impersonal, seeing that it makes sense to talk of the ethical only with reference to the personal and not to the impersonal. By no stretch of the imagination would it make sense to consider the ethical dimension with respect to an impersonal being; only with respect to a personal being can one raise the ethical possibility. Thus, by choosing to contrast not just monotheism as such but specifically ethical monotheism with polytheism, the distinction between the divine being as personal and as impersonal is inescapably being introduced.
4. In this connection, and in conclusion, let us point out that the statement which is generally taken as the quintessential articulation of the monotheistic faith of Judaism, the statement which, as such indeed, has been called the watchword of Judaism, i.e., the *Shema* (the Hear O Israel) makes precisely the point we are trying to make here. Namely, it is not, as usually presented, really stating that God is arithmetically one but rather that God *qua* ultimate being is a personal being. True, this is not readily evident. But this is so because of the custom in Judaism not to pronounce the Tetragammaton and therefore to substitute the appellation "Lord" whenever it appears. Thus, we usually articulate the *Shema* as stating "Hear O Israel, the Lord our God, the Lord is One," and this certainly gives the appearance that it states that God is arithmetically one.

   But if we stop to think for a minute we shall see that in this format the statement is really vacuous and tautologous. For, by saying that the Lord is God or that God (i.e., the ultimate being) is one, it does not say very much. Indeed, it does not establish anything new at all. It establishes, on the one hand, an equation between two appellations of the divine which as such is tantamount to saying that the ultimate is the ultimate.

   But the verse in Deuteronomy does not really say this. What it really says is "Hear O Israel YHWH is our Lord, YHWH is one." Now, YHWH is a proper-name which as such implies that the bearer of this name is a personal being (we affix proper names only to personal beings and when on some occasions they are affixed to impersonal beings this is only by poetic license, by extension through the process of personification, i.e., imagining a non-personal being as if it were personal). Thus, the verse in Deuteronomy, the watchword of the monotheism of Judaism, states that a personal being by the name of YHWH is our God; and that this personal being, this YHWH, is the ultimate being, the One, i.e., God *qua* the ultimate being, and not just another penultimate being, another of the gods of the pantheon.

5. If one wants to use these formulations in a precise way, this is indeed what they impinge upon. They both impinge upon the kind of *relation* that subsists between God and the word rather than on the kind of *being* God is.
6. Of course, in a way we can say that pantheism is but the limiting case for immanence; namely, when God becomes so immanent in the world that He becomes one with it, we have pantheism. As such, pantheism is but the end of the process of immanence (the end of the line, so to speak) and one can see and appreciate how on this basis people may be inclined to separate and withdraw immanence from the theistic alternative and equate it with the pantheistic alternative. Of course, if this is done then the immanent-transcendent contrast is, indeed, interchangeable with the pantheistic-theistic contrast (for clearly, there can be no question that transcendence falls with the theistic alternative). Indeed, the wide-spread practice of equating the two contrasts and using them interchangeably is most probably derived from this reasoning. But this reasoning, it would seem to us, is in the last analysis not really valid. For precisely as a limiting case it is no longer what it limits. Namely, when immanence is so maximal that God becomes one and the same with the world, i.e., when we have pantheism, we no longer really have immanence. No, immanence too belongs to the theistic alternative; and the immanence-transcendence alternative is but a further spelling out of this alternative in terms of its degree.
7. This should not be surprising at all seeing that the one and the many constitute a mutually exclusive contrast. For as such, this means that any further linkage would be possible only with regard to one of these two attributes but not with regard to both; indeed, the linkage to the one would clearly exclude the very possibility of also establishing a linkage to the other. Finally, by the same token, this also means that if a linkage to one of these two attributes by a third attribute can be established, this would suggest that its contrasting attribute can be linked to the other of the two attributes. Namely, if a linkage can be established between the attribute of the other and that of the one then this would immediately exclude the possibility of establishing a linkage also between the other and the many, and, furthermore, it would rather suggest that a linkage with the many would be possible for the attribute of the non-other, i.e., for the attribute of the same.
8. As argued above, there is no contradiction here in linking monotheism with theism and polytheism and pantheism, for in the context of the religious discourse the notions of monotheism and polytheism do not carry essentially an arithmetical signification. But, even if these notions are taken in their arithmetical significations, there would be no contradiction. But how is this possible seeing that the theistic view necessarily implicates a dualism and the pantheistic view necessarily implicates a monism? Do we not fall back into the contradiction discussed above

of linking one with twosome and many with oneness? The answer is no because the arithmetical oneness signified by monotheism and the arithmetical plurality signified by polytheism refer specifically to the divine being, i.e., to that which constitutes the ultimate principle, and not to the sum total of entities in the world; while the theistic view and the pantheistic view involve the totality of entities and not just those entities which constitute the ultimate principle. As such, there is really no contradiction, seeing that the oneness and the plurality involved in the linkage relate to different referents.

Furthermore, it will occur to some, no doubt, that linking monotheism with the theistic view may well give rise to the problem which so concerned philosophers belonging to the neo-Hegelian orientation, for example, F.H. Bradley. Thus, Bradley strongly insisted that an ultimate being, i.e., an absolute being, could not have relations. As such, in as much as monotheism refers to an ultimate being it could not be linked with a theistic stance, seeing that theism necessarily implicates a relation. But the reason for Bradley's opposition to this linkage is not determined by the problem of the arithmetical conflict, i.e., by the problems that you cannot be one and many at one and the same time. Rather, the reason is determined by his conviction that being in relation precludes the possibility of perfection, of absoluteness. For being in relation clearly implicates there being another entity outside the one which has the relation and this inescapably limits, and confines the latter. An entity being in relation cannot therefore be all-inclusive, unlimited.

But according to Bradley an absolute being must be all-inclusive and unlimited; if it is not it cannot be absolute. It follows, for him therefore, that if a being is in relation it cannot be absolute. Clearly, this argument revolves on equating absoluteness with all-inclusiveness, unlimitedness; only when the absolute is understood to signify all-inclusiveness and total lack of limitation is the argument valid.

But we would suggest that such an understanding of the absolute, i.e., that such an equation of the absolute with the all-inclusive and limitless, is possible only when our discourse is grounded in the dimension of power but not when it is grounded in the dimension of consciousness. Namely, the equation holds only with respect to an absolute being, i.e., to a God, who is constituted as a being-of-power, as an It; it does not hold with respect to an absolute being, i.e., to a God, who is constituted as a being–of–consciousness, as a Thou.

Bradley's objection, therefore, does not really undermine our position; indeed, it should not concern us seeing that it implicates an It-God while we are dealing with a Thou-god. And this response, by the way, would also apply to the attempts by some more recent philosophers, e.g., Whitehead, to overcome Bradley's objection. For much as they criticize and reject Bradley, they keep in common with him the It-God. Their alternative is also established on the basis of an It-God. As such, their "correction," so to speak is equally beside the point as far as we are concerned. They and Bradley are opposite teams but at least they play in the same field. We play in a different field altogether.

5

THE SELF AND NOT-SELF IN CHRISTIAN MYSTICISM

AUGUSTINE AND ECKHART

Ewert Cousins

THROUGHOUT THE CHRISTIAN TRADITION, there has been a strong affirmation of the self in philosophy, theology, and mysticism. Christians have focused on the self under the Biblical phrase "the image of God," which they draw from the first chapter of *Genesis*. There it is recorded that after creating the physical universe, with its vegetative and animal life, God said: "Let us make man in our image and likeness" (*Gen*.1:26). The Fathers of the Church, both East and West, employed the phrase "image of God" to describe the most central, basic, and distinctive dimension of the human person.

Note that the phrase "image of God" contains two positive affirmations: it identifies the human person as an image and, without any qualifications, makes a straightforward affirmation of God. This positive language implies a corresponding positive ontological perception that is supported by Christian theology and confirmed by Christian mysticism. It is true that, from all three perspectives, the human person is seen as radically relational. Nevertheless, because the self has its own ontological status, it is not identical with God nor absorbed into God. In a similar fashion, it is implied that God, too, has his own ontological status, which stands at an unfathomable distance from creatures, yet grounding them ontologically at the same time that it reflects them and, in the case of conscious creatures, reveals itself to their innermost depths. In the light of this experience and understanding, the Christian tradition would find it alien, inaccurate, and, if pressed, heretical to speak of a not-self.

In the present paper I will explore the notion of the self first in Augustine and then in Eckhart. Augustine provided the classical formulation of the self as image of God for Western Christianity in his extensive analysis of the soul in the second half of his treatise *On the Trinity*. His position became the common doctrine in the West through the Patristic period and into the Middle Ages, influencing, for example, Anselm in the eleventh and twelfth centuries and Bonaventure in the thirteenth. However in the fourteenth century there emerged a concept of the self which seems radically at odds with that of Augustine and his followers. In bold and even shocking terms, Meister Eckhart proposed a position which at least approximates a doctrine of the not-self. This position of Eckhart will be the object of our study in the latter part of this paper.

My paper will focus primarily on mystical experience, but will include the dimensions of philosophy and theology. Since I will be drawing from mystical texts and giving an interpretation of mystical experience, it seems wise to make some preliminary remarks on the nature of mysticism, as I am understanding it here, and on the methodology I intend to employ in its study. Concerning the first issue, I am taking mysticism to refer to that kind of human experience in which one has an immediate and intuitive consciousness of transcendence or the transpersonal, whether this be in the context of nature, the self, the divine, or what has been called emptiness or the void. As this formulation suggests, I am not limiting mysticism to an experience of the ontologically divine, although much of mystical experience in the world's religions is of this kind and has this as its goal. The minimal meaning I am giving to mystical experience is transcendence; namely, an experience which transcends the limits of ordinary, everyday forms of consciousness. With this as a general descriptive definition. I would like to make some more extended remarks on my methodology for the study of mysticism.

Methodology for Mysticism

The method I am proposing is akin to the phenomenology of Husserl, the German philosopher who flourished in the early decades of the 20th century.[1] My method is similar to his in that it proceeds by describing the contents of consciousness. However, it does not bracket and hold in abeyance the metaphysical content of the consciousness it is studying, although the observer may be called upon to bracket his own metaphysical presuppositions. Nor does the method adopt the model in which all intellectual content is derived from the interpretation of raw experience by subjective consciousness. On the contrary, my method is open to the possibility that the intellectual content of the experience can come from the very object of consciousness.

In the first stage, I am not concerned with establishing the method as universal, that is, as applying to all mysticism and to all religious traditions. Since I am focusing the method on two strands of the Christian tradition, I do not wish at the beginning even to ask the question whether it can apply to all forms of mysticism: to theistic and non-theistic, to Taoist and Buddhist mysticism, the mysticism of archaic peoples, to the experience of the prophet Isaiah and to that of Sankara. I believe that this method can be applied effectively to this wide variety of experiences and perhaps to mystical experience universally. However, to deal explicitly with this pluralism at the outset, I feel, would be too complex to control adequately. So if the method seems to be colored by certain Christian presuppositions, realize that these can be critically examined at a later stage.

I propose the following as stages of a journey into the study of mystical consciousness:

(1)The first stage is to encounter mystical consciousness. This may be a personal experience of the investigator that is reflected on later. Or it may be the experience of another which is described to the investigator either personally by the subject or through writings. The investigator might even be present during the mystical experience of the subject or learn of it later. Since in the present case I will focus on classical examples in a tradition, I will concentrate on written texts. Even here there is a variety of genres. Some mystical writings recount personal experience, for example those of Augustine, Bernard of Clairvaux, and Julian of Norwich. Others record the experience through a biographer, for example, in the ecstatic experience of Francis of Assisi when he received the stigmata. Or they may be works giving instruction in meditation, for example, Bonaventure's *The Tree of Life* with meditations on the life of

Christ; or instructions in the stages of mystical contemplation, for example, Bonaventure's *The Soul's Journey into God*; or sermons, like Eckhart's, which are intended to evoke in the listener levels of mystical consciousness.

(2)The second stage of the method is to enter into the consciousness of the mystic. This may seem impossible. Certain philosophical positions take a radically solipsistic stance claiming that we can know only the contents of our own consciousness and certainly that we cannot know the internal contents of another person's consciousness. This problem is compounded by the fact that we are not dealing here with everyday forms of consciousness, for example, of a tree or a hat, which we all can easily share, but rather altered states of consciousness which are contemplative or even ecstatic. How is it possible for us to share this experience? I believe that we can through the capacity for empathy which we all have and which some have cultivated to a high degree. If we hold, as I do, that we all have the capacity for contemplative and mystical experience, then we can have a spontaneous resonance with even high levels of mystical consciousness. And by our capacity for empathy, we can enter at least to some extent into the consciousness of another, even of a mystic.

(3)The third stage of the method involves describing the contents of consciousness of the mystic. Many elements fall within this stage: the mystic's experience of the self, for example, or, in the case of nature mysticism, the mystic's experience of sense objects or the universe as a whole. It would take much time to sort out all of these dimensions; I would like to focus here on a distinctive and crucial dimension: that of the divine, absolute reality in relation to the soul. I realize that I am speaking of a form of theistic mysticism. However I do not want to take theism in a narrow sense of a personal God, but in the sense of absolute reality, differing in ontological status from all other things and designated in some positive or affirmative fashion, not merely by silence or negative judgments. The point I wish to make here is that the ontological status of this reality must be taken into account seriously in dealing with the mystical experience.

I propose that intentionality is the perspective from which we can understand such mystical consciousness of the divine. Husserlian phenomenology drew the Aristotelian notion of the intentionality of consciousness from Franz Brentano. According to intentionality our consciousness "intends" in the Latin etymological root meaning of "stretching toward" an object. It is consciousness of something. In dealing with knowledge of the divine, we face the problem that the soul is finite and the divine infinite. This has led some to a radical apophatic theology, we might say a radical apophatic epistemology. However, if it is of the very nature of human consciousness to "intend" the divine, then the metaphysical distance is bridged by the intentionality of consciousness. This will be a crucial point in dealing with the self and not-self.

Here in the intentionality of consciousness we can ground knowledge of the ontological infinite. Once we establish that knowledge of the infinite is possible, the question arises as to the nature of that knowledge. I claim it is of the essence of the mystical experience of the divine to be conscious of and affirm the ontological reality of the divine—with all the divine attributes that the classical theologies have affirmed. This ontological affirmation cannot be bracketed nor can it be said to be merely the mystic's subjective interpretation. What makes God mysticism significant, what constitutes its distinctive character, is precisely the experience of God as the real, as that which is. This is not a mere interpretation of the experience; it constitutes the very essence of the experience.

Intentionality also can help answer the question that has been recently raised again by Steven Katz and others: namely, is there one form of mystical experience or many?[2] I believe that there has been a lack of critical reflection in posing the question. It has been formulated in terms derived from the finite realm of multiplicity. Instead, if it is explored through the very intentionality of God mysticism, then the ontological status of the object—the unique divinity—can provide the basis for the claim of unity. If God is perceived as being the one without a second, then when the mystic touches that reality, he or she realizes that they have reached the same realm that all other God mystics have reached. In this sense, at least, there is only one experience of the divine, since the divine is the uniquely one, although there may be diversities in the subjective paths, and even among the divine attributes. But even in the diversity of the divine attributes, the mystics perceive the divine nature which is the point where the intentionality of their experience converges.

The Self in Augustine

As indicated above, in patristic and in the major portion of medieval Christianity, the self is perceived primarily as the image of God. Although Augustine drew the terminology from verse 26 of the first chapter of *Genesis*, his understanding of this is based on his mystical experience which he records in his *Confessions*. He tells us how at a turning point in his life, he read "some books of the Platonists" (*quosdam*

Platonicorum libros). In them he found presented what the Christians believe as the mystery of the Trinity. Although he found the Trinity there, he did not find "that the Word was made flesh and dwelt among us" (*Jn.* 1:14). Augustine then tells us: "Being admonished by all this to return to myself, I entered into my inmost part" (*in intima mea*). He acknowledges that he was able to do this because God was his guide and helper. Within the inner chamber of himself, he perceived an unchangeable light: "I entered within and saw, with my soul's eye (such as it was), an unchangeable light (*lucem incommutabilem*). It was shining above the eye of my soul and above my mind." He realizes that this is no ordinary light, nor is it similar to physical light. Rather "it was higher than my soul because it made me, and I was below because I was made by it." He then identifies this light as God: "He who knows truth (*novit veritatem*) knows that Light, and whoever knows it, knows eternity (*novit aeternitatem*). Charity knows it (*caritas novit eam*). O eternal Truth and true Love and beloved Eternity! You are my God (*tu es Deus meus*), to you I sigh day and night."[3]

For Augustine this was an overwhelming mystical experience. It was catalytic and transformative, freeing him from the materialism and dualism of his previous Manichaean position. Mediated through Platonism and Neoplatonism, this experience led to his formal conversion to Christianity and his later life as a Christian bishop, philosopher, theologian, and spiritual teacher. It is the dramatic turning point in his autobiography *The Confessions*.

What was this experience? How to describe it phenomenologically? If we apply the method as presented above, we can say that Augustine experienced an immediate contact with the divine as eternity, truth, and goodness (love). This encounter took place in the depths of his soul, in the innermost recesses of his consciousness (*in intima mea*). As is clear from this text, its context, and Augustine's subsequent analysis, the soul or self does not disappear in this experience, although the intentionality of his consciousness is of God and not the soul. Rather he discovers that by journeying into the depths of himself that he himself is an image, or, as the medieval tradition emphasized, a mirror (*speculum*) of God. Thus the self retains its own intrinsic constitution ontologically, theologically, and mystically. However, it does not stand in radical isolation; on the contrary, in its very ontological and spiritual depths it is relational. Its very being is such that it has God at its center as the light of eternity, truth, and goodness.

Augustine calls this image or mirror dimension of the soul the *mens*. According to its etymology, we could translate this term by "mind," but this would not convey the proper meaning to a modern reader. What

Augustine means by *mens* is rather the highest, or deepest, portion of the soul which by its very nature reflects God. The *mens* is in what Augustine calls the superior reason (*ratio superior*). In his treatise *On the Trinity* he develops his understanding of the twofold perspective of *ratio* or reason. For him *ratio* is a single faculty with a double perspective. If reason turns its gaze on the phenomenal world—the realm of multiplicity, of finitude, of creatures—it is called inferior reason (*ratio inferior*). If, on the other hand, *ratio* turns its gaze to the realm above, specifically to the transcendent forms of the Platonists seen as the divine attributes of eternity, truth, goodness, and beauty, it is called superior reason (*ratio superior*). The Augustinian tradition used the term *intellectus*, or intellect, for this aspect of *ratio*, meaning by this a penetrating, intuitive grasp of the divine which is immediate and autonomous—not reasoned to by inferior reason.[4]

When one's consciousness of the *mens* is awakened, as happened in Augustine's mystical experience in the depths of the self, one comes to a simultaneous awareness of both the soul and of God. This is precisely the experience of the soul as image of God, for it has God present to itself as interpenetrating light, like light shining in a mirror. When we see light in a mirror, we first perceive the brightness of the light and do not immediately concentrate on the mirror itself. In a similar fashion, when Augustine experienced God as light shining in his soul, he first focused on God himself, saying: "You are my God, to you I sigh day and night."[5] Yet simultaneously he had an implicit awareness of his soul, or self, reflecting this divine light.

The Self as Image of the Trinity

Augustine devoted the last eight chapters of his treatise *On the Trinity* to bringing to reflective awareness the structure of the *mens*, or self as image of God, specifically, the image of the Trinity. This he did by analyzing the faculties of memory, understanding, and will. By retracing the memory to its ground, he discovered God as eternity; by retracing the understanding to its ground, he discovered God as truth; and by retracing the will to its ground, he discovered God as goodness or love. But eternity, truth, and goodness are not merely divine attributes; they lead the mystical soul into the very inner life of God, that is, the inner Trinitarian life of the Father, Son, and Holy Spirit. For eternity leads to the Father as the source of the Trinitarian processions, truth to the Son as the expressed Word and Image of the Father, and goodness to the Holy Spirit as the love between the Father and the Son. Thus the *mens* is more than an image of God; it is an image of the Trinity, with our memory reflecting the Father, our understanding the Son, and our will the Holy Spirit.

In a celebrated passage in *On the Trinity*, Augustine distinguishes two selves: that with one's self as object of consciousness, which he considered the image of stupidity; and that with God as object of consciousness, which he considered the image of wisdom:

> Now this trinity of the mind is the image of God, not because the mind remembers, understands, and loves itself, but because it also has the power to remember, understand, and love its Maker. And in doing this it attains wisdom. If it does not do this, the memory, understanding, and love of itself is no more than an act of folly. Therefore, let the mind remember its God, to whose image it was made, let it understand and love him.[6]

The image with one's self as object of consciousness is not the self of Christian mysticism. For this is the finite, superficial, self-contained self—the self of illusion which stands as an obstacle between the true self and God. The true self is fully itself when it reflects God, specifically when it reflects the Trinity, when the divine light of the Trinity shines in it as in a mirror.

When examining the question of the self and not-self in Christian mysticism, we must focus on the level of the image of God, and not on that of the superficial self. Of course, we could apply the notion of not-self to the superficial self, claiming that in the mystical experience the superficial self disappears or so sinks into the horizon of consciousness that it ceases to function significantly. Such a position would, I believe, be widely accepted. A more crucial issue arises on the level of the image of God: Does the self of the mystic remain when it reflects God as an image of God? Does the self perdure ontologically and psychologically, or is it absorbed into the divinity? In other words, does it become a not-self? I will examine this question by analyzing Augustine's mystical experience in the light of the notion of intentionality which I presented above.

In its deepest consciousness, the soul "intends" (stretches out to) God as its object. In its memory it intends God as eternity, in its understanding, as truth, in its will as goodness. These are three attributes of God, each of which is grounded in and manifests the divine nature. It is crucial to underscore that the intentionality of this consciousness is of the metaphysically ultimate: the really real, that which is. There is abundant evidence—both linguistic and experiential—that Augustine perceived the image of God in this way. The intentionality of the soul as image focuses on an object whose content is the divine, with all the metaphysical weight that the term carries in the traditional theology of the divine nature and the divine attributes. This mystical experience has a noetic or intellectual character and contains as its metaphysical content a grasp of ultimate reality itself. This means that the metaphysical ultimate is contained in the experience and is not brought in as a subjective interpretation of the mystic who is heir to a particular philosophical and religious tradition.

Furthermore, this metaphysical content of the divine reality is present in a positive or kataphatic fashion, and not merely in a negative or apophatic form. By that I mean that the intentionality of this consciousness tends not merely towards an unlimited horizon, an openness to infinity which breaks out of the limits of a circumscribed self but which does not necessarily touch the ontologically divine. On the contrary, the imagery of light, the affirmation of God in positive categories of Truth and Goodness, indicate that the intentionality of the image of God stands within the tradition of affirmative or kataphatic theology.

This leads to the question: Does the self remain in its mystical experience as image of God? I believe that it does because of the positive content of its intentionality. Since God is grasped in his positive perfection, the soul itself, though finite in its ontological structure, can extend to the positive absolute in its intentionality. Hence this absolute, as positive perfection, is reflected in the image. Although the self remains ontologically, on the psychological level of its intentionality it is so completely oriented to the divine that it may seem to be absorbed in the deity. Yet implicit in this consciousness is the ontological ground of its differentiated self, reflecting the positive perfection of the divinity.

Thus our phenomenological analysis has revealed that Augustine's mystical experience contains within itself philosophical and theological perceptions that the soul has an ontological status of its own, as does God himself. On the deepest level it has further revealed that by its very nature—by its innate intentionality—the soul is related to God as self-conscious image to its exemplar. Thus Augustine's mystical experience stands at a far remove from an experience of the not–self.

The Not-Self in Eckhart

While Augustine's mystical experience retains the self, Eckhart's seems to lose the self. In so doing Eckhart presents the most striking example within the Christian tradition of a doctrine of the not-self. It is important to call attention to the fact that Eckhart is heir to the tradition that Augustine inaugurated. He has a rich affirmative theology of the divinity and of the self as image of God. In fact, his major treatment of the soul is of the birth of the Son in the Soul. At the same time he experiences God as stripped of all positive attributes: as the Godhead above God, as the desert of the Godhead. It is this latter experience I will focus on here, as the basis for a doctrine of the not-self.

Eckhart moves towards the desert of the Godhead by a radical detachment. In a sermon on poverty, he distinguishes two kinds of poverty: external and internal. After external poverty, which he approves, he directs his attention to internal poverty. "A poor man," he says, "wants nothing, and knows nothing, and has nothing."[7] In Eckhart's era a lifestyle of external poverty had been extolled by Francis of Assisi and the Franciscan movement as the very essence of the Christian's following of Christ. Eckhart moves beyond the usual Franciscan position by advising a radical internal poverty. Of course, the Franciscans and the general monastic tradition practiced external poverty as a way toward and a symbol of internal poverty. But Eckhart goes much farther. The truly poor man, he says, must strip himself of absolutely everything, even of God!

He points out how "people say that a man is poor who wants nothing, but they interpret it in this way that a man ought to live so that he never fulfills his own will in anything, but that he ought to comport himself so that he may fulfill God's dearest will." But he says that such are not truly poor. "If a person wants really to have poverty," Eckhart says, "he ought to be as free of his own created will as he was when he did not exist." He goes on to say: "So long as you have a will to fulfill God's will and a longing for God and for eternity, then you are not poor; for a poor man is one who has a will and a longing for nothing."[8]

Eckhart then proceeds in his radical analysis, saying that we must be free from God himself. He speaks of his existence in his first cause, saying that there he had no God. "I wanted nothing, I longed for nothing, for I was an empty being. But when I went out from my own free will and received my created being, then I had a 'God,' for before there were any creatures, God was not 'God,' but he was what he was." He concludes: "So let us pray to God that we may be free of 'God,' and that we may apprehend and rejoice in that everlasting truth in which the highest angel and the fly and the soul are equal—there where I was established, where I wanted what I was and was what I wanted."[9]

Eckhart has become the truly poor man. He has stripped himself of all desire, of the desire to do God's will, even of God himself. In a similar vein, he strips himself of all knowledge, even knowledge of God; and then of all possessions, even of his own being and the being of God. In this state of radical poverty, he enters into the desert of the Godhead, where there is no differentiation, no distinction:

> I speak in all truth, truth that is eternal and enduring, that this same light [the spark of the soul] is not content with the simple divine essence in its repose, as it neither gives nor receives; but it wants to know the source of this essence, it wants to go into the simple ground, into the quiet desert, into which distinction never gazed, nor the Father, nor the Son, nor the Holy Spirit.[10]

In another passage, Eckhart calls forth the same experience of radical detachment by describing how the soul's naked being finds the naked being of the divine unity:

> But if all images are detached from the soul, and it contemplates only the Simple One, then the soul's naked being finds the naked, formless being of the divine unity, which is there a being above being, accepting and reposing in itself. Ah, marvel of marvels, how noble is that acceptance, when the soul's being can accept nothing else than the naked unity of God![11]

Let us apply the phenomenological method to Eckhart's experience of the desert of the Godhead. What is the intentionality of his consciousness? That towards which his consciousness tends is the emptiness of the Godhead—beyond the divine attributes, beyond the persons of the Trinity. It is the Godhead stripped of all positive perfection: the naked absolute. Eckhart has moved beyond the realm of finitude, beyond the intentionality of Augustine's mysticism: beyond God as truth and goodness into the divine abyss. But note that this consciousness is already on the level of the divine; it is not merely a negation of creatures, a negation of finitude, a negation of the superficial self. For Eckhart that would not be radical enough. He must penetrate into the divine realm itself and strip away all determinations. What he is left with is the desert, the abyss, the divine emptiness, the naked absolute. But remember that he never leaves the divine realm; rather he buries himself there in the desert of the Godhead.

Does the soul remain an image of God in that experience? Yes, but in a way that seems to erase its very status as image. For if the desert of the Godhead is the object of its intention, in this intentionality all ontological and psychological grounds of even a divinely imaged self seem to disappear. We may say that in that intentionality there is awakened the dimension of the soul that resembles the desert of the Godhead; and that abyss of the self plunges into the divine abyss, or better, finds itself undifferentiated from the divine abyss. There in that divine abyss questions of differentiation cannot arise. There is only the not-self.

Having explored these two strands of the Christian mystical tradition, we can open the discussion to interreligious dialogue. How are these notions of the self related to mystical perceptions of the self in other religions: in Hinduism, Buddhism, Islam, Judaism, Chinese religion?

Augustine can be a bridge to those traditions which affirm a position similar to the traditional Christian understanding of the self as image of God, and Eckhart may provide a bridge to those which hold a doctrine of the not–self. It is interesting that Christianity has produced versions of each position, although Eckhart's has often been considered of dubious orthodoxy within Christianity.

A further question arises: How are these two forms of mystical experience of the self related? Are they mutually contradictory? Does one supercede the other? I believe they are compatible within the same tradition and even within the same person. I believe, too, that they have been harmoniously integrated by certain Christian mystics, for example, Ruysbroeck. In an article entitled "Fullness and Emptiness in Bonaventure and Eckhart," I have explored this integration through the model of the coincidence of opposites of mutually affirming complementarity.[12] This model might prove helpful in dealing with the relation of these forms of mystical experience within the larger context of world religions.

NOTES

1. See my description of the method in my book *Global Spirituality: Toward the Meeting of Mystical Paths* (Madras: University of Madras, 1985), 18–38.
2. Steven T. Katz, "Language, Epistemology and Mysticism," in *Mysticism and Philosophical Analysis*, ed. Steven T. Katz (New York: Oxford University Press, 1978), 22–74; see also by the same author "The 'Conservative' Character of Mystical Experience," in *Mysticism and Religious Traditions*, ed. Steven T. Katz (New York: Oxford University Press, 1983), 3–60.
3. Augustine, *Confessions*, VII, 9–10; translations of Augustine are by Mary T. Clark, in *Augustine of Hippo: Selected Writings* in The Classics of Western Spirituality (New York: Paulist Press, 1984).
4. Augustine, *On the Trinity*, XII, 3, 3–4, 4; see also Bonaventure, *Disputed Questions on the Knowledge of Christ*, IV, corpus, and ad 7–9.
5. Augustine, *On the Trinity*, IV, 12, 15.
6. Augustine, *Confessions*, VII, 10.
7. Eckhart, *German Works: Sermon 52*; translations of Eckhart are by Edmund Colledge, in *Meister Eckhart The Essential Sermons, Commentaries, Treatises, and Defense*, eds. Edmund Colledge and Bernard McGinn, in *The Classics of Western Spirituality* (New York: Paulist Press, 1981).
8. Ibid.
9. Ibid.
10. Eckhart, *Sermon 48*
11. Eckhart, *Sermon 83*.
12. "Fulness and Emptiness in Bonaventure and Eckhart," *Dharma*, 6 (1981), 59–68; see also my book *Bonaventure and the Coincidence of Opposites* (Chicago: Franciscan Herald Press, 1978).

6

STEPS TOWARDS ECUMENISM

IN MEISTER ECKHART AND NICHOLAS OF CUSA

Emilie Zum Brunn

Meister Eckhart and the Universality of Human Nature

THOUGH IT IS UNHISTORICAL to speak of ecumenism before Nicholas of Cusa, one of Eckhart's great admirers in the 15th century, it seems to me that the works of the great Dominican theologian at once contain and suggest a series of considerations which are in direct relation with the ecumenical perspective. A sign of this is the way in which he was rediscovered, at the end of the 19th and beginning of the 20th century by three great comparatists: Rudolf Otto, Ananda Coomaraswamy and Daisetz Suzuki.[1] They were struck by the kinship of his thought with that of the East, i.e., with Hinduism as well as with Buddhism. This situates us straight away on a broader plane than that of the "religions of the Book," i.e., on a plane of a really universal ecumenism.

Eckhart's practice of inward life, as well as his speculative thought, together with his openness to the universal, is characterized by an extraordinary power of synthesis. Eckhart did not hesitate, as he tells us himself, to use what can be called a *comparative* method in order to find out the most direct *practical* approach to God:

> I have read many books as well of Pagan masters as of prophets of the Old and New Testaments, and I have searched very earnestly and with all my zeal which is the best virtue through which man may in the best and straitest way be united to God, and become by grace what God is by nature .... And when I penetrate all these writings as far as my understanding is capable, I find nothing but this: pure detachment is above all things, for all virtues have somewhat in view the creatures, but detachment is free from all creatures.[2]

So Eckhart tells us that the fundamental virtue or practice for converting wholly to God—the one he preaches all along his German Sermons and Treatises—*abegescheidenheit,* literally separation, i.e., detachment, is to be found both in the "Pagan" masters, i.e., the Greek philosophers, and in the revealed scriptures and in their commentators. Eckhart has always shown this attitude of freedom and objectivity towards his own religious tradition which is in keeping with the school of Koln, i.e., of Albert the Great and his followers who recognized, more or less explicitly, a double revelation: that of the *Book* and that of Reason (*Vernunft*) or *Intellect*, that is of the so-called pagan masters, especially Proclos and Hermes.[3]

Some may be surprised that Eckhart's fundamental aim should be "to become God in God" by returning, thanks to the virtue of detachment, to our original being in the Deity. It may seem more Hellenic than Christian—and indeed the concept of *deification* is of Greek and Oriental origin. But this remark could be extended to the Fathers of the Church as well as to the medieval Jewish and Islamic thinkers who, in the Middle Ages, adopted, together with the Christians, the *platonic* view of *epistrophe* or conversion, without hesitating to recuperate "the gold of the Egyptians." I have tried to show elsewhere that this common platonic language created the conditions for an authentic, though precarious, ecumenism in the Middle Ages, between some of the representatives of the "religions of the Book."[4]

After this example of practical ecumenism, let us now try and find out the *theoretical* justifications concerning it in the Master's works. This justification resides for him, as for most ancient and medieval thinkers, in the conviction of the *universality of truth*. But for Eckhart, this is not something merely abstract. It follows from the nature of God: *unus*, the One, and from that of man: *uni-versus*, turned towards the One, according to the symbolism of medieval etymology. This universality becomes even an identification with God when man is separated (*geschieden*), i.e., detached or liberated, as much from sin as from worldly aims: "In such a man, liberated from all alien and created things, God does not come, He is in him in His essence."[5]

Such is the noble man, an equivalent to the *noble soul*, an expression coming from Eckhart's predecessors, the great Rheno–Flemish beguines who first wrote of spiritual matters in the vernacular tongues, German, Flemish, and French, and adapted the courtly ideal of the knight wholly devoted to his lady to the relations between the soul and God.[6] This conception was diverted from its true meaning by the theoreticians of Nazism. They considered Eckhart as a precursor in the return of Germany to its Aryan (i.e., noble) origins, and exalted in quite a different spirit from his own the theme of the *noble man*. The way Alfred Rosenberg and others presented Eckhart's thought—and their interpretation still finds some followers—proceeds from a total inversion of the values which the Dominican Master defended, in accordance with the school of Koln and the Rheno-Flemish mystics. For them, the nobility of the human being resides in his/her nature or essence, beyond all individual, ecclesiastical, or social difference: "Humanity is in the poorest and most despised man as perfectly as in the Pope and in the Emperor."[7]

For in that tradition, that is, the foundation of our nobility, is *our original nature*. It is not our created nature, but its archetype or model in God. Therefore, it is by identifying ourselves to God, in the way mentioned at the beginning of this paper, through *abegescheidenheit*, detachment, that we may regain the purity, nobility, and freedom of this original nature, which alone is truly ours. At the end of his Odyssey, the noble man, who had "gone far away from himself," comes back to himself much richer. Having spoiled his created individuality, he recovers through this very fact the universality of human nature, i.e., equality and communion with the other humans who are *one* with him in this nature: "Do not accept yourself in any way as being *this* man or *that* man, but according to human nature, free and undivided."[8]

In fact, every human being is "accidental" in regard to human nature. Therefore it is by separating ourselves from that accidental aspect, submitted as such to laws which are foreign to our deepest being, that we are able to recover our essential freedom. Whereas the contrary would be to "will" one's difference, and to make of it an absolute, characterizes what scripture calls "the old man, the earthly man, the outward man, the inimical man, the man who is a slave."[9] It is by this prejudice against the One and the Universal that Eckhart defines *idolatry* and *injustice* as well as *heresy*.[10] So, if the Pangermanists who pretended to follow Eckhart had really understood his thought, they should have classified themselves in those categories—as should nowadays those who pretend to speak in the name of God, while condemning, torturing, and killing in the name of their "difference."

Meister Eckhart did not have to ponder over the diplomatic and institutional problems of ecumenism, concerning the relations of churches or nations of different religions, for which his time was not ripe. Nevertheless we find in his works important philosophical and theological presuppositions for an ecumenist charter. On one hand the doctrine of "double" revelation, founded on the catholicity of truth. On the other, a notion of human nature which can be extended to overlook any other "accidents" than those mentioned in his texts, such as that of race, for instance. It is, we could say, a universality *de jure*, since it is founded on human nature when, thanks to *abegescheidenheit*, it recovers its "kinship with God."

The Absolute as "The Cause of Our Errors" for Nicholas of Cusa

The cardinal of Cusa is one of Eckhart's spiritual heirs, especially concerning the theme of the return to God and negative theology. However, the continuity of spirit as regards the catholicity of truth gives place to a different perspective which could be characterized as being no longer *de jure* but *de facto*.

There are important reasons for this change. On the one hand, in spite of his links with the Rhenish tradition, Nicholas is a man of the Renaissance, strongly influenced by the Italian humanists and mathematicians. That is to say he is an empiricist and in some way a "relativist," i.e., he tries to make an epistemology of human knowledge. On the other hand, one of the chief events which marked his life and thought was the taking of Constantinople by the Turks, in 1453, an event which marks the end of the Middle Ages. The Christians found themselves faced with the necessity of negotiating with the Infidels and to try and propose an ecumenist charter. Nicholas was all the more ready to do that as he had written his *Concordia catholica* for the council of Basel, a proposal of Christian ecumenism which he now developed into a grandiose project of peace between all the religions of the world, the *De pace fidei*. This project was unfortunately of no effect and is perhaps reserved for more favorable times. Therefore it seems to me we should examine the great idea which presides in it and distinguish it from the way in which he conceived its realization, marked by the prejudices of his one faith as they existed still in his time.

The deep inspiration of this project is the explanation proposed by Nicholas to account for the errors and opposition which separate the diverse creeds. He considers the Absolute as, in a way, the *cause* of these errors and oppositions, since we cannot know the Absolute as it is in itself, and since we nevertheless identify it with our finite conceptions:

> To the diverse nations, You have sent diverse prophets and masters, at one time and at another. But it is a law of our condition of terrestrial men that a long habit becomes for us a second nature, is considered as truth and defended as such. Therefore great disputes arise, when each community opposes its own faith to the other faiths. So come to their help, You who alone can do so. For it is You alone whom they revere through all the outward objects of their cults and thus *it is because of You that the religious wars arise. For no one, in all things he desires, truly desires anything but the good that You are* ... so it is You whom through the diversity of their rites they all seem to search for diversely and *through the diversity of the divine names it is You whom they name for as You are in Yourself You remain unknown to all and ineffable*.[11]

Such is the fundamental presupposition of the *De pace fidei*, in a magnificent analysis which combines the negative theology inherited from Proclus and Denys with a new interest for human experience and epistemology. We find here the theological justification of what Eckhart called "the man who is an enemy" or "the man who is a slave." The latter, on the plane of religious epistemology, had chiefly developed the aspect *de jure*, or of what man is in the perspective of return: God in God. Whereas here, even in man's comprehension of God, what is developed is not the comprehension of the kingdom, but the *de facto* aspect, that of man against man, or at least of religion against religion. Thus we can understand the assurance man has of speaking in the name of God when, by his very condition, he is on the level of the *opposites* whose mysterious *coincidence* God alone knows and is.

We have here, as a complement to the ideal universality of human nature, an analysis which grounds, to my mind, any "Prolegomena to all future ecumenism." However, as has been said, the *De pace fidei* did not have, at the time, the least practical result. So we must now ask ourselves, whether or not this project, even independently of its historical circumstances, is not afflicted with some intrinsic defect which might hinder the achievement of the aim it proposes? That is to say, is the procedure proposed by Nicholas to establish his project of universal peace between all religions commensurate with his fundamental intuition? Let us therefore examine if he succeeds in what he proposes, i.e., in trying to show the *presuppositions* which are common to the diverse creeds.

In a first stage, Nicholas tries to show that all religions, even the polytheistic ones, have a common presupposition: that of *one sole Principle*, who is also Wisdom and the Word. This demonstration is easy and credible, at least in the Platonico–Christian perspective which is the Cardinal's.

In a second stage, Nicholas tries to show the rationality of the *Trinitarian dogma*. He develops there a ternarian dialectic inspired by Augustine. Here we go farther away from the initial intention of putting common presuppositions to light, in what Nicholas himself calls "intellectual reasoning."

There is a third stage in which the so-called common presupposition is yet more difficult to demonstrate, concerning the *Incarnation* of the Word. Here again Nicholas tries to solve the difficulty through a rational argumentation, i.e., through the notion of *homo maximum*, a kind of human asymptote towards the infinite.

In spite of his rational attempts, in the end Nicholas has recourse to religious faith, since he chiefly tries to convince the Moslems who recognize in Jesus a prophet having made miracles. And this discourse, so rationally begun, ends in an appeal to the *faith* in Christ, indispensable for salvation. At this point, we notice that what remains of the rationality aimed at by Nicholas is now reserved to the essentially *ethical* domain of the divine commandments: "They are brief, they are perfectly known to all and common to all nations," thanks to the light "innate in the rational soul."[12]

However, we must recognize that the unicity of the godly Principle, the trinitarian aspect of created things as of their uncreated Cause, and the notion of *homo maximum* are to be found in more creeds and philosophies than Nicholas could be aware at the time—so that in this he can be considered as a precursor in the search for the archetypes of the human mind, though of course our modern search for them takes a less rational turn.

On the other hand, we cannot ignore that Nicholas does not succeed in discovering effectively, as he had proposed in his treatise *De docta ignorantia* "doctrines more true and more correct," i.e., approximations which could be accepted by the one as by the others. In spite of his good intentions, it is in reality to the *Christian* religion, and particularly to the doctrine of the Word Incarnate, that the Cardinal tries to *reduce* the others. Without seeming to be aware of it, he returns to the dogmatic statement and its impenitent absolutism. Therefore, apart from the depth of his ecumenical use of the *coincidentia oppositorum*, the *De pace fidei* gives the same impression as the so-called dialogues between Jews, Christians, and Moslems which we meet in medieval literature and are usually but reductive attempts. Such are, in spite of the generosity and pacifism they express, *The Dialogue between a Philosopher, a Jew and a Christian*, of Pierre Abelard,[13] and *The Book against the Sect or Heresy of the Saracens* of Peter the Venerable.[14] The ecumenism they proposed was that of a reason which recognized the Christian dogma.

We discover in the *De pace fidei* still other infractions to the principle of *coincidentia*, even more shocking for us nowadays. As was taught in his day, Nicholas believed that the Jews would not be saved in the hereafter, since they refused to recognize Christ. Concerning the here and now, we are astounded to notice the indifference with which this religious man foresees the failure of his project with them. He says that it will be of no consequence for the universal peace he tries to promote, since the Jews, contrarily to the Moslems, do not have the means of waging war, when the proclaimed aim of the *De pace fidei* is to ground the peace of arms on the peace of minds!

Thus we see the reappearance of religious dogmatism and of the intolerance that accompanies it, in spite of Nicholas' relativistic position: a relativism which in the end he only accepts, only at the level of religious rites, which he carefully distinguishes from "the true faith." This aborted attempt is a renewed example of the tension of medieval Christian thought towards the catholicity of truth and its dogmatic incapacity to reach it. Such was the case, so to say paradigmatic, of Saint Augustine, in his desire for a "true philosophy" inspired by Platonic and Stoic universalism, to which he opposes the dogma of the one and only mediation of Christ and of the Church.

This should not prevent us from taking the grain and leaving the chaff. So we could take into account Eckhart's developments on the universality (diversity) of human nature, on the injustice and "heresy" of those who make an idol of their difference. We could also take into account the Cardinal's religious epistemology—which, in its principle, allows us to avoid both dogmatism and skepticism. Those thoughts might be helpful in some future charter of ecumenism.

NOTES

1. E. Zum Brunn, "L'ontologie de Maître Eckhart et la philosophie comparée, *Journal of the Faculty of Letters*, (The University of Tokyo, 1979) t. 4, 31–41. Reproduced in E. Zum Brunn and A. de Libera, *Maitre Eckhart. Métaphysique du Verbe et Théologie négative* (Paris: Beauchesne, 1984), 221–233. Also Japanese translation by Omori, (Tokyo: Kokubunsha, 1985).
2. Eckhart, *Von abegescheidenheit*, in *Die deutschen Werke*, ed. Deutsche Forschung-sgemeinschaft (Suttgart: Kohlhammer, 1936 etc.), t.5, 400, 2-401, 7.
3. L. Sturlese, "Alle origini della mistica speculative tedesca," t.3 (1977), 21–87. *Medioaevo*.
4. E. Zum Brunn, "Le néo-platonisme et les trois vérités, juive, chrétienne, musulmane," *Les Etudes Philosophiques*, t.4 (1982), 443–454.
5. Eckhart, *Predigt* 10s, *Die deutschen Werke*, t.1, 165, 13–15.
6. See G. Epiney-Burgard and E. Zum Brunn, *And the Art was Born Amongst Women. North European Poetesses and Mystics of the 12th and 13th Centuries*, transl. S. Hughes (New York: Paragon, 1987 or 1988).
7. Eckhart, *Predigt* 25, *Die deutschen Werke*, t.2, 18, 2–5.
8. Eckhart, *Predigt* 46, *Die deutschen Werke*, t.2, 382, 3–4.
9. Eckhart, *Vom edeln menschen, Die deutschen Werke*, t.5, 109–15.
10. See *Maitre Eckhart. Métaphysique du Verbe et Théologie négative*, Introduction and chap. 1.
11. *De pace fidei*, 6.
12. *De pace fidei*, 55. Cf. E. Zum Brunn, "Présupposés éthiques et coïncidence des opposés," *Freiburger Zeitschrift für Philosophie und Theologie*, 33 (1986), 111–128.
13. *Dialogus inter Philosophum, Judaeum et Christianum*, ed. R.Thomas (Stuttgart: Bad Cannstadt, 1970).
14. See J. Kritzec, *Peter the Venerable and Islam* (Princeton, 1964).

7

SELF, NOT-SELF, AND THE ULTIMATE

IN MARGUERITE PORETE'S "MIRROR OF ANNIHILATED SOULS"

Emilie Zum Brunn

LET ME BRIEFLY PRESENT Marguerite Porete, a béguine from Hainaut, in Northern France, who was a victim of the Inquisition under the reign of Philip the Fair. The only testimonies left concerning the author are her book, the acts of her trial, and, contrasting with the condemnations reported in them, the laudatory judgments of two contemporary friars, a Cistercian and a Franciscan, as well as of the famous theologian Godefroi de Fontaines, a former chancellor of the University of Paris. The true authorship of *Le Miroir des Simples Ames Anéanties* was rediscovered only in 1946, thanks to the perspicacity of Romana Guarnieri, the text itself having been rediscovered in 1876 and attributed for a long time to the holy Margaret of Hungary.[1]

We infer from these documents that Margaret taught pure love and persevered in this teaching, such as it is exposed in her book, though it had been condemned by Guido II, bishop of Cambrai, in the first years of the fourteenth century. Then Margaret was pursued by his successor, Philip of Marigny, "âme damnée" of King Philip, and afterwards accused by the provincial Inquisitor of Haute Lorraine. Finally, having refused to appear before the Inquisitor Guillaume of Paris and swear an oath of "truth" to him, Margaret was declared heretic and relapse by the Inquisition, i.e., by the theologians of the University of Paris—among whom were Jean de Gand and Nicolas de Lyre. She was burned alive, in the presence of the highest religious and secular authorities, on the first of June 1310, place de Grève (now place de l'Hôtel de Ville) in Paris.[2] This did not prevent her book from spreading rapidly all over Europe during the Middle Ages and up to the Renaissance. We still have Latin, old English, and old Italian versions. The *Mirror* seems to have disappeared from sight after the Renaissance, if we do not take into account the influence it still had anonymously—an anonymity which answered Marguerite's wishes—(according to R. Guarnieri this influence was not without effect on the Quaker movement). This book is now, at last, being rehabilitated both by Catholics and by Protestants, and has begun to be recognized for what it really is: a major spiritual work of French literature.

To be "With Ourselves" or "Without Ourselves"

Marguerite Porete is a typical representative of the Rheno-Flemish spirituality which united the *Minnemystik* (mysticism of Love) and the *Wesenmystik* (mysticism of Being). One, and perhaps the chief of its great precursors in the twelfth century, was the Cistercian Guillaume, abbot of Saint-Thierry, a friend of Saint Bernard's. He reintroduced into Latin theology important Greek themes which had been forgotten or left aside, in spite of Erigena's efforts in the ninth century.

The most important of these themes expresses the traditional doctrine of *deification*: the aim of the soul is not only considered to be an assimilation to God, as in the Latin tradition—i.e. to become *like* God—but, in Guillaume's own words, "to become *what God is*."[3] This is a reinterpretation, much more radical than Augustine's, of the return of the soul to its original reality in God. Thus for the great Rheno-Flemish beguines, such as Hadewijch of Antwerpen, Hadewijch II, and Marguerite Porete, as well as for the Cistercian Beatrice of Nazareth, the abandonment of the soul to God is expressed by an ontological dilemma: we must spoil what in us is purely created, and thus separated from Him, to be able to recover our true, "uncreated," unseparated being in God. Then shall we become *what God is*, or, in even bolder expressions, *God with God*, *God in God* or, simply, *God*.

Marguerite uses the word *self* ("soi") to describe the former, created, individualistic aspect of our being, which she calls a *naught* ("nient") or a *less* ("moins"). This naught also implies sin: considering her sins, she sees herself, not only as naught, but as *less than naught* ("moins que nient"). She uses the expression *to be with ourselves* or *with themselves* ("avec eux") or, specifically of the soul, *with herself* ("avec elle") to designate our attachment to this self. The opposite expression, to be *without herself* ("sans elle"), etc., conveys detachment from this self and its positive counterpart: attachment to God alone. This is obtained through *wishing no-thing* ("nient vouloir") which consists in having no other desire than that of loving God. Thus the full title of the book: *Le Mirouer des Simples Ames Anienties et qui seulement demourent en Vouloir et Désir d'Amour* (The Mirror of Simple Annihilated Souls who solely remain in Wishing and Desire of Love.) The practice of wishing no-thing leads to a true *annihilation* of the soul considered in its particular and selfish being, in its "less." But she thus loses herself only to find herself in a state of being incomparably higher, having "become God by condition of Love or justice of Love" (chap. 51).

This spoiling of self—which is really an identification with God's will—though it is the aim of the mystic's efforts and of the practice of wishing no-thing, is not a natural result of these efforts, but is given by God-Love in an "instant" or "moment of time," as in a flash of lightning. It places the soul in the sixth of the states or beings ("êtres") of grace, after the three deaths: to sin, to nature, to the spirit. This sixth state, the highest on this earth, is that of *annihilated illuminated life* ("vie anéantie illuminée"):

> At the beginning, this Soul lived the life of grace, which grace was born from the death of sin. Afterwards she lived the life of the spirit, which life was born from the death of nature; and now she lives the divine life, which divine life was born from the death of the spirit. This Soul, which lives divine life, is always *without herself* ... when she is nowhere by her own will, neither in God, nor in herself, nor in her neighbor, but in the annihilation which this lightning operates in her .... (chap. 59)

And the soul cannot describe this state, on reason of the forgetfulness produced in her "by the annihilation of the knowledge which this annihilation gives of itself." (ibid.)

> From now on, Love works in her *without herself* ("sans elle") .... This Soul can no longer speak of God, for she is annihilated in all her outward desires and in her inner feelings as well in all affection of her spirit ... for now the will is dead which kindled her desire. (chap. 7)

This annihilation of the selfish will (i.e., of desire and of fear which accompanies it), replaced by God's own will, brings the soul to a real freedom of autonomy. Having "become God" through the condition of Love, she need no longer long for Him as if He were separate from her. She does not *have* Love, she *is* Love. She no longer *has* Joy, she "swims in the sea of Joy" and therefore *is* Joy. (chap. 28)

This subject, especially the annihilation of will which does not suppress will in the Soul but transforms it in a superior essence, is explained very subtly in a series of Dialogues, in the medieval style, between the Soul, Lady Love, i.e., God, and Reason. The latter ends by dying of the shocks received all along, too hard for human understanding, and thus gives way to a higher comprehension of God, that of the Understanding of Love ("Entendement d'Amour"). It is the understanding or the "Fine Amour" of the only free souls, the *free annihilated* ("les francs anientis"), who are the *noble Souls*, i.e., the chivalrous souls, in the courtly language used as well by Marguerite as by the beguines mentioned above. These souls love God, as a knight loves his lady, in a totally disinterested way, *sans pourquoi* (without a why). To this Marguerite disdainfully contrasts the interested love of God of "common" Christians, whom she considers as villains. They save themselves, as she says, in a very uncourtly manner, because they are still "*with themselves*," i.e., encumbered with themselves ("encombrés d'eux-mêmes"). And so they will remain until death, unless they try and find "the straight kingly highway through the land of wishing no-thing."

Thus a capital distinction is drawn between the "*marred*," who are also called "villains, sheep, asses," i.e., all those who remain "with themselves" and the noble soul who is "without herself." This distinction, though resorting to feudal symbolism, has nothing to do with social, ecclesiastic or religious hierarchy. The "villains of heart," the "small minds," the "merchants," the "asses," and the "sheep" are for her, as well as the clerics of the university who condemned her, and those of the regular orders who misinterpreted her, and the beguines themselves who did not understand her:

> Friend, what will the beguines and the religious men say
> When they hear the excellency of your divine song?
> Beguines say I go astray,
> Thus do priests, clerics and preachers,
> Augustines, Carms and Franciscans,
> Because of what I write on the being of 'Fine Amour.'
> What they tell me does not save their Reason:
> Assuredly Desire, Will and Fear take away from them the knowledge
> And the riches and the union given by
> The high ardent light of divine Love. (chap. 122)

What has been most misunderstood by those clerics in Margaret's teaching is, it seems to me, the conception of *freedom* which characterizes it. In the state of union the soul is free *of the virtues* she in her turn commands them, because she has reached the state where her self no longer dictates her actions and has no longer to be curbed outwardly. Shocking also must have been the freedom of *indifference*: she neither desires or flees "masses and sermons," "honor and dishonor," "Paradise and Hell." This conception seems to be one of the chief points attacked by the Sorbonne and a little later, in 1311, by the Council of Vienne which more or less identified Eckhart's, as well as Marguerite's, teachings with those of the heresy of the Free Spirit. To what extent this concept of *freedom*, together with that of *poverty*, was a ferment as well of religious renewal as of heresy and of clerical persecution has been well shown in Umberto Eco's beautiful book, *The Name of the Rose*.[4]

The Ultimate or the "More" of God

What is the nature of the Ultimate, in this ontological view of participation which characterizes Rheno-Flemish mysticism?

God is considered, as is traditional in medieval Christianity, as *Being* par excellence, e.g., Marguerite Porete experiences that "He is ... and I am not," a sentence which we will also find in the writings of Saint Catherine of Sienna. God is the only true Being. Therefore climbing the steps of the spiritual ladder signifies climbing up the steps of being until the final identification with God. The seven states of grace are also called the seven beings ("êtres") of grace which the noble soul must acquire.

Simultaneously, God is *Love*. In Guillaume de Saint-Thierry, we already have this encounter of the metaphysics of Love with the metaphysics of Being. He reinforces it by an ontological grounding of the Persons in the Trinity—and by a direct participation of human creatures in trinitarian Love, through the link of unity which is the Holy Spirit.[5] On the other hand, Guillaume insists that Love only can attain to the knowledge of God, because she alone can penetrate His depths which transcend the powers of the intellect. *Amor ipse intellectus est*.

We find the same conception and experience of Love with our beguines. For them Love becomes *Lady Love* since they do not write in the Latin rhetoric of the theologians, but use the language of the *roman courtois* which they transpose spiritually. For them, as for Guillaume, "*To love ... is to be*, and to be one spirit with God."[6] And Marguerite links these concepts of Being, Love, and Trinity in one dense theological formula.

> *He is (He) who is*. Therefore He is what He is by Himself: *Lover, Beloved, Love* (chap. 113)

Such is, as it were, the knowable aspect of the Ultimate, accessible to the *intellectus fidei*. But, in the line of Denys the Areopagite, following

Proclus, there is also the unknowable, unparticipable aspect of the Ultimate. This aspect is very important in our beguines' writings, especially in those of the metaphysically minded Hadewijch II and Marguerite Porete. Both express beautifully the deepest theme of Rheno-Flemish mysticism, that of *overpassing* (Dutch: *overvaert*; German: *überfahrt*; French: *trépas*): even in the highest degrees or "beings" of grace, as well as in the beatific vision after death, the soul continually overpasses her own limits without ever being able to encompass the divine transcendence. However high our knowledge of God may be in contemplation, something of Him remains and will forever remain inaccessible to our grasp, and in this knowledge that in his transcendence God remains unknowable resides our highest joy. This inaccessibility is called in the Dutch tradition *ontbliven*: what *remains* (far from our grasp). It is generally translated by lack, perhaps more understandable for the modern reader. The excellence of this *rest*, which Marguerite calls the *more* ("plus")—God is *more* than what he communicates of Himself to us; he is also the *more* compared to our *less*—is one of the fundamental themes of the *Mirror*. When we have transcended rational knowledge as well as selfish desire, we find that we cannot either know, love, or praise God in the usual and human sense of these words:

> There is a very long way from the land of Virtues, where the marred reside, to that of the forgotten, naked, annihilated or glorified souls, who are in the highest state, where God is abandoned by Himself in Himself. Then He is neither known, nor loved, nor praised by these creatures, except for the fact that He cannot be known or loved or praised. This is the sum of all their love and the last stage on their way. (chap. 95)

This theme of Unknowing and of Overpassing, together with that of spiritual Poverty (of him who desires, knows and has no-thing), as expressed by Hadewijch II and by Marguerite Porete, has been pointed out as an important pre-Eckhartian witness in beguinal mysticism—the *Nonnenmystikk*, as the Germans say. Their thought and expression is very similar to that of the *Dreifaltigkeitslied* (Trinitarian Hymn), an anonymous poem of the end of the thirteenth century. Wilhelm Preger, in his *History of German Mysticism in the Middle Ages*, quotes this poem as an example of the development attained, before Eckhart, by the *Wesenmystik* or mysticism of Being.[8]

Conclusion

I fear that these brief notations do not convey in any adequate manner the precision and depth of the doctrine of Marguerite Porete, that "beguine clergeresse." The topics exposed here, in accordance with the proposed subject of this group, were, on one hand, ***annihilation*** of self in order for the soul to be completely identified to God, "to be God by condition of Love or justice of Love." On the other hand, this identification makes the soul which obtains it all the more conscious, and happily conscious, of the *Ultimate's ineffable transcendence*. Through the annihilation of self, the soul becomes passive to God until He sways her completely, and only at that moment does she enjoy true freedom—thanks to the non interference of her enslaving self.

There is ***no*** trace of ***quietism*** here, however. In a sentence which might easily be attributed to some Oriental teacher of non-action, Marguerite says: "And these Souls could govern a country if it were needed, but it would be ***without themselves*** (chap. 58). There is a balance between passivity to *God* and ***human*** activity and even initiatives swayed by him. The same balance is found, in Marguerite's doctrine of the Ultimate, between positive theology and mystic negativity. Her insistence on the Deity's ineffable transcendence is in itself an answer to the accusation of ***pantheism*** which, up to our day, has been made against the mystics who took up the Greek Fathers' conception of ontological participation in God. Thus, as shown by her doctrine and by the way it was attached, but also by the enormous influence she exerted in medieval Europe up to the Renaissance, Marguerite Porete is to be regarded among other spirituals of the twelfth and thirteenth centuries, as one of the parents of Rheno-Flemish mysticism, one of our deepest religious traditions, and perhaps of other grafts.

NOTES

1. See Romana Guarnieri, *Il Movimento del Libero Spirito. Testi e Documenti* (Roma: Edizioni di Storia e letteratura, 1965). Text of the Mirror after the Manuscript of Chantilly, 363–708. See also *Margaret Porete. "The Mirror of Simple Souls,"* ed. Marilyn Doiron (Roma: Edizioni di Soria e letteratura, 1968). Max Huot de Longchamp, *Marguerite Porete, Le Miroir des Ames Simples et Anéanties, Introduction, Traduction et Notes* (Paris: Albin Michel, 1984).
2. It is significant that the facts of Marguerite's trial should have been kept by the ministers of Philip the Fair: Guillaume of Nogaret and Guillaume of Plaisians. They are now in the *Layettes du Trésor des Chartes* (Paris, 1863–1909), t.2. They were partly published by Charles Lea, *A History of the Inquisition in the Middle Ages* (New York, 1888; repr. New York 1955) t.2, 575–578 and reproduced without corrections in Paul Fredericq, *Corpus documentorum inquisitionis haereticae pravitatis Neerlandicae* (Ghent, 1889) t.1, 155–160 and (Gent, 1896), t.2, 63–65.
3. Guillaume of Saint-Thierry, *Letter to the Friars of Mount–God*, PL 184, 307–354.
4. Umberto Eco, *Il Nome della Rosa* (Milan: Fabbri-Bompiani, 1980).
5. Guillaume establishes that the trinitarian relations are inherent to the mystery of divine *Being* by relating the verses of *Exodus* 3:14 ("I am he who is") with that of *John* 10:18 ("Do you not believe that I *am* in the Father and that the Father *is* in me?"). On the other hand, Guillaume shows that there is no other possibility of being than, for us, to *be in the Father*, while the Father is *in us*. But, whereas Christ *is* always that being, by nature, we must *become that being*, by grace. On this see Paul Verdeyen, "La théologie mystique de Guillaume de Saint-Thierry," *Ons Geestelijk Erf* (51, 1977) chap. 2, p. 175.
6. Guillaume of Saint-Thierry, *De contemplando Deo*, PL 184, 376 D–377A.
7. Hadewijch II is so called because the manuscripts and editions of Hadewijch of Antwerpen contain in their common *Mengeldichten* a series of poems, Mengeldichten XVII to XXIX, that have been recognized by the specialists as coming from a different pen. They have been translated in French by J.B. Porion, *Hadewijch d'Anvers, Poèms des Béguines*, (Paris: Seuil, 1954, repr. 1985), 131–185.
8. Wilhelm Preger, *Geschichte der deutschen Mystik nach den quelle untersucht und dargestellt*, t.1: *Geschichte der deutschen Mystik bis zum Tode Meister Eckharts* (Leipzig: Dörfling und Franke, 1874).

8

THE EPISTEMOLOGICAL ROLE OF LOVE IN KNOWING THE DIVINE

THE SHAPING OF THE CHRISTIAN TRADITION

Brian Gaybba

THE IDEA THAT LOVE offers insights, especially into the nature of personal and divine reality, is widespread and appealed to again and again in one way or another. It is an idea that dominated Western theological thinking until the thirteenth century, when the injection of Aristotelian epistemology into the theological academies pushed it into the background. Since then it has remained somewhat on the periphery of Christian theological interest and material on it is relatively meager, despite the attention paid to connatural knowledge in Catholic circles this century.

As regards this latter, attention has focused above all on Thomas Aquinas and on the role he assigned to connatural knowledge as regards making moral judgments. A good person could instinctively judge what was good because of a certain connaturality between such a person and goodness.

However, I believe that connatural knowledge should not be limited simply to moral judgments, and I suspect that Aquinas himself did not so limit it. Indeed, the classic Western tradition in this matter, reaching back at least to Augustine, granted love a role in understanding divine truth, and not just in making moral judgments. For this tradition, love formed an important part of theological method. Indeed, it was willing to grant love a role in understanding all truth, since all truth ultimately had reference to God.

Another area that could have done with more attention is that of *the way in which* love operates epistemologically. As Ri has noted, there has been little research on the matter[1] and among those who have dealt with it[2] most have granted love a role extrinsic to the act of knowing, viz., that of a motivating power.[3]

The purpose of this paper is therefore threefold. First of all, simply to raise the issue once again. Second, to take a broader look at its historical background in the Christian tradition. Third, to do so paying particular attention to the grounds adduced for love's epistemological role. I will conclude with some brief observations on the directions we should look to in the future for illuminating love's role.

Augustine

Western views on love's epistemological role were shaped by neo-Platonist metaphysics as christianized by Augustine[4] and Pseudo-Denys.

As for the metaphysics,[5] this saw all reality as deriving from a single source—the One, the Good. From that source successive levels of being proceed, each level participating in and therefore resembling the level preceding it. All along this chain of being there is an inner drive towards reestablishing the original unity. The human soul stands on the borderline between the spiritual and the material levels. To fulfil its yearning (its love!) for unity with its divine source, it must needs heed the presence of that source within it, purify itself of attachments to lower levels of being, focus on that presence and so open itself to it. As a result it will be transformed more and more into the likeness of its divine source, thereby knowing it better, since like can only be known by like. On the other hand, if the soul allows itself to be immersed in material reality, it will become increasingly conformed to it: viz., ephemeral, lacking the attributes of universality and unchangeability that characterize the divine.

The Augustinian view of love's illuminative role was rooted in the above framework. For him, love (which he calls the most 'luminous' of all realities[6]) operates epistemologically by purifying the soul's "eye,"[7] by focusing the thus-purified eye onto God,[8] and by transforming the soul more deeply into the likeness of God.

It is in this third ability of love—to conform the lover to the beloved—that the basic cause of its epistemological power resides. As for Plotinus, even more so for Augustine one becomes what one loves, an idea we find repeated again and again in his writings.[9] And here he deepens Plotinian metaphysics with his own Christian vision.

At the heart of that vision is the assertion that God is love. If the divinity's very essence is love, then the act of loving is itself God-like and as such conforms the soul to God. Love's conformity therefore is not derived simply from an *effect* of love, such as opening the lover to the influence of the beloved or effecting a transforming unity between lover and beloved. Instead such conformity comes into being the moment one loves. This is why, unlike in the case of Plotinus, love of neighbor and not just of God brings about the conformity with God that illuminates.[10] The love that illumines is not simply Plotinus' instinctive impulse but a moral reality.

Moreover, it is quite clear that for Augustine love enables one to ***understand*** divine realities and not simply to make moral judgments that are in tune with them. Love deepens our knowledge of what is loved. "When something partially known is loved, then that very love results in its being better and more fully known."[11] Love enables a person to understand the scriptures without error.[12] Love of neighbor enables us to understand even abstruse aspects of Trinitarian theology.[13] Indeed all truth can be grasped fully only by one who loves God and neighbor. This applies even to physics "since the causes of all natures are in God the creator" and logic "because only God is the truth and the light of the rational soul."[14] All truth is, for him, ultimately theological in character, since one only knows truth in its fullness when one sees reality in its relationship to God. This is the way God sees it. It is the way we should strive to see it. Seeing things from this perspective is "wisdom" (*sapientia*) as distinct from "knowledge" (*scientia*).

Augustine's baptizing of Plotinus, even though done unconsciously (or rather precisely because done unconsciously), was so effective that it passed into the mainstream of Christian thought, emerging as an articulate and dominant theological epistemology in twelfth century monastic theology.

Monastic Theology

"Monastic theology"[15] is the name given to a type of theology that was practiced particularly (but not exclusively[16]) by the monks. It represented what had become by then the traditional approach to theology in the West, one whose methodological heart was the epistemological role of love. As Leclercq[17] has pointed out, the whole aim of monastic life was unity with God, a knowledge of God derived from experiencing God. The theology inspired by that life gravitated therefore around that central idea.

The ways in which love operates epistemologically are basically the same as those outlined by Augustine (one way not stressed by Augustine is that love wins insight from God as a reward[18]). And, of those, it is love's ability to unite and to conform knower to known, to create the conditions for connatural knowledge to occur, that are most stressed.

The paradigm of this connatural knowledge was that which Father and Son had of each other within the Trinity: the latter knows the former perfectly because of being his perfect image, an idea that goes hand in hand with the two being one substance.[19] Knowledge, conformity, unity go hand in hand, then. Where one or other of these are perfect then all three are. Where any of them are lacking in perfection—as is the case with us in this life[20]—then to the same extent are the other two imperfect.

As noted above when dealing with Augustine, the very act of loving is divine-like. This idea is found also in monastic theology,[21] as is the idea that love has the power to make the lover become like that which is loved.[22] But William of St. Thierry, who is unquestionably *the* twelfth-century theologian of love's epistemological role, goes even deeper into the matter. He draws an explicit comparison between the way love operates and the senses do. The senses, as was widely believed in those days, emitted a ray that hit an object, became conformed to it and returned with its new shape to the mind. This enabled the principle that like can only be known by like to operate. Love operates like a ray. Moreover, it comes into contact not just with God but more specifically with the Holy Spirit (see above) and is molded into that Spirit's likeness.[23] On its return to the lover, it enables the latter to understand God the way the Spirit does. We therefore know God by "sensing" God.[24] Moreover, that Spirit is Love. Hence our love is shaped by the Spirit of Love and so participates in the epistemological power of that Love.[25]

By putting us into contact with the divine, love reaches beyond the visible realities of this world so as to touch their very source, thereby enabling us to understand them better.

It is at this point that Pseudo-Denys enters the picture. He bequeathed to monastic theology his typically hierarchically structured, symbolic view of reality—one in which not simply words but all objects were symbolic of higher realities. Every lower level of reality was, to use contemporary theological language, a real symbol of a higher one. Hence, the world we live in is but a symbol, the outer manifestation of, a higher one. To really understand the world therefore it was not enough to remain within its own categories, within the images, concepts, interrelationships found in it. Rather did one have to pass through it so as to grasp the world beyond, the divine world.

Between the symbol and its transcendent referent there was a relationship both of similarity (because of the ontological bond between them) and dissimilarity (because of the transcendence of the latter). This in turn meant that the symbol could only reveal its referent by being plastic, polyvalent. In other words, a symbol had to have many levels of meaning to it, each illuminating one or another aspect of its referent.

This had two important implications for theology's method. First of all, it meant that logical reasoning was not of much use. Logical reasoning demands conceptual precision, something that is anathema to a symbol. As Pseudo-Denys observed,[26] the method proper to a symbolist theology is non-demonstrative. Second, it meant that the symbol cannot have its meaning wrested from it by the analytical powers of the theologian.

Instead, the symbol must reveal its own meaning, its own referent: or rather the referent must reveal its true character through the symbol. It is the referent that gives understanding of the symbol rather than the other way around.[27] Hence to understand the symbol one has first of all to pass through it so as to experience that which it symbolizes.[28] And this is where love's purifying, unifying, and conforming powers enter into the picture.

In monastic theology the recognition, application, and analysis of love's epistemological role in knowing the divine, whether one was talking of mystical knowledge or even of doing theology (since the two were not separated,) achieved its zenith. The scholastic approach, marked by a stress on the role of logical reasoning, analytical techniques, precise definitions, had already raised the ire of monastic theologians such as Rupert of Deutz, William of St. Thierry, and Bernard of Clairvaux. Theology was becoming an academic discipline, and the monastic writers saw the dangers. As they saw it, reason was being enthroned in the place of love. They were not altogether correct. But neither were they altogether wrong.

The Thirteenth Century

To discover thirteenth-century views on love's epistemological role one has to study what it had to say about wisdom, as well as about the spiritual gift of understanding. However, I will focus here on wisdom, a procedure that also has the merit of highlighting where the change between the old and the new ways occurred.

Up until the time of Aquinas, the generally accepted view of wisdom remained the by-then traditional one: viz., that it was a way of knowing divine realities by means of savoring them. It was this that distinguished it from discursively acquired knowledge.

Discussions or comments on the nature of wisdom surfaced in two contexts especially. The first was that of the gifts of the Spirit, derived from *Isa*. 11:2. Three of the gifts listed there are wisdom, knowledge, and understanding. In his *Sentences*, Peter Lombard dealt with these gifts in general in book three, distinction 34, and in distinction 35 he discussed specifically the difference between the gift of wisdom and that of understanding. Hence, one can pursue the discussions on the topic by studying the commentaries on the *Sentences* that every theologian had to provide.

The second context was that of the question discussed as a prolegomenon to every theological *summa* of the period: Is theology a science? The two contexts were similar but nevertheless notably different. In the first case, all three, wisdom, knowledge, and understanding were seen as supernatural gifts. Hence love could play some role in all three, even though its role be the more extrinsic one of preparing for the gift.[29] In the second case, however, science, as distinguished from wisdom, was viewed as a purely natural product. But in both cases, up to the time of Aquinas, what was distinctive of wisdom was that it mediated a knowledge of the divine by means of savoring, experiencing it.

Of course, savoring the truth implies loving it. Hence such a view of wisdom implied a significant epistemological role for love. It would be unthinkable for a thirteenth-century theologian that one could savor divine realities without being united to them through love. Indeed, so important for understanding is this savoring via love that we find theologians such as Roland of Cremona insisting that

> those who do not have a formed faith [= a faith suffused with love] do not know theology...Without experience there is no art or science, and all intellectual knowledge flows from a prior sentient one. For just as someone who never tasted honey can never have a true knowledge of its taste ... so too is it impossible for someone who is not proficient in living out a faith suffused with

> love to know theology. Such a person may know how to talk about theology. But this is simply like the case of one born blind who can't know how to talk about colors without really knowing them.[30]

This text also makes clear that love contributes to the understanding of truth and not simply to the making of moral judgments.

Love does so, then, by means of its unitive powers. It allows an experiencing, a sort of sensing of divine realities to occur, which in turn is the basis for knowing them.

However, the link between love's unitive role and its ability to conform one to the divine is also maintained. A good example of this is to be found in the *Summa Halensis*. In book 3 the author argues that grace illuminates the believer's mind by conforming the soul more closely to God. The awakening of love in the believer is obviously part of this process.[31] And elsewhere Alexander observes that faith, hope, and love refashion us into God's image, giving rise to the sort of knowledge known as wisdom.[32]

The connection between love's unitive, conforming role with that of purification, so stressed by the monastic theologians, can also be found in writers of this period. One example is Odo Rigaldi's comment that purifying the heart and cleansing it of all earthly attachments will enable one "to see and know God as perfectly as can be hoped for in this life."[33] Another example can be found in Philip the Chancellor. He divides the activities of the believer's mind into three stages: primary, middle and final. The first stage is to be orientated to its end and this involves belief. The second stage "is to understand by tasting" ["intelligere cum sapore"]. The third is the vision of God that even in this life follows on the cleansing of the heart.[34]

So the basic elements of the old, Augustinian tradition continue to function, especially in the first half of the century. Indeed, though I have not yet been able to study the matter sufficiently, I suspect that that tradition achieved a scholasticised peak in the writings of Bonaventure (1221–1274). Bonaventurian scholasticism could be viewed as monastic theology's wedding with scholasticism and therefore as the former's true high point.[35] Bonaventure's epistemology is Augustinian. All knowledge is ultimately theological knowledge, since true understanding derives from a divine illumination enabling the mind to see the relation between all reality and the eternal reasons for them in God's mind. Hence the title of one of his works: "The resolution of all the arts into theology."[36]

However, in the midst of this ongoing tradition one can also witness the symptoms of tension and change.

The catalyst is, of course, Aristotelian epistemology. The Platonist world-view on which the older, Augustinian, tradition rested saw truth as something imparted from on high. To grasp it an illumination from on high was necessary. All being derived from a single transcendent source and sought reunion with it. Similarly all truth derived from that single source and one grasped the former in direct proportion to one's unity with the latter. Aristotle, however, saw truth as something the mind discovered in the visible world. It was something the mind gathered by means of its own inherent capacities. There was no need to appeal to a divine illumination, no need to appeal to love. The conformity to reality necessary for understanding to occur could be accounted for without love, since a conformity of the mind was sufficient. The mind abstracted the essences, the intelligible species, of the realities it came into contact with in the visible world, thereby forging a mental likeness of the object to be known. The conforming of one's entire self through love had no epistemological role to play, even though the unitive character of love, one that made direct experience of divine realities possible, continued to play some role. But it was one that would diminish as the Aristotelian epistemology took increasing root in the minds of theologians.

The methodological implications of such an epistemology therefore is that logic comes to play a predominant role in trying to understand the divine. All the reasons for a particular assertion are there for everyone to see and evaluate. There is no hidden factor that can be appealed to such as love, except to the extent that one granted it a value in mediating experience of the divine. However, even that became rather difficult in the Aristotelian system, which stressed that all knowledge took its origin in the senses—in direct opposition to the Platonic approach. In such a case, in what sense was the divine "experienced"? That it was experienced remained the firm conviction of all medieval theologians. However, the epistemological value of such an experience for understanding divine truths and therefore for doing theology was given increasingly little attention.

I mentioned above that the epistemological role of love comes to the fore especially in the idea that wisdom is experiential in nature, that it knows divine realities by savoring them. It is significant that the Aristotelian idea of wisdom was different. For Aristotle there was epistemologically speaking no fundamental difference between wisdom and knowledge. Neither operated by "savoring" the realities known (of course, all knowledge *began* for him in sentient experience). The difference was simply that the former dealt with the cause of all causes (i.e., the divine) and the latter with lower levels of reality. Hence for him metaphysics was wisdom.

In speaking of wisdom as involving a savoring of divine realities, the early thirteenth-century theologians had to take account of Aristotle's views on wisdom. Increasingly they recognized that wisdom could be used in his sense of the word, but insisted nevertheless that properly speaking wisdom involved experiential contact with the divine.[37]

Their having to take into account two notions of wisdom was itself indicative of the tension developing between the old and new approaches. For the old approach (still present in Bonaventure) there was only one kind of wisdom and therefore one route to it: graced love. For the newly developing approach there were two kinds—the old kind, increasingly confined to the area of a gift of the Holy Spirit; and the new Aristotelian kind, attainable by reason alone. Victory for the new approach was almost inevitable. Significantly it heralded itself in giving Aristotle's idea of wisdom precedence over the Augustinian one.

We see this process taking place in Aquinas, who also marks a high-point, different in stress to that of Bonaventure, of attempts to integrate the old and the new. In his system the Aristotelian idea of wisdom returns with full force. Experiential knowledge does indeed continue to play a role in his synthesis. But there is a clear change: the Aristotelian epistemology with its rationalist bent is to the fore; the experiential element with a role for love is in the background.

The change of direction is adumbrated already in his *Commentary on the Sentences*, book 3, d. 35. The issue is whether or not the contemplative life consists solely in cognition. He agrees that it does not—he would not gainsay the long tradition that it is a form of life that involves "savoring," love. But the role granted the latter is interesting: it is that of a motivating force, belonging to the volitional side of a person, enabling one to focus one's attention on the object loved (God). Contemplation, then, consists "essentially in cognitive activity" (sol 1). As Rimaud once pointed out, Thomas took over the Aristotelian sense of contemplation. This saw contemplation simply as the intellectual life in contrast to that of an artisan.[38]

This intellectualist bias is carried over into his discussion of the Spirit's gift of wisdom (q 2). He indeed repeats the idea that wisdom gives an insight into the divine because of a certain affinity with divine things brought about by love's unitive force (quaestiu. 3, sol 3). Wisdom involves judging things from the correct—i.e., the divine—perspective. To do so effectively the mind needs to be united to the divine, "a unity that takes place through love; therefore wisdom deals principally with divine things, and enjoys the delights thereof, delights caused by love."[39]

However, wisdom consists *essentially* in a knowledge that is distinguished from love. The traditional "savoring"[40] of truth is relegated to a love that precedes cognition, or which may follow on it. It is not part of the cognitive process itself.[41] Indeed, not only wisdom but also understanding can be accompanied by "savoring," by "delights." But the difference is not that wisdom's savoring is all that relevant epistemologically. Rather is the difference to be found in the fact that in wisdom the delight is focused on wisdom's objects (divine realities), whereas in the case of understanding the delight derives from the fulfillment brought about by the activity itself.[42]

The break with the past represented here is not as severe nor as noticeable as will occur later. Since he is talking about the infused gift of wisdom, he is still able to include some role for love. As was noted, he even spoke of love as bringing about an affinity with the divine that enabled a more accurate judgment of divine realities to occur. This stress on judgment is also interesting, as Aquinas will distinguish it clearly from understanding. It is the latter that is more associated with penetrating into the truth, with some sort of conscious insight. And this is a process in which love seems to play no epistemological role at all (see d 35, q 2, a 2, quaest. 3, sol). It is not surprising that he seems more at home with the idea of connatural knowledge in the sphere of moral judgment.

As I say, the break with the past in the *Commentary on the Sentences* is somewhat muted. However, the scene changes more dramatically when he has to deal with the issue whether theology is a science. Here the Aristotelian conception of wisdom comes into its own.

In his *Commentary on Boethius* (Proem q 2 a 2), he raises the objection that theology cannot be a science since it deals with divine realities; and that is the province of wisdom, not science. In his reply he points out that wisdom does not exclude science, but on the contrary it is the highest of the sciences, regulating all others. What is interesting about this is that the traditional distinction between wisdom and science is not even mentioned. Prior to Thomas, the stock answer to the objection that theology was not a science was that it was more than a science. It was wisdom and distinguished itself from science by the fact that it savored its object. In Thomas, however, theology's supremacy is here derived from the fact that the body of knowledge contained in it stands at the head of all the sciences. Aristotle's idea of wisdom has been allowed full citizenship in the land of theology.

In the *Summa Theologica* both views—the older and the Aristotelian—are discussed. The context is whether or not theology is wisdom (I, 1, a 6). One of the objections to its being wisdom is the fact that theology is acquired through study, while wisdom is an infused gift of the Spirit. In his reply Thomas naturally points out that the wisdom imparted by the Spirit is not the same as that acquired through study.

The former judges all things because of an affinity with their source, the divine. The latter judges all things because of the competence derived from study, and it is this latter wisdom that is the province of theology. Aristotle has not only been given the run of the house. He has also booted his rival out. His rival now belongs to the sphere of the supernaturally imparted gifts of the Holy Spirit.

However, that is not the end of the story. His rival is still around, even in theology. And indeed, the old epistemological role of love is brought back into the heart of Thomas's system. If Chenu is right, and I suspect he is, then love's illuminating power is summoned to form the core of his theory of theology as a subalternate science. Aristotle was allowed free reign of the house—but only the more effectively to tame him.

The thirteenth century was well known as the one in which theology's status as a science was debated by virtually every theologian. And by "science" was meant a body of knowledge rationally grounded according to the norms laid down by Aristotle for a science to exist. Thomas was the first to attempt to show how theology could claim to be a *subalternate* science in the Aristotelian sense of the term. A subalternate science takes its guiding principles from another one: e.g., engineering may take its principles from mathematics. Now such a science retains its scientific character even if the principles of the subalternating science are simply accepted on faith, so to speak.

The parallel with theology was brilliantly drawn by Aquinas: just as a subalternate science accepts its principles from elsewhere and then proceeds to draw conclusions from them, so too does theology accept its principles from elsewhere and proceed to draw conclusions from them. Theology's principles are the articles of faith, and these it gets from divine revelation. In theology's case the subalternating science is God's own knowledge and that which the blessed in heaven have of God.

However, the flaw in the system is obvious and Thomas was aware of it. For a subalternating science to be truly a science, its practitioners should in theory be able to analyze its principles and resolve them into their rational foundations. There should be a continuity then between the two sciences. How is this possible in theology? Strictly speaking, in this life it is not possible. However, there is, Thomas would say, *some* continuity, and it is here that the old Augustinian idea of love creating connatural knowledge plays its part.

The theologian's unity with God, experiential knowledge of God, provides the continuity between the principles accepted on faith and their divine source.[43] As Chenu has aptly commented, "that which makes theology a science is [for Thomas] precisely that which makes it mystical."[44] This also indicates that for Aquinas connatural knowledge and therefore love's epistemological role was in fact not limited simply to the sphere of making moral judgments. Instead it had a role to play in legitimating the insights of theologians into their subject. One of the arguments used for restricting his view of connatural knowledge to the moral sphere is the example he used in the *Summa* (I, 1, a 6: see above) to show how infused wisdom operated. The example was that of a moral judgment.

However, it is worth noting that the example was but an example: it does not explicitly limit connaturality to the moral sphere. It is true that Thomas' Aristotelian epistemology does shove him in the direction of associating connatural knowledge with moral judgments, because that was the area in which Aristotle himself acknowledged the role of connatural knowledge.[45] But the whole context of Thomas's discussion in the *Summa*—theology's character as wisdom—was all-encompassing and not simply limited to moral matters.

At any rate, to return to the way in which Thomas gave theology the necessary continuity with its subalternating science, some have argued that in his later work, the *Summa*, he abandoned this vestige of Augustinian epistemology.[46] In it the first principles are simply accepted on divine authority, without reference to any further illumination that could derive from an experiential unity with the divine.

Chenu[47] believes that there is no change—space and didactic reasons prompted Thomas to omit reference to it.

Whether Chenu is correct or not I do not know. What seems clear, however, is that the whole thrust of Thomas' approach was to push love's illuminating role into the background of theological work. The only place where it may fulfil a role was as regards the principles on which theology was based. After that, logic took over. Theology's conclusions were entitled to stand as scientifically established ones only if the logical coherence between them and the principles was perceptible. Of course, as a mystic Thomas appears to have continued to set store by the connatural knowledge made possible by love's unifying capacity. But his theological methodology moved in a different direction. Grace and nature are carefully distinguished. The unity of the older approach in this matter is effectively split.

Although the brand of theology to dominate the scene for the next few centuries was to be the Scotistic and not the Thomistic one, nevertheless the rationalist bias inherent in the scholastic approach from the beginning was triumphant. As far as I can judge, love ceased to fulfil a meaningful epistemological role in academic theology. Instead, it remained alive mainly in the mystical movement, one that became antagonistic to academic theology.[48] The increasing focus on logical interrelationships bore fruit in the nominalist movement and contributed to the decadence of scholasticism. Within such a perspective, one in which all the stress is on logic, love can have no meaningful role to play.

An adequate history of its role from this point on would therefore have to focus on the mystics and perhaps also on the pietist movements that gripped the popular imagination from the early fourteenth century onwards. Or at any rate, perhaps one should be examining treatises such as John of St. Thomas' classic on "The Gifts of the Holy Ghost." This seventeenth-century work by a devotee of Aquinas is well worth studying. He deals in some depth with the very issue of love's epistemological role. Moreover, it is crystal clear that it is a matter of understanding truth and not simply of making moral judgments—a standpoint he attributes to Aquinas. However, constraints of space make it impossible to go into his views here.

Concluding Remarks

That there is a long and strong tradition within Christian thought that love enables not just moral judgment but the understanding of divine truth to take place is undeniable. The basis of that ability is found in love's power to conform the believer to God. This conformity creates the connaturality that allows a deeper understanding of things divine to occur and therefore to judge more surely concerning them.

The type of knowledge acquired this way lacks any clear description, however. One does not necessarily experience the acquisition of new concepts thereby. On the contrary, the normal way in which it would seem to work is by a deeper understanding of concepts, images, symbols with which one is already familiar. The best word for it, I suspect, is "insight." William of St. Thierry compares it to the knowledge one has of a friend or spouse,[49] while Leclercq says it gives one a view of reality as a whole—which is a reversion to the old idea of wisdom.[50] Descriptions of it tend to stress its non-conceptual character. However, if it is to qualify as knowledge, understanding, insight, it must have some effect on the conceptual level: for example, a greater ability to distinguish concepts or see connections between them.

Ever since Aquinas there has been a tendency to split and oppose the two types of knowledge: reasoned and connatural. However, I believe that a holistic approach to knowledge will make room for both in such a way that the one aids the other. Connaturality will color the understanding of one's concepts, while conceptual and logical precision will provide the guidelines we need so as to avoid appeals to connaturality being simply a justification for the arbitrary. I also suspect that such a vision of the relationship between connatural and discursive knowledge will enable one to evaluate the traditional arguments for the existence of God. I seem to recall that in Frederick Copleston's famous BBC debate with Bertrand Russell on arguing for God's existence, Copleston's point was that you either saw intuitively the validity of the argument from contingency or you did not. Is there not perhaps a sort of connaturality operating here? Whether this is so or not, I do believe that both connatural and reasoned knowledge should be part of one's approach to reality,[51] even the same reality.

The classic approaches to love's role depend very heavily on a metaphysics that many today will find rather meaningless as a conceptual framework, even in the highly sophisticated and captivating version put forward by Karl Rahner, who so beautifully described love as "the lamp of knowledge."[52] Moreover, even for those (such as myself) who continue to find such a metaphysics meaningful, I cannot see that approach adding much more to our understanding than it has already contributed: viz., a knowledge acquired through ontological conformity to the object known, a conformity forged by love. I believe the past still needs to be retrieved, and that we will deepen our understanding of the issues as a result. But we will still be within basically the same conceptual framework. Is there any other framework, any other approach that can take us further?

I believe there is, though lack both of space and expertise necessitate my simply drawing attention to it and leaving the matter there. The approach in question is that of sociology, specifically the sociology of knowledge. The little I have read in that area has made me suspect that the forces structuring the way we know are but a social expression of the way love works. In both cases personal relationships, rather than bare logical interrelationships, play an important role in the process of understanding reality. I believe we will find there the practical fleshing out of the ontological skeleton constructed by our forebears.

Moreover, what is very interesting indeed is that the sociology of knowledge has been wedded to the epistemology of love in liberation theology's idea of praxis. For liberation theology, one must do what is right in order to know what is right. Orthodoxy is the product of orthopraxis, not the other way around—or rather there is a dialectical movement between the two. Certainly, the stress in liberation theology is on the social forces. But the religious input, the Christian dimension, is the idea that living the Gospel is essential for understanding it. After all, Jesus is recorded as having said that if anyone did his Father's will, then he would know that his teaching was from God. (*Jn*. 7:17) It is especially then in movements such as these that we must search for new insights into love's epistemological role.

NOTES

1. See Byung-Ho Vincent RI *La connaissance par connaturalité et son rôle dans la vie chrétienne selon Saint Thomas d'Aquin* (Thèse présentée pour l'obtention du Doctorate en Science Théologique du mème cycle), Institut Catholique de Paris, Paris: Copy Thèse Service (François Reder), 1982, 10, 11, 20.
2. See *op. cit*., first chapter, in which the author presents the views of the five main contributors to the discussion at the time he wrote.
3. See *op. cit*., 11.
4. I have already published a study of Augustine's views and so for more details the interested reader is referred to that work, the essential conclusions of which are reproduced here. See B. Gaybba, "Love and Know What You Will: the Epistemological Role of Love in Augustine." C. Landman and D. P. Whitelaw (Eds.), *Windows on Origins/Oorspronge in Oënskou*, Pretoria: University of South Africa, 1985, 107–133.
5. On this see A.H. Armstrong, *The architecture of the intelligible universe in the philosophy of Plotinus*. Amsterdam: Hakkert, 1967.
6. See *Sermo* CCCL. i; PL 39:1533.
7. *In epistolam Joannis ad Parthos* VII. iv. 10 - PL 35:2034; *ibid*, IX.x - PL 35:2052.
8. *Soliloquiorum* I.vi. 13; PL 32:876.
9. See, e.g., *De diversis quaestionibus* XXXV.ii - PL 4:24; *De trinitate* XI.ii.5 - PL 42:988; *In epistolam Joannis ad Parthos* II.ii 14 - PL 35:1997; *De moribus ecclesiae catholicae* I.xxi.39 - PL 32:1328.
10. See Gaybba *op. cit*., 124–125.
11. *In Joannis evangelium* XCVI.IV; PL 35:1876.
12. See *Sermo* CCCL.i; PL 39:1533.
13. See *Sermo* CXXVI.x; PL 38:705; see Gaybba *op. cit*., 109–110
14. *Epistola* CXXXVII.vii.17; PL 33:524.
15. Here too I must refer the interested reader to the more detailed study on Monastic theology that forms the opening chapter to my *Aspects of the Mediaeval History of Theology*, Pretoria: University of South Africa, 1988.
16. For example, I think Hugh and Richard of St. Victor are entitled to be regarded as practitioners of monastic theology, despite their not being monks and despite their very positive attitude to secular learning and the role of reason.
17. Leclercq, J. *L'amour des lettres et le désir de Dieu: initiation aux auteurs monastiques du Moyen Age*. Paris: du Cerf. 1957.
18. See e.g., William of St. Thierry *Speculum fidei*, PL 180:373, 383, 384, 394.
19. See William of St. Thierry, *Speculum fidei* - PL 180: 390.
20. See e.g., Bernard of Clairvaux, *Sermones in Cantica* XXXVIII - PL 183:977 and XXXI - PL 183:941.
21. See e.g., Rupert of Deutz, *De divinis officiis per anni circulum* XI.xvii - PL 170:309.
22. See e.g., Hugh of St. Victor, *Soliloquium de arrha animae*, PL 176:954.

23. This idea of love conforming the believer specifically to the Spirit cropped up in several thirteenth-century writers. See how it operates, e.g., in Thomas Aquinas' *Summa* I. 43. a 5. ad 2.
24. See William of St. Thierry, *Speculum fidei* - PL 180:391; L. Malevez, La Doctrine de l'image et la connaissance mystique chez Guillaume de Saint-Thierry. *Recherches de Science Religieuse*, 22 (1932) 189.
25. See William of St. Thierry, *Ad Fratres* II.iii - PL 184:349 and Malevez *op. cit.*, 200–201.
26. *Ep. IX*. J.-P Migne, *Patrologia Graeca*, 3:1106.
27. See R. Roques, Connaissance de Dieu et Théologie Symbolique d'après l' *In Hierarchiam Coelestem Sancti Dionysii* de Hugues de Saint Victor. *Rechérches de Philosophie*, 3–4 (1958) 190–191 and M.-D Chenu, *La Théologie au douzième siècle*. Paris: Vrin, 1957, 162.
28. This is especially clear in Hugh of St. Victor's method of *deductio* and *reductio*, on which see Roques *op. cit.*, 217–218 and 254–257.
29. See, e.g., how Albert the Great speaks of the necessity of purifying one's heart and dying to this world in order to be predisposed to the reception of the gift of understanding: In III Sent., d. 35, art. 10, ad. 4; *Opera omnia*, vol. 28, Paris: Vivès, 1894, 656.
30. "Ergo nesciunt theologiam qui non habent fidem formatem ... Sine experientia enim non habetur ars vel scientia, et omnis intellectiva cognitiio ex preexistenti cognitione sensitiva fit. Sicut enim qui nunquam gustavit mel, nunquam habet veridicam scientiam de sapore ejus...ita qui non est exercitatus in operibus fidei formate, theologie agnitionem non habet et tamen sciit loqui de theologia; similiter et cecus natus scit loqui de coloribus, et tamen scientiam eorum non habet." *Summa*, prol., q 2: as quoted in Chenu, *op. cit.*, 61–62.
31. *Summa theologica*, III, Florence: Quaracchi, 1948, q 6, c 1, sol.
32. *Glossa in quatuor libros sententiarium Petri Lombardi* Florence: Quaracchi, vol. 3 (in lib. zum), 1954, d 35, 7, 438.
33. *Comment in Sent*. III, d. 34; text as quoted in D.O. Lottin, Textes inédits relatifs aux dons du Saint-Esprit, in *Recherches de Thèologie Ancienne et Médievale*, I (1929), 89.
34. *Summa*, text in Lottin *op. cit.*, 79.
35. See e.g., C. Dumont, la réflexion sur la méthode théologique (suite), *Nouvelle Revue Théologique*, 84:17–35.
36. "De reductione artium ad theologiam."
37. See, e.g., Robert Kilwardby: "Scientia vero, quae est de causa causarum aut docet verum ut verum aut ut bonum. Illa quae docet de prima causarum verum ut verum metaphysica est, et spectat tantum ad aspectum. Illa quae docet de eadem verum ut bonum Sacra Scriptura est, et pertinet ad motionem affectus. Et haec proprie dicitur sapientia a sapore, quia facit cognitionem secundum gustum. Illa vero dicitur sapientia sed minus proprie, quia facit cognitionem secundum visum tantum" (*Quaestio de natura Theologiae*, ed. F. Stegmüller, Aschendorff, 1935, 49).
38. J. Rimaud, *Thomisme et Méthode*, Paris: 1925, 266–267.
39. "quae quidem unio ad divina per delectionem [sic] est; ideo sapientia circa divina principaliter est, et habet circa ea delectationem ex dilectione causatem." In librum III Sent., in *Commentum in libris IV Sententiarum*, Paris: Vivès, vol. 3, 1889, d

35, q 2 a 2 quaestiu 3, sol p. 593.

40. The idea of "savoring" became *the* image for experiential knowledge of God. Truth can be savored because Truth is also Goodness. The True and the Good are one. See Hugh of St. Victor, *Commentariorum in Hierarchiam Coelestem*, IV-PL, 175: 1001, 1002.
41. "Dicendum quod saporeum sapientia importat quantum ad dilectionem praecedentem, non quantum ad cognitionem sequentem, nisi ratione delectatiionis, quae ipsam cognitionem in actu exsequitur." In librum III sent., in *Commentum in libris IV Sententiarum*, Paris: Vivès, vol. 3, 1889, d 35, q 2 a l quaestiu 3, ad lum p. 591.
42. The delectation in *intellectus* "causatur ex congruentia operationis ad operantem; non autem ex dilectione ad ea circa quae est operatio, sicut est in sapientia" (*ibid.*, ad 2um).
43. "Et secundum hoc de divinis duplex scientia habetur. Una secundum modum nostrum... Alia secundum modum ipsorum divinorum, ut ipsa divina secundum se capiantur, quae quidem perfecte in statu viae nobis est impossibilis, sed fit nobis in statu viae quaedam illius cognitionis participatio et assimilatio ad cognitionem divinam, in quantum per fidem nobis infusam inhaeremus ipsi primae veritati propter se ipsam": (*Expositio super librum Boethii de Trinitate*, ed. B. Decker, altera, Leiden: Brill, 1959, q 2 a 2, resp). See also Chenu, *Op. cit.*, 73–74.
44. *Op. cit.*, 74.
45. For Aristotle the "good person" is the measure of virtuous actions, can judge what is or is not good by a sort of connaturality with what is right for a human being. See his *Ethics*, Book X, 1176.
46. See J. De Guibert, *Les doublets de Saint Thomas d'Aquin*, Paris 1926, 55–61; as quoted in Chenu *op. cit.*, 75.
47. *Op. cit.*, 75.
48. See on this Fr. Vanderbroucke, Le divorce entre théologie et mystique: ses origines. *Nouvelle Revue Théologique*, 72: 372–389.
49. *Speculum fide*i - PL 180: 392.
50. Leclercq, *op. cit.*, 205.
51. See K. Stern, *The Flight from Woman*, London: Allen & Unwin, 1966, 54–55.
52. K. Rahner, *Hearers of the Word*, London: Sheed & Ward, 1969, ch. 8, 100.

9

KIERKEGAARD'S TELEOLOGICAL SUSPENSION OF THE SELF

Nona R. Bolin

KIERKEGAARD'S TELEOLOGICAL SUSPENSION of the ethical announces his approach to the religious. The possibility of such a suspension is formulated within the broader question of time. From Kierkegaard's point of view as a religious writer, the tradition of philosophy and theology, onto-theology, has omitted a certain formulation of truth in its failure to consider the alternative answer to the Socratic question of whether truth can be learned. The coupling of the internal and the eternal in the tradition has obscured the experience of the religious moment when truth is learned and the temporal and the eternal collide. Onto-theology has quantified time and thus disassociated temporality from existence. It has lost sight of the existential experience of temporality and has laid its foundations in a theory of a subject that is always present to itself such that self-knowledge and truth are identical. Socratic truth has given the self a transcendent place and ignored the radical finitude of human existence. As the path to truth, self-knowledge takes on the timeless nature of the eternal. But for Kierkegaard, the "I" is not the principle of originary truth. Truth lies outside of the self, and thus disrupts the continuity of personal identity through the disruption of what Kierkegaard calls the "moment." Kierkegaard's investigation of the necessary relation of the self to temporal continuity pursues the question of time as simultaneously the question of the self.

The suspension of the ethical stage is impossible, an absurdity from the point of view of the understanding. The possibility of this impossibility, this unthinkable event, haunts all of Kierkegaard's writing and forms the question that impels his provisional query: "Is the teleological suspension of the ethical possible?" The necessary undecidability of this inquiry gives Kierkegaard's texts their uncanny structure. The question, while it has the form of an interrogative, is addressed to no one and solicits no answer. It is addressed to an anonymous 'We' whose status is effaced in the very asking. We address ourselves in the quiddity of our existence as those who are in question. But having arrived at its destination, the question inscribes an epitaph in the monumental moment of ethical decision, that signals the demise of the self. If the suspension of the ethical is possible, then it marks a death, the moment when there is no longer any choice. But the death of the self that is part of Kierkegaard's religious stage is not a physical death, not a recognizable death. It cannot be explained, this death in life. It can only take form "incognito."

Johannes de Silento, fascinated by the incognito, inquires into the suspension of the ethical in what Kierkegaard subtitles "a dialectical lyric." Johannes calls himself a "supplementary clerk" who dreads that some "gobbler of paragraphs" will cut up his corpus and expose his failure to construct a "tower," his inability to erect an architectonic that stands firm on its own foundation. Johannes concludes in the Preface (prefaces usually being those last minute additions) that he has failed to finish his tower and will be mocked by every "system ransacker." (*FT*:8) Nonetheless, he follows his fascination.

Johannes de Silento cannot think himself into Abraham. He cannot make the "movement of faith" that would give him some understanding of those events on Mount Moriah. Abraham cannot be understood. To understand Abraham requires that one lose one's understanding. (*FT*:36) Nothing is to be learned from Abraham. The knight of faith is never a teacher, never an exemplar. He is a mute witness to a paradox without resolution. His faith, as all faith, is the resignation to the paradox of existence. Who is Abraham? Johannes does not know. He can tell the story, describe how he loved Isaac and the event that took place that readily give themselves over to narrative investigation. Abraham defies representation. The proper name is but a placemark for an absence more radical than death. Neither exteriority nor interiority, a "Abraham" is the place of incommensurability between them, the interval between presence and absence, which Johannes describes as a "new interiority" that is not identical with the interiority that is binarily contrasted to exteriority.(*FT*:69) Abraham exists only as "Abraham" in God's calling. He exists incognito, in absolute relation to absolute otherness.

The suspension that creates the space for faith might be described as "uplifting" but not in term of the Hegelian "Aufhebung." It is not an elevation to a higher stage such as a synthesis of the esthetic and ethical stages. The suspension uplifts only in its indifference to dialectic, for Kierkegaard, an inaudible, invisible difference. Indeed the religious stage is not a summit. It is not the apex of the tower. It is not a place at all. Instead it is the "stage" that makes completion impossible. It is an uplifting that breaks with its ground, reveals the abyss over which the foundation is laid. Severed from the security of the universal, the religious stage is not a cohesive transition from the ethical, and Kierkegaard's rejection of Hegel's totalizing movement of the absolute makes this apparent. While extensive consideration of the Hegelian "Aufhebung" and Kierkegaard's suspension would facilitate some clarity on their respective differences, marking disjunctions of this kind is beyond the scope of this paper.

The notion of suspension is crucial in Kierkegaard's break from Hegel. In Hegel's dialectic the impasses of contradictory truths are relieved of their stasis, superceded through a movement of cancelling and a taking up or synthesizing a higher truth. Kierkegaard is not concerned with investing the religious with a higher truth in any progressive or additional sense. Kierkegaard's concern is focused toward the movement from the ethical to the religious, a movement not of transcendence but of delay and detour. The momentum of the movement is neither constant nor accelerated. Rather the motion of the movement to the religious is an infinitely finite motion, a "double-movement" where a fold insinuates itself in the temporal.(*FT*:36) Johannes can approximate the movements of faith but he cannot make them.

> In learning to go through the motions of swimming, one can be suspended from the ceiling in a harness and then presumably describe the movements, but one is not swimming. In the same way I can describe the movements of faith. If I am thrown out into the water, I presumably do swim (for I do not belong to the waders), but I make different movements, the movements of infinity, whereas faith makes the opposite movements; after having made the movements of infinity, it makes the movements of finitude. Fortunate is the person who can make these movements. He does the marvelous, and I shall ever weary

> of admiring him; it makes no difference to me whether it is Abraham or a slave in Abraham's house, whether it is a professor of philosophy or a poor servant girl—I pay attention only to the movements.(*FT*:37–38)

The movement is enigmatic and cannot be contained in any theoretical application of mechanics. The motion which defies Johannes credulity is a comportment that reveals a way of being, a way of commitment towards a paradox. Motion and time are co-extensive in the paradox. But linear calculation is out of the question in their measurement. (*FT*:35) This spatio/temporal movement that Johannes characterizes as a "leap" is a leap like that of the ballet dancer. But unlike the dancer who is unable to instantaneously reassume his posture as soon as he descends, the knight of faith never wavers.

> One does not need to see them in the air; one needs only to see them the instant they touch and have touched the earth—and then one recognizes them. But to be able to come down in such a way that instantaneously one seems to stand and to walk, to change the leap into life into walking, absolutely to express the sublime in the pedestrian—only that knight can do it, and this is the one and only marvel.(*FT*:41)

The movement to faith is preceded by resignation wherein choice is relinquished. But resignation is not faith, and does not require it. Resignation is an "infinite movement" that yields eternal consciousness. Johannes describes it as "a purely philosophical movement."(*FT*:48) There is a following movement that yields "a little bit more" than eternal consciousness, an excess, a supplement, an otherness. (*FT*: 48) This is the movement of faith, and this other is the paradox. Acknowledging the possibility of what is impossible from the point of view of the understanding, the religious knight embraces the absurd. This movement takes place instantaneously, in what Kierkegaard calls the "moment" [ojeblikket]. Just as the movement toward eternal consciousness is a different movement from the religious movement, the moments are different as well, and Kierkegaard's writings are pervaded with these moments. The radical disjunction of these moments binds Kierkegaard's thought, but they present the reader with a double bind. One seeks to analyze their differences, which marks the differences between the ethical and the religious stages. But in the very stasis of analysis, the movement and moment of faith inevitably escape. The understanding cannot incorporate the excess of faith. "The absurd does not belong to the differences that lie within the proper domain of the understanding. It is not identical with the improbable, the unexpected, the unforseen." (*FT*:46) The escape is inevitable in the approach. Nonetheless, the understanding is drawn by the paradox, and as such pursues its hiddenness.

It is the inevitable aporia that Johannes de Silento forecasts in his Preface, the project that guides his inquiry: seeking the success of a failure, a difference that yields no differences.

The religious maintains no contiguity with the ethical. They are separated from each other by a "chasmal abyss."(*FT*:20) It is not a movement from a state of presence to another state of presence. Rather it is a movement of disjunction from presence to a cancellation of both presence and absence, although not dialectical cancellation. (Dialectics cancels the present for Presence.) The movement demands a leap such that the logic of identity is bracketed. The ethical is the domain of ontological identity. It is the region where Law is the authority. There the universal commands the whole rhetoric of uplifting or edification and describes the essence of all ethical activity. The religious raises itself above the Law but not for its own edification and justification. There is not, nor can there be, any justification of the religious.

> Faith is precisely the paradox that the single individual as the single individual is higher than the universal, is justified before it, not as inferior to it but as superior—but in such a way, please note, that it is the single individual who, after being subordinate as the single individual to the universal, now by means of the universal becomes the single individual who as the single individual is superior, that the single individual as the single individual stands in an absolute relation to the absolute. This position cannot be mediated, for all mediation takes place only by virtue of the universal; it is and remains for all eternity a paradox, impervious to thought.(*FI*:56-56)

The ethical consciousness, represented by Judge Wilhelm in *Either/ Or*, finds its strength and legitimation in universal righteousness. It is the refuge of the good conscience that harbors its extreme possibility in the tragic hero. It is also the place where faith and reason find compatibility in eternal consciousness. Here the understanding comprehends all existence and faith along with it. Such is the proclivity of German Idealists who serve as Kierkegaard's foils in developing his description of the ethical stage. The dissolution of faith into the ethical is the work of the philosopher and is first and always a self-edification. Indeed, it is only at the stage of the ethical that a "self" is possible. In Judge Wilhelm's solicitation of Johannes the esthete, Wilhelm chastises Johannes for his inability to form a commitment and express the universal in his love for another. In the Judge's rhetoric, the parameters of the commitment take the form of the legal and ethical validity of marriage. Wilhelm argues that the esthetics of romantic love, pursued to the exclusion of all else by Johannes, is not cancelled in marriage as the esthete would maintain. On the contrary, in time the esthetic ideal is sustained and even perfected by the lawful commitment of marriage. A true "reconciliation" between art and life, the professed ideal of the esthete, is achieved only in marriage. In marriage, conquest and possession are merged. The movement of this merger takes place in what Wilhelm describes as the moment of decision. So Wilhelm's main consideration is that of time, more specifically the moment that gives life genuine value. Absent in the life of the esthete who lives in the multiplicity of the immediate, the moment is pertinent only to internal history.

> Internal history is the only true history; but true history contends with that which is the life principle of history, i.e., with time.... Whenever the internal process of blossoming in the individual has not yet begun and the individual is shut, there can only be external history. (*E/O*:137)

Conjugal love begins as possession while romantic love begins and ends as conquest. Since the esthete is concerned with conquest, his nature is constantly outside himself, whereas in the ethical the possessive creates an opening where the individual is concerned with an interiority that is constitutive of personal identity. Without the commitment to the universal, the esthete has no inner self. He is simply a shell, a shadowgraph [symparanekromenoi] and for him time is circumstantial. In the ethical the importance of time is that it is no longer fleeting immediacy. While Johannes can practice his art he cannot live it. Art must be reconciled with life, and they can reconcile only through the mediation of the universal, transfiguring the esthete and supplying him with an inward history. Without this metamorphosis, the individual remains a "practiced actor who has lived himself into his part and into his lines." (*E/O*:140) The esthete is never in himself, but constantly outside himself.(*E/O*:142)

While the esthete is a victim of time, the married man who incorporates first love and fidelity has triumphed over time. "The married man, being a true conqueror, has not killed time but has saved it and preserved it in all eternity."(*E/O*:141) The ethical individual does not fight with external factors like the false conqueror but with himself, "fights out love from within him."(*E/O*:142) Through the mediation of the universal, conjugal love repeats itself everyday, and is "divine...by reason of its occurrence everyday. Conjugal love...is the imperishable nature of a quiet spirit." (*E/O*:142) Marriage is also the state of a free individual for it is a freedom made possible by the necessity of the Law. The esthete understands true freedom to consist of the absence of external restraint. He misunderstands duty as constraint and the enemy of love. When duty appears, love becomes monotony. But Wilhelm argues that duty makes love "the true temperate climate" and unites the spontaneity of the esthetical with the commitment of the ethical.(*E/O*:150) To love truly can only be an inner movement of the heart. Thus while the esthete claims his very existence to be a dedication to love, Wilhelm maintains that Johannes is instead the enemy of love. Only dutiful possession permits its continuance in time. The separation of love and duty relegates the esthete to a life of constant self-contradiction making authentic selfhood impossible.

> It is as if in the word 'be' a man were to separate 'b' and 'e' and so would have no 'e' but would maintain that 'b' was the whole. The moment he pronounces it he utters the 'e' along with it. So it is the true love: it is not a dumb and unutterable letter, but neither is it a soft and inapprehensible indefiniteness. It is an articulate sound, a letter. Is duty hard? 'Eh bien,' then love pronounces it, it realizes it, and thereby does more than its duty. Is love by way of becoming so soft that it cannot be held fast? Well then, duty imposes upon it boundaries.(*E/O*:151–2)

The ethical self aspires to total adequation with the universal. Here the self takes itself to be its own possibility. It is its own project and the vehicle of actualization is choice. The ethical choice is an absolute choice of the absolute.

> I choose the absolute. And what is the absolute? It is I myself in my eternal validity. Anything else but myself I never choose as the absolute, for if I choose something else, I choose it as a finite thing and so do not choose it absolutely. Even the Jew who chose God did not choose absolutely, for he chose, indeed, the absolute, but died not choosing it absolutely, and thereby it ceased to be the absolute and became a finite thing.(*E/O*:21)

The self chooses itself according to the validity of the universal, for should the individual choose himself in a finite sense, this self would be particular and just one finite thing among others. Hence the ethical individual chooses himself absolutely, and in so doing the self comes into existence absolutely, absolutely distinct from his former existence. He has chosen absolutely. The moment of choice is absolutely decisive for it does the following:

> It performs at one and the same time the two dialectical movements: that which is chosen does not exist and comes into existence with the choice; that which is chosen exists, otherwise there would not be a choice. For in case what I chose did not exist but absolutely came into existence with the choice, I would not be choosing, I would be creating: but I do not create myself, I choose myself.(*E/O*:219–20)

Choice is the expression of freedom, and the free spirit or the ethical spirit is born from the absolute choice of choosing oneself. While the esthete thinks himself free and unbridled by commitment, in actuality, he is unfree. He cannot actualize the moment of choice. Instead that moment is perpetually delayed in the pursuit of immediacy. Thus the moment of decision, the absolute choice of the absolute, is postponed. The inevitable result, according to Judge Wilhelm, is despair. The esthete is eccentric for he has his center in his periphery. He who is not himself, who has no self, has no continuity and lives as a multiplicity. He fails to catch up with himself.(*ET*:46) Disoriented, the esthete 'goes in halves.'(*E/O*:275)

In choosing oneself absolutely the "I" infinitizes itself absolutely, for it is only the self who one can choose absolutely, nothing other can be chosen absolutely. The absolute choice of oneself is one's ownmost freedom. But this absolute choice of choosing oneself absolutely does not render "self" an empty abstraction. The ethical realm is not concerned with the external but only with the internal. No matter how the external may change the moral remains the same. It resides in internal time, namely, as intentional determination. In that it is a creation produced by a choice, this self is free and distinct. It has taken up the ideal of the esthetical in all its rich variations and yet has bound it by the monumental decisiveness of the moment. In the moment, the personality issues forth and concertizes itself as internal history. Through the universal the individual retains the richness of the esthetical while at the same time is transformed into a new self, for freedom now permeates all of his being. "Thus his finite personality is infinitized by the choice whereby he infinitely chooses himself."(*E/O*:227) Within the ethical, the individual is in possession of himself, he "gathers" himself in all his finite concretions. The ethical is that in a man whereby he immediately becomes what he becomes and in so doing becomes "transparent." The transparency reflects his own self-knowledge. But self-knowledge is not merely a procedure of contemplation. Indeed self-knowledge, as Wilhelm expresses it, is much more a matter of acquaintance.(*E/O*:263)

> He who lives ethically has seen himself, knows himself, penetrates with his consciousness his whole concretion, does not allow indefinite thoughts to potter about within him, nor tempting possibilities to distract him with their jugglery; he is not like a witch's letter from which one sense can be got now and then another, depending on how one turns it. He knows himself. (*E/O*:263)

Judge Wilhelm's concept of selfhood is a composite of the Kantian/Hegelian theory of self-consciousness. While each person is a determinate individual, each shares the essential human characteristic of agency. Agency presupposes that rationality is the definitive characteristic of personhood. As agents, persons are accountable for their choices. The recognition of the inevitable conjunction of choice and the universal principles of moral law is what gives cohesion to the formation of the self. Selfhood emerges by mean of enlightened choice based on the universal applicability of moral principles. The self binds itself to the universal by virtue of its capacity to reason.

Wilhelm believes himself to have achieved authenticity in the universal. He is "comfortable" in his own ethical edification and is characterized in much the same manner that Kierkegaard characterizes the contemporary Christian living in the spiritlessness of the social institution of Christendom, content in the assurance that he lives according to universal righteousness. "Christendom is comfortable—from this comes this tendency toward unity....[W]ith the coming of this unity, restlessness and striving, and fear and trembling, which should obtain for the entire life, go out." (*J&P*, 77:10-A 185:63) With this dominance of unity, the absolute difference between God and man is obliterated, and man, in his natural inclination to relegate all experience to some category of the understanding, turns faith into doctrine and passes it on like real estate to all who so gratefully accept transitive edification. Nonetheless, all who are as comfortable as Judge Wilhelm must be shaken by the ultimatum of the Jutland Priest: that before God we are always in the wrong. While the Judge can convincingly plead his case before men, in the face of what man is not, all justification is mere pretentious arrogance. Before God: "There is only one way of supporting the claim that you are in the right...learning that you are in the wrong." (*E/O*:346)

This recognition brings with it a certain uplifting in that it allows for the possibility of an infinite relationship, and, as Wilhelm himself persuasively argues, it is only the infinite that edifies. Wilhelm's shortsightedness has placed the religious alongside the ethical, and, as with Kant, has rendered faith and reason completely compatible by the mediation of the universal. But from the point of view of Kierkegaard as religious writer, truth does not and cannot lie within the recesses of the individual. Truth must be encountered and the encounter is not something that can be shared collectively. The ethical man claims an infinite relationship with the universal, concretized in his own self-choosing. At the moment of the ethical choice, the absolute self is actualized. But there is another moment [objeblikket] in Kierkegaard's writings that is inconceivable within the time frame of the ethical, a moment of which Judge Wilhelm knows nothing. It is a moment so inconceivable that can be given no possible space. Impossible and absurd within the ethical understanding that gives justification to its choices, it is a moment of madness. Beyond the boundaries of the ethical, the understanding is rendered absurd.

Kierkegaard investigates the tension between the ethical and the religious stages and the latter's challenge to the absoluteness of universal duty and the necessity of coupling of faith and reason. His investigation is often incorporated within an explicit or implicit rejection of German Idealism. In a kingdom of absolute and universal values, one cannot even ask Johannes de Silento's question: "Is the teleological suspension of the ethical possible?" Within this domain there is no conceivable reason to suspend the ethical, no justifiable violation of the Law. But in his consideration of the religious, reason and Law are suspended. Thus the very question exiles the examiner from the community of the universal and renders him solitary and indeterminate. While one may take the question to be voiced from the depths of the irrational and the unethical, such a dismissal would neglect the radicality of Kierkegaard's thinking.

Such characterizations cannot explain the suspension of which Johannes de Silento speaks. The question echoes in its own suspension for the religious consciousness has no tools of verification or falsification. Beyond the limits of the understanding, beyond Good and Evil, the religious consciousness has no voice. It is a question asked with inevitable irony, for the very asking shatters the enclosures where rationality reigns. But certainly it would be an egregious misconception to maintain that the question betrays its own irrationality, for this classification only finds its legitimacy within the ethical. It loses all import in the suspension. The suspension of the ethical abates the very operation of the binary opposition of rational/irrational, ethical/unethical for it cannot be placed within a category of the understanding nor can it be situated within the temporal parameters that constitute the ethical self.

In *Philosophical Fragments* Johannes Climacus proclaims himself the exponent of a dialectical puzzle. He describes his thinking as a "thought experiment," a "dance" that sidesteps the traditional privilege of Reason. In it most abbreviated form the paradox can be called the "moment." But it is not the decisive moment of selfhood explicated by Judge Wilhelm. It is not a moment of choice. Instead it is the uncanny moment when the self becomes untruth, and in place of self-knowledge there is an atopos self-absurdity.

This moment is the "cornerstone" of Kierkegaard's philosophy.[1] It is crucial in understanding the self-negation of the religious consciousness. While it occupies a pivotal place in many of his works, it comes to prominence in *Philosophical Fragments*. In his experiment, Climacus seeks another approach to truth than the traditional Socratic notion of truth. But having no access to that truth, the experiment is always precarious. The moment is not one that initiates internal history as does the ethical moment and is not a point of continuity that joins the ideal of a previous stage with a higher consciousness. The non-dialectical religious moment does not join past and future nows in the teleological movement of the before to the after that necessarily constitutes the internal integrity of selfhood. The religious moment, decisively different from the ethical, is incisive. It opens up a gap or a "breach" of continuity that can occur only at the limits of choice where a strange "otherness" calls. But this difference cannot be heard by the understanding except as an "acoustical illusion."(*PF*:49) It cannot be marked by the understanding as an item of reflection. Only a presence, a subject or object, can be marked with the distinction of identity. Only that which is present to the understanding can be identified. Consequently, the moment of encounter with "God," as absolute otherness, cannot be marked. The "reasons" for the disjunction between the ethical and the otherness that Kierkegaard calls "God" is not recoverable by way of any historical evidence. "God" cannot be understood in any traditional way, not even in terms of the mystical tradition. "God" is the unknowable, "but what is this unknown...? It is the unknown...so let us call it 'God.' This is the only name we give it."(*PF*:49) The epistemological difficulty is necessary, but not in terms of any logical or historical necessity. The incompatibility is with the generality of all meaning and thus all ways of calculating time. The other cannot be measured. While this religious moment as the 'fullness of time' makes all the difference, it cannot be grasped. It has no "distinguishing mark" [Kjendetegn].

> ...one waits and watches and the moment is supposed to be something of great importance, worth watching for, but since the paradox has made the understanding absurd, what the understanding regards as very important is no distinguishing mark.(*PF*:52)

The teleological suspension of the ethical is neither temporal nor atemporal. It is *both* temporal *and* atemporal, the merging of the finite and the eternal that defies every classification of time which is necessarily understood in terms of a harmonious unity. With the suspension of the ethical, time is split by otherness, interrupted by that which cannot be measured as a present 'now.' The suspension of the ethical and the movement to the religious does not transpire as a relation between two presents, nor from a present to an absence. From a religious point of view, the incarnation is the event that insinuates into time's ever-present now an inexplicable but irrevocable disruption wherein the finite and the eternal are conjoined in the god/man. As the conjunction of contradictions, the incarnation defies the authority of the logic of identity or even the concept of time.

But unlike Hegel's theory of Christianity, Christ, for Kierkegaard, is not a synthesis who overcomes contradiction and mediates God and Man. There is no ontotheological overcoming of man's difference from God. God is not the full presence of the Absolute. Consequently, this difference cannot be mediated through any presence, even by a god/man. Unlike the both/and of the universal and the particular that forms the unity of the ethical, the both/and conjunction of the religious maintains the incommensurability. The incarnation is an "existence communication" that speaks of the paradox of all existence. It does not convey the homogeneity of the divine and human, not even their heterogeneity (which owes its difference to the principle of identity). The incarnation communicates the irresolvable paradox, a paradox that cannot be incorporated into any quantitative or qualitative measurement of continuous 'nows' that excludes difference in favor of identity. However, it is not a question of the negation of time, absence, of a cessation of time in a present or a simultaneity. It is a question of a different structure, a different stratification of time.

Based on what Kierkegaard calls a "self-contradiction," the incarnation orients itself towards the future of its own enactment. Just as the emergence of the god/man is unfathomable, all existence arises from an abyss and a radical uncertainty connects with the event of becoming. Contrary to the reductive demands of the understanding, being cannot be reduced to the reflective gaze of the understanding. The inevitable excess that is existence preserves the paradox. The inexplicable becoming that is the incarnation communicates with each individual temporal being. But this temporal becoming is neither the immediate and indeterminate multiplicity of the esthete nor the decisiveness of an ethical self. Through the incarnation one understands oneself as a finite, singular individual through the paradox of existence. Filled with the eternal, the religious moment puts one in touch with the radical contingency of one's own temporality. The incarnation draws the I to its own limits. Obliged to recognize something greater and other, the unity of selfhood is fractured by otherness. This otherness exceeds the wholeness of the human, an otherness that is in its singularity greater than the whole. All existence is uncanny, arising from an abyss and opening upon an unknowable destiny. As otherness, Christ remains illusive.

Yet his presence among men was a historical event. Recovery of his being is not essentially oriented toward a past that is deemed to have factual integrity. Rather, his existence engages a future. Thus Kierkegaard maintains that Christ's contemporaries had no advantage in terms of faith. Faith has no need to be nostalgic for a past when it is the future that is at stake. History teaches nothing about the god/man except a few notations concerning a historical existence. But history never captures any existence. History cannot accommodate the paradox from which all existence precedes. As a narrative of continuous presence, history cannot incorporate aporetic becoming. This disruption is that about which everything turns for each individual, and for the Christian the incarnation is the truth of existence that carries all finitude toward a commitment that transgresses the universal. We are committed to the truth of that which we are not, that which draws us to a future that never will occur as present, always remaining a 'to come.' The suspension anticipates the inevitable deferment of the selfhood.

Truth enters history only by way of rupture. Every attempt to heal this wound within or outside of time is sheer folly. Truth comes from without, from a place that cannot take its place within internal history. Thus truth precludes any anamnesic totalization of selfhood. In *Philosophical Fragments* Climacus contrasts the ramifications of the externality of truth to the Socratic tradition that interiorizes truth. Socrates has found the self to be the place of truth. Since all knowledge is recollection, the learner is himself the place of truth. At the time one discovers the truth, one also comes to know oneself, for all knowledge is ultimately self-knowledge. This recognition is recollection, the knowledge that identity is eternal. Thus in the Socratic there is no historical starting point.

> The dialectic of the moment is not difficult. From the Socratic point of view, the moment is not to be seen or to be distinguished; it does not exist, has not been, and will not come. Therefore, the learner himself is the truth, and the moment of occasion is merely a jest, like an end-sheet half-title that does not essentially belong to a book.(*PF*:51–52)

But if the eternal remains outside the individual, as Climacus' thought experiment proposes, then interiority cannot be the locus of truth. Truth is absolutely different and the moment of its occurrence cannot be swallowed up by eternity. To know the truth that stands outside Socratic self-knowledge becomes the obsession of the understanding. Drawn by the allurement of the paradox, the understanding can either relinquish its claims to mastery or it can attempt to solve the paradox. The former Climacus calls "faith," the latter he calls "offense." Either way, the paradox of otherness consumes all thinking. The paradox is the point of departure for the religious. However, this departure is terrifying for it is a departure of self from self. It commences from a place where understanding must confront that which it is not and cannot choose to be. The I confronts its own delimitation such that it is what it is only through the experience of what it is not. This negative is not the inter-subjective other who is a component of the universal "We," but the other who never conforms to the insistence of the understanding. At its limit, the topological structure of the ethical, namely the universal, reveals a dislocation that renders unity impossible and self-identity self-deception. For Kierkegaard, self-deception is the mark of Christendom. In the face of the religious a self is never in itself. Self-reflection can never close the circle of its own contemplation.

While Kierkegaard has often been understood to have commonalities with the Christian tradition either as a mystic or as a theistic existentialist, it is questionable that any of these classifications unproblematically apply. The radicality of his thinking was revealed in his refusal to accept the traditional theories of time, self, and God. In thinking the necessity of the inter-relatedness of key concepts in the Western onto-theological tradition, Kierkegaard's thinking sought a departure from the tradition by provocatively calling these concepts into question. But Kierkegaard understood this questioning to penetrate the very style in which the inquiry was to be pursued. Thus Kierkegaard's thinking can be said to usher in many of the concerns of what is now called "Post-modernism." As post-moderns demand style to be rethought, Kierkegaard, the religious writer, allows his work to break with its own ground. Authorship always remains undecidable, retaining the paradox against all self-edification and entreating the otherness that appears in the gaps of writing.

The suspension that imperceivably marks the "inbetweeness" [Mellemvaerende] of human existence does not form itself out of argumentation or refutation. These philosophical tools are abandoned at the boundaries of the ethical. Rather the suspension forms itself in the unanswerable question of its own possibility. Kierkegaard's writing opens itself up to the interrogation of the very occurrence of inquiry rather than any attempted resolution. By maintaining the hiddenness of the paradox that makes the question possible, Kierkegaard can be taken at his word when in *The Point of View of My Work as an Author: A Report to History* he describes himself as always having been a writer of the religious. Faith is not professed. Faith is enacted in his writing. In the unconditional acceptance of the paradox, Kierkegaard relinquishes himself, his signature, to the otherness he names "God."

NOTES

1. Mark C. Taylor, *Journey's to Selfhood: Hegel and Kierkegaard* (Berkeley: University of California Press, 1980), 124.

REFERENCES

Søren Kierkegaard

E/O Either/Or, Vols. I & II, translated by Swenson and Swenson (Princeton: Princeton University Press, 1971).

FT Fear and Trembling, translated by Hong and Hong (Princeton: Princeton University Press, 1983).

PF Philosophical Fragments, translated by Hong and Hong (Princeton: Princeton University Press, 1985)

J&P Journals and Papers, translated and edited by Hong and Hong (Bloomington: Indiana University Press, 1967).

10

A SPECULATION ABOUT THE TRINITY DOCTRINE

Ninian Smart

IT IS TIME FOR CROSS-CULTURAL Christian theology to be the normal way for Christians, trying to think about the Divine. There are great and dynamic cultural traditions which can provide insights into Truth. In this paper I shall consider the Trinity doctrine from the angle of Indian philosophy and doctrine. I shall sketch some thoughts from the tradition of Rāmānuja to throw light upon the Trinity. But at the same time I want to make use of a speculative method which will give a fresh perspective on our topic.

It might be considered by some that the idea of the Trinity is not a unifying one. It is a teaching which in one form or another is rejected by Muslims, for instance, while it does not make much sense to Theravadin Buddhists. My belief is that we cannot buy unity by imposing too rigid a view on the religions. They may all search for Truth, but their ways are complementary rather than directly unified. Maybe in some future condition of the world they will come to unity, but the time is not yet. So I recognize that in putting forward a vision of the Trinity I am not directly promoting the unity of religions; but we need to know where we stand, and knowing this we can enter into fruitful collaboration with others in the onward search. But: Who are we?

I take it as important that doctrines tend to be doctrines of religious communities (to borrow the title of a marvelously clear book published recently, by William A. Christian Sr., through Yale University Press [Christian, 1987]). In presenting this paper I speak out of the Christian tradition and in particular the Episcopalian branch, though I have been much influenced by my collaborator, Mr. Steven Konstantine, who is Orthodox, and with whom I have helped to fashion a book expounding a Christian systematic theology in world perspective. But as hinted above I have also been influenced by Rāmānuja. So in speculating about the Trinity I come from the wider Christian community, but in dialogue with the wider community of theism. We are entering a period when the lines defining the limits of communities are getting fainter and even breaking up. But still, the typical situation is one in which communities generate their several doctrines and narratives, their values and their norms of practice. It is in this spirit that I wish here to project a vision of the Trinity, not expecting those who do not accept it to agree with this vision; but maybe hoping that they may be moved by it and understand Christian traditional faith better.

A Speculation About Creation

We most often look at the Lord from the under side, so to speak: looking up and marveling at the glory and awe-inspiring power. But there are uses to looking down: imagining ourselves to be Creator. Think what it means, the inward imagination of a cosmos, vast, swirling, evolving, giving birth to life, then to feeling, then to clear consciousness and wondrous ingenious joys and unspeakable horrors of suffering. How can a God have the terrible impulse to create a cosmos where creatures will suffer so? It is of course an old question, and it lies at the dark heart of the problem of evil.

There may be logical palliatives. After all free-ranging creatures are by definition liable to come into collision with their environment—to fall from cliffs, to drown in floods, to burn themselves in fires, to be crushed by rocks, and to be tormented by diseases. So it is not feasible to make free creatures in a material environment who will not suffer to some extent (and yet what of heaven: Is there suffering there?). Let us suppose that this is so, that Creation of free beings inevitably means some suffering. Let us for the moment neglect the surplus, the degree of suffering. The palliative argument still poses a question, as to whether after all Creation can be justified. Before pursuing this directly, let us just for a moment reflect on the issue of freedom.

It is evident that a materially embedded person with freedom cannot be protected from both the conditions and the consequences of her freedom. It is part of the conditions of freedom that there should be capacity for action, and that implies a material interplay between the environment and the individual. This cannot be altered at will so to speak by the Creator without inducing miraculous chaos and thus the destruction of the very regularity which enables an intelligent and conscious being to exercise her freedom. Nor can the Creator interfere continuously to stop free creatures from doing things dangerous to one another and to themselves. In short freedom sets its price.

It might be thought however that the mode of Creation, that is via a long evolutionary process, is cruel. I do not wish here to minimize the miseries of living beings in the vastly long process from amoebas to humanity. But it obeys the anthropic principle that the cosmos is just sufficiently orderly to produce consciousness and human beings. The evolutionary way is one which does not cut off the individual from her environment: we are part of the warp and woof of the cosmos. So if you were going to produce a material cosmos which managed to exhibit free creatures, then this cosmos fits that bill.

It may open to the Lord to produce other realms less material: to play with angels and golden glory as well as this beautiful but less obviously wonderful world. But angels are so close to God that they can do nothing but praise him. Lucifer's act of imagination was almost unimaginable. Angels are not free creatures the way we are: and perfect behavior without adventure is fairly good, but maybe not in the long run as good as sainthood in the conditions of this world. Anyway even if God can create better worlds, that is no cause of complaint for us in this world.

These palliatives of the problem of evil however do not dispose of the problem confronting a Creator. Let us imagine we are embarking on that task: Would we dare to create a world where jaguars break their legs and humans die in forest fires? Well, it would be said by some that it is not for us to enter into the mind of God, and my way of posing the question is dangerously anthropomorphic. But my thought experiment recognizes that we do use human concepts and analogies with human persons in speaking and thinking about the Lord. I realize well that there is an unspoken side of God, and that our metaphors are fragile. But still, to get a greater insight, why not imagine that we are Divine?

It is in my view a strength of the Christian faith (though this does not mean that it does not have other weaknesses) that we envisage the Creator as saying: I would not make a world I would not enter into myself. The Lord has her *avatāra*. She is prepared to suffer in the world. It is a problem for a Creator to make creatures detached, knowing that conscious creatures will suffer somewhat and some terribly. I do not say that it is necessary for a theist to believe in incarnation, but the belief makes a lot of sense, independently of the question of God's reconciliation with alienated humanity, as according to older ideas of the Atonement.

And so already in this very speculation there are the seeds of the Trinity doctrine. Before I go on to the place of the Spirit in such a speculation, let me now turn to the Indian interpretation of Christian ideas. I offer this as part of the process of globalizing the faith, so that it does not become too dependent on European and Western thought. For we live in a multicultural world: and we therefore need a multicultural faith. In setting forth these ideas I shall be drawing on ideas expressed earlier by me in *The Yogi and the Devotee* (Smart, 1968) and also by Eric Lott in his writings about Rāmānuja (e.g. Lott, 1976). I owe much also to John Carman's writing (Carman, 1974).

The Cosmos as the Lord's Body

Rāmānuja used the analogy of an embodied spirit to describe the God-cosmos relationship – the cosmos being God's body. It is an analogy which Christians have sometimes shied away from because they may think that it is pantheistic, and pantheism is anathema. But attention to Rāmānuja's meaning would dispel such a fear, which in any event relates to ideas that the cosmos *is* God, which is not Rāmānuja's position (any more than I am just my body). For Rāmānuja the body is the instrument of the soul or spirit through which it acts. In the case of God, his or her body is perfectly under divine control, whereas we have only partial control over our bodily aspects. I can waggle my fingers and maybe even my ears, but cannot get my gall-bladder to do things. So saying the world is God's body does not detract from God's omnipotence in relation to it. So karma for instance becomes an expression of God's will for his multitudinous creatures. The system of Rāmānuja deeply emphasizes God's grace.

The analogy of the body in using the notion of absolute divine control does everything, too, which the notion of Creation out of nothing intends. This Christian idea is meant to combat the idea of inherent limitation and evil in the material world. In the Indian tradition there is not however much credence given to the belief in a beginning of the temporal processes of the cosmos. This seems to me to be consonant with one strand of Western thought. There is no reason why God was not always Creating: the cosmos is like a tune always played upon God's violin. But the matter is open: if we wish to think of the world as having a beginning in – or rather with – time, that is fine, and we do not need to enter into disputation on the matter here.

The self-body analogy emphasizes the combination of transcendence and omnipresence which I think any live conception of God must contain. As the *Īśa Upaniṣad* says, Brahman is both within all this and outside of all this (that is, of the cosmos). Of course, reflection will tell us that when we say that the Divine is "within" all this we do not mean it literally, as if cutting open a piece of wood will reveal Brahman. It is a metaphor or analogy and so with the "outside" or the "beyond" implicit in the concept of transcendence. This is perhaps why we feel the image of the soul and body apt: my thoughts cannot be found by cutting open my head, and I can conceive my soul existing after the disappearance of my body.

For Rāmānuja there was a sharp difference between souls and bodies, but yet souls are creatures of God as well as the material cosmos. So how does the Lord stand in relation to souls? As he stands in relation to the material cosmos, the supersoul (Brahman) is the soul of souls. He is the inner controller or *antaryāmin*. And thus it is that we can think of Brahman as out there "beyond" what we see and yet embedded within it—the moving spirit of the material world and soul of what is out there and yet also as secretly at the depth of each person's soul.

The Inner Controller and the Idea of the Spirit

In the Christian tradition the Holy Spirit has special significance in being the divine Person who among other things informs and guides the Church. This guidance involves too the notion, in classical forms of the faith, that the body of Christians becomes as it were an extension of the Incarnation. The Church carries on the work of Christ, and, through it, Christ's body and blood are projected into the lives of those who follow Christ in faith and partake of the blessed Sacrament. It is an interesting side observation that both the concept of the Son and that of the Spirit seems to presuppose the existence of the material cosmos: that is we explain it to ourselves in terms of features of this-worldly history. This is not to say that we do not envisage the Incarnate Son and the Spirit as existing from before the beginning of the world.

But the fact that the Spirit's primary function from our point of view is the guidance of the faithful does not entail that she is not active in some much wider sense. Here as *antaryāmin* we can see her secretly controlling conscious beings from within. She is the refraction of the divine Being in consciousness. And from this point of view, the Brahman enters into the world, not only as avatar, but also in the guise of the soul of souls.

A Footnote on the Creation and Consciousness

It is often thought that the way to understand the cosmos is through reducing it (so to speak) to its basic stuff—the rudimentary and beautiful patterns which lie beneath the surface of matter as we perceive it. But the universe seems to be destined to evolve: material energies do not stay still but evolve their way to more complex forms, and from inert-seeming matter to conscious beings. It is as if cats and Chinese are already implicit in the quarks and molecules. So why not estimate the universe by the significant forms it evolves into, by the orchids and conscious beings which emerge from the evolutionary soup? Anyway: the fact is that there are conscious beings, and in this leap to a "higher" stage of existence they display the novel properties of mind-based events. If the Lord lies within the world, he lies behind consciousness perhaps in a special way.

In other words while God is present everywhere, he is specially present within each living being's consciousness, as the ***antaryāmin***. The practical side of this is that the individual can by, exploring her own consciousness, penetrate to the divine within—which is where in experience the person meets, so to speak, the Spirit. In exploring consciousness we are having a clearer view of this aspect of the cosmos. All this would imply that the Spirit acts in particular through history, which is, so to say, the ongoing unfolding of human consciousness through the acts of human agents.

Concealment and Human Freedom

It is a recurrent motif in Indian thinking that we are plunged in ignorance. It is ignorance which keeps us away from realizing our communion (or in Advaita union or identity) with the Divine Being. Our interpretation of this, from the angle of a Christian ***darśana***, is that the self-revelation of God through the Creation is opaque, obscure. It is obscure because creatures need a screen, so to speak, between themselves and the Divine Power if they are to have freedom. So Brahman is concealed behind the world or buried deep within it. Where the environment is not opaque, perhaps in heaven, as we imagine, it is hardly possible for any freedom to exist. This is no doubt why we think of heaven as a final resting place in the journey back to God.

All this reinforces the point we made earlier. A world of material freedom is bound to be a painful one. This is one reason why we can look on it as characterized as the Buddhists say by ***duḥkha***, by illfare. Moreover, the bright Light which we can only glimpse is so glorious that by contrast everything in this world seems to be unsatisfactory.

Incidentally, the Christian emphasis on sin is overdone, if by that there is the suggestion that most of our problems flow from bad acts and ill will: stupidity and lack of vision are quite as important in the causation of misery. The element of ignorance which Indian philosophy underlines is rightly there. The Indian analysis of the problems of the world is realistic.

But it is a commonplace of Buddhist teaching that insight and compassion have to go together. Many debates within the Buddhist tradition turned on their apparent separability. That they do in fact go together can be explained at least in part by the following considerations, which help to illuminate the Trinity doctrine for us.

Selflessness and Insight: Compassion and Knowledge

The Buddhist analysis of persons seems at first sight something which might be good if autobiographically applied but not if heterobiographically. What I mean is this: The thought that I have no soul may be good for me, but the thought that others do not have souls does not in the same way encourage moral action. But if we contemplate the issues a bit more deeply we shall see that the Buddhist analysis implies that individuals are made up of patterns of cloud-like, short-lived events (five clouds: of physical events, of perceptual events, of volitional events, of feeling events and of conscious events). When I think about this, I see that my sole difference from my neighbor is that I affect "my" future events more than, but only more than, I affect my neighbor's. I have no inner bond with my past or future, beyond the casual link. So in effect I merge with my environment and overlap with other people. In this way any narrow view of continuity with what I ordinarily take myself to be is misconceived. As I achieve a detached appraisal of myself and the "self-less" character of my world, so I note two things: first that suffering still happens, and second that a self-less person ought to take her wider role in diminishing it. In short, insight does have solidarity with compassion and benevolence.

In this way the dispersal of an ignorant narrowness of analysis of the self is a stimulus to compassion. If one were to sum up the point: in so far as one sees the interpenetration of persons, one has a sense of a new compassion. This is the pragmatic meaning of *anattā* or the non-self doctrine. In principle the strictures of Mahāyāna Buddhists on the Theravada are not really justified if this account of non-self is correct. Nevertheless the *Bodhisattva* ideal gives an expanded and indeed glorious image of moral self-sacrifice.

We shall now turn to observe the effect of this analysis upon the doctrine of the Trinity.

The Trinity and the Notion of Anattā-pneuma

I shall here take it as axiomatic that the Trinity consists in three centers of consciousness united in a sense of single identity. There are other views, but I do not here propose to argue for this version of the social Trinity. But it is perhaps important to explore how it is that three centers of consciousness can coinhere. Following a thought of Lynn de Silva, we may see each center of consciousness as being modeled after the attitude of selflessness which we have just explored. That is, as human beings may come to be selfless in their outward acts and thoughts, and find their truth in a kind of merger with others, so the members of the Trinity merge their actions together in a spirit of selflessness. In a manner not fully imaginable by us, they may feel their identity while remaining three centers of consciousness, as Father, Son, and Holy Spirit.

From our point of view the three persons can be thought of as having somewhat differing functions—as Creator who creates and continuously sustains (is involved we may say with Augustine in continuous creation); as Son who reconciles; and as Spirit who guides.

The vision of the Trinity is important from a practical point of view, since the model of social life bonded together in love and selflessness gives inspiration to those who follow this vision and sets before them an ideal which means that not only is God Love but this becomes the highest virtue of the Christian. We have used a piece of partly Buddhist language in order to show that the famous *Bodhisattva* ideal in Mahāyāna Buddhism is a fine image of the attitude which we should inculcate in ourselves. If anyone wishes to see Christ as *Bodhisattva*, that is a fine image. If there is perhaps a weakness in the *avatāra* model in the Hindu tradition it is that not all the avatars have an easily identifiable moral message. The Buddhist *Bodhisattva* is much more luminous in his dedication to fellow creatures.

The Son and Particularity

The Trinity is reflected in and present to the created cosmos. The traditional Christian view is that there is a strong particularity or uniqueness in the circumstances in which Jesus enters the world. If human beings so to speak represent the middle ground of the universe, with their highly concentrated consciousness, then it is appropriate that God's entry into the cosmos should be through a human being. Now as far as we can see there is no consciousness which is not somehow concentrated. It may be that following the Buddhists we may emphasize its lack of self—no permanent soul, unchanging, which underlies it (though in the case of the Divine Consciousness there is a hidden side about which we cannot speak and which has therefore neither change nor lack of change). Though we wish, then, to stress the changeable and flickering characteristics of consciousness, it is also important to stress its concentration: its emanating outward so to speak from a center. If the Brahman is to be incarnated and perform its descent or *avatāra* into human form, it must incorporate itself in a particular body and a particular consciousness. This involves it in the particularities of history: hence the "scandal" of the Christian faith. It seems to me that a really whole plunge into life involves this descent into a human being, and this is one main reason why there is emphasis among past theologians on the uniqueness of Christ. This is where the *Īśvara* has a particular consciousness and through that enters into, and suffers in, the world which has been created. But because we argue for the Spirit as *antaryāmin*, we think of her as guiding history, both in the community which flows from the *avatāra* of the Lord and in the wider world of history.

The Antaryāmin and the Meaning of Global History

The fact that I have tried to express the Trinity doctrine in terms which are drawn from the Indian tradition, both Hindu and Buddhist, means that I suppose that truth is to be found in traditions far beyond the Christian. The Christian vision should be able to draw on the insights of history, both Western and Eastern, both Northern and Southern. But it is not reasonable to try to synthesize traditions in a mechanical way. I regard the relations between diverse cultures as dialectical. It is not realistic to look on the diverse traditions and subtraditions as simply pointing to some single Truth. For one thing there is a vast gulf fixed between the underlying assumptions of the Theravada and those of the theistic religions of the West. It is better to see the differing traditions as having lessons for one another and as presenting visions which may help to correct one another. So the older idea of a natural theology (in the Catholic tradition) or natural religion which is a kind of *praeparatio evangelii* is too simplistic. But in a more dialectical fashion we can see other faiths sometimes as challenges which can be authentic challenges to one's own tradition.

This is in accord with various strands of thought about the epistemology of worldviews. We have already argued that worldviews cannot be proved except on their own premises. This does not mean that we cannot have reasons for faith: but a certain opacity is essentially the essence of worldviews. In other words, the divine revelation itself does not shine out with luminous certainty. And so we may in fact have erroneous thoughts and feelings about the Ultimate. So corrective views which come from other cultures are healthy critiques of our convictions. To give some examples about Christian beliefs: the Indian tradition has a strong emphasis on the *via negativa*, which is very largely ignored in many ways of Christian speaking. Again the idea of rebirth suggests a gradualist aspect of moral improvement, and this may be a good model of the future life for Christians. Buddhist non-substantialism is a good corrective to the Western Aristotelian tradition to which Western theology is still a little in thrall. So we take a Popperian position: that criticism is good in the advance of knowledge. Therefore we may see the work of the Spirit dialectically in history.

In this way we do not have to distort other cultures to bend them all into a model of spurious unity. We do not have to worry about differences. We also can respect other cultural traditions themselves as exhibiting the work of the Spirit.

So we have a model of the Spirit as working in a rich and pluralist way, inspiring the diverse creativities of human cultures. On our view of the essential opacity of Truth we do not even need to be dogmatic in interpretation of the Spirit's detailed work, beyond saying that the life of the Buddha (for instance) and the thought of Rāmānuja seem to be more clearly than some other manifestations of South Asia the work of the Spirit.

Moreover, we can see the Buddha's experience of Enlightenment as awareness of the Light within, the inner controller, which has two faces. For those who approach it suffused with the atmosphere of love and devotion, it can indeed appear as the Person within. For those who for whatever reason are not drenched in *bhakti* but train themselves calmly in yoga (as did the Buddha) the inner controller no longer appears as a kind of divine being but as the transcendent and supremely immanent nirvana. In the varying impact of different kinds of religious experience, we see the glittering themes of diverse religious and doctrinal claims.

A differing way of talking about the dialectical relations between different cultures is to say that the differing traditions are complementary. This complementarity gives a warmer and easier mode interpreting human history.

Another aspect of this way of looking at the Trinity is that the particularity of incarnation is balanced by the universality (in a way) of the Spirit's work: that is the spark which lights every person is part of the fabric of universal human history. So the Divine is specially present in living beings and above all in humanity: each particular individual mirrors Christ and the Father, through the light which is the Spirit.

The Question of "Secular" Knowledge

Naturally, our religious faith has to take account of secular knowledge. The advance of the sciences occurs dialectically and by imagination and criticism of theories as well as through the probing of nature. Nature indeed is one of the great critics of theories—*the* great critic one might say. We can see a dialectic at work between mysterious nature and our delving curiosity. Our attitude to supposedly scientific theories has to be critical. One of the ways in which other traditions can keep us honest is by showing that they have other cosmologies, some of which may be nearer to modern knowledge than our traditional Christian cosmologies. Buddhist ideas of the flux of nature are very consonant with modern pictures of the world.

But we need not be fooled by the wonders of modern scientific knowledge into adopting a form of scientism. The secular worldviews have quite as much opacity as our more spiritual and traditional worldviews. In the face of the secular worldviews we simply put forward our *darśana*. Does it grip people? The test of such a vision is in the long run its power over people, which will wither if it becomes too remote from modern knowledge.

This is where it is impossible for Christian theology, if it wishes to be realistic, to cut itself off from the wider study of religion, or religious studies, which itself is a modern invention. It tries in the first instance to describe religion and religions as clearly and accurately and as empathetically as possible, without making value judgments, because it is concerned with presenting some important human facts. It is concerned with the power of religions independently of their truth. It is an attempt to hold mirrors up to various cultures. As such it becomes something of a broker between cultures, helping mutual introductions. Moreover it stimulates self-consciousness among traditions. It therefore plays a part in the creation of a multicultural work, in which the various movements, traditions, subtraditions and trends interact with one another.

Christian theology, proceeding according to the old confines of European or Western values, is left behind in this world: it has to face up to the global character of life. Moreover, it must surely reflect that though the real meeting with Buddhism, sensitively understood, is a recent phenomenon, the challenge of Buddhism (and the others) was for ages there. When Jesus wandered with his followers by the blue waters of Galilee, there were carved monasteries in the rocky hills of

India and in Sri Lanka. It was about to move into China. And its questions were therefore waiting for Christians to hear, just as Christianity was preparing some questions too for the Buddhists in their other world. Maybe this was why St. Thomas went to India, it is said he was the doubting one, prone to question.

Thus religious studies is in many ways the most vital of the various branches of secular knowledge for Christian theology to come to terms with.

Secular knowledge itself is one of the great achievements of the human race. Its dialectical struggles with nature, both human and nature out there, are part of the ongoing work of the Holy Spirit, according to this interpretation that I am offering of the Trinity doctrine. Science is part of the holy work of the *antaryāmin*. So it is that we look upon the inner controller also working in the poetic fancies of W.H. Auden or the music of Prokofiev and Mozart, in the paintings of Paul Klee and Pablo Picasso, and in the cultural creations of all countries and times.

A Summary of the Trinity

The position outlined here can be summarized as follows. The threefold Divine Being has three centers of consciousness, one being the *Īśvara*, another the *avatāra*, and the third the *antaryāmin*. Of course God transcends these forms which are here stated from the angle of this cosmos. Beyond the way we relate to Her, God is unspeakable: She is the Brahman which is without form. She is the Void, emptiness. She is Suchness, *tathatā*. She is that at which the finger points, the dark side of the moon. But in his face towards us the Lord is creative (and destructive), incarnate, and secretly present behind the surface of consciousness.

In stating matters this way, I am looking at Christian faith from the direction of Melkote or Srirangam, from Nagarjunikonda or Kandy. In brief, from India: and we could look at it from China and the ideas of Hua-yen and Neoconfucianism. We could see the Trinity in the Great Ultimate and work of the Creator in the great jewel-net of Indra, by which the Hua-yen school poetically models the world. We could draw on African spirituality, or Japanese, or Native American. And in due course there would be a many-faced Christian theology, in which the complementary questions of other traditions would enliven the categories of Europe and the West.

All this is already happening in different parts of the Christian movement. The movement flowed through Christ as a central figure in the historical process that has now come together as global history. I think it is obvious in many ways that the work of the Christian Church remains very incomplete unless we work out a way of presenting it as a vision which can take seriously the unification of the world, yet without imposing uniformity.

For no faith, whether secular or religious, will in the foreseeable future come to dominate our globe. It will long remain plural. So we need a view of the Trinity, which is after all the central notion in the Christian faith, which will not be a false way of trying to impose a vision which is foreign to others in this world, lying beyond the faith. By seeing all history as the sphere of the *antaryāmin* and by abandoning the epistemology of certainty which continues to dominate many appeals to revelation, we have a humbler view, which sees the Christian movement as one among many, which yet can strive towards a way of generating a dialectic in which other values can take part.

I have presented these ideas from a Christian angle. I well know that this is only one perspective. Others, such as Jews and Buddhists, ought too to draw upon their fundamental features and practices, with a view to presenting alternative, but possibly congruent, visions: that is, ones which are complementary and which can both question and support the visions of others. Then maybe we can all climb up higher, to those higher-order values which in a sense may unify the world: but unify it by agreements in toleration and in pluralism, rather than some imposed unity which even if it were effected would only drive the differences of vision underground, where they would flicker and contend in a greater darkness than that cloud of unknowing which of course envelops us all.

References

Carman, John B., *The Theology of Rāmānuja* (New Haven: Yale University Press, 1974).

Christian, William A. Sr., *Doctrines of Religious Communities* (New Haven: Yale University Press, 1987).

Lott, Eric J., *God and the Universe in the Vedantic Theology of Rāmānuja* (Madras: Ramanuja Research Society, 1976).

Smart, Ninian, *The Yogi and the Devotee* (London: Allen and Unwin, 1968).

Smart, Ninian, *Beyond Ideology* (London: Collins, 1981).

Eastern Reflections

11

GOD, NOTHING AND THE ULTIMATE

A HINDU PERSPECTIVE

S.P. Banerjee

Introduction

DISCUSSION ON THE CONCEPT of God has been a perennial pastime in the arena of philosophy. Both in the Oriental and in the Occidental systems of thought the discussion about God has occupied a prominent place. Even though practi-centric systems have challenged not only the concept of God, but also the very validity and justification of religion, there is no reason to think that interest in the discussion of the concept of God has declined in recent times. Positivistic and materialistic criticisms notwithstanding, philosophy of religion still constitutes an important section of the discipline, and it is worthwhile taking a close look at the shape of things in this field of study in these days of the triumphant march of science.

A few centuries back it was thought that science would displace religion. Since that time, sectors of the cosmos which had been thought to constitute the domain of religion have been correctly identified as domains of science. In spite of this, science did not replace religion. The demarcation of the domains of religion and science in Western philosophy can be credited to Kant. Consequently the idea of God and the attributes assignable to him have been re-assessed and understood in a characteristically Western way.

In the context of Indian thinking, the situation is a bit different. This paper will present the Hindu point of view, discussing the idea of God and his attributes as it emerges in the practices and beliefs undertaken or entertained in contemporary Indian society. In this context it is certainly not possible to describe the genesis and growth of Hinduism, its diverse views and practices and its philosophical implications. However the general Hindu attitude to religion is easily discernible.

In the language of Radhakrishnan, "The Hindu attitude to religion is interesting. While fixed intellectual beliefs mark off one religion from another, Hinduism sets itself no such limits. Intellect is subordinated to intuition, dogma to experience, outer expression to inward realization. It is insight into the nature of reality (*darsana*) or experience of reality (*anubhava*).... Religious experience is of 'self-certifying' character. It is *svatasidha*."[1]

It is also important to remember in this context that the Hindu philosophy of religion starts from and returns to an experiential basis. This is true of all the important sects, e.g., Sakta, Saiva, Vaisnava etc. It is also equally true irrespective of the *marga* or *prasthana* (way) followed for the attainment of the final goal—*jnana (knowledge), bhakti (devotion)* and *karma (action) (prasthana-trava, the "triple")*. The *Svetasvatara Upanisad*[2] declares, "God the maker of All, the great spirit ever seated in the hearts of creatures, is fashioned by the heart, the understanding, and the will. They who know it become immortal." It was well understood that as religious experience is always psychologically mediated, the human mind in its craving for the ultimate tries to perceive it in a form easily intelligible to it and thus limits the Supreme to finite forms and actions. This explains the multiplicity of gods at a certain stage of religious practice and experience.

However, the easy Western inclination to designate Hinduism as polytheistic is not acceptable. The idea of God as Supreme has not been challenged by Hinduism. The concept of a limited God is inconsistent, and polytheism ultimately is not viable, logically or emotionally. The peculiarity of the Vedic concept of many Gods can be stated thus: when a God such as Indra, Varuna, or Agne is worshipped, he is worshipped as the Supreme Lord. This is not polytheism. Rather it is best expressed by Max Muller's term, *henotheism*. In the Vedic literature, both the aspects of unity and diversity have been fully acknowledged, and this is expressed through adoring and worshipping the ultimate Godhead in different forms and locations. One may understand this apparently paradoxical position by remembering that there are stages in the progress of human religious experience on the one hand, and there are diverse manifestations of the same Godhead on the other. This diversity and unity of the Supreme has been excellently brought out in the *Bhagavad Gita* in the eleventh canto (adhaya) called *Visvarupa-darsana* (Arjuna's vision of the universe).[3] It is important, in considering the Hindu perspective on God and the Ultimate, to note that through the different forms and practices of worship, there is a progressive march toward the Supreme Lord.

These prefatory remarks will, it is hoped, give us the proper perspective of understanding how the Ultimate has been treated in the different forms and practices of Hinduism. As for the concept of "nothing," it is difficult to identify its exact connotation and position in any sect of Hinduism, though in one School of Buddhism (Sūnyavāda or Mādhyamika School of Buddhism) the concept of *śūnya* (Void or Nothing) plays the pivotal role.

The Nature of the Ultimate

One may think of the Trinity of Brahma, Visnu, and Mahesvara in the context of God, Nothing, and the Ultimate. But such a position is not justified. Brahma, Visnu, and Mahesvara or Siva are different from one point of view; but, from another, they are the different manifestations (creator, sustainer and the destroyer) of the same Supreme God, who has been identified as Visnu. For the Saivas, it is the Siva who has all the three qualities. And this Ultimate is Truth, Beauty, and Goodness (Satya, Siva, and Sundara).

A very legitimate problem may be raised regarding the notion of God and the Ultimate in Hindu philosophy of religion, for a distinction is found in some trends of thought between Saguna Brahman and Nirguna Brahman—between the God with attributes and the attributeless Absolute (i.e., between Isvara and Brahman). It is maintained in Advaita Vedanta that Isavara, or the God of religion, cannot be the Ultimate/Absolute of philosophy, since God cannot be thought of without attributes, whereas the Ultimate cannot be thought of with attributes. To associate attributes with a being is to qualify it and thereby to limit it. One may find a similar approach in a much later Western philosopher (Spinoza) who holds that to qualify is to negate, *determinatio est negatio* and hence Substance cannot be qualified.

If this is so, the question of the attributes of God seems to be very important and therefore analysis of them in the context of the dominant Hindu views is in order. An accepted practice in the West is to classify the attributes of God into metaphysical and moral: infinity, unity, simplicity, incorporeality, immutability, impassibility, eternity, goodness, omniscience, omnipotence, personality.[4] We also come across the concepts of absolute, unlimited, creator, merciful, just, perfect, etc. Of the above attributes, goodness, mercy and justice would constitute moral attributes and the rest metaphysical attributes. There may be some problems regarding the classification of personality without which the moral attributes are not applicable to God. Let us discuss the Hindu way of associating some of the attributes with God (Isvara, Brahman, Purusottama, Visnu, Narayana, Siva, Sakti) and the problems which may emerge from this association.

Even though there is some unity in the core of the theistic systems there is no uniformity regarding the analysis and attribution of the divine qualities among the Indian systems of philosophy. To illustrate this, a little digression on the relationship between the systems of philosophy and the theistic systems may be needed. It is known that the Indian systems of philosophy assume a concretization of the philosophical ideas present in the Vedas and the Upanisads. Six major systems of philosophy developed out of the Vedic tradition, and they have been paired because of the closeness of their philosophical views.

We thus have Nyaya and Visesika systems, Sāmkhya and Yoga systems and Purva Mimamsa and Uttara Mimamsa (widely known as Vedanta) systems. These systems do not have a uniform view about God nor do all of them believe in God, though in some form or other the notion of the Ultimate is present in each. These systems are predominantly philosophical in nature, but as has been pointed out, philosophy (the Indian expression is "*Darśana*") is never merely a conceptual/intellectual game. It is always aimed at final liberation (*moksa*) of a person, and so every philosophical system is practical in outlook. Since philosophy is practical in nature and is aimed at attaining the goal of liberation it can never be strictly separated from religion.

But there may be a difference in emphasis. While philosophical systems, as their nature demands, are logical and argumentative; religion is primarily practical and based on revelation and intuition. However, in spite of this difference, there need not be any conflict or discord between the two. We may note that the Nyaya system in its early phase was distinctly colored by the Saiva view, for some of the early Maiyayikas were Saivas in their religious beliefs, just as Vaisesikas were Pasupatas (Pasupati is another name of Siva). Sāmkhya was colored by Vaisanavism.[5] Purva Mimamsa, generally known as Nimamsa or Vedanta in its different schools, has different notions about God and the Absolute.

God as Creator

As for the idea of God as Creator, we come across three sorts of views or models—two of which are Hindu and one Christian. We have (a) the potter model, (b) the magician model, and (c) the spider model. In the potter model God is likened to the potter who, as the efficient cause, *creates* the pot out of the material (clay) available to him. Thus the potter is not the material cause, but he is the efficient cause in bringing about the pot or pitcher out of pre-existent matter. In the Nyaya-Vaisesika system, God is regarded as the ***nimittakarana*** (efficient cause) who creates the world out of the material (***padarthas-dravya guna, karma etc.***) available to him. The creation depends not only on the materials but also on the moral stock of actions performed by persons (jivas) which determine the nature of the creation. But the mediacy of God as the ***nimittakarana*** is an absolute necessity for the appearance of the world. So the potter theory negates the view that God creates the world out of nothing.

Creation of the world out of nothing has been designated here as the magician's model in which the magician brings into existence something out of nothing, as it were. This is generally taken as the Christian view in which God is regarded as the unconditioned creator, dependent on nothing for creation. Needless to say, the Christian does not employ the magician model in describing God as creator.

The third model is the spider model, which is another Hindu view. It is maintained here that God creates the world out of himself just as the spider spins out its own web without depending on anything else outside itself. The particular Hindu view referred to here maintains that God creates, not out of any impulsion or compulsion, but spontaneously out of his own will. It is his Lilà; his particular way of acting. This is generally accepted by the principal theistic schools like Vaisnavas, Saktas, and the Saivas.

It is clearly stated in Visnu Purana that Visnu, or Narayana, or Krishna, as creator, brings about the universe out of himself. In the tenth and eleventh cantos of the Bhagavad Gita, after describing his own qualities, Krishna reminds Arjuna that he (Arjuna) need not know so many details; it would suffice that he know that the world is only one part of Krishna's creation.[6]

In the Visnu Purana, Maitreya, one sage, asks another—the great sage Parasara—how can the attributeless Brahman, who is above everything, be the creator, sustainer, and the destroyer? Parasara replies that as the burning power is natural to fire so are these qualities natural to Brahman.

In the Sakta system the Supreme Reality Sakti is also called Samvit. In the Samvit, power exists in the interplay of two conditions; those of creation and dissolution. Samvit is always active, and its activity is expressed in two ways—Tirodhana (self-limitation involving appearance (srsti) or creation) and disappearance [samhara—dissolution]. Maintenance (Sthiti) of the world represents an intermediate state between samhara and srsti. Samvit has the ***power of actualization*** (maya). The many actualizations are real, but the Reality as universal being is one. We may confront three problems in relation to creation/actualization:

(a) Samvit alone is real, but not the appearances.
(b) Samvit as well as the world shining within it are real but it is without external protection (ànanda).
(c) Samvit, the world within it, and its protection outside (icchà) are real.[7]

While the Advaita Vedanta maintains that the appearance of many from one is only an illusion, the attitude of Sakta Agama is different. "It believes in the power of Samvit to generate movement, though it is only abhasa, and externality is not apparent. The universe is within this power and power is within the Absolute."[8] But generation or creation is not unreal.

In the Saiva theory also, Siva is the ultimate creator, sustainer, and destroyer. There is a close relationship between the Sakta and the Saiva views regarding the relation between Siva and Sakti for the creation (Srsti), sustenance (Sthiti), and destruction (Pralaya) of the world. The common core of all the three views—Vaisnava, Sakta, and Saiva—is that creation (appearance/generation) of many from one is real and it is not, as Advaita Vedanta holds, an illusion.

Difficulties

In briefly assessing the three models discussed above, one notes some difficulties in each of them. In the potter's model we have the concept of a limited God who creates, as a potter does, from the material supplied to him. Such a God cannot be claimed as omnipotent nor as the Ultimate or Absolute. The problem of evil may not be a problem for such a theory, but a limited God does not answer the needs of the worshipper. It may also be argued that a person can attain his ultimate goal, viz perfection, even without accepting such a God. For in the magician's model (in which God is not only the creator but the omnipotent creator), there is difficulty in accepting creation as the bringing into being of the world out of nothing. The argument *ex nihilo nihil fit* may not be brushed away easily. If one further develops the Deistic position, a form of relationship between God and the world where both are independent of one another, serious difficulties are encountered. The question as to what God was doing before creating the world, or what impelled him to create the world, cannot be easily answered. The problem of evil in such a theory becomes almost insoluble unless one takes recourse in the doubtful way of thinking away evil in the fashion of 'it is good in the wrong place.' The spider model is placed a little better, for here the question of first creation does not arise at all. If the process of creation and destruction is beginningless, then the question of the motive behind this process does not occur. It is in the nature of the Ultimate, Vishnu, or Sakti, or Sivad—to have this Lila, manifesting itself in diverse forms and names. But all such manifestations are real. The difficulty here concerns the exact nature of the reality of the many. The problem of evil is cast in the form of a retributive theory of punishment in which neither evil, nor freedom of choice, nor the action of an agent is denied. At the same time, the omnipotence and goodness of God is affirmed. The suggestion however, that it is the Lila of God to indulge in creation and destruction may be as vulnerable to logical questioning, as to say that God creates out of nothing at his fiat.

In Hinduism, the major theistic schools as well as some philosophical systems accept creation as real. The theistic schools generally maintain that the relationship between the one and the many is one in which the same Supreme Reality exists as one in many, and the many exist in one. There is no mystery in such a relationship. "The error is to make an unbridgeable gulf between God and man, Brahman and the world.... We have arrived at an affirmation and some conception of the divine and creative Supermind in which all is one in being, consciousness, will and delight, yet with an infinite capacity of differentiation that deploys but does not destroy the unity."[9]

For the system of Advaita Vedanta, however, the emergence of the many from the one is unreal. It is an illusion.

Consequently, the conception of God, the Creator, is not finally acceptable. In contrast to the theistic systems, God (Isvara) and the Ultimate (Brahman) are not identical. From the ultimate point of view (paramarthika drsti) even God is negated along with the negation of multiplicity (nana). Multiplicity in any form may be denied—*neha nana asti kincana*—there is no "many" here. The appearance of many is illusory. This way of thinking culminates in Advaita Vedanta where after liberation (moksa) the liberated soul and the ultimated reality become identical, shorn of any form of distinction. If the soul and the ultimate reality are identical—*atman* and *Brahman* being *advaya* ("not two")—there cannot be any distinction between the worshipper and the worshipped (*bhakta and Bhagawan*), and as such the very basis of theism is lost. The Advaitin aspires to liberation through jnana and the final state he wants to achieve is that of *Satcit-ananda* (Existence—consciousness—bliss).

But for any theist this way of conceiving is not adequate to the possibility of worship for which a distinction between the worshipper and the worshipped is the minimum prerequisite. True, it is that the many (worshipper included) is the creation of the one (Isvara or God), and the relation between the two can never be one of total separation; but it is this distinction which makes religion possible.

Even though we find in the Gita an attempt at a synthesis of the three ways—*prasthanatrayas: jnana, bhakti*, and *karma*—the Gita favors bhakti rather than the other two ways. Of the philosophical systems, Vedanta (Advaita Vedanta especially) is a strong supporter of jnana as the way of liberation while Mimasa (Purva Mimasa) puts emphasis upon Karma for attaining the same objective. Among the theistic schools, the Vaisnavas are the strongest advocates of the bhakti marga. In Gaudiya Vaisnaism, particularly after the advent of Sri Caitanya, bhakti has not only been advocated as the principal way to worship God, it has been upheld as the highest ideal—the summum bonum of life—even higher than moksa. In Indian philosophy, in general, four ideals (purusarthas) are accepted: dharma, artha, kama and moksa. Moksa is generally considered to be the highest ideal. The Gaudiya Vaisnavas hold bhakti to be the fifth and highest of the purusarthas, considering even the aspiration to the attainment of moksa to be demonic.[10] The practitioner of Vaisnavism may worship his Lord Krishna/Vishnu/Narayam any one of the bhavas (ways). These bhavas, attained through bhakti, can be of five types: calmness and composure (santa), service like a servant (dasya), friendship (sakhya), affection for the offspring (vatsalya), and blissful sweet, relation (Madhura). The worshipper's highest aim is to remain in eternal relationship with his God in any one of the above ways.[11]

In the Sakta system, however, this exclusive emphasis on bhakti is not to be found. Saktas believe in moksa as the ultimate object or goal to be achieved, and in moksa we reach the sakti stage. Self-realization is a means to reach moksa. The order of progression in spiritual experience, as pointed out by Svatantrananda in the *Matrkak-Cakra-Viveka*, starts with the rise of pure knowledge in which knowables begin to disappear. But as the world still continues to exist for the worshipper the distinction 'thisness' does not altogether vanish.

The next position is that of Isvara when the motor organs in which the movable objects are similarly absorbed become one with the cosmic body with which the subject as the agent is identified. The Yogin in this stage is associated not only with an individual body but with the entire universe. In the state of Sada-Siva which follows, the senses, in which the knowable have been absorbed, become one with the self, the true subject. It represents a state of omniscience. In the Sakti stage, the universe body and the omniscient self become unified—this is a condition of undistributed equilibrium between spirit and matter (cit and a-cit).[12]

The Attributes of God

In the light of the above discussion, we may now briefly consider the significance of such attributes of God as omnipotence, omniscience, omnipresence, and goodness, and mercifulness. So far as the Advaita theory is concerned, the question of attributes relates only to Isvara who is not the Ultimate. For theistic systems God is the Ultimate and the above attributes are justifiably associated with Him. In the Nyaya-Vaisesika system, even though we cannot attach omnipotence to God, God is omniscience (*Sarvajna*) and is omnipresent (*bibhu*), since there is no obstacle to his knowledge or presence. In the Yoga system we have a rather uncommon notion of God. God is to be worshipped (upasya), but he does nothing in any way. So, he is neither the creator, nor sustainer, nor destroyer. We may note that in the theistic systems God has been endowed with all the positive qualities. He is unbounded and from our study of the relationship between one and many, we have already noticed that many is in one as one is also in many. God is not only good but also merciful. Without his karuna (kindness) no one can have the ultimate religious experience. This is specially true in relation to Vaisnavism. Isvara is associated with five types of activities (*panca krtya*)— creation, sustenance, destruction, kindness, and is the arbiter of punishment (Srsti, Sthiti, Laya, Anugraha, Nigraha). So, God, over and above being the creator, sustainer, and destroyer, also is a *Person* who bestows His karuna (anugraha) on the deserving worshipper. He also punishes (nigraha) the person who deserves punishment.

In this context notice some important points and problems associated with them. The attributes which are attached to God in Vaisnavism or in other Hindu theistic systems are more or less the same as they are in Christianity. Omnipotence, omniscience, and omnipresence, ultimateness, unlimitedness, personality and goodness have all been associated with God. This becomes very clear if one carefully reads the Gita, especially the tenth and eleventh cantos—*Bibhuti Yoga and Visvarupa Darśana*.[13] There are some logical and ethical problems associated with religious beliefs. If God is both a person and is omnipresent this presents a difficulty. If we attempt to solve this difficulty by proposing a concept of a person without a body this leads to other difficulties. Both in Vaisnava and Sakta systems it has been suggested that the whole of the universe is Isvara's/Sakti's body. But this is altogether a different concept of body and runs counter to our common understanding. That God's omnipotence and the existence of evil do coexist comfortably has been pointed out long ago. The retributive theory of punishment may be the best solution, but this theory has to grant freedom of choice and action to human agents. Otherwise we cannot ever become moral agents.

But, exactly here we have a problem. If we look carefully to the Gita, especially to the slokas 33–34 in the canto eleven, we find that Lord Krishna urges Arjuna to take arms in the Kurukshetra War and to kill the enemies who are his kith and kin. The justification of such an action is that these people have already been killed by the Lord, and Arjuna has only to be his *nimitta* (medium) in the ordinary world. This raises the serious problem of the reality of the aham—I, the bhakta—without whose reality, the existence of self-consciousness, freedom, religion and morality become impossible. There is here an ambivalence regarding the nature of reality and freedom granted toward the human agent. The extent of freedom of the agent may mark out the extent of the limitation of God's sphere of activities. This however is not an acceptable position in a theory where God is the Ultimate. The general Hindu attempt has been to maintain that this problem arises only from the ordinary point of view. Once the worshipper makes some progress in his/her religious march, she/he realizes that in spiritual experience it is futile to maintain such a rigid dichotomy between the *Bhakta* and the *Bhagawan*. The real crux of the problem lies in the relationship between the one and the many. Absolute reality of the many as individual, free agents in the fashion of the Existentialist model does not seem to have been favored. But the total identity between the many and the one—in the fashion of Advaita Vedanta—also has been ruled out.

The Concept of Nothing in the Hindu System

It may be noted that there is no mention of any absolute void in Hindu Systems, although in one School of Buddhism, the *Mādyamika or Sunyavada* School (associated with the famous scholar Nāgārjuna), the notion of void (sunya) plays an important role. Nāgārjuna, through his fourfold dialectical reasoning, tries to establish the unreality of everything we come across. So, with the establishment of the unreality of everything, including the self/I, we are left only with the void. This sort of a view is not found in the Hindu theistic schools nor even in the six systems of philosophy. We may, however, try to analyze the notion.

Nothing is neither a subject, nor an object nor is it the content of consciousness. Advaita Vedanta argues through the negative dialectic (neti, neti) to establish the non-dual Brahman.

The negation/nothing, therefore, is only methodological or transitory leading finally to the establishment of something positive—Brahman. We have already noted that Advaita Vedanta ends in establishing complete identity between I (aham) and the Ultimate (Brahman).

In the Tantra Systems there is a conception like *Purnahamta* (Purna + aham + ta) which is attained through relative negation or nothingness. This is regarded as the final state reached through Yoga and Sadhana in which the I (aham) exists as fullness (purna).

To the question whether the many are totally negated in such a state, the answer is both yes and no. Everything exists, not as this or that (idam) but as I (aham). I (aham) may be of two types—one as fullness (purna aham) and the other as the doer, enjoyer, etc. (grahakarupi). So far as the Purnaham is concerned, it is pure consciousness without any distinction, action, or limitation. But the vivisected aham is the ordinary I which is the doer, the enjoyer, etc. A passage from the vivisected embodied I to the unlimited, unbounded I (cit, pure consciousness) is the object of Tantra Sadhana. For attaining this ideal, as the Tantra would enjoin, strength (sakti) of mind and person is necessary. Tantra accepts the aphorism that the fullness of the aham cannot be achieved by the powerless, (nayamatma balahinena labhya) and they prescribe a very stiff sadhana for acquiring sakti and arousing the Kundalini for achieving the goal. It is also maintained that the final stage can be reached through sadhana in accordance with Tantrika prescription and Krpa (kindness) or Mahasakti. In the stage of Purnahanta, existence is bracketed, so to say, but *no* eidetic reduction reaches the unreal. The Kandita ("limited I") I is suspended, not totally negated or destroyed, in the full I. So, whatever negation is there, is relative only and not total. Different stages in this march to Purnahamta have been very carefully and clearly identified in the Tantrika literature.[14] The final realization depends on one's realizing Matrka.

This brief reference to the analysis of the concept of nothing demonstrates in the Hindu theistic systems and even in the traditional six Indian Systems (sad darsana) that the concept of nothing is found, if at all, in a relative way. In Nāgārjuna's philosophy, however, it is the culmination of philosophical dialectic. In that Buddhistic system also, it is suspected, the Sunya is not the final goal of philosophy. It is observed by many that Sunyavada is only parasitical on something positive which has not been elaborately stated by Nāgārjuna, keeping in view the Buddhistic negative dialectic and Nirvana as the final stage to be reached. However a detailed discussion of this is not needed in the present context.

As far as the Hindu religious practices of the common person are concerned, it may not be inaccurate to say, that the majority of the Hindus are either Vaisnavas or Saktas or Saivas and that they worship their Isvara Visnu/Narayana or Sakti/Kali/Durga/Camunda or Siva/Mahadeva/Viswanatha taking him/her as the ultimate—the creator, sustainer, and destroyer of the universe. Though all the ways (*margas*) of Sadhana (worship)—jana, bhakti, and karma—are practiced, there is no doubt that for the overwhelming majority of the worshippers, the person, the principal path followed is bhakti. Whatever the philosophical findings and conclusions, the bhakta holds fast to his/her God primarily through devotion (bhakti) and the actions resulting from it. But this devotion is not blind, for it is blended with knowledge as well.

NOTES AND REFERENCES

1. *The Hindu View of Life*, George Allen & Unwin Ltd., Great Britain, 1927, 15.
2. *Svetasvatara Upanisad*, iv. 7. (esa devo visvakarma mahatma sada jnanam hrdaye Sannivistah hrda manisa/manasabhiklpto ya enam vidur amrtas te bhavanti).
3. (For the English version) Robert N. Minor, *Bhagavad Gita*, Heritage Publishers, New Delhi, 1982.
4. Paul Edwards, *The Encyclopedia of Philosophy*. Macmillan Publishing Co., New York & London, 1972, Vol. Three, 346–47.
5. Gopinath Kaviraj, *Aspects of Indian Thought*, The University of Burdwan, Burdwan, West Bengal, 1966, 70–71.
6. *Bhagavad Gita*, any edition, tenth canto sloka 41, Athaba bahunaitena kina jnatena tabarjuna/ Bistavyaha-midam Krtsnamakamsena sthitojagat.
7. Please see Gopinath Kaviraj, *Aspects of Indian Thought*, The University of Burdwan, Burdwan, 1966, 181–85.
8. *Ibid*. p. 183.
9. Sri Aurobindo, *The Life Divine*, Sri Aurobindo Ashram, Pondicherry, 1960, 155.
10. Sri Rupa Goswami in *Bhakti*, Rasamrta says, "Bhakti mukti sprha yavad pisaci hrdi bartate. Tabat bhakti sukhsyatra Kathamuvyadayo bhalnt." It means that so long as the heart is full of the demonic desire for enjoyment and liberation, there is no chance of drawing real bhakti in the heart.
11. Cp. Mahamahopadhyaya Pramathanath Tarkabhusan, *Banglar Vaisnay Darsana*, Sri Guru Library, Calcutta, Bengali, Year 1370.
12. Mahamahopadhyaya Gopinath Kaviraj, *Aspects of Indian Thought*, The University of Burdwan, 1966, 214.
13. *Bhagavad Gita*. 10th canto, Slokas 8–11, 20, 39, 42, and 11th Canto, Slokas 18–20, 33–34.
14. Mahamahopadhyaya Gopinath Kaviraj, *Tantrika Sadhana O Siddhanta* (in Bengali) Vol. I & II, especially Vol. II, University of Burdwan, 1975, pp. 68–84.

12

GOD-LANGUAGE AND THE LANGUAGE OF NOTHING

IN HINDU AND BUDDHIST THINKING

Krishna Sivaraman

THE PAPER IS AN ATTEMPT to think out the inter-relations of God and Nothing along the lines of the reflective and meditative spiritualities of Vedanta Hinduism and Mahāyāna Buddhism, the two most representative and inter-related phases of Eastern religion and thought. Theistic motifs which find expression in 'God' and trans-theistic motifs verbalized negatively as the Absolute criss-cross the frontiers of the two traditions influencing each other conceptually and semantically in the different phases of their development.

The religious history of India is marked by the conflict and interaction of two major approaches to the holy or the divine: to conceive and envision it as the absolute or the unconditional in terms of a mystical state of being or in straight theistic terms as a personal God. Both trends have their root in the Vedic foundations of Hinduism appearing as two aspects of one conception. Hinduism, as Vedanta related back to the Vedas with its concentration on the impersonal facets of the Vedic religion and the spiritual premises that are involved in such re-integrated approach, include the following: ***brahman***, the ground of all positivity which is mystically experienced, ***samsāra***, which is an intuitive estimation of man's empirical situation governed by the laws of necessity and consequent unfreedom and finitude, and a cognitive, reflective approach involving pre-eminently negation in respect of *samsāra*, buttressed by systematized spiritual exercises (*yoga*) leading to the state of liberation (*moksa*). Buddhism, which originated closely on the heels of Vedanta, eschewed all links with the older tradition and developed a more non-theistic orientation involving the religious premises of ***nirvāṇa***, ***duhkha***, or ***samsāra*** and ***dhyana***.

Both these expressions of a new spirituality emerging on the scene of the history of India, well before the Common Era, come to share through inter-action, both negative and positive, the same ideology and outlook in respect of the transcendent. This paper attempts to focus on what is intrinsic to this outlook, viz., the verbalization and conceptualization of Nothing as a category of religious meaning. What are the religious implications of the ontological language of 'nothing' which is so central to Eastern religiosity and in what precise sense can they be contemplated as counterparts of the biblical approaches to an encounter with the Holy? This latter part of the question is not addressed here as an issue, but is merely proposed as worth pondering for comparativists and those interested in global spirituality. Such a proposal of course assumes that the two spheres, Hindu-Buddhist and the Western-Christian, are commensurable in respect of the very languages that are often thought to divide them into worlds of meaning apart. It may not be a common universe of discourse, but neither is it a case of languages reciprocally opaque.

An important aspect of the contemporary rediscovery of the ontological question (vis-a-vis pre-Socratic philosophy, especially Parmenides) is the emphasis on the problem of nothing.[1] While the modern focus is more on the experience of nothingness as a starting place for reopening in an authentic way, the enquiry into the nature of man and his becoming, this paper aims at presenting profiles of existential analyses from Eastern religious thought. It may, hopefully, shed some light not only on the experience of nothingness as a mode of human consciousness but also on negation and, as earlier stated, its scope as a category of religious meaning. The approach may be described as one of a hermeneutic, in a cross-cultural and contemporary setting, of the meaning of 'God.' The term 'nothing,' as well as the terms 'God' and 'the Ultimate,' are significant descriptions of the divine, the three terms corresponding to three perspectives, the non-theistic, the theistic, and the trans-theistic, which span the vast and complex Indian religious landscape, Buddhist as well as Hindu.

The God-language itself is, it may be noted, but one of the descriptive modes of speaking of the divine or the transcendent and is characteristic of the general approach of Hinduism. One of the several meanings of the term 'orthodox' (*āstika*) given is acceptance of God, which means acknowledging that God-language is intelligible. It is also freely utilized, albeit in a restricted sense in Mahāyāna Buddhism where Buddha becomes deified. The language preferred by the generality of Buddhist thinking, however, is 'emptiness,' 'voidity.' Buddhism as distinct from the general Hindu approach considers the divine, not in reference to the cosmic manifestations, not as ontological cause and anthropomorphic personification, not as the ground of knowing and speaking but as supraexistential state, a state which appears as a Nothing when seen from the point of view of the false plenitude of existence (*samsāra*).

Hindu religious thinking in the course of its history, was profoundly influenced by the impact of Buddhism even though the latter was, itself, one may say, a spiritual spinoff of Upanisadic Hinduism and an inheritor of its implicit negative theology.[2] The conflict and tension between Hinduism and Buddhism is in a sense the conflict and tension between the negative and affirmative approaches to the divine. The latter verbalizes it as God and/or the ultimate, not as thus speakable literally or conceptually but as symbolic. Likewise, though not experientially certified like an empirical object, it is identifiable in experience of a special kind. Buddhism verbalizes the divine paradoxically as what is not verbalized and experienced as what is not identifiable in experience, and, therefore, as nothing more than Nothing. Buddha's celebrated silence to certain 'metaphysical' questions put to him is an eloquent paraphrase of the meaning of nothing,[3] more eloquent one may say than the valiant efforts of the negative dialectics of Nāgārjuna, the greatest Buddhist thinker and often hailed as the second Buddha. It is significant to remember that the final outcome of this historic conflict on the Indian scene was the disappearance of Buddhism as a separate religion (though not as a configuration of spirituality) and the transformation of Hinduism itself from its earlier theistic and pan-theistic phases into a trans-theistic metaphysics of realization.[4]

It will, however, be somewhat of an over-simplification to describe the culminating overview of Hindu spirituality as trans-theistic. Theism or theology is an essential and integral element of Hinduism. The issue that has been the subject of fierce and even acrimonious debate for over a millennium and still continues to be debated is how the *theion* is to be understood and interpreted: Is it a 'personal' God with super-personal depths in it beyond all description, a being who can be loved and prayed to and who is directly and centrally revelation, grace, incarnation (*avatāra*), Teacher, etc.

Or is it an 'impersonal' Absolute, which is approached primarily in noetic terms as something whose existence requires no explanation and which is the presupposition of all other existences, something which cannot be known because it is knowledge itself, the light by which things become known at all, something which is an end-value in the sense of what is invariably and implicitly valued in all valuations, the dearmost without which nothing at all is or can be dear.[5] God thus conceived as the vehicle of ontological, noetic and axiological perfection must be 'trans-personal.' It is the ultimate in the sense of the unconditional and it is God, but in the sense that it is as much all positivity as it is also all-cancelling negativity. It is the Great I, but by that is meant that it is not an I over or against you and me; its trans-personal depth opens itself but only when it is realized as thus intrinsically transcending the personal and inter-personal dimensions, in terms of what they and their world are *not*.

The polarity of theism and absolutism colors all the phases of the development of Hinduism and to minimize the significance of either is to miss the true core of Hindu spirituality. The Vedas which are the fountainhead of all forms of Hinduism are essentially God-intoxicated, grasping Him now as Fire (Agni), now as the Majestic (Indra), now as the Terrible (Rudra), and the Just (Varuna). These are not substantive things, or personifications of natural forces, but predicates of the Godhead referred to as the One. Hinduism, as Vedic religion, consists essentially of rapport with the transcendent Being 'ever free and ever the Lord,' and this consciousness has never left it at any stage of its history. Theism, therefore one may say, with Otto, constitutes the core and substructure of Hindu religiosity.[6]

However, there soon builds up a dialectic in a manner uniquely identifiable as of Hindu religious thought, between a personal God and the impersonal ultimate. The quest for Godhead behind the manifestations, That One (*tad ekam*)[7] for which the gods truly stand, finds its explicit articulation in the Vedanta (Upanisads), literally, the goal of the Veda. The problematic of Vedanta which finds expression on almost every page of the Upanisads, is really the problem of deity and deitas, concreteness and ultimacy, God and 'the God beyond God,' their relation and balance. God's nature is not exhausted in his relationship to man as Creator or Providence. He is also something in himself out of all relations and functions, even the most internal of them. This is the Absolute. He is not merely a term of the relation of difference between God and the world. He is also the being of all things. In this sense as the foundational and only Being (*sad eva*)[8] God cannot be distinguished from anything as there is no other beside him. Vedanta, therefore, understands God as the Great Being (Brahman) without a second. Even the relation of 'I' and 'thou,' which is the relation entailed in worship and prayer, is possible because of a common, unobtrusive platform on which, as it were, both of them stand, which is therefore, not merely more ulterior or ultimate but the very principle of ultimacy itself, the original and inexhaustible source of being which cannot be described more specifically than simply as what is (or rather the being of what is).[9] As the universal being without divisions, not even the division of subject and object, it does not stand in need of being evidenced because it is self-evidently immediate. As Being without an other facing it, as therefore lacking in nothing as full being, it is Plenteousness or Bliss itself.

The complexity of Hindu experience over the millennia and proliferation into luxuriant cults, rites, and mythologies, as well as diversely articulated theologies, are commonplace information with which a student of Hindu religious history is acquainted. But it is not as readily acknowledged that it has also been part of Hindu self-understanding that such diversities and manifoldness are accepted and worked into an interpretive theorizing as part of religious life. Both the theistic and absolutistic motifs with cosmic affirmative approaches and acosmic, negativistic ones are incorporated in different degrees into the different schools of Vedanta which, avowedly, represent the mature self-expression of Hindu religious thought

But let us first study what the ontological language of 'nothing' can really mean as shedding some light on the negativistic concepts like *śūnya* and *nirvāṇa* of Buddhism which assumes the intelligibility of 'nothing' and builds on it. It may also throw some light on the Hindu application of the sense of 'nothing' in talking about the world as *māyā* or *ajnāna* and in its negative theology with its approach to Reality as 'not this,' 'not this.'[10]

The locution of 'nothing' that is common to these religious languages is not an abstract metaphysical language standing for some general idea of negativity but presupposes confrontation with nullity as intrinsic to existence itself. In the case of Buddhism the confrontation is characteristically in the sphere of practical life with the focus on suffering in its typically human form, which pervasive factor renders life in its everydayness nugatory. With Vedantic Hinduism the confrontation takes the form of what is a commonplace of theoretical life, viz., error or illusion. It is the experience of a theoretic lie, something turning out to be quite unsuspectedly other than what it pretended to be, thus providing a true edge for 'contradicting,' i.e., saying 'no' to what is experienced, that brings home to one at least as a very real possibility, the null character of cognitive experience as such and of a practical life that is based on it. The Hindu scripture when it speaks the language of 'not this, not this,' presupposes on the part of the receiver who harkens to the word thus spoken, an experience of negation.

The ontological character of 'nothing' or non-being is highlighted by the dialectical sense that attaches to it in the hands of those who use it as a means of referring to what is not on the surface, but makes its presence felt to sensitive eyes. It is dialectical in nature so that one may not place 'to be' (being) and 'to be nothing' (non-being) in absolute contrast. The mystery of 'being nothing' cannot be trivialized by transforming it into a simple case of a judgment or proposition in which a possible or real assertion is merely denied. The relevant question to ask here is not whether negation of a judgment is not also, after all, a kind of judgment but the following: What is the structure which makes negation of a judgment possible? This question will take one into ontology ('what is'), may be an ontology of non-being ('what is not'), encountering which, and participation in which, makes it possible to say 'it is not.' Negation of judgment is not merely a negative judgment.

There is a tendency on the part of modern interpreters of Eastern thought to assimilate it to contemporary trends of analytic philosophy with its logic which bases everything on ultimate, contingent, matters of fact. Questions of 'being' and 'non-being' in the sense intended by classical philosophers are considered as lacking theoretical significance and as only misleadingly ontological. Answers to such questions (if they be questions at all) can only mean the decision adopted concerning the use of language. The function of analysis itself as ontologically neutral is pure and simple negation and does not amount to any positive gain to the stock of knowledge. Negation merely separates what has been uncritically held together and merely removes the appearance or illusion of gain in knowledge. Negation has no ontological entailment.

But is this claim valid? The contemporary Western reaction against justifying philosophy as primarily concerned with being is understandable as an aspect of the 'waves of modernity' sweeping in the wake of 'that revolt against Heaven which began with Renaissance in the West and is now invading the whole globe.'[11] But to draw strength and support for this modernist reaction from an essentially pre-modern religious system like Buddhism, is to distort the existential approach and the soteriological intention of the latter. Distortion apart, one may ask whether some standard of ontological commitment is not implied even to say meaningfully that a given theory depends on or dispenses with the assumptions of such and such objects.

The attitude of the logicist which prohibits and vetoes questions of a certain kind, in so far as it is not arbitrary whim, is, after all, based on or committed to certain tacit assumptions and evaluations about being. Being has a character which makes this attitude the only legitimate method of cognitive approach. Being itself cannot be approached cognitively except in those of its manifestations which are theoretically significant in the sense of being open to analysis and verification. Being may thus be shown to be a necessary concept even for those who reject philosophy with arguments derived as they are, from an implicit understanding of what it means to have being.[12]

What has been set forth should not be mistaken as a polemic against logic or as insinuating that Eastern religions are illogical, irrational and dogmatic. Logicism is surely questioned, specially in the context of the talk of 'nothing,' as negation as implied in the talk (in the Indian religious context) presupposes an encounter which is pre-logical but still within the scope of *logos*. The encounter with 'nullity' (*tuccha*) is an experience where we find ourselves at the very boundary of existence and strike against what in some sense may be called the transcendent or absolute dimension. Talks or utterances of 'nothing' and their dialectical implication of an unutterable being in the hands of Buddhist philosophers as also, less equivocally, with the Hindu Vedantins derive their sense from the context of situations which have in them an absolute dimension that differentiates such situations from those of every-day existence. The absolute or the total, as it were, gets opened up in a negative way. In such "limit-situations"[13] existence becomes shipwrecked, comes to the end of its resources, is reduced to 'nothing,' when, so to speak, confrontation with 'what is' (Being) takes place. By 'what is' is meant what *is* absolutely and totally as distinguished from 'existence,' what *is* so absolutely and totally that it can be identified only negatively, as the further side of 'nothing.' It thus follows that the language of 'nothing' that is employed in a spontaneous manner in Eastern religious thought with reference to transcendence, is not one that could be assessed or assimilated to a mere logical or syntactical analysis in abstraction from the specific discourse situation to which the language belongs. Once we are able to discern, at least imaginatively if not by existential encounter, such situations, it should not be difficult to find an appropriate meaning for 'nothing.'

What we are here referring to as limit-situations constitute the counter-part of biblical examples of encounter with the Holy in which the believer assumes the role of humility and supplication and openness in relation to God and hopes for His incursion in a dramatic, unpredictable uncanny way. The latter may appear exceptional and unique historically speaking but so is the case with 'limit situations' which are by no means commonplace of normal experiences. One may ask: Who does not have an experience of existence coming to the end of its resources sometime or other in one's life? True, but it is also significant that to a fortunate few only, like Buddha himself, it amounts to a religious experience in which the way is immediately opened to bringing into existence an absolute character that could not be achieved in any other way. The point is that as Jaspers says "what has happened may pass without anything happening to us men as men, without our hearing the voice of transcendence, without our attaining to any insight and acting with 'insight.'"[14] A so-called limit-situation may happen and one without an inner, invisible preparedness for it may treat it as still a species only of the familiar and the manageable. One may pass it on with a mere shrug. The transcendent dimension does not disclose itself. Misfortune befalls us, or one comes close to death, or alternately speaking, to the sharp edge of an experience of disappointment. But these experiences do not trigger off automatically in a predictable manner confrontation with the transcendent or the holy.

The situation preeminently includes the response also. The situation, therefore, may be said to comprise a region lying on both sides of the experiencing subject and the object that is experienced.[15] Religious faith has a two-way character: it is always contextual to a typical situation and it is non-available save as the element of response within the situation.

Let us now isolate some meanings of 'nothing' extracting them from the negativistic concepts and terms that are used in Buddhist religion and are also adopted with qualification in Hinduism. As it was shown in the earlier section, 'nothing' as a significant religious term means not sheer negativity but nullity or the stuff of nothingness that we find in and around us, within our existence. In characteristic Buddhist language it refers in ontological terms to 'that which never is but is forever changing,' not enduring even from one moment to another. 'Nothing' designates the character of all this world of experience as a Becoming and never attaining to Being, and is indicative of the utter vanity in clinging to what cannot be grasped and is entirely void. Buddha's own term which he uses in his very first sermon[16] is *duhkha* which is used in the vogue of therapeutic language as both a symptom and a disease. It is all possible physical and mental loss, the imperfection itself which is endemic to humanity, to living beings, and even to gods. As a disease it means the possibility and the liability of loss, of ceasing to be in the very moment of coming to be what we are as inseparable from individual existence. This liability is what is disclosed to us in the experience of '*duhkha*.'

Closely associated with this sense of nullity is the sense of the wilting away of the familiar world which though normally preoccupies and absorbs our total attention finally sinks to the level of nothing in the face of the 'end.' The valuable suddenly appears as nothing in the context of death. What one prizes and cherishes with all one's zeal and involvement sinks to nothing and is, in a dramatic mood of transvaluation of values, suddenly held of no account.

When Buddha drove out as a young prince to visit the pleasure gardens he encounters sickness, old age, and death. He also met a hermit self-possessed, serene, and carrying a beggar's bowl. The charioteer describes him to the curious prince as one who has abandoned all belongings and leads a life of austerity, living without passion or envy and begging his daily food. Buddha muses: "This is well done and makes me eager for the same course of life: to become religious has never been praised by the wise and this shall be my refuge and the refuge of others and shall yield the fruit of life and immortality."[17]

The meaning of 'nothing' in the sense of 'no value' is closely related to the *eschaton*. In early Christian eschatology we are familiar with St. Paul's advice that time is short and those who deal with the world should live as if they had no dealings with it.[18] In Eastern religions the 'end' is all the time there is and at no time in particular. It is a 'now' in the face of which one's appropriate response should be to demonstrate a new sense of urgency through a denial, symbolically at least, of worth or meaning or existence to everything. This is the celebrated theory of detachment (*vairagya*) or renunciation so central to Eastern religiosity in general. Renunciation, one may say, is the living of a transvaluation of all values previously cherished and an existential acknowledgment of the nugatory nature of worldly goals.[19]

In the shades of meaning thus far listed, 'nothing' does not carry, except in very muted form as glimpsing an as yet unclear end, any overtone of positivity. For a full emergence of the positive significance one should, of course, turn to Hinduism which uses it as necessarily interchangeable with the language of bliss and plenitude.[20] Denial of what is 'limited' (*alpa*) space-wise, time-wise and thing-or person-wise, is either the cause or consequence of the affirmation of the limitless ultimate (*anantam*). But one does not have to turn to the Vedanta doctrine of God/ultimate. There are 'positive' meanings connoted by 'nothing' itself that one can find in the Mahāyāna reconstructions of Buddha's teaching,[21] and, also of course, in the post-Buddhist developments of Vedanta where the term becomes, in one sense, even synonymous with Brahman and, conversely, all positive terms used to refer to it become understood as negation of negation.

One such positive meaning is that nothing refers to an experience which, while essentially negative in the sense of denying ultimate *rationale* to existence, at the same time becomes, so to speak, the foil for Being. It makes it possible for one to recognize that things are things. As Heidegger, who gives a classic expression to this idea would say, it is only when things are seen against the abyss of nothing that for the first time we notice the 'wonder' of Being. For the first time we ask ourselves with Leibnitz, 'Why is there anything at all, and not just nothing?'[22]

The 'abyss of nothing' takes on various forms and admits to diverse interpretations in Buddhism. Śūnyatā, 'voidity,' does not connote one single meaning. The so-called Hīnayāna Buddhism understands it to mean voidity of the substantial and the whole. The perception of a whole, identical and permanent amid change and difference, is the work of construction which imposes a configurated wholeness (*pudgala*) on the real elements of existence. It is against the perception of them as unreal fictions that the 'events' or real, temporally discrete elements (*dharma*) stand out as real (*aśūnya*).[23] Mahāyāna deepened the sense of *śūnyatā* in terms of 'essencelessness' which should not be confined to any particular aspect of experience as the Hinayanists do but apply to the whole of experience. Experience itself in its entirety is void; (*śūnya*) has no real existence. Strangely enough *śūnya* here connotes not only unreality but reality also. Against the experience of the abysmal character of experience as such, reality stands out precisely as what cannot be expressed through conceptualization, affirmative or negative (*dṛṣṭi śūnya*).[24] For the other school of Mahāyāna, namely the *vijnāna vāda*, unreality pertains not to experience as such but only to what is confronted as object in experience. The perception of the objective side of experience as 'nothing' serves as a foil for understanding the experiencing consciousness itself as ontologically real.[25]

Buddha, compassionate that he was (*upāya kauśalya*), had to appeal to the understanding of the person that he addressed and could not, therefore, always express his innermost convictions. So the Mahayanists appealed to the doctrine of two kinds of utterances of Buddha, those which are true only of the empirical world and are not to be understood literally, and those which speak of the ultimate truth. The latter being too deep for comprehension are not delivered to the ordinary people.[26] One such ultimate truth as Nāgārjuna would say, is the perfectly symmetrical relation between the affirmative and the negative, as entailed in the concepts of *Nirvāṇa* and *Śamsāra*, as if saying '*nirvāṇa* if and only if *samsāra*.' Expressing it thus in terms of a material bi-conditional is warranted by his words: "There is no specific difference whatever between nirvāṇa and samsāra; there is no specific difference between samsāra and nirvāṇa."

One of the most paradoxical aspects of 'nothing' is not mere entailment of but equation with Being itself. This has given rise to misinterpretations of Buddhism which does not have two sets of terms to refer to Being and Nothing. Hinduism has, and espouses rigorous non-dualism but as compatible with its admission of a dualism of the negative and the positive.

Whatever we think of or talk about we do it as something which is. We do this, however, only implicitly and not with explicit awareness. It leaps into our thematic awareness only on occasions when we explicitly deny that what we think of or talk about has being as, e.g., in our contemplation of dream experience, in our recovering our composure with the negative insight, 'it was only a dream' or 'this is not a snake.'[27] That things *are*, quite escapes our notice until such occasions, when through explicit negations we come to apperceive that things *are*. Only when some experience shakes us out of our normal attitude of everydayness do we become aware of Being.

Buddhism distinctly from Hindu Vedanta, does not have recourse to the language of Being but uses the same expression 'voidity' to point to or imply the 'is-hood' in virtue of which anything that is *is*. It does it for the simple reason that 'Being' cannot possibly itself be regarded as an entity as *something* which is. However one may seek to conceptualize it, it has to be contemplated as void of it. It is equatable with the denial alike of 'is,' 'is not,' 'is both' and 'is neither' (*catuṣkoṭi vinirmuktam*).[28] Vedanta, however, speaks of it as Being (*sat*) but is careful to interpret it to mean 'a denial of what is not,' to indicate that it is not equating it with 'is'.

Otherwise it will be constrained to say 'Being is.' There is a paradox involved in saying 'Being is' like the paradox involved in saying that the knower, or rather that by which one knows, is, or can be, known. The knower, surely is known but not as an object: it is immediate. The same with Being. It is what makes it possible that something is. It itself is not *something*. The issue here is one of distinguishing between entities and the condition which renders it at all possible that these are or should be entities. Being is that kind. One can itemize and make an inventory of the contents in a room: tables, chairs, people even the most minute of the things that ordinarily escape notice; these are all entities, and we implicitly think of 'being' with them. We do not include 'being' as an item in our list. If we have to use only the language of entities or things, we can only point to 'being' as no-thing.[29] The Vedantic slant can be brought out by an emendation of this example: in the contents of the room that are itemized, the light or visibility will not be included, not because it is not there but because it is there not as a thing but as the condition. Without light nothing conceivably can be present or manifest in order to be counted. Being should be understood on the model of light. The example has the advantage of making it possible to see what it would be without the condition. Darkness is a datum of perception and likewise spiritual darkness (*ajnāna*) too, paradoxically, is a datum of cognitive experience.

Coomaraswamy quotes from Behmen's *Dialogues*, two passages which explain precisely what 'nothing' signifies. It is worth repeating as underscoring the wealth of 'nothing' as co-ordinate with God the ultimate:

> Lastly, whereas I said, Whosoever finds it finds Nothing and all Things; that is also certain and true. But how finds he Nothing? Why, I will tell thee how He that findeth it findeth a supernatural, supersensual Abyss, which hath no ground or Byss to stand on, and where there is no place to dwell in; and he findeth also nothing is like unto it and therefore it may fitly be compared to Nothing, for it is deeper than any Thing, and it is as Nothing with respect to All Things, forasmuch as it is not comprehensible by any of them. And because it is Nothing respectively, it is therefore free from All Things, and is that only Good, which a man cannot express or utter what it is, there being Nothing to which it may be compared, to express it by.

> But in that I lastly said: Whosoever finds it finds All Things; there is nothing can be more true than this assertion. It hath been the Beginning of All Things; and it ruleth All Things. It is also the End of All Things; and will thence comprehend All Things within its circle. All Things are from it, and in it, and by it. If thou findest it thou comest into that ground from whence All Things are proceeded, and wherein they subsist; and thou art in it a King over all the works of God.[30]

It is needless to be reminded of the very real problems that are involved in 'inter-faith' translations. Translations as such are, in effect, interpretations; and, when the 'ultimate realities' of one tradition or one family of traditions are sought to be rendered into the language of a totally different family, interpretations become 'over-interpreted.' The Buddhist śūnya becoming 'nothing' or 'nothingness' and the Vedantist *Brahman* becoming God or Godhead are, perhaps, good examples. Steven Katz warns us that 'nothing can make sense but only within the syntactical and semantic structures of English, 'which in turn receive their English meaning only in relation to a given ontology (or ontologies).'[31]

The genius of Sanskrit and also other Indian languages which are 'calibrated alike' (whorf), in which meaning is determined in relation to ontologies but with a clearly discernible family resemblance, provides the possibility, like in the case of the Greek language, of distinguishing the dialectical from the formal meanings of 'nothing.' 'Nothing,' which has no relation to being which, indeed means the very negation of being (*a-bhāva*), is distinguished from a 'nothing' which has a dialectical relation to being, which is different from (*bhinna*) *and* yet similar to (*sadṛśa*) being. The words beginning with negative pre-fix sometimes instead of emphasizing differences serve to underline or insinuate complementariness. In calling a thing 'unblue,' for example, we emphasize its similarity to the other unblue things as well as its differences from blue things.

In some of the Sanskritic terms which are part of theological repertoire, in which negation prefix is built-in, nihilation does not have the same function of simply rejecting a suggested description: *a-vidyā* (*nañ* + *vidyā*) *a-jñāna* (*nañ* + *jñāna*), both meaning 'nescience' which term would include not only the avowedly false and the erroneous knowledge, but also knowledge claiming to be 'valid' or validated by the standard means of verification. The so-called *vidyā* or *vidyās*, also are *a-vidyā*, *jñāna*, also *ajñāna*—cases of 'learned ignorance.' *Ajñāna* is understood on parity with *jñāna* as a positive something rather than as the privation or absence of *jñāna*. Nescience or ignorance marks the sphere which is the opposite of 'knowledge' in the sense of relational, discursive knowledge. Consciousness of ignorance is a paradox as when one says 'I am ignorant.' It is as if one were to say 'I am asleep' while asleep. The Vedantist would say concerning the latter that 'I did not know anything in sleep,' is the more appropriate form of knowledge that one has on awakening in retrospect of one's state of sleep. Not because consciousness is switched off in sleep but because consciousness which was present was merely a witness to the 'nothing' that ennucleates the world that is about to unfold in wakeful life. The important point is the claim that 'knowledge' and ignorance can be compatible with regard to the same context, knowledge in the sense of relational knowledge, a knowing subject in relation to an object known. Indeed, because of it, there is consciousness of ignorance. The same content may be known negatively as well as positively, as unknown and known.[32]

Avidyā—or *ajñāna*, the more positively coined expressions *māyā*, *samsāra* and their experiential equivalent *duhkha*, are all expressive of the slant on 'nothing' which means that it is just what it is and nothing more, i.e., that is not *real*. The Hindu Vedantist would be careful to add that it is not also unreal. It is most correctly interpreted as a 'false' appearance (*mithyā*) or 'false' perspective (*mithyā dṛṣṭi*) (as in the case of a 'false' coin, a counterfeit pretending to be what it is not.) It is false from the point of view of man, himself, preeminently though not in essence, a part and parcel of it. The image of the rope and snake which is the favorite of the Hindu Vedantist is that something is taken for what it is not. The rope is taken for a 'snake.' It is not that there is nothing. The rope is. It is merely that because of *avidyā* the 'snake' is superimposed on the rope. The snake corresponds to the world as it presents itself in its contingency as the world of multiplicity and difference: i.e., where what *was* then *is not* now, 'what *is here* is *not there*,' and more existentially, where '*I* am *not you*,' as also their converse, viz., what *is* now *is not* then, what *is there* is not *here* and *you* are not *I*.

The logical thrust of a thinking that is intrinsic to the religious outlook of both Hinduism and Buddhism is to deny ontological status to contingency, a logic which finds its most consistent expression in the theories and conceptualizations stemming from 'nothing.' The absolute ('being') lies within as immanent, and the world it presents, itself, in its contingency is, therefore, experienced as an impediment to its realization. Whether it is through a concentration on the unreality of contingency as in Buddhism or centering on the reality within as in Vedanta, through a process of quietening and rendering transparent of the contingent world, the goal aimed at is a positive realization.

The language of 'nothing' is not one that calls for understanding and assessment in mere syntactical analysis and the question of translation and over-interpretation should not be allowed to obscure the fact that the issue involved here is not merely linguistic but conceptual and even existential. The language must be seen as arising in the existential situation in which human existence knows itself to be given over to finitude. The existential situation is also what is called a revelatory situation by theology where one moves through the awareness of finitude to confrontation with Being which Hindu theology calls 'God,' the 'ultimate' and Buddhism would rest content to label as 'nothing.'

The Buddhist was cognizant of the possibility that talk about 'nothing' can be easily misunderstood to mean nothing is said. Experience of nothing normally means no experience unless it is supposed that nothing is really something, which is, logically speaking, an absurdity. Alternatively, when the Buddhist teacher preaches or proclaims 'nothing' to consist in the exhaustion of all views (*dṛṣṭi śūnya*), one may understand the 'nothing,' i.e., the absence of being as itself a view. As Candrakirti explains, it is as if one said to another, 'I have *nothing* to sell you' and the other asks in reply 'sell me that nothing.'[33] Nāgārjuna calls such men 'incurable.' He says: just like a snake or a science taken in a wrong way, the *śūnyatā* being misunderstood brings about one's own destruction.[34] If 'nothing' is discerned in its actual sense intended as entailed in the daily praxis, there is no room for misunderstanding it to imply nihilism.

Truly speaking, says Nāgārjuna, concluding his famous discourse on the 'centrality of the significance of Nothing' (*Mādhyamika Kārikā*), 'no truth indeed has been taught by a Buddha for anyone, anywhere.' The commentator cites a Sutra which elaborates thus:

> Not one syllable was uttered nor used by the perfected one, neither did he address anyone nor will he. Yet all creatures, according to their propensities perceive the voice of the perfected one as if it issues forth in the various dialects of their homelands; for them it takes special forms 'this revered one is teaching this doctrine for our benefit' or 'we are hearing the doctrine of the perfected one.' Inexpressive, beyond language are the elements of existence, tranquil, pure and devoid of Being; one who knows them so is called a Buddha.[35]

Buddha's performatory 'non-discourse' proved, nevertheless, "the dharma–shower by which all his disciples became refreshed." (Tucci)

There is an equally picturesque description, imparted as a challenge to understanding in respect of the teaching of Nothing, in the Hindu tradition also. The celebrated commentator of Vedanta (Sānkara) relates a conversation between teacher and pupil as reportedly narrated in the Upanisads, how Bahva, questioned about Brahman by Vaskalin, explained it to him by silence: "He said to him, 'learn Brahman O friend' and became silent. Then on a second and third time when questioned he replied, 'I am teaching you, indeed, but you do not understand. Silence is the self.' The famous Vedantic image of a teacher imparting the highest teaching to his pupils in a solemn setting is well known: "How strange! Under the banyan tree are old men. Their teacher is only a boy. His explanation consists in silence yet the pupils have been made free from doubts through correct understanding."[37]

NOTES AND REFERENCES

1. *Early Greek Thinking*, David Farell and Frank A. Capuzzi, trans., New York, Harper & Row, 1975, translations of Heidegger's essays on Pre-Socratics.
2. Radhakrishnan, *Indian Philosophy*, Vol. 1, New York, The Macmillan Co., 1927, 611ff.
3. *Majjhima Nikaya Suttas* 63, 72; *Prasannapada*, Candrakirti, Poussin's ed., 446. See also Murti, T. R. V., *The Central Philosophy of Buddhism*, London, Allen & Unwin, 1961, 47ff.
4. For a general discussion of the influence of Buddhism on Vedanta, see Murti, T. R. V., *Vedanta and Buddhism*, Seminar Papers, the Center of Advanced Study in Philosophy, Banaras Hindu University, Varanasi, 1968.
5. *Brahadaranyaka Upanisad*, 2, 4, 1–7.
6. Cf. Rudolf Otto, *Mysticism East and West*, Ch. X, 103–123, New York, Meridian, 1957.
7. *Rg Veda*, 1, 164, 46.
8. *Chandogya Upanisad*, 6, 2, 1.
9. *Katha Upanisad*, 6, 13.
10. Brahadaranyaka Upanisad 3, 8, 8; 4, 4, 15.
11. Nasr, *Knowledge and the Sacred*, New York, Crossroad, 84.
12. K. Sivaraman, *Method as a Philosophical Problem*, in *Indian Philosophical Annual*, Madras, Center of Advanced Study on Philosophy, 1968, 117ff.
13. For my interpretation of the existential orientation of 'Absolutisms' Hindu and Buddhist and their built-in negation, I am indebted to John Macquarrie's paper on *The Language of Being*, in his *Studies in Christian Existentialism*, New York, S.C.M. Press, 1965, utilized throughout this section.
14. Karl Jaspers, *The Perennial Scope of Philosophy*, London, Routledge and Kegan Paul, 1950, 162.
15. Karl Jaspers term for it is the 'comprehensive', *op. cit.*, 160.
16. *Majjhima Nikaya*, 1, 140.
17. *Coomaraswamy, Buddha and the Gospel of Buddhism*, New York, Harper Torch Books, 1964, 20.
18. I Corinthians, 7, 31.
19. L. Drummond, *World-Renunciation in Indian Religion in Contributions to Indian Sociology*, Vol. 1, 1957 (Delhi).
20. Buddhism also makes uses of the language of 'bliss' (*sivam*) as in the last verse of *Madhyamika Karika*, but as Candrakirti points out its meaning is still negative implying the dying away of all objects of knowledge and of *knowledge also*. Cf. Mervin Sprung, *Lucid Exposition of the Middle Way*, London, Routledge, and Kegan Paul, 262.

    For a well-documented study in contrast of the goals of *nirvana* and *moksa*, see Krishna Warrior, *The Concept of Mukti in Advaita Vedanta*, University of Madras, 1961, 74–111; 469–528.
21. For a scholarly study of the subject, the classical work still not superseded in terms of conclusions, is Dutt, *Aspects of Mahayana Buddhism*.
22. Macquarrie, *op. cit.*, 85.
23. Chatterjee, A. K., *Yogacara Idealism*, Varanasi, 1967.
24. Murti, T. R. V., *The Metaphysical Schools of Buddhism in History of Philosophy*,

Eastern and Western, London, George Allen & Unwin, 1967, 297.

25. *Ibid.*, 210.
26. *Madhyamika Karika*, 17, 8-11. Mervin Sprung, *op. cit.*, 230–233.
27. *Ibid.*, 19, 19, 25.
28. Mervyn Sprung, *op. cit.*, 181.
29. Macquarrie, *op. cit.*, 88.
30. Coomaraswamy, *op. cit.*, 125, 126.
31. Steven Katz, *Mysticism and Religious Traditions*, Toronto, Oxford University Press, 1938, 25.
32. For a good and critical account of *Advaita Vedanta* theory of Nescience, see Radhakrishnan, *Indian Philosophy*, Vol. 2, New York, The Macmillan Company, 1927, 587–608.
33. Mervin Sprung, *op. cit.*, 150.
34. *Madhyamika Karika*, 24, 11.
35. Mervin Sprung, *op. cit.*, 263.
36. The *Brahma Sutra*, 3, 2, 17, commentary.
37. *Daksinamurtistotra*, Masson & Pat Wardhan.

13

THE ULTIMATE GOAL OF BUDDHISM AND THE DOCTRINE OF NO-SELF

P.D. Premasiri

BUDDHISM AS IT IS PRESERVED in at least one stratum of the religious literature which represents its cardinal doctrines can without hesitation be called a non-theistic religion. There are good grounds to conclude that the bulk of the doctrine preserved in the five Nikayas or collections of the Suttapitaka of the Pali canonical tradition form the core of the original teachings of the Buddha. No one who becomes intensely familiar with the Buddhist teachings confined in these sources would be inclined to doubt their deep spiritual significance. They present a specific world view, an account of the human predicament as well as a spiritual goal for man conceived as liberation or salvation. The attainment of this goal is believed to be a consequence of a systematic transformation of the person by means of a graduated path of moral training and perfection.

Most people brought up in theistic spiritual traditions find it difficult to conceive of any religious morality or spirituality in the absence of a theocentric conception of reality. All finite things in the universe including human souls are believed by them to be created by God according to a certain teleological plan. Salvation is conceived as the attainment of the eternal felicity of the soul as a consequence of obedience to God and the fulfillment of the divine purpose. The human being is believed to be incapable of working out his own salvation without God's grace due to man's inherent moral weakness. The type of Buddhism that will be elaborated in the sequel is an obvious exception to such a theocentric view of spirituality. For Buddhism represented in the Pali canonical tradition speaks of no creator God, of no creation, of no teleological plan, and above all of no substantial entity called an individual self or soul, awaiting to be redeemed by the grace of God. One may therefore wonder how such a doctrine is to be differentiated from an atheistic materialism which has no conception of a life beyond death and be described as propounding a religious ideal.

However, the Buddha, as represented in the Pali canonical tradition explicitly denies that his world view can be identified with the nihilism attributed to an atheistic materialism. He described his own teaching as one which steers clear of two familiar ways in which reality is conceived. According to the Buddha, speculation about the nature of things generally leads to one of two mutually contradictory positions, namely externalism (*sassatavada*) and annihilationism (*ucchedavada*). The eternalist doctrine is an attempt to explain reality in terms of enduring substances. An ontological theory according to which all change and plurality or diversity is considered to be illusory, or one which posits an unchanging and absolute substantial reality behind the appearance of the fleeting variety of existence falls under the doctrine which Buddhism described as externalism. Vedantic Brahman, Sankhya Purusa, the God of some theistic religions or eternal and enduring subject of experience in many religious and philosophical systems are examples of what Buddhism described as externalism.

Externalism, when applied to the nature of the individual self, admits that the soul and the body are distinct and that the human soul cannot be destroyed even though the body it occupies is subject to change and destruction. The soul is said to be unborn or without beginning (*ajo*), permanent (*nityah*), eternal (*sasvato*), and primeval (*purano*).[1] Buddhism viewed this kind of doctrine as one which commits itself to the theory that life or the sentient or animate aspect of existence (*jiva*) is distinct and separable from the corporeal or the physical aspect of existence (*sarira*). It was described as the doctrine which asserted that the *jiva* and *sarira* are two distinct realities and that *jiva* (soul) is an eternal principle whereas *sarira* (body) which is composed of the material elements is dissolved at death. Buddhism represented the annihilationist as one who asserted that *jiva* and *sarira* are identical. Those who committed themselves to this belief were not concerned with life beyond death, for they believed death to be a total annihilation of personality.

Two familiar expressions of the question regarding the relationship between life and matter, mind and body and the psychical and the physical aspects of living being were: (1) Are mind and body identical? (2) Are mind and body distinct? (*tam jivam tam sariram va annam jivam annam sariram va.*) The Buddha refused to commit himself to an affirmative answer to both questions suggesting that it would be misleading to do so and that it would be a futile exercise to attempt to discover which answer was correct. He left this question aside as an undeterminable one along with a number of other metaphysical questions of the same nature.

To the first question the materialist does not hesitate to give an affirmative answer. For he does not believe in any independence of mental functions from bodily functions. The modern behaviorist analysis of mental conduct concepts can be considered as a sophisticated form of the same thesis. The eternalist metaphysician does not hesitate to give an affirmative answer to the second question. For he believes in an indestructible principle in man which is differentiated from the physical body which obviously disintegrates at death. The Buddha's position was that both theses are oversimplifications of the actual facts.

Leaving aside externalism and annihilationism, the Buddha presented the doctrine of *paticcasamuppada* (dependent-co-origination) as an alternative principle through which the nature of reality could be comprehended. According to this doctrine, no uncaused first cause was to be postulated. No self-existent or self-subsistent eternal entities were to be recognized. All existence was to be understood as relative existence. All origination was to be seen as dependent origination, dependent not on a single ultimate cause but a plurality of co-existing and co-related conditions. The Buddha believed that wherever an intelligible explanation is possible it has to be in terms of a plurality of observable or discoverable conditions. The Buddha attempted to explain the process of life by the application of this principle of dependent-co-origination as a process of becoming (*bhava*) avoiding the doctrines which asserted the two extreme viewpoints, (1) that what really exists exists eternally and (2) that what does not have eternal existence does not have any existence at all.

The first premise on which the soteriological goal of Buddhism is founded is the truth of the unsatisfactoriness of life lived by man in his unenlightened condition. While refusing to solve metaphysical questions commonly raised about the first beginnings of life and the universe, its spatial dimensions and the nature of ultimate reality, the

Buddha claimed that he taught four fundamental truths, namely (1) the truth about unsatisfactoriness (*dukkha*), (2) the truth about the causal origin of this unsatisfactoriness (*samudaya*), (3) the truth about the cessation of this unsatisfactoriness (*nirodha*), and (4) the truth about the means by which this unsatisfactoriness is to be overcome (*magga*). Buddhism made no ontological claims of a metaphysical nature. It did not attempt to explain the ultimate origin of existence by positing an absolute substance, but spoke of the related existence of things in cyclic processes of evolution and dissolution. The Buddhist quest for right knowledge is not an attempt to grasp an ontological absolute in terms of which everything else is to be looked upon as illusory or non-existent, but to understand the nature of the very things that we encounter in ordinary experience in a certain perspective that conduces to the elimination of *dukkha* (unsatisfactoriness). The cyclic process of *dukkha* ceases to continue not when we have discovered some actual and Absolute Being which is not subject to change, but when we have given up the very pursuit of something which is not subject to change. Emancipating knowledge (*vimuttinanadassana*) for Buddhism is not insight into some nominal reality which is over and above the fleeting things of the empirical world, but the change of attitude towards those fleeting things.

Responding to those things as if they are permanent, unchanging realities (*nicca*), as if they give us lasting satisfaction (*sukha*) and as if they are identical with our very being (*atta*), is the delusion that creates suffering. To overcome this it is necessary to cultivate what Buddhism calls "knowledge and insight into things as they have come to be" (*yathabhutananadassana*). All things have come to be with a complex variety of interdependence. All existence is relative existence, and therefore, empty of substantial reality or own being (*svabhava*) as the later Buddhist philosophers expressed in terms of their concept of *sunyata* (emptiness).

The attempt to transcend the fluxional world of sense experience in order to attain a state of permanent being and to pass from phenomenal to nominal existence has characterized the key approaches of many metaphysically inclined philosophical and religious systems. Buddhism too admits the universality of change and believes that whatever is subject to change cannot be productive of happiness (*yadaniccam tam dukkham*). However, the unique feature of Buddhism is that it seeks emancipation not in discovering an entity that does not change, (which according to Buddhism one can under no circumstance find) but in changing our attitude towards what by nature is subject to change. Consequently, the early Buddhist doctrine lacks metaphysical concepts which are comparable to Platonic forms, Vedantic Brahman, God of monotheistic religions and the immortal soul of many a religious system.

According to the Buddha, everything that exists, or that is knowable, or that is communicable in language, falls within the senses and their corresponding data. If someone questions "What is everything?" it is fitting to reply, "Everything is eye and material objects, ear and sounds, nose and smells, tongue and tastes, body and tactile sensations, mind and thoughts." In the opinion of the Buddha, if anyone were to speak of anything other than these and was challenged to explain what he meant he would be at a loss to explain himself.[2]

There are, according to Buddhism, three fundamental characteristics of all existent things that fall into the above categorization in terms of the senses and their data. The first characteristic is that everything is subject to change. The second follows from the first in that the absence of permanent and enduring entities causes suffering and frustration. Neither any physical object sought after by pleasure-seeking individuals nor any mental state attained as a result of a pleasure-seeking endeavor, such as the gratification of a sensuous desire gives lasting happiness. Therefore, the more one hankers after sensuous pleasure, the more one is likely to be frustrated.

The third characteristic is that nothing can be conceived as a self entity or an enduring soul. For an enduring soul (or *atman*, as conceived by metaphysicians of the time) was by definition an intransigent changeless substance.

It is this third characteristic, soullessness (*anatta*), which is unique in Buddhism, for there is no other religious tradition which upholds a doctrine of no-self in the sense and manner in which Buddhism did. Unlike in theistic religious systems, the essence of the human person is not a simple entity created by God on whose grace salvation depends. In the Pali canon the individual and the external world are treated as analyzable into simpler constituents called aggregates (*khandha*) spheres of sense (*ayatana*) and elements (*dhatu*). In the third book of the Pali Suttapitaka called the Samyuttanikaya there are three sections (khandhasamyutta, salayatanasamyutta, and dhatusamyutta) devoted to the analysis of the constituents of reality in terms of these three modes. The point of this analysis was not to reach some simple unanalyzable constituents of being, but to give analytical insight into the compounded and interdependent nature of all empirical existence including our own selves and to destroy the illusion that there is any underlying simple and uncompounded substratum.

The analysis into five aggregates is often used in the Pali suttas to show that there is no component in what we conventionally call our 'self' that has an enduring nature. The self is the organic unity of the psychophysical organism consisting of the mental and material processes (*namarupa*). This is further analyzable into five aggregates as *rupa* (material form), *vedana* (sensation), *sanna* (perception), *sankhara* (dispositions or habitual tendencies) and *vinnana* (consciousness).

Taken separately, it is an observable fact that each of these factors of personality is in a process of constant change. The Buddha repeatedly advised his disciples to reflect on the three characteristics of these aggregates, their transient nature, their unsatisfactoriness and their unsubstantiality.[3] These three characteristics of the aggregates should be wisely seen (*sammappannaya datthabbam*) in order to remove the attachment and to avoid clinging to them, which is the root cause of suffering. When wisdom dawns, one gets disenchanted with these aggregates and one's passion is destroyed and the mind is emancipated.

> When the learned noble disciple sees in this way he is disenchanted with material form, sensation, perception, dispositions and consciousness. When he is disenchanted he becomes detached. Through detachment he is emancipated. When he is emancipated there arises the knowledge that he is emancipated.[4]

In the Buddha's analytical treatment of factors of personality, he makes use of the definition of the traditional metaphysical concept of a changeless soul (*atman*) to show that none of the observable constituents of personality conforms to that definition. The real self as traditionally understood was believed to be eternally blissful, not subject to change, disease, or destruction. The Buddha, unlike other philosophers, did not commit himself to an affirmation of the existence of an entity or entities conforming to that definition but applied that definition to show that the observable elements of existent reality do not conform to it. Addressing his first five disciples, the Buddha says:

> Monks, material form is not atman. If material form were atman it would not be subject to disease, and it would be possible to say with regard to material form 'Let my material form be thus and let my material form not be thus!..Is it proper to look upon that which is impermanent, and unsatisfactory and having the nature of transience as 'This is mine, this am I, this is my self?'[5]

The Buddha frequently advised his disciples to give up the aggregates saying that they are not one's own:

> Monks, give up that which is not yours. When you give it up it will be to your well-being and happiness for a long time. What, monks, is not yours? Material form is not yours.... sensation...perception...dispositions...consciousness is not yours....Suppose monks, if some one were to take away or burn or deal according to his wish with the grass, wood, branches and leaves of this Jeta

grove will it occur to you monks 'Someone is taking us away, burning us, or dealing according to his wish with us?'[6]

The Buddha believed that among recluses and brahmans (*samana-brahmana*, an expression used to refer to the various religious teachers of the Buddha's time) those who held diverse conceptions of self considered one or the other of the five aggregates of personality as the self.[7] The continuity of selfhood or personhood could be conceived only in terms of the continuity of the aggregates of personality. Where there is no material or mental element left there is no sense in talking about the continuity or survival of a person. The material and mental aggregates have no permanent existence. Yet they are constantly grasped and clung to as belonging to an imagined permanent 'I.' The experiential basis for the notion of 'I' is the existence of the transient material and mental processes. But the self-consciousness arising on this basis separates itself in the imagination into a distinct entity which is supposed now to be the permanent bearer of those mental and physical properties. The notion of 'I' so generated in turn becomes the source of anxiety and tension. One begins to see the material body as the self (*rupam attato samanupassati*), or the self as consisting of the material body (*rupavantam va attanam*), or the material body as within the self (*attani va rupam*), or as the self within the material body (*rupasmim va attanam*). He becomes obsessed by the idea 'I am material body,' 'material body is mine' (*aham rupam mama rupanti pariyutthayi hoti*). While he is in this manner obsessed with this idea, the body changes. When this happens there arises grief, lamentation, anguish, frustration and anxiety.[8] The same is true of other aggregates of personality as well.

The Buddha's repeated exhortation is to abandon the notion of self, and to give up all phenomena which are supposed to be identical with or belonging to the self. For what arises in this process of misconception and mistaken identification is nothing but frustration and anxiety. When the Buddha is accused of teaching a thesis about the annihilation of an existing being (*sato sattassa ucchedam vinasam pannapeti*), his response to the accusation is that he is not talking about the arising or annihilation of any eternal being but merely the arising and cessation of *dukkha*.

According to Buddhism, over and above the personality factors analyzed under the five aggregates, there is no entity which may be called the pure ego or a transcendental self which is neither matter nor mind. The human personality is the organic unity of the personality factors operating in accordance with certain causal patterns as a complex and dynamic organism. Personal identity does not consist in the persistence of an underlying indestructible entity over and above the changing factors of personality. 'I' in our linguistic usage does not refer to an enduring entity but to a changing psychophysical process. However, Buddhism does not subscribe to the materialist position that the identity of a person can continue only as long as a spatiotemporally continuous body lasts. Since for purposes of personal identity, the psychic components of personality such as continuity of memory and character traits are considered in Buddhism to be even more important than the material components, personal identity may be established even beyond the disintegration of an individual's body.

In the twelve-fold formula of dependent origination, the Buddha presents the cyclic process of existence in a depersonalized form. The concept of an experiencing subject is completely ignored in this analysis. The static concept of an experiencing subject is dissolved into a dynamic causal and conditioned process resulting in the generation of the experience of *dukkha*. In the twelve fold formula of dependent-co-origination accepted by all schools of Buddhist thought, there is no attempt to explain the ultimate origins. It takes the psychophysical reality of the empirical individual in existential terms and explains how the cyclic process of *dukkha* rolls on, depending on a number of experientially identifiable conditions.[10]

The reversal of this process occurs as a result of the breaking of two crucial links. They are ignorance and craving. The destruction of ignorance and craving is the way to attain the ultimate goal of Buddhism. Human suffering is due to the presence of a triad of evil which has to be overcome by following the Buddhist path of spiritual culture. The triad consists of *lobha* (greed), *dosa* (hatred), and *moha* (delusion). According to Buddhism, the evil mental traits that cause human suffering function concomitantly at the two main levels of the human psyche. At the emotional level are *lobha* and *dosa* and at the cognitive level is *moha*. All human suffering, whether it is at the individual level, or at the societal level is a consequence of these three psychological traits. An enlightened one is a person who completely eliminates these traits and such a person is regarded as one who has attained *Nibbana*.

How is the doctrine of no-self related to the Buddhist notion of the ultimate goal as outlined above? According to Buddhism, the crucial element in *moha* (delusion) or *avijja* (ignorance) is the delusive notion of a self. Attachment and repulsion, the two major psychological responses of the individual to the stimuli of the external world, spring from the ego notion. Craving cannot be overcome without overcoming the tendency to make the distinction between what one conceives as the self and the not–self. The source of all evil lies in the tendency to feed and nourish what is conceived as the self at the expense of everything else conceived as the not-self. The self becomes the pivotal point round which many other things conceived to belong to it are gathered and clung to with tremendous attachment. The initial stage of acquiring the notion of selfhood begins with the identification of oneself with the factors of personality (*khandha*). So the Buddha emphatically exhorted his disciples to reflect on the fact that the personality factors cannot be identified with a really existent self.

Man enters the cycle of *dukkha* by making the initial mistake of grasping the factors of personality as the self. From this point onwards he gradually expands his ego, constructing around it other identities such as caste, race, religion, political ideologies, etc. These ramifications of the basic consciousness of a differentiated self begin to entangle the person in diverse conflicts. The anxieties and frustrations produced in any individual mental series on the one hand and the diverse conflicts with the resultant acts of violence and brutality causing immense suffering at the societal level on the other, can, according to Buddhism, be traced to our involvement with the notion of an ego.

The view that there is a self, and the attempt on our part to speculatively identify it with some factor of our experience is, according to the Buddha, the result of clinging to a harmful dogma. In order to reach the peace of *Nibbana*, one has to dissolve the notion of the self. The thought 'I am' (*manta ham asmi*) has to be completely destroyed in order to overcome *dukkha*. The ultimate goal of Buddhism was not conceived as the survival of an individual self in any form. Buddhism conceives of the ultimate attainment neither as the absorption of an individual finite self in a macrocosmic absolute, nor as the survival of a self-monad in some union with its original creator.

Nibbana, or the ultimate in spiritual transformation in Buddhism, is the final ending of all unsatisfactoriness (*dukkha*). It is described as the highest bliss that man can attain. This blissful experience is attained not in another life, but immediately here and now. The blissfulness of the attainment as far as the living person is concerned consists of the freedom he attains from the deep-rooted evil traits of his mind described in Buddhism as the three roots of evil, (*akusalamula*), the cankers, (*asava*), the dormant evil traits, (*anusaya*), and defilements (*kilesa*). Such a person is at peace with himself as well as with the rest of society. He, therefore, is not instrumental in creating suffering either for himself or for others. He is called a worthy one (*arahanta*), a person who is accomplished (*katakaraniya*), one who has reached the noble goal (*anuppattasadattha*). According to Buddhism, he does not come back to the tormenting cycle of *dukkha* any more, for he has completely dissolved the personality factors in such a way that they will not arise again.

Buddhism is content to call its final state of liberation *Nibbana*, which means tranquility within, appeasement of the disturbing passions. Buddhist *Nibbana*, understood in these terms, is not an entity or an object. It is senseless to ask whether it has real being or not, for it is what happens to a person, not a spatiotemporally located something. It is due to this reason that the ultimate goal of Buddhism is characterized primarily in ethical and psychological terms, although the use of figurative expressions to talk about this attainment is not lacking in the early Buddhist scriptures. Unlike most religious systems, Buddhism preferred the use of the ontologically neutral term *Nibbana* which literally meant 'peace' or 'calm' to describe its ultimate attainment. What corresponds in Buddhism to that which theistic religious systems describe as coming to God is the cessation of the cyclic process of suffering, the appeasement of greed, hatred, and delusion. This transformation could be effected here and now by following the path of moral perfection, the Middle Way of the Buddha consisting of the Noble Eightfold Path.

When the Buddha was asked what the after-death state of the person who has attained this *Nibbanic* bliss in this immediate life is, the only reply that he gave was that he becomes like the flame of a lamp which is blown out. The question as to whether he arises again, or does not arise, or both arises and not arises, or neither arises nor does not arise, is considered to be an irrelevant question. The fires of passion and the flames of *dukkha* persist as long as they are continually fed by the conditions necessary for their persistence. When those conditions are no more, these fires are extinguished. Questions regarding the existence or non-existence of a self-entity are irrelevant.[11] This position of the Buddha is consistent with the stance that even while the individual personality series is going on, there is no substantial entity to be referred to as the self. If there is no such entity even while a person is living and the personality factors are rolling on, there is no sense in asking what happens to that entity when the personality factors cease to roll on. To give a categorical answer to an inappropriate question is only to mislead the questioner. Therefore, early Buddhism maintained that the question itself is an unanswerable one, because it is itself misconstrued.

The Buddha's explanation of the issue in reply to a question posed by Anuradha, one of his disciples, is conclusive regarding the early Buddhist position about the nature of the emancipated person (*Tathagata*). Anuradha, on being questioned by other religious teachers about the destiny of the *Tathagata*, after death consults the Buddha regarding the appropriate answer in that connection. The Buddha explains to Anuradha that neither the aggregates of personality taken separately and singly, nor the mere collection of the five aggregates, can be conceived as the *Tathagata*. He also says quite specifically that there is no *Tathagata* apart from those aggregates, thereby rejecting the idea of a pure ego which exists independently of the observable aggregates of personality. The Buddha goes on to say that even in this life there is no *Tathagata* in the sense of a truly existent substantial entity.

Therefore, the question about his existence or non-existence after death cannot arise.[12] The Buddha's statement in the Alagaddupama sutta that he speaks only of the arising of *dukkha* and the cessation of *dukkha*, and that, even in this very existence the *Tathagata* cannot be known has to be understood not in terms of some mystical interpretation which postulates a transcendent metaphysical Being, but in conformity with his view that all existence is relative existence, and that 'existence' and 'non-existence' have no application once we cease to talk about relative existence. In this manner the Buddhist middle position of avoiding the extremes of externalism and annihilationism is reasserted with reference to the nature of the goal of the spiritual path as well.

Nibbana is not conceived as the original substance from which the phenomenal world evolves or is created or is produced. It is not an eternal condition of Being, or a timeless self. However, there are instances in which metaphysical interpretations have been erroneously attributed to the Buddhist doctrine due to the influence of other non-Buddhist metaphysical and pantheistic teachings. One such instance is Radhakrishnan's interpretation of *Nibbana* as absolute metaphysical Being. According to him:

> Nirvana is an eternal condition of being, for it is not a sanskara, or what is made or put together, which is impermanent. It continues while its expressions change. This is what lies behind the skandhas, which are subject to birth and decay. The illusion of becoming is founded on the reality of Nirvana. Buddha does not attempt to define it, since it is the root principle of all and so is indefinable.[13]

However, the doctrines represented in the Pali canonical sources have nothing to suggest any such interpretation of *Nibbana*, although, on the contrary, there is much evidence against such an interpretation.

One might suggest that the Buddha's intention in talking about no-self was to prevent people from mistaking something which is not the real self for the real self. This is the opinion of those who subscribe to a position similar to Radhakrishnan's. According to them, although the Buddha denied that changing processes of mind and matter constituting the five aggregates of personality are the real self, he admitted a real self transcending these phenomenal processes. But no evidence in favor of such a conclusion can be adduced from the Pali scriptural sources.

Radhakrishnan says:

> Nirvana is timeless existence, and so Buddha must admit the reality of a timeless self. There is a being at the back of all life which is unconditioned, above all empirical categories, something which does not give rise to any effect and is not the effect of anything else.[14]

It has already been pointed out that in early Buddhism the question regarding the existence of an eternal and timeless soul in a transcendental realm after the death of the person who attains *Nibbana* was considered to be an inappropriate one in that even in this very life the existence of any such identifiable entity is not admitted.

Radhakrishnan is not alone in giving metaphysical and pantheistic interpretations to the Buddhist goal of *Nibbana*. P.J. Saher for instance believes that Buddhism speaks of the possibility of "withdrawing into ourselves, into our real self that is free from all attributes, into the primary ground of being-in-itself, into nirvana."[15] Attainment of *Nibbana* is explained by Saher as a man's finding his way back to the primary ground of being.[16]

However, the question is whether such interpretations are in accordance with what the Buddha conceived as the goal. Although it may not be true of all strata of Buddhist literature that represent the Buddha's teachings, with respect to the Pali canonical scriptural tradition, it is obviously true that the Buddha refused to engage in speculative discussions. His concern was with the immediate problem that every rational being was confronted with, namely, the problem of *dukkha*. It can be overcome by transforming one's psychological traits. *Nibbana* was conceived as the peace that one can experientially attain as a result of such transformation. It is a bliss that is not to be awaited in another world. Not only is it the case that this bliss is immediate but also the eradication of all anxieties about future becoming forms part of this bliss.

NOTES

1. Bhagavadgita II.20
2. Samyuttanikaya (Pali Text Society, London) IV.15.
3. *Ibid*. III.21
4. *Ibid*.
5. *Ibid*. III.66
6. *Ibid*. III.33
7. *Ibid*. III.46
8. *Ibid*. III.3
9. Majjhimanikaya (Pali Text Society, London) I.140
10. Samyuttanikaya (S) II.l
11. Majjhimanikaya I.487
12. S.IV.384.
13. Radhakrishnan S., *Indian Philosophy* (London: George Allen and Unwin Ltd. 1929, Vol I), 449.
14. *Ibid*. 452
15. Saher, P.J., *Happiness and Immortality* (London: George Allen and Unwin Ltd. 1970), 67.
16. *Ibid*. 68

14

THE BUDDHA'S CONCEPTIONS OF REALITY AND MORALITY

David J. Kalupahana

THOMAS NAGEL BEGINS his recent work, *The View from Nowhere* (Oxford, 1986) with a criticism of the perennial search for objectivity, not only in relation to our conception of the object, but also relating to our conceptions of the subject as well as the moral life. Philosophers, starting with the obvious distinction between subjective life and objective experience, have moved in different directions in formulating their views of the world. The pendulum has swung in different directions. If we start from the subjective side, we are said to be confronted with the problems of skepticism, idealism, or solipsism. If we are to begin with the objective side, we are faced with a different set of problems. We need to accommodate the individual, his perspective, as well as the perspectives of others in a world that is generally looked upon as being neutral, objective, and perspectiveless. Nagel focuses on the second approach.

> It is this second version of the problem that particularly interests me. It is the obverse of skepticism because the *given* is the objective reality—or the idea of an objective reality—and what is problematic by contrast is subjective reality. Without receiving full acknowledgment this approach has been very influential

in recent analytic philosophy. It accords well with a bias toward physical science as a paradigm of understanding.

But if under the pressure of realism we admit that there are things which cannot be understood in this way, then other ways of understanding must be sought. One way is to enrich the notion of objectivity. But to insist in every case that the most objective and detached account of a phenomenon is the correct one is likely to lead to reductive conclusions. I have argued that the seductive appeal of objective reality depends on a mistake. It is not the given. Reality is not just objective reality. Sometimes, in the philosophy of mind but also elsewhere, the truth is not to be found by travelling as far away from one's personal perspective as possible.[1]

Nagel's effort to resurrect the human perspective without, at the same time, allowing it to deteriorate into an idealism or a form of solipsism, will certainly be in conformity with the teachings of the Buddha. The reason is that the philosophical atmosphere in India before and during the 6th century B.C. to which the Buddha was responding was not very different from the gestalt against which Nagel is reacting, even though the former may not appear to be as sophisticated as the latter. The search for ultimate objectivity and the need to accommodate the subject within that objective perspective, as it was in the Cartesian enterprise in Western philosophy, led some of the Upanisadic thinkers to rely upon some form of intuition to establish the ultimate reality of the self (*ātman*).

In the beginning this was only the self (*ātman*) in the form of a person. Looking around he saw nothing else than the self. He first said "I am." Therefore, even to this day when one is addressed he says that "this is I" and speaks whatever other names he may have.[2]

This does not look very different from the Cartesian enterprise. Here we find the ordinary self-awareness being placed inside a casket made of stainless steel and preserved as a permanent and eternal mental substance, a self that can be comprehended through an intuition that allows no room for doubt. However, in the Indian speculation, unlike in the Cartesian system, it was this very same ultimately real self that also constituted the reality of everything in the universe. The realization of the oneness or unity of the self (*ātman*) therefore implies an intuitive understanding that the mysterious entity within the individual is identical with the mystery that is inherent in all phenomena.

In more recent times, the Cartesian "ghost in the machine" came to be repudiated as a result of a landmark treatise by Gilbert Ryle entitled *The Concept of Mind* (Hutchinson, 1949).[3] The private metaphysical subject, the agent behind human experience and action, came to be abandoned in favor of a public *concept* which the community of philosophers, leaving all their prejudices behind, were able to analyze and for which they could assign publicly verifiable meaning. In that process the ghost in the machine was eliminated along with certain parts of the machine. This positivistic approach is what contributed to the behavioristic model of explanation adopted by the psychologists with a scientific bent of mind, and which is now being challenged by people like Nagel. In the ancient Indian tradition, a similar attempt to eliminate the Upanisadic version of the "ghost in the machine" led to an equally positivistic doctrine propounded by the Materialists. For the Materialists, the objective reality consists not simply of matter, but also of the principle that governs the behavior of material bodies. This mysterious principle is referred to as "nature" (*svabhāva*).[4] As in the positivist tradition in the West, the Materialists were enthusiastic about eliminating not only the "ghost in the machine" but even a part of the machine, that is, the psychological and moral experiences of humanity.

Nagel would be pleased to learn that his problem was also the Buddha's problem, even though the solutions are not the same. The Buddha was confronted with theories, some of which were the results of individual perspective (*diṭṭhi*), such as those of the Upanisadic thinkers, and some others which supposedly avoided any such individual perspective (*adiṭṭhi*), like those of the Materialists.[5] No doubt, the middle path between the two extremes of individual perspective and no perspective is not an easily circumscribed perspective so long as our attempt is to achieve ultimate objectivity. This means that there is something radically wrong with our search for ultimate objectivity itself.

The first attempt on the part of the Buddha was to avoid the search for ultimate objectivity regarding the subject. This is one aspect of his doctrine of non-self or non-soul (*anatta*). It is intended to get rid of the "ghost in the machine" without, at the same time, abandoning any part of the machine. The machine is the psycho-physical personality consisting of the five basic constituents: the physical body (*rūpa*), feeling or sensation (*vedanā*), perception (*saññā), dispositions (saṇkhāra*), and consciousness (*viññāṇa*).[6] These are not radically distinguishable ultimate elements. Instead, they represent five mutually dependent aspects of the conscious human personality.

The Buddha's definition of the physical body has objective as well as subjective features. Objectively, it is made up of the four primary elements (*mahābhūta*) and the derived elements (*upādāya-rūpa*).[7] Subjectively, it represents the function of being affected. This function is explained by the use of the verb *ruppati*, "is affected," in the definition of the concept of *rūpa* or physical form.[8] This twofold definition, objective and subjective, enabled the Buddha to retain the physical personality as a necessary condition for the objective identification of a human person while at the same time allowing that objective personality to be related to the subjective aspects of human life. The Buddha seems to be reluctant to speak of a human person independent of a physical organism. A purely immaterial (*arūpa*) personality is a mental fabrication (*manomaya*). Physical identification is thus one of the important means of preserving the objectivity of the human person. The sensations and perceptions, understood in a non-reductive way, account for the shared experiences of human beings. Being dependent upon the physical personality for their occurrence, these sensational and perceptual experiences have their limitations. Such limitations provide the occasion for the generation of what the Buddha called dispositions (*saṇkhāra*), and these dispositions represent a watershed between the subjective and objective aspects of the self. Serving as the most important factor in the individuation of a human personality, the dispositions account for the fact of subjectivity.

At the same time, by placing its indelible impression upon the objectively identifiable physical personality as well as the commonly shared sensations and perceptions, these dispositions enable a human person to reveal the objectivity of that subjective self. The Buddha's explanation of this most significant aspect of the personality reads as follows:

> Disposition is so-called because it processes material form (*rūpa*)... feeling (*vedanā*)... perception (*saññā*), ...disposition (*saṅkhāra*), ...consciousness (*viññana*) which has already been dispositionally conditioned, into its present form.[10]

In other words, the personality consisting of the five aggregates that has come to be as a result of past dispositional conditioning (*abhisaṅkhataṃ*) is continually provided with an individuality or unity by the activity of the dispositions.

According to Nagel, "We are in a sense trying to climb outside of our own minds, an effort that some would regard as insane and that I regard as philosophically fundamental."[11] For the Buddha, such stepping out can be achieved only by a careful examination of the dispositional tendencies that bring about the unity as well as the individuality of a person. The individual is not merely a "bundle of perceptions," but also a bundle that is integrated by the dispositional tendencies.

Finally, we are left with the problem of re-identification. The physical body certainly helps in the objective re-identification of the human personality. Yet that objective re-identification can turn out to be extremely superficial and could be even misleading if we are to ignore the re-identification that takes place subjectively on the basis of consciousness (*viññāṇa*). The Buddha characterized this constant process of re-identification as the "stream of consciousness" (viññāṇa-sota),[12] an idea that was to become the central theme of William James when he tried to dispose of the metaphysical conception of self.[13]

Once again, the dispositions (*saṅkhāra*) that are responsible for the individuation of the subjective stream of consciousness also turn out to be the mirror through which the objectivity of that stream is reflected. It is for this reason that the Buddha combined the dispositions and the stream of consciousness to speak of the "stream of becoming" (*bhavasota*),[14] which is another way of explaining the psychophysical personality.

The doctrine of the five aggregates (*khandha*), therefore, represents two important aspects or processes, one of deconstruction intended to show the absence of a permanent and mysterious self or a ghost in the machine, and the other of reconstruction or re-integration that attempts to retain the entire machinery without leaving behind what Nagel calls the "irreducible feature of reality," namely, consciousness.[15] The manner in which these elements are defined, as explained above, eliminated the possibility of their reduction into ultimately further unanalyzable constituents as material and mental substances.

It is significant to note that even though the five aggregates – physical form, feeling, perception, disposition and consciousness – can be looked upon or are understood as concepts, that very function of conceiving is not included among the aggregates.

As pointed out earlier, the Buddha was willing to provide a subjective definition even of the physical body. However, he avoids doing so in the case of conception. Here one may notice an important point of comparison (or even contrast) between the Buddha and the psychologist James. James, the psychologist, was reluctant to use the word 'concept' because it "is often used as if it stood for the object of discourse itself,...."[16] He therefore speaks of the "conceiving state of mind."[17] If that were the case, in the Buddhist scheme, it could find a more appropriate place among the aggregates. Yet it did not. James himself proceeds to qualify his statement immediately, saying: "It (the conceiving state of mind) properly denotes neither the mental state nor what the mental state signifies, but the relation between the two, namely, the function of the mental state in signifying just that particular thing."[18] The Buddha's definition of conception is less complicated and is couched in rather impersonal terminology. Instead of speaking about a conceiving state of mind or the individual act of conceiving, the Buddha speaks of "conception taking place" (*saṇkhaṃ gacchati*).[19] The reason for this definition will become evident as we proceed with the analysis of the various conceptions. This impersonal definition of conception will also have significant implications for the Buddhist philosophy of language which is beyond the scope of this paper.

With this explanation of the human personality or the subject, it will be possible to move on to the Buddhist conception of the object. The Buddhist view of the object bears little resemblance to what is available in the more recent philosophical traditions, and may even appear to be rather exotic, especially after the Western tradition has come to bury the contributions of a philosopher like George Berkeley.

To return to Nagel: "The aim of objectivity would be to reach a conception of the world, including oneself, which involved one's own point of view not essentially, but only instrumentally, so to speak: so that the form of our understanding would be specific to ours, *but its contents would not be*."[20]

In spite of Nagel's attempt in the earlier part of the book to remain satisfied with limited objectivity, especially in the explanation of the human self, ethics as well as science, he seems to be determined to adopt an extremely rationalist approach toward the object. "What there is and what we, in virtue of our nature, can think about are different things."[21] He says: "I want to resist the natural tendency to identify the idea of the world as it really is with the idea of what can be revealed, at the limit, by an indefinite increase in objectivity of standpoints."[22]

Indeed the tone in which Nagel began his work, namely, a criticism of positivist science that does not allow room for "the subjectivity of consciousness as an irreducible feature of reality," seems to change as he proceeds to analyze the nature of the objective world. While he was willing to let go the ghost in the human machine, he is not prepared to let loose the ghost in the world machine. The early Indian thinkers as well as Descartes were consistent in their philosophical enterprise in trying to retain the ghosts in every instance.

In contrast to these different theories, including Nagel's, the Buddha, who abandoned the ghost in the human machine with his theory of non-self (*anatta*), was, both for the sake of consistency as well as for epistemological reasons, equally prepared to renounce any conception of mystery associated with the objective world. According to him, just as much as stepping outside of oneself will enable one to understand and appreciate the truth about the individual subject, a similar stepping out of the object will be conducive to the better understanding and appreciation of the object itself. This is the reason for the Buddha's extension of the doctrine of non-self (*anatta*) to the objective world as well. The de-mystification of the self or the de-solidification of the concept of self went hand in hand with the de-mystification and de-solidification of the concept of the object.

In order to restrain the tendency toward solidification of the objective experience into incorruptible and ultimately real objects, the Buddha recommended the adoption of a perspective that resembles the Berkeley method in Western philosophy. According to Buddhism, in the meditations that eventually bring about more accurate knowledge and understanding, the initial as well as the most essential step is the avoidance of the substance/quality or primary/secondary distinction. Explaining the restraint of the sense faculties, the Buddha says:

> Having perceived a material form with the eye, a person remains non-grasping on to a substance or mysterious cause (*nimitta*) and perceivable qualities (*anuvyañjana*). If he dwells with the faculty of sight uncontrolled, covetousness and dejection, evil unhealthy states of mind, might predominate. So he fares along controlling it; he guards the faculty of sight, he comes to control over the faculty of sight. (This statement is repeated with regard to the other senses as well, including mind, *mano*.)[23]

This does not mean the transcendence of sense experience, as some interpreters of Buddhism make it out to be, for the restraint is called for after the complete act of perception has taken place, not before. It is only an admonition to give up the wild-goose chase, that is, the search for a mysterious entity or cause (*nimitta*) to which the perceived qualities (*anuvyañjana*) are supposed to belong. A Berkeleyan approach is further reflected when the Buddha advised one of his disciples, Bāhiya, to adopt the following method:

> Then, Bāhiya, thus must you train yourself: "In the seen there will be just the seen; in the heard just the heard; in the reflected just the reflected; in the cognized just the cognized." That is how, Bāhiya, you must train yourself. Now, Bāhiya when in the seen there will be to you just the seen;... just the heard;... just the reflected;... just the cognized, then, Bāhiya, you will not identify yourself with it. When you do not identify yourself with it, you will not locate yourself therein. When you do not locate yourself therein, it follows that you will have no "here" or "beyond" or "midway between," and this would be the end of suffering.[24]

This Buddhist approach, however, differs from that of Berkeley in that the elimination of a mysterious substance to account for the identity and the re-identification of the object is not followed by the introduction of an equally mysterious conception of God. The identity as well as the continuity of the object is explained in terms of the principle of dependence (*paṭiccasamuppāda*), to which we shall return soon.

For the Buddha, the constant attempt to introduce a mysterious substance in the explanation of the subjective life as well as objective experience is the work of the tender-minded. The tender-minded are the victims of anxiety (*paritassanā*) in relation to things that do not exist either subjectively or objectively. The tough-minded approach is to renounce the search for "things as they are" and confine oneself to what is given, i.e., "things as they have come to be" (*yathābhūtaṃ*).[26]

The psychologist *par excellence* of the Buddhist tradition, Vasubandhu has characterized the object as a concept (*vijñapti*). We have already pointed out the manner in which the Buddha described a concept (*saṅkhā*) as something that is neither ultimately subjective nor ultimately objective. We also compared the Buddha's view of concepts with that of William James. A conception is thus distinguishable from imagination or day dreaming. A genuine concept is not simply the arbitrary creation of the individual's mind; it is also dependent upon the object of experience as well as recognition and agreement by a community of intelligent human beings. Looking upon conception in this manner the Buddha was able to step outside both the subject and the object. It also enabled him to deal with new situations and new perspectives without falling into any dogmatic slumber. Dogmatism (*diṭṭhi*) is the result of allowing the vehicle of conception, namely the concept, to be solidified through a process of reification.

James struck a similar note when he maintained: "The facts are unquestionable; our knowledge does grow and change by rational and inward processes, as well as by empirical discoveries. Where the discoveries are empirical, no one pretends that the propulsive agency, the force that makes the knowledge develop is *mere conception*."[27] Unfortunately, James was unaware that the Buddhist psychologist of the 4th century A.C., Vasubandhu, had compiled a whole treatise entitled the "Establishment of Mere Conception" (*Vijñaptimātratāsiddhi*), not to justify any form of idealism, but to elaborate upon the Buddha's view of conception as a means of stepping outside the metaphysical subject (*pudgala-nairātmya*), as well as the metaphysical object (*dharma-nairātmya*).[28] Here again, Vasubandhu was preceded by his illustrious co-religionist, Nāgārjuna, who equated conception (*prajñapti*) with dependent arising (*pratītyasamutpāda*), for it is a way of emptying the subject and object of substantialized implications (=emptiness, *śūnyatā*) and representing a middle standpoint between extremes (*madhyamā pratipat*).[29]

If the negative doctrine of non-substantialism (*anātmavāda*) that represents a stepping outside of both subject and object may sound unfamiliar to the modern Western student of philosophy, more cumbersome is the positive doctrine of dependent arising (*pratītyasamutpāda*). Yet, it can be understood in terms of the more familiar category of causation provided one is prepared to shed the substantialized or essentialist perspectives.

Skepticism regarding causal explanations, especially in the area of perceptual experience, is rampant in the traditional Indian schools as well as in some of the modern Western philosophical traditions. Once again such skepticism is the result of the pursuit of excess objectivity that Nagel is complaining about. In the modern world, the most prominent advocate of such skepticism has been Bertrand Russell. Nagel expresses this dilemma when he says: "The same ideas that make the pursuit of objectivity seem necessary for knowledge make both objectivity and knowledge seem, on reflection, unattainable."[30] This dilemma is inevitable so long as we deal with an objectivity that is excessive to the point of being absolute, while human knowledge remains undeniably limited and relative. If objectivity is not as excessive and absolute, skepticism may not appear to be so troublesome.

Here the problem is created by the science of logic that derived its inspiration from the two-valued logic of Aristotle. In this particular system, which incidentally is not so alien to the traditional Indian logical system where absolutism reigned supreme in discussions relating to 'existence,' it is possible to speak of the true and the false distinction appearing in the following form. If the statement: "All swans are white," is true, the statement: "Some swans are not white," is false in the sense that the latter contradicts the former. Here, the term "all" (*sarvaṃ*) is used in an absolute sense. Thus, whenever there is a need to account for possibilities (which may be otherwise), it is necessary to introduce counterfactual after counterfactual, an attempt that some modern philosophers now look upon as being futile.[31]

The Buddha was clearly aware of the problems relating to the absolutist conception of "all" or "everything" (*sabbaṃ*). His empiricism as well as his explanation of conception, as mentioned earlier, prevented him from absolutizing even the conception of "all." Questioned by a metaphysician by the name of Janussoni specifically on the problem of "all" (*sabbaṃ*), the Buddha replied that as far as he is concerned "all" means the eye and material form, ear, and sound, nose and smell, tongue and taste, body and tangible, mind and concept, that is, the six forms of sense experience. Pressed by Janussoni with questions regarding other definitions of "all," the Buddha insisted that he would avoid any such definition, the reason being that they would be beyond experience (*avisaya*).[32] It is for this reason that whenever the Buddha was compelled to utilize universal terms, that is to use the conception of "all," he, as far as we can know from the available discourses, always qualified it as "all this" (*sabbam idaṃ*). Modern Buddhist scholars, misled by medieval Hindu thinkers like Udayana Āchārya, have failed to realize the epistemological significance of this qualification.

The avoidance of any absolutistic notions of truth does not mean the wholehearted sponsorship of skepticism, either in its absolute form, as reflected in a philosopher like Sañjaya, or in its less severe form as portrayed in the Jaina logic of *syādvāda*, where everything is a possibility or a "maybe," until the attainment of "omniscience" (*kaivalya*). The difficulty consists in discovering a middle path between these extremes. In the first place, the Buddha had to admit that every rational human being needs to recognize certain things as being true and others as being false. Otherwise human life would be chaotic. Therefore, to the question as to whether there is a variety of truths (regarding the same matter), the Buddha declared that "truth is one and there is no second," (*ekaṃ hi saccaṃ na dutīyam atthi*).[33] Second, it was necessary to prevent this truth from deteriorating into an absolute truth as reflected in the statement: "This alone is true, everything else is false," (*idam eva saccaṃ mogham aññaṃ*),[34] which leaves no room for change as well as possibilities. The Buddha realized the necessity to account for change as well as creativity and novelty in the explanation of experience. His conception of truth and the method by which that truth is to be clarified, namely, logic, had to accommodate such creativity and novelty.

This task was accomplished by the Buddha by dissolving the absolutistic true/false dichotomy and replacing it with a trichotomy: the true, the confused, and the false, the first accounting for what is available in the present context, the second allowing for the possible, and the third explaining the impossible. The Buddha refers to truth as *sacca*, the confusion or the confused as *musā* and the false as *kali*.

This repudiation of the absolute true/false distinction, comparable to one unsuccessfully attempted by William James in Western philosophy,[35] seems to leave the Buddha with a method of providing truth-value to propositions that appears very different from the methods adopted in the essentialist or absolutistic systems.

An extremely interesting passage in the *Aṅguttara-nikāya* (misinterpreted by K. N. Jayatilleke[36] because of his careless handling of the terminology used by the Buddha) illustrates the Buddha's standpoint.

The passage reads as follows:

> I *know* what has been seen, heard, thought, cognized, attained, sought and reflected upon by the people including the ascetics and brahmans. If I *know* what has been seen... by the people... and I were to say: " I do not know it," that would be confusion (*musā*) on my part. And if I were to say: "I know it and I do not know it," that too would be confusion on my part. However, if I were to say: "I neither know it nor do not know it," I would be committing a sin (*kali*) on my part.[37]

The truth-values assigned to the last three statements by Jayatilleke seems to be inconsistent with the terminology used by the Buddha to characterize them. The four statements may be summarized as follows:

I. I know p.
II. I do not know p.
III. I know and do not know p.
IV. I neither know nor do not know p.

According to the Buddha, if I is true, both II and III are confusions (*musā*) and IV alone is false (*kali*). Compared with the term *musā*, the term *kali* expresses the heightened sense of epistemological sin. If proposition II were to be characterized as the contrary of I, as Jayatilleke does, then even III would be a contrary, and IV alone would be a contradiction.

The four propositions may be stated as follows:

I. p (true)
II. $\sim$p (contrary)
III. (p.$\sim$ p) (contrary)
IV. $\sim$(p. $\sim$p) (contradictory)

The question remains as to why the Buddha did not characterize III as contradiction (*kali*), even though Jayatilleke seems to interpret it as such. Jayatilleke formulates them as follows, leaving room for assigning truth-value to each one of them:

I. p (true)
II. not p (contrary)
III. both p and not p [?]
IV. neither p nor not p [?]

It is our contention that the conclusions derived by Jayatilleke from an analysis of the Buddha's statement reflects not only his failure to observe the important distinction between the two terms "confusion" (*musā*) and "sin" (*kali*) but also his enthusiasm to adopt the essentialist true/false dichotomy, as well as the method of providing truth-value to propositions rather indiscriminately. For the Buddha the true/false dichotomy needs to be modified whenever the evaluation involves both knowledge and description, that is empirical statements. An empirical statement would be contradicted only by a statement that represents a *total negation* of both knowledge and description, and for the Buddha this would also involve a denial of all possibilities of knowing or describing, which is the effect of the fourth proposition. By describing the fourth proposition as "(epistemological) sin" (*kali*), the Buddha was probably condemning the Jainas for giving truth-value to it. For the Buddha a truly contradictory statement implies not only indescribability as this or that but also the absence of any possibility of knowing through empirical means. Therefore, Jayatilleke's attempt to give truth-value to proposition IV [~ (p. ~ p)][38] is based upon the true/false distinction as well as the system of evaluation adopted in the essentialist systems of epistemology and would not be appropriate in the Buddha's anti-essentialist teachings. Proposition III, (p. ~ p), does not rule out the possibility of knowledge altogether and is therefore a contrary rather than a contradiction.

With such a definition of existence or truth, the Buddha could formulate a theory of causation or dependence and even utilize counterfactuals without making them overwork. This fact is clearly expressed in his general formulation of the principle of dependence:

> When that exists, this comes to be; on the arising of that, this arises. When that does not exist, this does not come to be; on the cessation of that, this ceases.[39]

It may be noted that the second statement above serves the function of a counterfactual.

What is most important in the above analysis is that the truth-value of a concept, a statement, or a proposition, is determined on a contextual basis, rather than in an absolute way. This has important bearings on the Buddhist theory of linguistic convention, a subject that is outside the scope of the present paper. We will focus our attention on its significance in the area of ethics or moral discourse.

In the *Upaniṣads* while the search for ultimate objectivity reached its culmination in the conception of *ātman*, the ultimate reality of the subject as well as the object, a similar search in the area of ethics gave rise to the conception of *brahman*.[40] *Brahman* was the source of the fourfold caste-system: The creation of the *dharma* or the moral law being subsequent to the creation of the caste-system, the latter is seen to take precedence over the former. Therefore, the caste specifies the duty which serves as the foundation of morality. This conception of duty came to be elaborated in the *Bhagavadgītā*, where its ontological status is preserved leaving no room for the human perspective.

The Buddha was inclined to use the term *dharma* to refer to the moral ideal since he had very little sympathy with the Hindu caste-system which gave meaning to the Upaniṣadic term *brahman*. For him, the term *dharma*, used in an ethical sense, denoted good, both in its concrete and ideal forms.[41] Its negation, *a-dharma* meant bad or evil. For the Buddha, good is what produces good consequences (*attha*),[42] and such consequences are dependently arisen, i.e., depend upon various factors operating within each context. A pragmatic criterion of good, therefore, has to be contextual as well. For this reason, *dharma* as the moral ideal was never looked upon as an Absolute. Indeed, grasping on to any conception of good as the ultimately real, the universally valid and eternally existent is criticized by the Buddha. This idea is clearly expressed by him in his discourse on the "snake-simile" addressed to a monk named Arittha available both in Pali and Chinese.[43] He insists that a person has to "abandon even the good, let alone evil." Utilizing an appropriate simile, the simile of the raft (*kulla*), the Buddha argues that a person builds a raft only for the purpose of crossing over a stream. If, after crossing over, the person were to carry the raft on his shoulders wherever he goes insisting that the raft was useful and, therefore, he should not abandon it, that person would not understand the function of the raft.[44] This means that the usefulness of the raft is contextual and concrete. Apart from the context, the raft has no meaning, and it is not possessed of absolute value. The pragmatist James struck a similar note when he said that "there is always a pinch between the actual and the ideal which can be gotten rid of by leaving part of the ideal behind."[45]

What does the Buddha mean by abandoning the good? Most scholars take this to mean the transcendence of both good and evil and the attainment of an ineffable state comparable to the *brahman*. If this interpretation is correct, it would mean that the epistemology and the conceptual analysis which were adopted in determining the subject and object are inappropriate in the sphere of moral discourse, and the Buddha can be rightly accused of being inconsistent. Therefore, "abandoning the good" needs to be understood in a totally different way.

The raw materials on the basis of which we arrived at a reasonable conception of a human person were subjective as well as objective. Similar facts served as the raw material for our conception of the object. The very same epistemology and conception call for the preservation of three factors in arriving at any conception of morality. These are: (1) the conception of the individual human person, which we have already arrived at as a viable philosophical concept without having to sacrifice the human perspective; (2) the conception of the objective world, including other human persons, for objectivity is not completely abandoned, and (3) the reality of new and varying contextual situations (that is, the possibilities) that continue to unfold before humanity as a result of dependent arising and which need to be accounted for. These constitute the raw material that go to produce a reasonable conception whenever human beings are called upon to make moral decisions or judgments.

Thus, a reasonable moral judgment will require a careful decision regarding the manner in which we incorporate any one of these factors whenever that particular factor becomes relevant to the situation without ruling it out beforehand. This can be done only when we realize that, as in the case of factual truths, what is involved in a moral decision is also a conception. The Buddha used the term *vohāra* (=*vyavahāra*) to refer to moral conception,[46] while he reserved the term *saṅkhā*, as noted earlier, to refer to conception relating to facts. Realizing that moral conceptions are more variable than conceptions relating to facts, the Buddha was willing to speak of an ideal moral standard as a useful guide. Thus, we have the term *dhamma* used in the plural to refer to concrete conceptions of the good, while the same term used in the singular as *dhammo* refers to the ideal good. It is only the need to modify the ideal (*dhammo*) when that ideal comes into conflict with the concrete good (*dhamma*) that is implied in the Buddha's admonition to "abandon the good." It is not a call to renounce any and every conception of the good. This is the reason for the Buddha's statement that a person should aspire to be moral or virtuous (*sīlavā*) rather than being one who is made up of morals or virtues (*sīlamaya*).[47] It is another way of stating the fact that concrete moral situations are not derived from ultimate and absolute moral laws. Instead, the so-called absolutely objective moral laws are abstractions from concrete moral situations.

The above understanding of the subject, the object and morals will enable us to appreciate the contents of the Buddha's first discourse to the world. In this discourse, popularly known as the "Establishment of the Conception of Righteousness" (*Dhammacappavattana*), the Buddha speaks of two extremes of behavior: self-indulgence and self-mortification.[48] Self-indulgence is characterized as being low, vulgar, individualist, ignoble and unfruitful (in the long run). It represents excessive selfishness stemming from a perspective that leaves no room for the objective reality of other human persons or of the world at large. Contrasted with this form of behavior is self-mortification, described as being painful, ignoble, and unfruitful. This is the result of excessive altruism that tends to ignore the objectivity of the human person, to dissolve him completely in an excessively objective world. Selfishness and altruism in their extreme forms therefore represent two different extremes with which we perceive the individual and the world.

An extreme form of selfishness is easily condemned. Yet a similarly extreme form of altruism is rarely denounced. The Buddha was aware of this when he characterized selfishness as being low, vulgar, individualist, and described self-mortification as being simply painful. Excessive altruism may eventually be traced back to excessive skepticism regarding human knowledge which, in turn, can feed heroism. In the Indian context, this position is reflected in the Hindu religious text, the *Bhagavadgītā* as well as the Buddhist text, the *Śaddharmapuṇḍarika-sūtra*.

Rationalist Nagel believes that truth must lie either in skepticism or in heroism or in both.[49] Hence he is able to justify a position where the so-called moral life can override the good life.[50] If by the moral life, Nagel means an excessively objective moral principle comparable to one sought for by Kant, with whom he has great sympathy, the good life would represent the concrete life of human happiness, whether it be of an individual person or a specific community of persons. Indeed, it is the excessive objectivity of that moral life that compels Nagel to favor the overriding of the good life by the moral life. The Buddha, who was less inclined to adopt such a rationalist position and favored the modification of the ideal when it comes into conflict with the concrete, looked upon both selfishness and altruism as being ignoble and unfruitful. For him, the noble and the fruitful way of life is represented by a carefully conceived middle path that will contribute to the welfare of oneself as well as of others.[51] This is a more enlightened form of ethical pragmatism.

NOTES

1. Thomas Nagel, *The View From Nowhere*, New York & Oxford: Oxford University Press, 1986, 27.
2. *Bṛhadāraṇyaka Upaniṣad* 1.4.1 (edited and translated by S. Radhakrishnan, *The Principal Upanisads*, London: Allen & Unwin, 1953).
3. Gilbert Ryle, *The Conception of Mind*, London: Hutchinson, 1949, 15–16.
4. *Svetāśvatara Upaniṣad* 1.2 (see Radhakrishnan).
5. *Sutta-nipāta*, ed. D. Anderson and H. Smith, London: Pali Text Society, 1913, 840.
6. *Saṃyutta-nikāya*, ed. L. Feer, London: Pali Text Society, 1884–1904, 3.86.
7. *Ibid*., 3.68.
8. *Ibid*., 3.86.
9. *Dīgha-nikāya*, ed. T.W. Rhys Davis and J. E. Carpenter, London: Pali Text Society, 1890–1911, 1.77.
10. *Saṃyutta-nikāya* 3.87.
11. Nagel, op. cit., 11.
12. *Dīgha-nikāya* 3.105.
13. William James, *The Principles of Psychology*, Cambridge, Massachusetts: Harvard University Press, 1983, 219–278.
14. *Saṃyutta-nikāya* 1.15.
15. Nagel, op.cit., 7.
16. James, *The Principles*, 436.
17. *Ibid*.
18. *Ibid*.
19. *Dīgha-nikāya* 1.202; *Majjhima-nikāya* ed. V. Trenckner and R. Chalmers, London: Pali Text Society, 1887–1901, 1.190.

20. Nagel, op.cit., 74 (emphasis mine).
21. *Ibid.*, 91.
22. *Ibid.*
23. *Dīgha-nikāya* 1.70; *Majjhima-nikāya* 1.180 ff.
24. *Udāna*, ed. P. Steinthal, London: Pali Text Society, 1948, 8.
25. *Majjhima-nikāya* 1.136.
26. *Saṃyutta-nikāya* 2.17.
27. James, *Principles* 439.
28. *Viṃśatikā* 10 (see Kalupahana, *The Principles of Buddhist Psychology*, Albany: State University of New York Press, 1987).
29. *Kārikā* XXIV.18 (see Kalupahana, *Nāgārjuna. The Philosophy of the Middle Way*, Albany: State University of New York Press, 1986).
30. Nagel, op. cit., 67.
31. Kripke, Saul, "Counterfactual Theories of Knowledge," paper read before the University of Hawaii, Department of Philosophy Colloquim, January 22–23, 1987.
32. *Saṃyutta-nikāya* 4.15; see Kalupahana, "A Buddhist Tract on Empiricism," *Philosophy East and West*. Honolulu, 19 (1969):65–67.
33. *Sutta-nipāta* 884.
34. *Majjhima-nikāya* 1.169.
35. See James, *The Will to Believe* Cambridge, Mass.: Harvard University Press, 1979, 89.
36. *Early Buddhist Theory of Knowledge*, London: Allen & Unwin, 1963, 346.
37. *Aṅguttara-nikāya*, ed. R. Morris and E. Hardy, London: Pali Text Society, 1885–1900, 2.25.
38. Jayatilleke, op. cit., 345.
39. *Majjhima-nikāya* 1.262–264, etc.
40. *Bṛhadāraṇyaka Upaniṣad*. 1.4.11 ff.
41. *Majjhima-nikāya* 1.415–417; *Theragāthā*, ed. H. Oldenberg and R. Pischel, London: Pali Text Society, 1883, 304.
42. See Kalupahana, *A Path of Righteousness* (*Dhammapada*), Lanham: University Press of America, 39–40.
43. *Majjhima-nikāya* 1.130–142; *Chung Ā-han Ching 54.1 (Taishō* 1.763–766b).
44. *Majjhima-nikāya* 1.135; *Chung Ā-han Ching* 54.I (*Taishō 1.764c).*
45. James, *The Will to Believe*, 153.
46. *Saṃyutta-nikāya* 1.14–15.
47. *Majjhima-nikāya* 2.27.
48. *Saṃyutta-nikāya* 5.420.
49. Nagel, op. cit., 69.
50. *Ibid.*, 169.
51. *Dhammapada* 166 (ed. Kalupahana, *A Path of Righteousness*).

15

NISHITANI'S CONCEPTION OF TIME

AND HIS CRITIQUE OF THE WESTERN NOTION OF HISTORY

John R. Mayer

THE CONVENTIONAL CHARACTERIZATION of the principal contrasts between Buddhist and Christian fundamental approaches—almost presuppositional approaches—to ultimate reality has two principal points. One is the Buddhist preference for an impersonal understanding of the absolute; in contrast with the Judeo-Christian notion of a personal God: the other is the absence of a fundamentally linear or telic conception of time among the Buddhists, in contrast with the Western notion of an eschatological history.

Of course it is true that in the modern centuries, when there was considerable interaction between the cultures of West and East, there are evidences of the appeal of the contrasting tradition. In the West Schopenhauer introduces an impersonal Will as Absolute; there are many ordinary folk who deem the personification of the Divine as mere primitive anthropomorphism, and understand God as the vast impersonal energies out of which the cosmos evolves and which keep the structures in their natural place, moving within orderly patterns.

In the East we have the notion of a future Buddha, Maitreya, whose anticipation is made analogous to the expected second coming of Christ among the Christians, or the return of an Imam or Mahdi at the end of the world as taught by the Shi'ite Muslims. There is also plenty of evidence, for example in Tibetan iconography, that in spite of the presence of sophisticated teachings among the Mahayanists that *samsara* is *nirvana*, there is nonetheless an unsophisticated understanding of *nirvana* as outside and beyond the six created realms and, that the enlightened one as a Buddha leaves the *samsaric* realm; and as a *Bodhisattva*, forgoes leaving the same until all living beings are empowered to do so. Surely such a view is itself eschatological, implying that eventually the merits of all the *Bodhisattvas*, coupled with the success of their teaching and guidance, will finally liberate all sentience. Furthermore, understanding Buddha-nature as universally inherent in all sentience, but paradigmatically inherent in Amida, those resolutions and practices have resulted in his having salvific powers for all those who turn to him. This is singularly analogous to Christian notions.

Nonetheless, the point is well taken that in more sophisticated Buddhist traditions, such as the one espoused by Keiji Nishitani, there is a resistance to and critique of Western notions of personhood and historicity, and that thus his approach to Buddhism does not include a quasi-Western Buddhist eschatology, nor a quasi-Western Buddhist theology.

In the present paper we shall discuss Nishitani's conception of the role of person *vis-à-vis* the absolute or ultimate only to the point that it relates to and is interdependent with his conception of time and history and focus our attention primarily on his view of these, as found in the last two chapters of *Religion and Nothingness*, entitled "Sunyata and Time" and "Sunyata and History" respectively. Because these texts are dense, rich, and difficult, our method is going to be not an analytic retelling of the same in the same order as Nishitani presents his ideas, but a hermeneutic designed at the same time to make the argument easier to follow for the ordinary Western reader not intimately familiar with all the Eastern and Western references that Nishitani employs in his text.

Let us then look at the Western tradition and the conventional analysis of the two traditions, whose spokesman in Nishitani's text is Arnold Toynbee. We know that Western civilization has two roots—one in Athens and the other in Jerusalem. In fact the Greek sources of Western tradition are not that different from the Eastern views, as will emerge in this presentation. After all, we know from the Greek texts about the *gymnosophists*, the naked wise men from the East, as we also know that Plotinus, a principal founder of the Neoplatonic tradition, studied Plato from Ammonius Saccas for ten years, and then traveled to the East to Iran and India to gain access to Eastern wisdom before formulating his doctrine in the *Enneads*.

The principal fundamental fact for the Greek—in which the human finds himself—is the cosmos. The Greek has a clear sense of nature and its cyclic order; the birth, life, death, and rebirth is frequently alluded to even in Plato's dialogues. In contrast, the Jewish heritage, with its fundamental concept of a covenant religion, sees all as history: as the unfolding and fulfillment of promises and conditions that emerge in time as God deals with His people. In fact there is not much biblical evidence of the awareness of cosmos and seasonal cycles. Of course, it is not the case that the ancient Jew was unaware of these, but, rather, that he did not attribute much significance to them. This is why there is practically no evidence of science in the Old Testament.

In contrast, the Greek did not have a real sense of history. We know that there are classical Greek historians: indeed, Herodotus is called "The Father of History" because for the Greeks he "invented" history. The Homeric epics are also historical tales, centered around the Trojan War, its causes and consequences. But the Greeks have no sense of a historical destiny: events come and events go; the Peloponnesian wars are documented by Herodotus so that in case similar incidents arise in the future, people may learn from the records of the past. The Greek history is not like Jewish history. Historic events are imbedded in, and elements of, the cyclic order of nature.

The Hindu traditions about history are explicitly analogous to natural cycles. The tradition talks about six great eras or *kalpas* following one another in rigorous cyclic order: three ascending eras, during which life and virtue increase and enhance spontaneously, followed by three descending ages, in which virtue and the human lot deteriorate and decline. There is no absolute beginning and no absolute end. That the cycle is envisioned in very long terms—far more generous quantitatively than even modern geological history—is not an argument against the fundamentally natural character of history for the Indians. In contrast, we have the Judeo-Christian view of history as once-and-for-all; each event is unique in its particularity, making a contribution to a singular unfolding or fulfillment.

Indeed, there are many Western scholars who would so restrict the use of the words "history" and "historical" as to deny that the Easterner has a sense of history, since his sense is only cyclic, and hence not "historical" at all. The more generous alternative to this is to grant the words "history" and "historical" to the cyclic envisionment though fully recognizing its difference from the typically Western notion.

This, then, is the background to which Keiji Nishitani addresses himself in his essays. It may perhaps also help if we are to make explicit that the objective of the essays contained in *Religion and Nothingness* is to explicate and develop an adequate understanding of a late 20th-century metaphysics, which will gain insights from both the Western Christian tradition and from Buddhist sources. The two traditions are treated as sufficiently complex and rich as to be both mutually complementary and contrasting at the same time. Nishitani cites both Eastern and Western texts for supporting his claims and is at the same time critical of, and concerned about, nihilism and secularization both in the West and in modern Japan.

It is true, however, that he sees Western nihilism and the anomie that it produces as the direct consequence and outcome of Western religious traditions. He believes, however, that historically Buddhism has also encountered a despair and a nihilism analogous to the modern predicament, but that it has managed to overcome it not so much by rebutting it, or avoiding it, but by taking it even more seriously than the European nihilists and secularists do. This has resulted in the Buddhists arriving at a spiritually sustaining doctrine of *sunyata* or *zettai mu*, absolute nothingness.

This absolute nothingness is not to be envisioned as mere emptiness, a static, hollow non-being; rather, as the French word *le neant* also implies from its participial structure, an emptying, a nihilating, a self-overcoming and self-negation which, when all is said and done, is paradoxical enough to embrace and become its very opposite; fullness, life, being, *Tathata*, suchness.

This is arrived at by citing the emptiness of emptiness; and by Nishitani's use of the dialectic by linking opposites with the Japanese term *soku*. The English translation uses the Latin word "*sive*": this is not much help of course to those who do not have a good command of Latin. The closest English term would be "as." More fully, it is really closer to "such as" or "as is exemplified by." In the conventional use, as one would ordinarily expect to find this term, we might have: "a vehicle, *sive* a car" or "a challenge, *sive* being slapped with a white glove." But Nishitani uses *sive*, invariably in a paradoxical, dialectical way, linking opposites with *sive*, rather than linking an abstract, general term to a more concrete example of it. Thus we find personal-impersonal, finite-infinite, *samsara-nirvana,* life-death as the terms linked by "*sive*"; and the fascinating fact is that Nishitani manages to convince his readers, who at first find this deliberate irrationality unintelligible, intelligible after all. Thus, Nishitani's technique is highly reminiscent of that of Nicholas of Cusa, who asserts the coincidence of opposites. The principal difference between them is that "coincidence" is a symmetrical term, while "*sive*" is asymmetric. This signifies that "personal–*sive*–impersonal" is not identical with "impersonal–*sive*–personal."

Nishitani does not deny the linearity, the unfolding of time: the stretching of time endlessly backward from some present and its simultaneous stretching endlessly forward. This is time in the sense of historicity, in which events occur once only, uniquely, as part of a history of progress. Time, from this perspective, is asymmetric, irreversible, flowing ever forward, disclosing being in ever new forms. All this is all too familiar to Westerners; and, Nishitani asserts, if taken as the adequate and exhaustive paradigm of time, leads one not only to Western religiosity but also to its loss to modern secularism. We have to recognize at least a couple of additional dimensions of time in order to come closer to a more enlightened spiritual position.

If the temporal flow is envisioned as a horizontal vectorial line (by "vectorial" we mean "directional," "asymmetric"), in which an ever-moving point, the present, divides the past from the future, there is a new perspective we can gain if we consider the dynamic point only. It is always the present (granted, a different "present" at each moment), but whatever is, is only here. This is the eternal present. Behind it, but no longer existent, the past; in front of it, but not yet, the future. The natural flow of English would have inserted two "is"es into the previous sentence. These were deliberately eliminated to draw attention to the fact that only the dynamic point *is*. Any past makes sense only in reference to one static point, as does any future.

But once the point is seen as dynamic, the very line we have postulated in the earlier image, we must now admit, does not exist, is not, is not time. Time past and time future are relative to a moment, but all that ever is, is the eternal present, the dynamic point. This is in contradistinction to the transient, the momentary present. This eternal present stands not in relation to an antecedent past and a sequent future; no; it stands in contrast with, and hence in relation to, an abyss, a nihility, which discloses the contingency of the eternal moment. The nihility on which the moment rests, so to speak, is vertically rather than horizontally envisioned. In the moment, the present, nihility is disclosed in the contingency of all particularity. But this is not a threatening nihility, or, better still, it is not merely a threatening nihility. It is a reassuring nihility which fulfills itself with the transient content of the ever-present present. Nothing in particular empties itself of its own nothingness to be momentarily disclosed as a this and a now. And the very evanescence of the this and now is the nihilating rather than the becoming of the fundamental structure of reality.

But we better get back to the cavalierly treated question of whether this dynamic self-emptying nihility is threatening or not. Clearly, the transitoriness of life, of projects, of all that which is valued by the human, is the source of nausea in the existentialist nihilism of Sartre; of the ominous and menacing absurdity of the world of Franz Kafka. It is also the intent of the first of the Four Noble Truths of Buddhism, namely that all is *dhukkha*. The *dhukkha* nature of all that is implies simultaneously its capacity to be given to experience as suffering and its transitory character. The Buddhist encounters transitoriness as in some sense unsatisfactory.

But then the question arises: Who is it that suffers? To whom is the transitory nature of all that is unsatisfactory? Who is threatened or made nauseous by absurdity. Clearly, the answer is "I," the human subject, the entity who is the victim of time and history. But, Nishitani is quick to point out, here is the rub; here is the central problem of all Western religions. In making the person of ultimate value, in focusing the quest on personal salvation and personal relation with a personal absolute, there is an insufficient recognition of the necessity of letting go of that person and personality. Nishitani is convinced, and finds many Western exemplars supporting his conviction, that for spiritual growth and development the self must be overcome, annihilated, emptied of its self and personhood in order to gain the famous victory *dhukkha* that is the promise of the Buddha. It is not faith in the consoling belief that the transient is somehow magically preserved in some permanency after all, restored from death to endless existence, which begins with the end of time, that is the key to overcoming the suffering caused by the impermanence of life, the imminence of the shadow of death; rather, with the withering of the false sense of self-importance, the discernment of the self-emptying character of all that is the self-imposed distortion which judges the transitory as unsatisfactory also vanishes. The *samsaric* freedom from *dhukkha* is possible, provided that one lets go of the sufferer, the one whose presumed needs are not adequately met in *samsara*. *Samsara* becomes *nirvana*; and the thusness of this thus merges into the thusness as emptiness of Buddha-nature, which, in its eternal self-emptying, empties itself both of selfhood and of suffering.

Time, according to Nishitani, is not merely cyclic for the Buddhists. The cyclic character is seen and affirmed through all the natural processes which are aspects of time. That is the consequence of belief in an ordered cosmos. But time is not exhausted therewith. There is another temporal dimension relating the moment to an abyss, a field of emptiness whose dizzying richness brooks the subject-object distinction, bringing about an abandonment of clinging to particularity and personhood encouraged by traditional Western theology. This abandonment is dubbed The Great Death. But it is exactly through this Great Death that one approximates the realization that there is nothing but the whole, and the whole is essentially self-emptying. The cult of person and personality, which, even if directed toward a Divinity, is, when all is said and done, a clinging to an "I" in a pre-liberated, pre-enlightened manner. The development beyond such a perspective leads to The Great Liberation. Thus Nishitani finds official Western theology, with its emphasis on covenant, eschalogy, personal salvation, and the preservation of individual particulars beyond their temporal existence into an eternity that is understood as an "over yonder," a transcendence outside and above the natural order; a dysfunctional metaphysics.

He would rather urge the recognition of a transcendence which situates the transcendent not over and above the natural order, but on its "hither" side: closer, nearer, in such a way that person and personality are left as "too far," "yonder." Closer, nearer, on the hither side rather than yonder side, is the language Nishitani uses to attempt to convey that the Westerner situates transcendence in the wrong place. It is really right here and right now. Redemptive time is not future time. There can be no eventual compensation for a misspent now. The present can be saved only in the present. The present is shot through and through with the eternal—as abyss or emptiness on which the mere thusness of the thus rests. This is given expression by the conception of transdescendence. And in this sense every present moment is but repetition. Each moment is whole, whose ending is coincident with its beginning: each is complete in itself. Time is not thought of as asymmetric in this mode of its apprehension; rather, it is eternal recurrence—the same forward or backward, here or there. Nishitani finds Western examples of the awareness of this type of temporality. Interestingly, he cites the example of original sin (using a Kierkegaardian interpretation of it), wherein Adam's sin is all humankind's sin: similarly the notion that at all times all creatures are sustained by the power of God is an instance of the conception of a non-progressive time, an everlasting present in which the Divine and the human are in functioning contact. And in its multiple finitude and diversity it is but an expression of the infinite in its potentially indeterminate sense.

Now we begin to understand how Nishitani uses *sive*. Not merely logically, and methodologically, but evocatively, intelligibly, making us stretch our conventional rationality well beyond its conventional limits.

And the sympathetic, reflective reader, perhaps not on first reading, but on the second or third, gets a strong sense of saying "yes, that is right, it must be so."

Finally, then, the issue is not whether the East or the West has been right about time and history. The Western model, the progressive, linear, eschatological, telic model, with its unique moments, need not be denied. But it cannot be deemed exhaustive or adequate. Its inadequacies lead exactly to those imponderable absurdities about the beginning or the end of time, which in Western religious history has had so many relatively foolish and embarrassing interpretations. We know that the end times were expected in the time of Christ when it was rumored that the second coming was due before the then living generation had expired. Thereafter the end times were expected with surprising regularity. Nishitani suggests that the encounter with a more cyclic, repetitive conception of time, if taken seriously, has the potential of leading us into greater awareness of the simultaneity of the eternal with the temporal. It will also disclose the true meaning of the Buddhist notion of the impersonal aspect of the ultimate, which Nishitani describes as the impersonally personal.

By this he means that the ultimate is characterized by an indifference that is supported by such biblical claims as that the rain falls evenly on the just and the unjust. This ultimately discloses that the conventional Western understanding of the Buddhist notion of the impersonal character of the ultimate is a flawed one, which should be replaced with a "hither side of the personal" notion of the impersonal. This is best characterized as universal compassion indifferent to the happenstantial qualities of the focus of that compassion.

It is exactly the impersonality of the universal compassion that assures the simultaneous and absolute efficacy of the compassion for enlightenment and thus the Buddhahood of the *Bodhisattvas* and the Buddha-nature of all sentience. What arise as past and future, as cause and effect, as intent and fulfillment, in a sequential form of temporality turn out to be related to one another in the mode of "circuminsessionial interpenetration." This is the English phrase used by Father Van Bragt in the translation of the Japanese *egoteki shonyu*. The Pali equivalent, *pratitya samutpada*, has often been translated as "co-dependent co-origination." Obviously both of these are unusual English expressions, which require reflection by the thoughtful interpreter. Both locutions attempt to formulate the symmetry rather than asymmetry of the temporal dimension. It is not merely that death presupposes birth, or that birth leads to death, in a linear, asymmetric way; no, birth and death are but two aspects of the same reality: each is part and parcel of the other.

It is exactly thought and language which create the difference and opposition between them. It is because of that the Buddhist recognizes the inadequacy of thought and language to the task of encapsulating truth. Language can, of course, function as a useful indexical, pointing attention this way or that. But it cannot capture or contain the truth; especially not when language restricts itself to asserting the clearly thinkable. Only when language frees itself from the strict requirements of logic does it gain the power to enlighten. Exactly as it draws us to the realization of the unity of opposites, and the richness of that emptiness *sunyata*, which grounds each and every interpenetrating particularity, does language serve to drive a wedge between conventional, habitual thought-patterns and the spiritual potential of lived contact and oneness with the whole.

We do not have to choose between models of time as developed in the East and West. We must, instead, see that only the affirmation of both can disclose adequately the human situation in its simultaneous condition of depravity and enlightenment. The latter is not flight from the former; it is a compassionate acceptance of it through which our depravity is emptied of its whatness, quiddity.

Nishitani is singularly well equipped to carry contemporary thought beyond its present limits. He is thoroughly familiar with primitive Buddhism in its Indian origins; at home with the Chinese developments of the *Mahāyāna* tradition; a living embodiment of the Japanese reception of that heritage; and also an intelligent, sensitive, susceptible modern, who knows through his own being the lure and allure of Western nihilism—not as the despair-evoking pathology which calls for flight from reality, but as the passionate call for celebration of the here and now, life as freedom, creativity, and responsibility. But when fully developed, such a celebration is not centered in the pointless clingings of the ego; it is the free dance of the spirit in its self-spending *kenosis*, or self-emptying. Thus the path through nihilism ends not in despair, but in enlightenment.

My only reservation about Nishitani's claims is that I do not think he fully understood or appreciated Nietzsche. He wants to see the European philosophical acumen as spent and shortstopped at the point of despair and clinging. While he is generous about such figures as St. John of the Cross and Meister Eckhart, he is critical of the negativity of the existential tradition, especially as it was found in wartime and post-war Europe. He does not fully appreciate the genius of such spirits as Nietzsche, who surely intended to go beyond negative nihilism, and who surely succeeded in so doing, if one reads such texts as *The Joyful Wisdom* sympathetically.

16

NISHITANI ON THE SELF

SELFLESSNESS AND HISTORICITY

Daniel Charles

1

IN PROFESSOR MASAO ABE'S PAPER of 1969 about "God, Emptiness and the True Self,"[1] we find a significant statement about Nothingness as the Ultimate according to Zen Buddhism:

> The ground of our existence is nothingness, *sunyata* because it can never be objectified. This *sunyata* is deep enough to encompass even God, the "object" of mystical union as well as the object of faith. (...) *Sunyata* or nothingness in Zen is not a "nothing" out of which all things were created by God, but a "nothing" from which God himself emerged.[2]

Such a doctrine, Professor Abe argues, might recall Pseudo-Dionysius' Christian mysticism:

> In Pseudo-Dionysius, identification or *union* with God means that man enters the godhead by getting rid of what is man—a process called *theosis*, i.e., deification. This position of Pseudo-Dionysius became the basis of subsequent

> Christian mysticism. It may not be wrong to say that for him the Godhead in which one is united is the "emptiness" of the indefinable One.[3]

But if read carefully Pseudo-Dionysius' *Mystical Theology*, we may notice that there is an essential difference between Zen and Christian mysticism: if we adopt the Christian standpoint, we run the risk of subjectivizing and humanizing God:

> Pseudo-Dionysius calls that which is beyond all affirmation and all negation by the term *him*. Many Christian mystics call God "Thou." In Zen, however, what is beyond all affirmation and all negation—that is, Ultimate Reality—should not be "him" or "thou" but "self," or one's "true self."
>
> I am not concerned here with verbal expressions but with the reality behind the words. If Ultimate Reality, while being taken as nothingness or emptiness, should be called "him" or "thou," it is, from the Zen point of view, no longer ultimate.[4]

2

As early as 1960, an attempt was made by Keiji Nishitani, the well-known philosopher of the Kyoto school, to find a kind of compromise between Zen and Christian mysticism. To the ordinary Christian way of thinking, he says, the transcendence of God is represented as a separation: God is "up in the heavens," i.e., aloof from the world. Yet every Christian claims that, together with all the created beings, he has been created by God. In that sense, God is omnipresent. But he is not the world, or the life of the world: such a view would lead to pantheism. Rather, he is immanent as well as transcendent. Now, if the encounter with God as transcendent is to be seen as a "personal relationship with God through the awareness of sin," how is it possible to describe the relationship with God as immanent? The Christian doctrine can but recognize the privilege of Nothingness:

> That a thing is created *ex nihilo* means that this *nihil* is more immanent in that thing than the very being of that thing is "immanent" in the thing itself. (...) It is an immanence of absolute negation, for the being of the created is grounded upon a *nothingness* and seen fundamentally to be a nothingness. At the same time, it is an immanence of pure and absolute affirmation, for the nothingness of the created is the ground of its *being*. This is the omnipresence of God in all things that have their beings as a *creatio ex nihilo*. It follows that this omnipresence can be said to represent for man the dynamic *motif* of the transportation of absolute negation and absolute affirmation. To entrust the self to this *motif*, to let oneself be driven by it so as to die to the self and live in God, is what constitutes faith.[5]

As a result, whereas pantheism remains an "impersonal" relationship,

> when the omnipresence of God is encountered existentially as the absolute negation of the being of all creatures, and presents itself as an iron wall that blocks all movement forward or backward, it is not impersonal in that usual sense.[6]

We should call such a relationship an "impersonally personal" or "personally impersonal" one or, better yet, as expressed in Daisetz Teitaro Suzuki's "logic of *soku-hi* (=*sive/non*), where *soku* (*sive*) means the inseparability of two entities and *hi* the negativity, a "personal–*sive*–impersonal" as well as "impersonal–*sive*–personal" relationship. In Suzuki's terms, "A is not A and therefore A is A. A is A because it is non-A."[7] Nishitani's argument relies on the etymological explanation of "person" as deriving from *persona* – which means "mask" in Latin. When we speak of a mask, Nishitani says, we do not imply that there is an actor behind it; in a similar way, the following is true:

> Person is an appearance with nothing at all behind it to make an appearance. That is to say, "nothing at all" is what is behind person; complete nothingness, not one single thing, occupies the position behind person.
>
> While this complete nothingness is wholly other than person and means the absolute negation of person, it is not some "thing" or some entity different from person. It brings into being the thing called person and becomes one with it. Accordingly, it is inaccurate to say that complete nothingness "is" behind person.
>
> Nothingness is not a "thing" that *is* nothingness. Or again, to speak of nothingness as standing "behind" person does not imply a duality between nothingness and person. In describing this nothingness as "something" wholly other, we do not mean that there is actually some "thing" that is wholly other. Rather, true nothingness means that there is nothing that is nothingness, and this is *absolute nothingness*.[8]

The existential encounter with God's omnipresence means an actualization and realization of nothingness in the self, so that the self

> does not cease being a personal being. (...) When person-centered self-prehension is broken down and nothingness is really actualized in the self, personal existence also comes really and truly to actualization in the self. This is what is meant by absolute negation-*sive*-affirmation, and it is here that some 'thing' called personality is constituted in unison with absolute nothingness. Without a nothingness that is living and a conversion that is existential, this would make no sense.[9]

In sum, Nishitani's reasoning shows that "a good bit of the suspicion that the impersonal – OK, more generally, negation – is the dominant notion in Zen Buddhism" has to be "laid to rest."[10]

3

If Nishitani's argument about the reciprocal interpenetration of presence and absence in the self describes, not a theoretical compromise, but the result of an existential conversion, such a conversion is in itself an event which is to be grasped historically. Why? First, as a student of Heidegger, Nishitani knows that our understanding is always historically situated and conditioned. Second, his teacher Hajime Tanabe and his colleague Yoshinori Takeuchi, both involved not in Zen but in Shinran and the Buddhism of Pure Land, have insisted on the "opening up" of history from the existential and individual reality into world history, so that the religious meaning of history may be preserved. As John C. Maraldo has shown in a remarkable paper,[11] even if Nishitani does not share exactly their views, he seeks, like them, "a sense of history that realizes the absoluteness and incomparability of each moment."[12]

In other terms, history takes root in a transhistorical realm, the realm of the mutual interpenetration of every particular with other particulars, so that

> while A is A itself and B is B itself (A = A, B = B), yet at the same time, A and B penetrate each other. This is what we call "*jitafuni*: (self and others are not two). A and B are not fixed; they are *yuzumuge*, interpenetrating and reciprocal (...). This is, in formal logic, a contradiction. In "natural being," however, this is not a contradiction but two sides of the same coin.[13]

Man's emergence as man from this field of interpenetration without obstruction confirms the uniqueness of his destiny as man—a uniqueness he possesses in its entirety, even if simultaneously he shares it with all other beings:

> There is, so to speak, a circumference-less center, a center which is a center only, a center on the fields of emptiness. That is to say, on the field of *sunyata*, *the center is everywhere*. Each thing is its own selfness and shows the mode of being of the center of all things. Each and every thing becomes the center of all things and, in that sense, becomes an absolute center. This is the absolute uniqueness of things, their reality.
>
> Still, to treat each thing as an absolute center is not to imply an absolute dispersion. Quite to the contrary, as a totality of absolute centers, the All is one.(...) "All are One" can only really be conceived in terms of a gathering of things together, each of which is by itself the All, each of which is an absolute center.(...)
>
> "All are One" signifies the "world" as the unifying order or system of all that is.[14]

Thus to the extent that the self is "present in the home-ground of all other things," the self is not the self; but as soon as we begin to consider it differently, i.e., not as a "small, self-centered circle," but as being in unison with emptiness, the self becomes an absolute center. The circle is open, the circumference has disappeared, and yet everything is "in order," i.e., gathered together with all the other things into a reciprocal relationship (*egoteki kankei*, translated by Jan Van Bragt as "circum-insessional relationship," a concept drawn from the doctrine of the Trinity, which uses it to describe the highest reciprocity between the divine Persons in the Trinity; in fact, a word constructed by Nishitani from *e* = "*circum*, around," *go* = "one another, mutually" and *teki* = "back and forth," hence *e-go-teki* = "back and forth around one another").[15]

Now we reach the core of Nishitani's thesis about historicity: for him, the same *egoteki kankei* obtains *between the different dimensions and epochs of time*. In this sense, it opens the way toward a transhistorical understanding of history; and Nishitani's argument is not so far from the views of the Zen thinker Shin'ichi Hisamutsu, who considered in 1979 that the emergence of the true self "is not achieved in the movement of history, that is, through the historical dialectic," but "is accomplished at the root-source of history, which is prior to the birth of history:—and brings about the necessity of a "supra-historical history," or of an "history that transcends history."[16]

But let us listen to Keiji Nishitani:

> The roothold of the possibility of the world and of the existence of things, namely, the place where the world and the existence of things "take hold of their ground," can be said to lie in the home-ground of each man, underfoot and right at hand.
>
> In this way, the selfness of the self—insofar as the self is said to "be a self"—lies radically in *time*, or, rather, is bottomlessly in time. At the same time, on the field of *sunyata*—insofar as the being of the self is at bottom only being in unison with emptiness, insofar as the self is said "not to be a self"—the self is, at every moment of time, ecstatically outside of time. It was in this sense that we spoke above of the self of each man as at bottom preceding the world and things.[17]

Now, how to proceed from the "historical" self to the "transhistorical" "not-self," the vice-versa? Nishitani's answer is decisive, for it shows the relativity of the difference between derived time (or, in Heidegger's terms, the "ordinary conception of time") and primordial time (Heidegger's *Gleichursprüngzeit-lichkeit* or "equi-temporality"). First, Nishitani says, we are simultaneously *inside* and *outside* time:

> We are born in time and we die in time. "To be in time" means to be constantly within the cycle of birth-and-death. But we are not merely within time and within the cycle of birth-and-death. On our own home-ground, we are not simply drifting about in birth-and-death: we live and die birth-and-death. We do not simply live in time: we live time. From one moment in time to the next we are making time to be time, we are bringing time to the "fullness of time." That is the sense of what we referred to earlier as "being bottomlessly in time."
>
> But now, thus to be bottomlessly within time and within the cycle of birth-and-death means to stand ecstatically outside of time and outside of that cycle. It means to precede the world and things, to be their master. This, at bottom, is the sort of things we "are" in our home-ground, in our selfness. And when we become aware of that fact, namely, when we truly *are* in our own home-ground, we stand from one moment of time to the next *outside* of time, even as we rest from one moment to the next bottomlessly *inside* of time. Even as we stand radically, or rather bottomlessly (groundlessly and with nothing to rely on), inside the world, we stand at the same time outside of it. In this case, having nothing to rely on means absolute freedom.[18]

Second, the simultaneity of the inside and of the outside leads to the realization of a kind of "geology" of time, i.e., to the integration of the various possible time-stratas according to the *egoteki* principle which may very well interpenetrate without obstruction:

> On the field of emptiness, all time enters into each moment of time passing from done moment to the next. In this circuminsessional interpenetration of time, or in time itself that only comes about as such an interpenetration, namely, in the *absolute relativity* of time on the field of *sunyata*, the whole of time is phantom-like, and the whole of the being of things in time is no less phantom-like.
>
> (...) We might say, in other words, that because in the field of *sunyata* each time is bottomlessly in time, all times enter into each time. And only as something bottomless that all times can enter into, does each time actually emerge in its manifestation as this or that time, such as it is. This suchness and phantom-likeness must need be one. Therein, to be sure, lies the essence of time.[19]

Third, Nishitani shows that the logic of *soku-hi* or *sive-non* holds good in the case of the antinomy of simultaneity and linearity: Kierkegaard, he argues, spoke of a simultaneity occurring in the "moment"; in a similar manner,

> past and present can be simultaneous without "destroying" the temporal sequence of before and after. Without such a field of simultaneity not even culture, let alone religion, could come into being. We can encounter Sakyamuni and Jesus, Basho and Beethoven in the present. That religion and culture can arise within and be handed down historically through time points to the very essence of time.[20]

> But in Buddhism, time is circular, because all its time systems are simultaneous; and, as a continuum of individual "nows" wherein the systems are simultaneous, it is *rectilinear* as well. Time is at once circular and rectilinear.[21]

4

In the last section of the Part V of *Religion and Nothingness*, entitled *Sunyata and Time*, as well as in the Part VI (*Sunyata and History*), Nishitani tests his philosophy of self and selflessness by confronting it with the "concrete" history of the emergence and development of the historical consciousness.

His point of departure is the suggestion made by Arnold Toynbee in *An Historian's Approach to Religion*, that the opposition between liberalism and communism, since it concerns two movements which rely on the same Judeo-Christian (or "Western Judaic") religious tradition, will become less and less important in the future, once "Western Judaism" and "Buddhaic" thought will have come really face to face.

Toynbee's analysis of "Buddhaic" thought shows that it holds the movements of nature and cosmos to be cyclical, and in parallel the order which rules the human world to be impersonal. In sum, in a world where the individual is dissolved into the universal, self-centeredness tends to be ignored, but nothing new can occur.

On the contrary, "Western Judaism" as seen by Toynbee professes that the history of humanity is linear, because it reproduces on whatever scale there may be, the rhythms of the individual. Accordingly, history must depend upon the will of a personal being, God. Thus it is difficult, if not impossible, to avoid self-centeredness. The religion of the Prophets of Israel provides the best example of such a self-centeredness; being a chosen people, the Jews consider their selfishness as dictated by God's will.

Such a view is of course oversimplifying: Nishitani would never go bail for Toynbee's fancies. He criticizes Toynbee's interpretation of the conception of time in Mahāyāna Buddhism, because to assume only the circular character of time leads to a denial of any possibility of historical consciousness.[22] And in a similar way, "the claim that historical consciousness originated with the Jewish people contains serious problems."[23]

Nevertheless, Toynbee's thesis seems to Nishitani "to put its finger on the core of the matter. History is essentially bound up with the fact that the self, here described as self-centered, comes to act from within itself in a certain sense as a *personality*."[24]

The example of Christianity is convincing. Like Judaic thought, Christianity teaches the highest respect for the Divine Order. But since man has rebelled at the beginning against that very Order, i.e., against God's will, the awareness of freedom, together with the awareness of sin, both confirm the utmost importance of the self-centeredness and the possibility of occurrence of new events, i.e., the affinity of historical consciousness with linear time. The first coming of Christ, as an irrevocable historical event, "prepares" his second coming; similarly, the redemption and the last judgment are or will be irrevocable—simultaneously necessary and unforeseeable.

Now, self-centeredness appears as consolidating and securing its positions when we consider the next step in the development of historical consciousness, namely the European Enlightenment. According to Nishitani, Christianity and Enlightenment have in common their prejudice about the meaning of history; but whereas Christianity attributed such a meaning to God's will and defined it in eschatological terms, Enlightenment ascribes it to man's intellect and describes it as an historical progress.

Of course, modern historiography has given up the idea of progress and consequently the very conception of an historical meaning or teleology. But it has been left the burden of one-dimensional linearity of time by the Enlightenment, i.e., in fact, by Christianity. As such, it has inherited the self-centeredness of "Western Judaism," and can but develop it.

Nishitani's position is now clear: he intends to go beyond the opposition, described by the historian, between the Enlightenment which sees history "as a continuum of moments objectively equal in time, in which each moment may be subjectively heightened by the sum of lived experience, personal and historical," and millenarianism, which conceives the moment "as the sum of all time contained in one lived experience."[25]

5

In lieu of conclusion, we will set up here some remarks about the meaning of Nishitani's conception of self and historicity in an hermeneutical perspective.

1) For Nishitani, the standpoint of ***sunyata***, as developed by Zen Buddhism, is "the standpoint of radical deliverance from self-centeredness."[26] A "bottomlessness," it is "the standpoint of the Existence of non-ego":

> In the Existence of non-ego, non-ego does not mean simply that self is not ego. It has also to mean at the same time that non-ego is the self. It must reach self-awareness as something come from the self's absolute negation of itself. It is not the case that the self is merely not self (that is non-ego). It must be the case, rather, that the self is the self because it is not the self. Were it simply a matter of the self not being the self, the way would still be open to follow Nietzsche in taking the Will to Power as the true self, or the "selfness" of the self. (...) Or again, the real self might be sought in the union with some absolute being like God, or the One of Western mysticism (...) Yet in all of these, the standpoint of the true non-ego is still incapable of appearing in complete fashion. Only by going a step further does the standpoint of true non-ego appear in the reversal, "self is not self (self is non-ego), therefore it is self." This reversal is precisely that existential self-awareness wherein the self is *realized* (manifested-*sive*-apprehended) as an emergence into its nature from non-ego.[27]

The hermeneutical orientation of Nishitani's research appears immediately, if we notice that for him, in Jan Van Bragt's words, the question "comes down to this: the West has nowhere to go but in the direction of the Eastern (Buddhist) ideal; but it cannot do so, except from its own Western (Christian) premises."[28]

2) Nishitani is less interested by history than by historicity.[29] His problem concerns time as such or temporality, and he solves it by showing that we are situated both inside and outside time. Consequently, he holds that hermeneutics and historiography cannot be really separated. But the hermeneutics as he foresees it demands a redefinition of historiography itself, since the hermeneutical situation of contemporary historiography is far from clear, due to the Christian prejudices it harbors. Nishitani's hermeneutical approach, since it eschews allegiance to Western methodology, has also to be redefined under a *Buddhist* perspective.[30]

3) Heidegger is present everywhere in Nishitani's work even if he is not quoted frequently. A remarkable feature of Nishitani's developments consists in their concern with the lack of a hermeneutical self-interpretive stance in Heidegger's last writings. Marlene Zarader, for instance, has noticed that if the references to Greek thought abound in Heidegger, Christian thought is progressively abandoned, and Jewish thought entirely "silenced."[31] While Nishitani does not necessarily agree with Heidegger's positions, he appears to fill some of the most crucial gaps in Heidegger's self-reflection upon his own hermeneutical strategy. To begin with, he suggests for the first time the outlines of a dialogue between Heidegger and the East; but the dialogue with Christianity and "Western Judaism" in general, if it sorely lacks in Heidegger, exists—and frequently in Heideggerian terms—in *Religion and Nothingness*.

4) The commentators have noticed that Nishitani's aim is to preserve the religious aspect of history. Such an attitude obtains its object when Nishitani speaks of the necessity of considering the solemnity that certain special moments—when God created the world, when Adam sinned, when Christ was born and raised from the dead, when he will come for the second time—possess in Christianity the very same solemnity that each "individual moment of unending time" possesses in the *Bodhisattva* Path.[32] Perhaps Nishitani adds, "it is when the self experiences the *metanoia* to faith" that the solemnity of the other moments is "truly realized."[33]

An "edifying" hermeneutics—a meta-noetical hermeneutics—which would contribute to a real existential conversion, and not primarily to an augmentation of our knowledge, may be reconstructed from *Religion and Nothingness*. Shall we compare it to Richard Rorty's definition of hermeneutics as an "edifying" discipline?

NOTES

1. *The Eastern Buddhist*, II/2 (1969): 15-30. Reprinted in Frederick Franck's anthology of the Kyoto school, *The Buddha Eye*, New York, Crossroad, 1982, 62–74. We quote from this latter version.
2. Abe, 72 and 71.
3. Abe, 68.
4. Abe, 68–69.
5. Keiji Nishitani, *Religion and Nothingness* (transl. Jan Van Bragt), Berkeley, University of California Press, 1982, 40. (To be quoted here as RN).
6. *RN* 40.
7. Daisetz Teitaro Suzuki, quoted in Nishitani, *RN* 291, n.19.
8. *RN* 70.
9. *RN* 71.
10. Hans Waldenfels, *Absolute Nothingness, Foundations for a Buddhist-Christian Dialogue* (transl. J.W. Heisig), New York, Paulist Press, 1980, 142.
11. John C. Maraldo, "Hermeneutics and Historicity in the Study of Buddhism," *The Eastern Buddhist*, XIX/1 (1986), 17–43.
12. Maraldo, *op. cit.*, 39.
13. Keiji Nishitani, "On Modernization and Tradition in Japan," N. Kobayashi and Y. Kuyama, eds., *Modernization and Tradition in Japan*, Nishinomiya, International Institute for Japan Studies, 1969, 92. Quoted in Waldenfels, *op. cit.*., 103.
14. *RN*, 146–147.
15. Waldenfels, *op. cit.*, 105; cf. also 180, note 32.
16. Maraldo, *op. cit.*, 37.
17. *RN*, 159.
18. *RN*, 159–160.
19. *RN*, 161.

20. *RN*, *ibid*.
21. *RN*, 219.
22. *RN*, 204.
23. *RN*, 206.
24. *RN*, 203.
25. Leonard Marsak, *The Enlightenment*, New York, John Wiley & Sons, 1972, 7. Quoted in Maraldo, *op. cit*., 39, note 56.
26. *RN* 250.
27. *RN*, 251.
28. Jan Van Bragt, Introduction to *RN*, XXXVII.
29. Cf. his declaration to John C. Maraldo in Maraldo, *op. cit*., 40.
30. Cf. Maraldo's conclusion, *op. cit*., 41–43.
31. Cf. Marlene Zarader, *Heidegger et les paroles de l'origine*, Paris, Vrin, 1986, 278–282.
32. *RN*, 272.
33. *RN*, *ibid*.; cf. Hajime Tanabe, *Philosophy as Metanoetics* transl. Yoshinori Takeuchi with Valdo Viglielmo and James W. Heisig, Berkeley, University of California Press, 1986, *passim*.

17

NOTHINGNESS AS THE ULTIMATE

Daniel Charles

WHEN AT THE BEGINNING of the present century, the Japanese philosopher Nishida Kitarō attempted to develop a link between Western philosophy and modern Japanese thought, he decided to draw into the discussion "that which (or the one who) is addressed in Christianity as ultimate principle, namely God," with "that which in Buddhist tradition is addressed as *sunyata*," and may be "named in a terminology closer to the West (...) as 'absolute nothingness' (Jap., *zettai mu*)."[1] In order not so much to develop Nishida's point than to throw light on what is at stake in such a comparison, let us enumerate five considerations by another Japanese philosopher, Abe Masao, who explores the basic differences between Eastern and Western conceptions of nothingness.

1. From the Buddhist perspective, if "ultimate Reality, wondrous being, is to be disclosed," the "existential realization of absolute *Mu*" (or "true *sunyata*") is requested; with only relative *mu*, "there is no awakening to ultimate Reality."

2. The realization of absolute nothingness is not "a gate through which one reaches the hall of ultimate Reality," but "it in itself is the hall of ultimate Reality, because absolute *Mu* or true *sunyata* is existentially realized as such through overcoming *Mu* or *sunyata* as a third category standing beyond relative *u* (being) and *mu* (non-being), and through returning to and affirming relative *u* and *mu* as they are."

3. The Buddhist idea of wondrous being cannot be equated with the Western idea of "Being," since this latter is "neither non-dualistic (unlike absolute Nothingness) nor realized through the realization of Emptiness," but "rather gains its ultimate status by virtue of its being ontologically prior to non-being."

4. The "difference between Western intellectual traditions and Buddhism in their respective understanding of 'Being' as the ultimate reality depends on whether or not the realization of absolute *Mu* is essential for its disclosure and whether or not relative *mu* (non-being) is understood as completely equal and reciprocal to relative *u* (being)."

5. When being is taken as ontologically prior to nonbeing, negativity "is no more than something to be overcome by positivity." When on the contrary "positivity (or *u*) and negativity (or *mu*) are equal and reciprocal, it is the antinomic and contradictory tension between positivity and negativity that is to be overcome." True liberation does not consist of giving to being the ontological priority over nonbeing, but in "emptying" Emptiness "as the final step." The "dynamism of 'Emptiness' (...) is simultaneously Fullness." Life has no priority over death: the oneness of life and death, as antinomic and self-contradictory, may be broken through by the "Great Death" which negates life-and-death and "is beyond a realization of death as distinguished from life." *Nirvana* or liberation does not consist in an overcoming of death by means of the power of life but in an awakening to freedom here and now.[2]

Thus, according to Abe's view, "the ultimate which is beyond the opposition between positive and negative is realized in the East in terms of negativity, and in the West in terms of positivity." But one should not overlook the historical instances in which the Western tradition has seen that ultimate as negative or nothingness. For example, Christian mysticism and negative theology, as forerunners of Nietzsche and Heidegger, "unorthodox" as they are since they represent merely "a strand within Christianity," offer something "strikingly similar to the Buddhist understanding of Emptiness."[3] In Christian mysticism, "which is based on experience of God's uniting directly with the soul, God is not a transcendental, personal being over against the soul, called 'Thou,' but the Godhead from which the personal God emerges. As Pseudo-Dionysius the Areopagite wrote in his *Mystical Theology*, the Godhead is undefinable, unnameable, and unknowable, beyond dark and light, true and untrue, affirmation and negation. Only the *via negativa* provides a way to reach the ineffable God."[4]

However, in another text of the same period, the tune is not the same. "Pseudo-Dionysius," Abe Masao argues, "calls that which is beyond all affirmation and all negation by the term 'Him,' and other Christian mystics call God 'Thou.' In Zen, however, what is beyond all affirmation and negation – that is, ultimate Reality – should not be 'Him' or 'Thou' but 'Self' or one's 'True Self.' (...) If ultimate Reality, while being taken as Nothingness or Emptiness, should be called 'Him' or 'Thou' it is (...) no longer ultimate."[5]

Nothingness and Negative (Mystical) Theology

According to John D. Jones, who is the author of the most recent (and audacious) translation of the Areopagitic writings, the majority of translations and commentaries on these writings have been elaborated according to a traditional framework which is not congruent with Pseudo-Dionysius' *non-metaphysical* way of arguing, or at least "rests on a metaphysics which is significantly different from Pseudo-Dionysius,' and which has been the source of systematic mistranslation and misinterpretation of his writings."[6]

Let us recall first the main features of Pseudo-Dionysius' thesis. For him, the divinity of all, is the cause of all that is, and apart from all that is, there is nothing. But since this "nothing" is truly nothing, i.e., "real" nothingness, we cannot even say that *there is* nothing. Jones suggests that the text should be understood as follows: "apart from all that is: nothing." The major emanation is the use of the colon, which yields a reading quite different from the traditional. Hence the basic formula: "the divinity is all that is. Apart from all that is: nothing. (The) divinity: nothing."

The first affirmation "the divinity is all that is," or "all as cause of all" – is unfolded by *affirmative* theology, which, in order to celebrate the divinity as cause of all that is, "embraces Trinitarian theology (the theology of Father, Son and Spirit), metaphysics and symbolic theology (the interpretation of sensible symbols as they apply to what is divine)." As differentiating itself in the totality of beings, the divinity "causes" them, i.e., makes them exist "as both the same as, and different from," itself; and as understood in reference to beings, the divinity is in itself both the same and different from beings. Thus, since this affirmative theology affirms not only the sameness of the divinity and beings, but their difference as well, it may be called, in so far as it deals with that difference, *negative* theology – that is, negative *within affirmative* theology.

The task of this negative theology is to "express the preeminence and simplicity of the divine cause."[7] The divine cause brings all beings into being: beings proceed from God (procession) and they return to and subsist in Him (reversion, *mone*), allowing the divinity itself to abide preeminently beyond multiplicity. In terms of affirmative theology, the divinity is interpreted to be *the* being of beings, i.e., "the first, highest and most real being (*ens realissimum*) existing in itself (*per se*) apart from other beings." In terms of negative theology, the divinity is seen as not being a being, but as being beyond being, beyond unity, and beyond multiplicity as well: it is not an *ipsum esse per se subsistens* but the being of beings, which "lets be a hierarchically ordered totality of beings."[8]

Now Pseudo-Dionysius affirms that it is possible to unite oneself with the divinity: beyond affirmative theology, and beyond the negative-within-affirmative theology, it is possible to "stand out of the light of beings, abandon all knowledge of beings, and plunge into a darkness of unknowing." Such an unknowing is the requisite for an immediate experiencing of divinity as pure nothingness. It has to be cautiously distinguished from "the function of negative theology within affirmative theology and metaphysics."[9]

> Within metaphysics, negative theology expresses divine causal preeminence by denying that it is anything like what is. Nevertheless, although this serves to deny that the divinity is any intelligible or sensible being, the divinity is still rendered intelligible within this denial, for the denial expresses the divinity in reference to beings as the ultimate cause and source of beings. (...) However, negative (mystical) theology requires the denial of all reference to beings and of every attempt at making the divinity intelligible to us. Thus it requires that we deny affirmative theology and the divine cause (and Trinity). Culminating in ecstatic unity with the divinity, negative (mystical) theology requires that one deny the sameness and difference which prevail between beings and the divinity. In this radical denial, affirmative theology, and, more particularly, metaphysics are not declared to be false. For unlike affirmative theology, which offers an explanation of and discourse about what is, negative (mystical) theology requires the abandonment and indifference towards every explanation and discourse. In the cessation of all discourse, this denial makes possible unity with nothing: (the) non-same and non-other.[10]

Only negative (mystical) theology is able to lead us toward the "nothing" which the divinity "is," once totally emptied of itself. Only negative (mystical) theology ultimately denies divine causality and preeminence, i.e., metaphysics, for the benefit of a "knowledge (as divine unknowing): nothing."[11] Such a "no-thing" is not to be understood "simply as no-thing or no-being, so that we understand nothing as be-ing itself (*ipsum esse*), or as simply and unlimitedly being. Rather, nothing: beyond being and hence, beyond cause."[12] As Pseudo-Dionysius himself says in incandescent words, "no unity or trinity or numbers, or oneness, or anything among beings, or anything known among being, brings down the hidden-ness—beyond all and beyond logos and intellect—of the beyond divinity beyond be-ing beyond be-ingly beyond all."[13] The divinity cannot receive any of the divine names; then it ceases to differentiate itself from the various beings. One has to "abandon all sensation and all intellectual activities, all that is sensed and intelligible, and all non-beings and all beings."[14] One must deny all eminence and support, e.g., all metaphysical interpretation of why beings are. One becomes free to enter the realm of what Emilie Zum Brunn, in referring to Suzuki Daisetz Teitaro's commentaries on Meister Eckhart, calls "translinguistic reality."[15] As Jones says, "negative (mystical) theology is not one logos among many; negative (mystical) theology culminates in the denial of all logos. Negative (mystical) theology does not take up a standpoint which is opposed to the standpoint of metaphysics; negative (mystical) theology demands the denial of every standpoint."[16]

Nothingness and Eschatology

If we attempt to summarize Jones' teachings about Pseudo-Dionysius, we can but confirm, as it seems, Abe Masao's appreciation about nothingness in Christian mysticism: the West does not yield precedence to the East in this matter, and the Areopagitic writings counterbalance easily the five considerations of Abe Masao about Buddhist emptiness. We may profitably think of Pseudo-Dionysius as the "missing link" between Plotinus and Eckhart.[17] But we are still faced with Abe Masao's observation about the lack of radical justification of "Him" or "Thou." In front of the designation ultimate reality, Christian mystical thought seems to shrink from the true encounter with nothingness and rests reassured when the darkness of unknowability melts away to reveal, in full light, the hidden face of God as a human being or person.

Yet the solution to this remark has been given in the midst of the Kyoto school of philosophers itself, by Nishitani Keiji. When we meet a God of "absolute negativity" which "presents itself as an iron wall that prevents us from all further movement, forwards or backwards, it is not impersonal in the usual sense of the word." Between "him" and "us," Nishitani argues, there exists an "im-*personally* personal relationship," or a "*personally* impersonal relationship."[18] We have to remember that "person" comes from *persona* (mask), and that there is nothing behind a person; "that is, behind it lies absolute nothingness. While this absolute nothingness is wholly other to his person and means an absolute negation of the person, it is not some*thing* different from the person. Absolute nothingness is that which, becoming one with that 'being' called person, brings into being that person. (...) Nothingness is not a thing which *is* nothingness... Rather, there not being even any nothingness is true nothingness, absolute nothingness."[19]

Nishitani's thesis has been confirmed by Abe himself, who recognized as important the fact that St. Paul as well as Buddhism have considered *death* as "an essential element for true religion."[20] In this sense, the death of Jesus unites him with nothingness, and his resurrection appears as a procession or emergence from nothingness. Moreover, when we define ourselves as beings-toward-death, we underline our dying and awakening at every moment. Thus, even if "Christian spirituality does not lead to *nirvana* but to a state in which, and in union with God, the human person is re-established with all his faculties,"[21] there is no less profoundness in Christian "personal" mysticism than in the Oriental quest of impersonality.

It is worth noting that R. Schurmann insists as well that Plotinus, too, claimed a "very personal and dated experience of the One," and quotes Plotinus' own description of the "union with the divine" as leading toward an "awakening to oneself" and as "above the other intelligible beings."[22] According to Porphyry, Plotinus experienced such an "awakening" four times in his life.[23] However, when Plotinus speaks of these experiences, he insists on the necessity of getting rid of his own body, and in so doing he opens the way to an "intellectualist" (or nominalist) interpretation of the union with God. But another interpretation of this is possible, i.e., in a realist sense—one for which the body, far from being separated from the soul, is to be divinized as well as the soul itself. The absence of a Christology in form seems to have given its ambivalent character to the *Corpus Areopagiticum* and to have allotted "both nominalists and realists to make use of it";[24] for instance when Barlaam tried to reject any participation of the body in prayer and opposed the hesychast tradition, he quoted Dionysius as his authority for adopting nominalism, i.e., a dualistic anthropology of body and soul.

Gregory Palamas answered that "to make the mind 'go out,' not only from fleshly thoughts, but out of the body itself, with the aim of contemplating intelligible visions—that is the greatest of the Hellenic errors."[25] In this sense, it is clear that Gregory Palamas achieves "the fundamental Christian correction of the dualism of much Greek thought, especially Platonism."[26] But he does not hesitate to "follow the great Dionysius" as well as the Platonists Evagrius and Gregory of Nyssa in building a "synthetic" anthropology which will overcome Barlaam's dualism. For instance, he insists on the importance of calling the union with God of the hesychasts, "spiritual sensation," "a phrase appropriate to, and somehow more expressive of, that mystical and ineffable contemplation. For at such a time man truly sees neither by the intellect nor by the body but by the Spirit, and he knows that he sees supernaturally a light which surpasses light. But at that moment he does not know by what organ he sees this light, nor can he search out its nature, for the Spirit through whom he sees is untraceable."[27] Such ecstasy, since it entails a perception through the Holy Spirit, "implies a God-inspired love in man," and *the experience of a corresponding ecstasy in God himself.*[28] It is only "through the descending ecstasy of God and the transcendent ecstasy of man" that "their mystical meeting and union is achieved."[29] Man's *theosis* or deification involves God's humanization.

If this is so, then Christology becomes central and decisive. In Palamas' perspective, "the deification of human nature was accomplished for the first time in the person of Christ," and in a reciprocal manner "Christ's uncreated life and energy become the property of the man who is united with Him, and in whose person the Christ Himself lives and operates."[30] The historical dimension becomes essential;[31] "for Dionysius' closed and 'anagogic' universe," Palamas "substitutes a theology of history."[32] According to this theology, Christ's death appears as a turning point: it is the death of the "only man who was not conceived in iniquity, nor born in sin,"[33] and who "alone could inaugurate a new race of humanity, into which man enters by the new birth of baptism."[34] And it is also the death of God, "which finds expression in the outcry of abandonment by God from Jesus on the cross: 'My God, my God, why have you deserted me?' (Mk. 15, 34). The paradox of this outcry consists in that the very absent God who is addressed in these words himself becomes present, so that the distance and proximity of God are in some strange way mutually conditioning."[35]

To sum up: Since the deification of man or *theosis*, i.e., the Western version of the encounter with absolute nothingness, is made possible by the coincidence of the self-emptying of God and of the self-emptying of man in Jesus, "what the Christian seeks in spiritual life is not a spatial or material 'beyond,' but a *future*, the Kingdom of God, already present in the sacramental mystery. (...) The Christ whom the hesychast seeks and finds within himself is thus the king of the future, and the divine light which he sees is the 'light of the time to come'; all Christian spirituality can have no other foundation but this eschatological reality, anticipated in the sacraments."[36] Therefore we live *already* in the realm of "realized eschatology,"[37] where, as Wolfhart Pannenberg says, "the differences of present, past and future are overcome in the *eschaton*."[38]

NOTES

1. Hans Waldenfels, *Absolute Nothingness, Foundations for a Buddhist-Christian Dialogue*. tr. J.W. Heisig (New York, Paulist Press, 1980), 39.
2. Masao Abe, *Zen and Western Thought*. ed. William R. La Fleur (London: Macmillan, 1985), 130–131.
3. Masao Abe, *op. cit.*, 134.
4. Masao Abe, *op. cit.*, 133.
5. Masao, Abe, "God, Emptiness and the True Self," *The Eastern Buddhist*. 11/2, 1969, 22; quoted by H. Waldenfels, *op. cit.*, 141.
6. John D. Jones. *Pseudo-Dionysius Areopagite, The Divine Names and Mystical Theology*. Introduction (Milwaukee, Wisconsin: Marquette University Press, 1980), 2.
7. J.D. Jones, *op. cit.*, 3.
8. J.D. Jones, *op. cit.*, 4.
9. J.D. Jones, *op. cit.*, 4-5.
10. J.D. Jones, *op. cit.*, 5.
11. J.D. Jones, *op. cit.*, 26.
12. J.D. Jones, *op. cit.*, 91.
13. Pseudo-Dionysius Areopagite, *The Divine Names*. XIII, 3 (980 D–981 A); quoted in J.D. Jones, *op. cit.*, *ibid.*
14. Pseudo-Dionysius Areopagite, *Mystical Theology*. I, 1 (997 – 999 A); quoted in J.D. Jones, *op. cit.*, 96.
15. Emilie Zum Brunn, "L'ontologie de Maitre Eckhart et la philosophie comparee," *Journal of the Faculty of Letters*, The University of Tokyo (Aesthetics), Vol. 4 (1979), 41; reed. In Emilie Zum Brunn and Alain de Libera, *Maitre Eckhart, Metaphysique du Verbe et Theologie Negative* Paris: Beauchesne, 1984), 233.
16. J.D. Jones, *op. cit.*, pp. 101–102.
17. Cf. R. Schurmann: *op. cit.*, p. 347, note 59.
18. Keiji Nishitani, quoted in H. Waldenfels, *op. cit.*, 142.
19. Keiji Nishitani, quoted in H. Waldenfels, *op. cit.*, 81.
20. Masao Abe, *Zen and Western Thought*. *op. cit.*, 236.
21. John Meyendorff, *A Study of Gregory Palamas*. tr. G. Lawrence (London: The Faith Press, 1974), 169.
22. Plotinus, *Enneads*. IV, 8, 1; quoted in R. Schurmann, *op. cit.*, 349.
23. Porphyry, *Life of Plotinus*, 23; quoted in R. Schurmann, *op. cit.*, *ibid.*
24. J. Meyendorff, *op. cit.*, 209.
25. Gregory Palamas, *The Triads*, I, ii, 4, tr. J. Meyendorff (London: S.P.C.K., 1983), 44.
26. J. Meyendorff, In Gregory Palamas, *The Triads*. *op. cit.*, 126, note 36.
27. Gregory Palamas, *The Triads*. I, iii, 21, *op. cit.*, 37–38.
28. Georgios I. Mantzaridis, *The Deification of Man*. tr. Liadain Sherrard (Crestwood, New York: St. Vladimir's Seminary Press, 1984), 103.
29. *Ibid.*
30. G.I. Mantzaridis, *op. cit.*, 128.
31. Cf. J. Meyendorff, *A Study of Gregory Palamas*. *op. cit.*, 186.
32. J. Meyendorff, *op. cit.*, 189.
33. Gregory Palamas, *Hom. 16*. 192 C, quoted in J. Meyendorff, *op. cit.*, 126.
34. J. Meyendorff, *op. cit.*, 126.
35. H. Waldenfels, *op. cit.*, 158–159.

36 J. Meyendorff, *op. cit.*, 193.
37 J. Meyendorff, *op. cit.* p. 194; cf. also G.I. Mantzaridis, *op. cit.*, 123.
38 Wolfhart Pannenberg, *Theology and the Kingdom of God* (Philadelphia: The Westminster Press, 1969), 65.

18

RALPH WALDO EMERSON'S ZEN UNIVERSALISM

Sōiku Shigematsu

Introduction

MENTAL ENERGY OFTEN TENDS in two opposite directions: sometimes as a centripetal force, sometimes as a centrifugal. When it works centripetally, our consciousness is directed inward and goes deeper and deeper into our own self until it finally touches the very bottom of existence. This is a typical mode of self-inquiry, which takes us back to the simplest but most essential questions: 'Who am I?' or 'What am I?' It also involves the problems: 'What is self?' and 'Who acknowledges whom?' Confronted with such ultimate questions, intellectual analysis is without exception thoroughly incompetent, because the questions belong to the boundary of intuition – to religion.

When, on the other hand, our consciousness turns outward and works centrifugally, our attention extends to things other than ourselves, that is, to the whole world outside ourselves. It is then focused on surrounding nature: first our own body, then others such as our wives, children, and friends, and then objects such as this pebble, that tree, this river, that mountain, the great earth, that star far in the sky, and finally the entire universe. Thus, the outward movement of consciousness brings us to another simple, and essential, question: 'What is the universe?'

It is true that this kind of intellectual activity has created the magnificent world of human civilization, which is the product of science. Still, when Emerson says that "science must be studied humanly," he suggests that our attitude in investigating scientific matters should not be only intellectual but also egoless.[1] That is, we must not only treat things objectively, seeing each object of the intellect dualistically with the seer and the seen divided, but also religiously, seeing them monastically with the seer and the seen undivided, thereby viewing them from inside where the objects are related to what is at the very foundation of human existence. If we follow Emerson's suggestion and study science "humanly," the question 'What is the universe?' may be paraphrased as 'What is the relationship between the universe and ourselves?'

Emerson knew that when the universe is studied with such religious eyes, centrifugal attention goes farther and farther, making a huge circle, and finally returning to its starting point. Or, to use his favorite metaphor, the two arcs stretch themselves in opposing directions, eventually meeting each other to form a complete circle. Undoubtedly, it is true that centrifugal attention is also one of the best ways to forget the human ego that usually veils the truth. As Emerson often suggested, the best way to dispel egotism is to look up far into the sky. The major problem here lies in whether one is a believer or not. Believers will believe this, but unbelievers will never do so. At one time, Emerson had to sigh with despair: "Men seem to be constitutionally believers and unbelievers. There is no bridge that can cross from a mind in one state to a mind in the other."[2]

Emerson was quite sure that the two contrasting mental movements, centripetal and centrifugal, would come finally to one question 'Who and what am I?' When he was 25 years old, he wrote in his *Journals*:

> The great business of life is to learn ourselves. We may read history but this is what we learn there or we learn nothing. We may explore the sciences but they are naught, if they do not end in being aids to this. We may engage in professions, we may manage affairs, make fortunes, build houses, navigate ships, enact laws, till the earth, but these are but various ways of learning the same lesson. He that explores the principles of architecture and detects the beauty of the proportion of a column, what doth he but ascertain one of the laws of his own mind?[3]

Later he repeatedly stresses this truth, saying that "wherever we go, whatever we do, self is the sole subject we study and learn."[4] This principle, which he believed until his death, is also the basic attitude traditionally emphasized in the Zen monastery. Eihei Dōgen (1200–1253), founder of Japanese Soto Zen, says, for example, that "to learn the Buddhist Way is to learn oneself."[5] Also, Dōkyo Etan (1642–1721), Japanese Rinzai master, insists that "the greatest thing to be concerned with is our mind right now today."[6]

Self Knowledge

How, then, can we learn ourselves? "Self-negation" is recorded by Emerson as the first step in his pilgrimage of self-inquiry. After reading the biographies of religious enthusiasts such as Swedenborg, Guyon, Fox, Luther, and Boehme, Emerson was struck with the similarity between them and wrote in his diary:

> Each owes all to the discovery that God must be sought within, not without. This is the discovery of Jesus. Each perceives the worthlessness of all instruction, and the infinity of wisdom that issues from meditation. Each perceives the nullity of all conditions but one, innocence; and the absolute submission which attends it.[7]

These geniuses revealed the two basic elements of religion. The first is that "God must be sought within." As Lin-chi I-hsuan (?–867), a famous Chinese Zen master, always admonished his students, "Don't seek truth outside yourself?"[8] The second is the importance of "innocence" and "absolute submission," within. The first thing we must do to achieve this is to dispel our daily consciousness which is always at the mercy of egotism. This involves emptying oneself as if one were to pour out a bowl filled with old dirty water. One must then wait in "innocence" and "absolute submission" until one comes to touch one's own original identity.

In *Nature*, his first published book (1836), Emerson tried to describe this process of religious metamorphosis. In his youth, he had two soul-stirring experiences, which exerted a great influence on his later life. One of them was the so-called "transparent eyeball" experience. The entry in his *Journals* goes:

> As I walked in the woods I felt what I often feel, that nothing can befall me in life, no calamity, no disgrace, (leaving me my eyes) to which Nature will not offer a sweet consolation. Standing on the bare ground with my head bathed by the blithe air, and uplifted into the infinite space, I become happy in my universal relations.[9]

This passage was slightly modified and crystallized into the famous (for some people "notorious") "transparent eyeball" experience recorded in *Nature*.

> Standing on the bare ground,—my head bathed by the blithe air and uplifted into infinite space,—all mean egotism vanishes. I become a transparent eyeball; I am nothing; I see all; the currents of the Universal Being circulate through me; I am part or parcel of God.[10]

This invaluable experience not only constitutes the essence of *Nature*, it also expresses the whole of Emerson's philosophy. When the author looks up into infinite space, standing alone in the midst of nature, away from the crowd, his "mean egotism" utterly disappears and his whole existence turns into "a transparent eyeball." At that moment, he exclaims: "I am nothing; I see all." Who is it who cried out?

Who is this I? What is nothing? What is all? Undoubtedly, here is the key to understanding Emerson's "Zen Universalism."

There have been various responses to *Nature*. Soon after its publication, there was sharp disagreement among his contemporary readers. Some critics valued it as "a gem throughout" and an anonymous reviewer called it "a prose poem." But other critics attacked it on doctrinal grounds while some suggested neglecting it as "mere moonshine."[11] Here is a recent and typical example of unfavorable criticism of the "notorious eyeball experience." The critic, Jonathan Bishop, first says that one of the "bad" descriptions found in Emerson's *Nature* "is the 'transparent eyeball' sentence, perhaps the best-known sentence among readers who wish to make fun of him."[12] Then he introduces a caricature drawn by Emerson's contemporary.

> Christopher Cranch unerringly picked this image out to caricature; his drawing...shows the one concrete picture these words irresistibly muster up, a preacherly eyeball staring into the heavens.... But the speaker, the I, is innocently absurd at best.[13]

Unfortunately, however, the author of this caricature has missed the point. The "transparent eyeball" cannot be given an adequate image precisely because it is transparent. It is formless and invisible. It has neither color, nor size, nor weight. It has no discernible features at all—because it is transparent. A Zen master might have drawn a circle to express Emerson's point. But, strictly speaking, there is some responsibility on Emerson's side for this kind of misunderstanding.

Emerson insists, as Zen thinkers do, that "a foolish consistency is the hobgoblin of little minds," and that "to be great is to be misunderstood."[14] What Emerson says is true enough; but it also involves a confession of his own lack of logical ability which he referred to in the *Journals* of his younger days.[15] On the other hand, it may be true that, had he known the methodology and philosophy of Zen practice, he could have constructed and expressed his thought much more consistently.

Zen Universalism

Traditionally, Zen has been viewed from three angles of vision: Universalism (tai), Individualism (so), and Vitalism (yu).[16] The following passage by Dōgen, which follows right after the line already quoted, ("To learn the Buddhist Way is to learn oneself") perfectly summarizes the way of Zen:

> To learn oneself is to forget oneself. To forget oneself is to perceive oneself confirmed by the All. Confirmation by the All is to return the body, and mind of the self and the others to original freedom.[17]

The first sentence explains what I call Zen Universalism; the second, Zen Individualism, the third, Zen Vitalism.

"To forget oneself" is the first step into Zen Universalism. Most of us live every day, believing that the I or self of which each of us is conscious, this self we regard as our own identity is unfortunately no other than the ego: the illusory self that derives from our fundamental ignorance of the true nature of existence. This ego is self-centered and completely separate from all the other existences that surround it. To live according to this egocentric I is to always be at the mercy of the waves of illusion. Unless we live at a deeper level than this our:

> Life's but a walking shadow, a poor player
> That struts and frets his hour upon the stage
> And then is heard no more; it is a tale
> Told by an idiot, full of sound and fury,
> Signifying nothing.[18]

"To forget oneself," therefore, is the first essential step toward self-realization. When human egotism vanishes through the exercise of self-negation (in practice, by remaining uninvolved in the activity of the ego), one becomes "nothing." Deep within, at the bottom of existence, one suddenly "perceives oneself confirmed." This often occurs when some impulse from outside, e.g., a click of a stone hitting a bamboo stalk, shakes one's consciousness. Right then and there, enlightened eyes see a huge "transparent eyeball," which is formless, invisible, and as large as the universe.

To grasp such a world of Zen Universalism, each Zen student is expected to undergo the kōan practice of Hosshin (Dharma Body), beginning, for example, with the Mu (Nothing) kōan or the Sekishu no Onjo (The sound of the One Hand) kōan. These kōan are very elaborately and subtly devised to give each student a chance to catch a glimpse of satori.

Someone who may be in a position to easily understand Zen Universalism is an astronaut. Antoine De Saint-Exupery, the pilot and author of *The Little Prince*, is a good example because he knew what it is to look down on human beings from a perspective high above the earth. How often have I admired his penetrating insight into Zen Universalism as I have re-read his work! In his eyes, every distinction disappears. Looked at from afar and above, every difference vanishes at once. Or, as Emerson says:

> Every violation, every suicide, every miracle, every willfulness however large it may show near us, melts quickly into the All, and at a distance is not seen. The outline is as smooth as the curve of the moon.[19]

To see things "at a distance" is to escape the superficial ego, which creates every mean distinction—every yes or no, mine or yours, this or that. It is to see with a "transparent eyeball," completely apart from human rootless illusion—that is, it is to see the "All" of the universe just as it is.

Suppose there is a round jewel at the bottom of a stream. When there is no breeze, we can see it clearly through the current. But when the wind ripples its surface, it is not easy to see the gem through the disturbed water. The very moment the wind blows, the gem seemingly disfigures itself, although it in fact remains round as ever. To one person it may appear square; to another, oval or even triangular. To see a thing exactly as it is, we must dispel the wind of egotism and make the rippled surface of the water, our blurred eyes, smooth, clear, and calm. It is human egotism that provokes distorted perception and biased vision. When it is not present, our existence returns to its original Mu or Nothing, which forms the basis of each and every thing.

Huan-po Hsi-yen (?-857?), a Chinese Zen master, calls this egoless state "Mind."

> This Mind, from the beginningless beginning, is unborn and indestructible, not green or yellow, without form or appearance. It belongs neither to the categories of existence nor non-existence and cannot be defined as new or old. It is neither long or short, big or small, for it transcends all measurement, expression, survey, and approach.[20]

Lin-chi, his disciple, puts it in another way:

> Over a mass of reddish flesh there sits a true man who has no title; he is all the time coming in and out of your sense-organs. If you have not yet confirmed this fact. Look! Look![21]

The "true man who has no title" is invisible to the eye because he is no other than the subjectivity of Nothing, the identity of Mu, or perfect non-individuality and non-discrimination.

A Zen saying that expresses this is that: "From the origins nothing exists."[22] It is a fundamental belief of all Buddhists that all the forms of existence are conditional; they come and go, appear, and disappear. Phenomenal things are thus impermanent and have no substance. Everything exists only in interdependence. Behind, no, right in the midst of these phenomena, the Nothing, subjectivity of the man without any title, prevails throughout the universe. It is this Nothing that makes all existences perfectly equal. Nothing, however, is not a mere void. The penetrating eye undoubtedly can see the following truth.

In Nothing
everything is contained:
limitless –
Flowers,
moon,
pavilions....[23]

This Nothing, containing everything limitlessly, is in a state of perfect stillness just before everything appears. It is, as it were, a top spinning at full speed, which seems as if motionless. From here, the world of Zen Individualism unfolds itself. Dōgen is truly right when he says: "To forget oneself is to perceive oneself confirmed by the All."

Emerson's Zen Universalism

Now we have surely come a step closer to understanding Emerson's "transparent eyeball" experience.

> In Man the perpetual progress is from the Individual to the Universal, from that which is human, to that which is divine, "Self dies, and dies perpetually." The circumstances, the persons, the body, the world, the memory are forever perishing as the bark peels off the expanding tree.[24]

This is where Emerson's Zen Universalism starts. Exactly as Zen students do, he moves along the way of ego-negation in an effort to empty himself. His *Journals* abound with passages that illustrate this effort.

> In listening more intently to our own reason, we are not becoming in the ordinary sense more selfish, but are departing more from what is all, and falling back on truth itself and God.[25]

> A trust in yourself is the height not of pride but of piety, an unwillingness to learn of any but God himself. It will come only to one who feels that he is nothing.[26]

> Touch the deep heart and all these listless stingy beefeating bystanders will see the dignity of a sentiment, will say This is good and all I have I will give for that. Excite the soul, and the weather and the town and your condition in the world all disappear, the world itself loses its solidarity, nothing remains but the soul and the Divine Presence in which it lives.[27]

> Proud may be the bard among his fellow men, but when he sits waiting his inspiration he is a child, humble, reverent, watching for the thoughts as they flow to him from their unknown source. The moment of inspiration I am its reverent slave.[28]

And the following description originated in an actual experience:

> In the instant you leave far behind all human relations, wife, mother, and child, and live only with the savages—water, air, light, carbon, lime, and granite.... I become a moist cold element... I have died out of the human world and come to feel a strange cold, aqueous, terraqueous, aerial, ethereal sympathy and existence.[29]

Each of the above quotations describes what I call Emerson's "Zen Universalism." The last one is, as it were, another "transparent eyeball" experience. Again, his I, the ego, dies out of this human world. Or in Emerson's words: "Exactly proportionate is the merit of the self-denial and the power it confers."[30] Herein lies the key that resolves the seeming paradox between Zen Universalism and Individualism. "I am no-thing, I see all," says Emerson. "To forget oneself is to perceive oneself confirmed by the All." says Dōgen. Zen experience teaches that when one is nothing one is all.

As Shākyamuni sat in samādhi under the Bodhi tree, there was no heaven, no earth, no self, nothing at all. He was no other than the Nothing. Passersby with an eye may have felt a huge transparent body sitting where Shākyamuni sat. Night deepened. Then at last, he noticed the morning star in the sky. The moment its light entered his eyes, it awakened his own sense of sight. At that instant, his consciousness came to life with prajñā intuition. This is exactly the moment of satori experience.

Here, total self-negation, in the actual process of experience is directed toward perfect self-affirmation. To Shākyamuni's eyes, everything was shining and looked completely new and beautiful. Shākyamuni, now the 'Buddha' (Awakened One), must have exclaimed: "That morning star is myself! I'm shining!" A Zen saying goes:

Heaven, earth, and I
    the same root.
Everything and I:
    one thing.[31]

This is true because, as Emerson observed, "Nature, God, has put no being alone, but has established relations among them all."[32] Or, as another Zen saying puts it:

Self and other
    are not two:
Illusory
    you and I.[33]

Everything is myself. Indeed in Zen experience, "nothing" is exactly "everything."

The following passage describes another important experience of Emerson's that had a great influence on the formation of his thought, together with the "transparent eyeball" experience. In 1833, he journeyed to Europe where he visited the Cabinet of Natural History in the Garden of Plants. His entry runs:

> Not a form so grotesque, so savage, nor so beautiful but is an expression of some property inherent in man the observer—an occult relation between the very scorpions and man. I feel the centipede in me—cayman, carp, eagle, and fox. I am moved by strange sympathies.[34]

"I feel the centipede in me—cayman, carp, eagle, and fox," says Emerson, just as the Buddha might have uttered: "That morning star is myself! I'm shining." Originally, self and every other self are one. From this experience Emerson develops his theory of "correspondence," which cannot be considered here.

Returning to his "transparent eyeball" experience: What is the landscape seen with "a transparent eyeball?"

> Warm, pleasant, misty weather which the great mountain amphitheater seemed to drink in with gladness. A crow's voice filled all the miles of air with sound. A bird's voice, even a piping frog enlivens a solitude and makes world enough for us.[35]

> In the wood, God was very manifest as he surely was not in the sermon. In the cathedralled larches the wild ground pine crept him, the thrush sung him, the robin complained him, the catbird mewed him, the anemone vibrated him, the wild apple bloomed him; the ants built their little Timbuctoo wide abroad; the wild grape budded; the rye was in the blade; high overhead, high over cloud the faint sharphorned moon sailed steadily west through fleets of little clouds; the sheafs of the birch brightened into green below. The pines kneaded their aromatics in the sun. All prepared itself for the warm thunderdays of July.[36]

The world goes on in this way. This is the original landscape—without any human coloring and defilement of egotism. Here, someone might recall Robert Browning's "Pippa Passes:"

The year's at the spring,
And day's at the morn;
Morning's at seven;
The hill-side's dew-pearled;

The lark's on the wing;
The snail's on the thorn;
God is in heaven
All's right with the world![37]

"Who" is it then that sees the landscape in this way? It is the very same "transparent eyeball," the I that is "backed by the Universe of beings" and that "lean(s) on omnipotence."[38] Or, as Emerson noted later, it is "God in us" who "worships God."[39] Emerson's God is none other than the "transparent eyeball."

NOTES

1. *The Journals and Miscellaneous Notebooks of Ralph Waldo Emerson*, ed., W.H.Gilman, *et. al.*, (Harvard University Press, 1961), Vol. V, 169. (June 4, 1936).
2. *JMN*, IV, 88. (September 17, 1833).
3. *JMN*, III, 144, (September 1, 1828).
4. *JMN*, IV, 67–68. (February 10, 1833).
5. See Dōgen: Shōbōgenzō, "Genjō Kōan."
6. Shōju-Rōjin-Shu, ed., Shinano Board of Education (Shigensha, 1975), 103.
7. *JMN*, V, 5. (January 7, 1835).
8. *The Record of Lin-chi*, trans. by Ruth Fuller Sasaki (Kyoto: The Institute for Zen Studies, 1975), 16.
9. *JMN*, V, 18. (March 19, 1835).
10. *The Complete Works of Ralph Waldo Emerson*, ed., Edward Waldo Emerson (Centenary Edition), V ol. I, 10.
11. See *Emerson's Nature: Origin, Growth, Meaning*, ed., Merton M. Sealts, Jr. and Alfred R. Furguson (Southern Illinois University Press, 1969).
12. *Jonathan Bishop: Emerson on the Soul* (Harvard University Press, 1964), 10.
13. *Op. cit.*, 15.
14. *The Complete Works of Emerson*, II, 57.
15. *JMN*, II, 238. (April 18, 1824).
16. See Sōiku Shigematsu: *A Zen Forest: Sayings of the Masters* (Weatherhill, 1981) and Sōiku Shigematsu: *A Zen Harvest: Japanese Folk Zen Sayings* (North Point Press, 1988). In the introductions, I have explained these three viewpoints of Zen.
17. See Shōbōgenzō, "Genjō Kōan."
18. William Shakespeare, *Macbeth*, V, v.24–28.
19. *JMN*, V, 164, (May 28, 1836).
20. See Denshin-hoyo (Transmission of Mind).
21. *The Record of Lin-chi*, 3.
22. *A Zen Forest*, poem no. 1094.
23. *Ibid.*, no. 1107.
24. *JMN*, V, 229. (October 25, 1836).
25. *JMN*, III, 199. (September 27, 1830).
26. *JMN*, IV, 279. (July 29, 1931).
27. *JMN*, IV, 383. (December 29, 1934).
28. *JMN*, V, 13. (January 14, 1835).
29. *JMN*, V, 496-7. (May 11, 1938).
30. *JMN*, III, 266. (June 29, 1831).
31. *A Zen Forest*, no. 835.
32. *JMN*, III, 186. (June 7, 1830).
33. *A Zen Forest*, no. 490.
34. *JMN*, IV, 199–200. (July 13, 1833).
35. *JMN*, V, 480. (April 26, 1838).
36. *JMN*, V, 503–04. (May 22, 1838).
37. *Selected Poetry of Robert Browning* (Modern Library), 3.
38. *JMN*, III, 130. (May 9, 1828).
39. *JMN*, III, 273. (July 15, 1831).

19

PARADOX, LANGUAGE, AND REALITY

Robert E. Carter

THE DECONSTRUCTION AND RECONSTRUCTION of the history of thought will doubtless continue in our "post-modern" world, and there is every reason to suspect that Heraclitus may become a major figure in this scatter-pattern of re-appropriation. Heraclitus, the odd man out in the history of Western philosophy, confounded his contemporaries with his enigmatic utterances. He continues to confound with the cryptic and inscrutable tone of the handful of fragments left to us from his writings. Yet it is Heraclitus who may come to stand strong and tall as the precursor of post-modernism, and a key bridge between the philosophical cultures of East and West. What is clearly focal in Heraclitus' philosophy is the affirmation that *paradox* is not incomplete and premature understanding, but a deep and profound indication of what reality itself is most nearly like for a rationally linguistic being!

Philip Wheelwright stresses this point in his small volume on Heraclitus:

> ... Heraclitus regards the paradox itself, and not its logical transformation, as more truly representing the true state of affairs.

> It is this acceptance of the ontological status of paradox—an acceptance, that is to say, of the view that paradox lies inextricably at the very heart of reality—that gave Heraclitus his ancient reputation for obscurity.[1]

It is important to recognize that Heraclitus is not to be seen as the hopelessly confused relativist whose position a Socrates can easily expose as a vicious skepticism, with no epistemological ground to stand on. Heraclitus' stand was epistemological to the core, and his charge was that to adopt a univocal and nonparadoxical logic is to *distort* our knowledge of things. It is non-paradoxicality that wrests things from the flow of real experience and places them in a conceptual realm of human forms where they are harmlessly pinned down like a collection of butterflies. More on this notion of distortion shortly, but let me quote Wheelwright again to support my interpretation to this point:

> The most characteristic difficulty in Heraclitus' philosophy lies in the demand which it makes upon its hearers to transcend the "either-or" type of thinking and to recognize in each phase of experience that a relationship of "both-and" may be present in subtle ways that escape a dulled intelligence.... To him nothing is exclusively this or that; in various ways he affirms something to be *both* of two disparates or two contraries, leaving the reader to contemplate the paradox, the full semantic possibilities of which can never be exhausted by plain prose statements.[2]

The clarity and precision of either-or logic, i.e., of the Laws of Identity and Non-contradiction, make it impossible to give expression to the flux, the shifting and paradoxically this–and–yet–not–this (or that) manifested in the flow of experience. The paradoxicality is not to be taken as a confusion, temporary or otherwise. Rather, the paradox is itself the only way that we, as rationally-linguistic beings, can express the inherent complexity and ambiguity given in experience. Furthermore, this very paradoxicality serves to lead us on to the search for a deeper understanding which scholars of Heraclitus term "the unity of opposition."

Kahn writes that "the unity of opposites stands" as a "truth whose primary application for human beings lies in a deeper understanding of their own experience of life and death, sleeping and waking, youth and old age."[3] The opposites are one, just as the opposing tensions comprising the bow and the lyre (fragment 51) are complementary, and it is such unified tension in complementary opposition which makes them the entities they are. It is this seeming opposition itself which is, in fact, the unity. In Kahn's words, "the opposites are one; and this deathless structure of life-and-death is deity itself."[4] But this pulling in opposite directions is mistakenly taken as strife or antagonism, for "the real constitution of things is accustomed to hide itself" (fr. 123; tr. Kirk).

All things are themselves unities of opposition, and, in our sense, must be thought of as processes, as continually changing rivers or streams of consciousness.

Pure Experience

It is the Japanese philosopher Nishida Kitarō who is the major player in this essay, but Heraclitus provides interesting insight into Nishidean thought, for Heraclitus and Nishida share much in common. So it is with Nishida and William James. Nishida credits James with supplying him (through his writings) with the key concept in Nishida's own philosophical development, "pure experience." And pure experience will lead us to paradoxicality once more. James maintained that there was heuristic value in the supposition that there is a single, "primal" stuff of which all things are composed. Consciousness, matter, and whatever else one supposes to be in the world are but manifestations of this original stuff. Yet, as Charlene Seigfried warns:

> James's thesis of "one primal stuff or material in the world" is meant as a counter-assertion to those who hold to an aboriginal dualism of consciousness. James is not asserting a metaphysical sub-stratum, but he is denying the subject-object distinction as irreducible. Pure experience is neither monistic nor dualistic, it is undifferentiated.[5]

Reality is "a that, an Absolute, a 'pure' experience on an enormous scale, undifferentiated and undifferentiable into thought and thing."[6] It is precisely this sense of pure experience as undifferentiated, undichotomized, conceptually neutral, ambiguous and prior to the subject/object distinction that Nishida intended by his unity of the undifferentiated. It is a fact or conscious awareness prior to all cognition and to all physical traits. "It is plain, unqualified actuality, or existence, a simple *that*."[7] Thomas R. Maitland, Jr. amplifies the point that for James pure experience is a unity underlying conceptual distinction making:

> Another revealing but difficult to understand characteristic of pure experience is its "much at onceness" that transcends all separation. As such it is similar to the impression made on the conscious level if a number of impressions, from any number of sensory sources, fall simultaneously on a mind which had not yet experienced them separately. Such a mind would fuse them into a single undivided object. In this case, and in that of pure experience there is no meaning, only a "big blooming buzzing confusion." But in another sense there is meaning because all there is in each case is pure experience... on the level of pure experience they mean everything they are. On that level things compensate each other, are alive and fuse into each other....[8]

On the question of *meaning* and its relation to pure experience, Nishida contends that when the unity–as–undifferentiated pure experience is broken, "i.e., when one enters into relationship with something else, meaning is born, judgment is created."[9] Meaning and judgment are always and necessarily states of disunity. In the state of pure experience, self and other, subject and object, true and false, meaning and the meaningless, "are mutually submerged, and the universe as unity is the only reality...."[10]

Building on what has been said thus far about James' notion of pure experience, we are now in a position to show why it does seem evident that he presupposes "richer unity behind the thinner and more abstract editions of perception and thought." Quite explicitly James maintains that the division of pure experience into consciousness and content "*comes, not by way of subtraction, but by way of addition....*"[11] Edward I. Moore summarizes James' position when he writes:

> For James the world consists of a flux of pure experience out of which man—by observation and inspiration—carves isolable chunks to which he gives names. These chunks have no identity in reality as chunks. They are simply artificial cuts out of what is in reality a continuum. Man cuts them out for purposes of thought and purposes of behavior. But the cuts are *his* cuts, not nature's.[12]

He adds the following:

> Out of this aboriginal sensible muchness attention carves out objects, which conception then names and identifies forever—in the sky "constellations," on the earth "beach," "sea," "cliff," "bushes," "grass." Out of time we cut "days" and "nights," "summers" and "winters." We say *what* each part of the sensible continuum is, and all these abstracted *whats* are concepts.[13]

What was once a unified and undivided whole of experience becomes separated into parts, concepts, relations, according to human needs and purposes. But pure experience is never so divided. It is always and everywhere "the instant field of the present."[14] So it is that we discover that reality and the immediately sensible are one and the same: "Reality is apperception itself."[15] Experience is reality as it presents itself to us.

Conception halts the flow of pure experience, isolates one or more aspects of it, abstracts these from the whole for practical purposes, and thereby harnesses reality.[16] These selective abstractions "must never be taken as the full equivalent of reality,"[17] partly because they are partial selections from the whole, and partly because they are static fixations of a reality which is always and everywhere a flux, a changing flow. James presupposes the eternal flux of reality as apprehended in pure experience, much as the Buddhist affirms that reality, the Buddha, is impermanence. James stresses that concepts cannot change, they can only cease to be: "They form an essentially discontinuous system, and translate the process of our perceptual experience, which is naturally a flux into a set of stagnant and petrified terms."[18]

In one sense, conception adds to reality as perceived, for concepts "bring new values into our perceptual life,"[19] e.g., sublimity, power, admiration, etc. Nevertheless, the "shortcomings" of the "conceptual transformation" include the rendering of a map "superficial through the abstractness, and false through the discreetness of its elements.... Conceptual knowledge is forever inadequate to the fullness of the reality to be known."[20] Concepts are just "secondary formations, inadequate, and only ministerial."[21]

Still, concepts are as real as perceptual experience, but "the 'eternal' kind of being which they enjoy is inferior to the temporal kind, because it is so static and schematic and lacks so many characteristics which temporal reality possesses."[22]

Thus James concludes that "the deeper features of reality are found only in perceptual experience."[23]

> Here alone do we acquaint ourselves with continuity, or the immersion of one thing in another, here alone with self, with substance, with qualities, with activity in its various modes, with time, with cause, with change, with novelty, with tendency, and with freedom. Against all such features of reality the method of conceptual translation, when candidly and critically followed out, can only raise its *non possumus*, and brand them as unreal or absurd.[24]

Still, James warns that as finite beings, we are able to encompass but a few passing moments of pure experience. But in a footnote he adds that in "'mystical' ways, he may extend his vision to an even wider perceptual panorama than that usually open to the scientific mind."[25] And while Nishida resists the "mystical" label, he does assume that such extensions of vision are readily open to us, and that it is in the religious life that they are most distinctively found.

James and Nishida appear to share the insight that rational and transcendental attempts, in the history of philosophical thought, to understand or grasp reality-as-experience in conceptual and linguistic terms, "draws the dynamic continuity out of nature as you draw the thread out of a string of beads."[26] In words that would gain immediate endorsement from Nishida, James urges that if this "continuity and flow mean logical self contradiction, the logic must go."[27]

The human mind draws out of pure experience what it needs, or prefers, to achieve certain practical ends. It does this by making distinctions within the undifferentiated whole of pure experience. Such drawing out, fixing, staying the flow of lived experience, and "holding fast to meanings, has no significance apart from the fact that the conceiver is a creature with a partial purpose and private ends."[28] We are responsible for carving out this partial practical truth from the richer unity behind our pragmatic purposes, concepts, and conscious experiences.

A Limit Concept

As soon as we are able to talk about pure experience, to conceptualize and "language" it, it thereby becomes a mixture of perceptual and conceptual awareness. This, of course, leads us to more sharply distinguish the conceptual as subjective, and the perceptual as objective. Yet, the worrisome question remains, can we, in fact, speak philosophically meaningfully about nonexperiential experience? "If pure experience is never pure as experienced, then in what sense can it be spoken of meaningfully at all?"[29] Seigfried answers this question by taking pure experience to be itself a *posited* limit concept "which enables James to dethrone dualism as the primordial beginning of all experience."[30] Ontological dualism is perhaps the key assumption which Zen Buddhists, too, seek to question and undermine in the attempt to push back behind conceptualization and thought to the immediately given. "This temptingly plausible dualistic explanation can be overcome by hypothesizing that the primary reality is of a neutral nature and can be designated by an ambiguous name like 'phenomenon' or 'datum'."[31] It is interesting to note how often the term "field" is used in Jamesian interpretation, for Nishida, too, writes of the field of the immediate:

> Pure experience can be defined as the instant field of the present, the immediate flux of life before categorization. Its purity is a relative term, denoting the proportion of unverbalized absorption in the present sensation.[32]

Pure experience is an heuristic limiting concept for James, whereas it appears to be an actual and direct experience for Nishida. Indeed, a culture of meditation, of silence, and emptiness would not find pure experience a speculative matter, but an original experience out of, or from which conceptual experience is carved. As Nishida observes, "that within meaning or judgment is a part which has been abstracted from the original experience, and in its content it is, on the contrary, a poorer thing than the original experience."[33] Yet it is not to be concluded so quickly that James, unlike Nishida, was unable to find a direct experience of pure experience. He does not state that it is not experienced, but only that it is not conceptually graspable and communicable, for to do so is already to break it up into categories.

Instead, as Seigfried remarks, it is "the immediate flux of life which furnishes the raw material to later reflection."[34] Nevertheless, James does hedge his bets in concluding that "only new-born babes, or men in semi-coma from sleep, drugs, illnesses, or blows, may be assumed to have an experience pure in the literal sense of a *that* which is not yet any definite what...."[35]

Yet, even though James assumes that totally pure experience is rare, and at that available only to those whose intellectual capacity is minuscule or damaged, he also states that "namelessness is compatible with experience," and in his study of religious experience he lists ineffability as one of the characteristics of mystical experience.[36]

Furthermore, in his *The Varieties of Religious Experience*, he clearly leaves open the door for pure experience to enter in issuing this warning:

> ...our normal waking consciousness, rational consciousness as we call it, is but one special type of consciousness, whilst all about it, parted from it by the filmiest of screens, there lie potential forms of consciousness entirely different.... No account of the universe in its totality can be final which leaves these other forms of consciousness quite disregarded.[37]

Then, as if speaking directly to our point, he reflects autobiographically that,

> Looking back on my own experiences (with nitrous oxide), they all converge towards a kind of insight to which I cannot help ascribing some metaphysical significance. The keynote of it is invariably a reconciliation. It is as if the opposites of the world, whose contradictoriness and conflict make all our difficulties and troubles, were melted into unity.[38]

A Normatively "Richest" Experience

It may well be that the greatest difference between James and Nishida is what Dilworth correctly describes as "the concept of a 'richest' experience in Nishida's mind which might best be understood in terms of the Zen notions of 'emptiness' or 'nothingness'."[39] Nishida began *A Study of Good* with the claim that to experience means to know events precisely as they are.[40] Reality, as it is in itself, can be directly apprehended, and without distortion, so long as the experience keeps out of the way, and simply passively *mirrors* reality. James is an advocate of the active mind, and in addition to the inclusion of the activities of the mind in virtually all "somewhat" pure experience, he warns that, "all present beliefs are subject to revision in the light of future experiences,"[41] including pure experience, precisely because it is never completely pure. Inescapably, experience is filtered through the categories of intellect and distinction. Still, it is the uncut "big blooming buzzing confusion" which is the methodological whole out of which the parts are cut.

James was emphatic in pointing out that relations among things in experience are "just as much matters of direct particular experience, neither more so nor less so, than the things themselves."[42] We experience the "and" of two things in relation, and the "if" of uncertainty or potential sequence as in "if-then," just as much as we do the substantive matters being related. In short, "the relations that connect experiences must themselves be experienced relations, and any kind of relation experienced must be accounted as 'real' as anything else in the system."[43] As immediately apprehended, experience is not a dualism composed of thought and thing, subjective and objective elements, but is undifferentiated, as we have seen.

Even in his early *Principles of Psychology*, James compares the flow or stream of conscious awareness (stream of thought; stream of consciousness) to the pattern or flight of a bird. "Like a bird's life, it seems to be made of an alternation of flights and perchings."[44] The "resting-places" are the "sensorial imaginations," arresting the flow-of-flight and providing images which are capable of being held before the mind indefinitely, and contemplated without change occurring. The flow-as-flight is filled with "thoughts of relations" which apply between the fixed matters for contemplation. We can experience just as directly "if," "but," and "by" as readily as "blue" or "cold."[45]

But we are habituated, for so many reasons of cultural habitation, to focus on, ("perch on") "the substantive parts."[46] We select from the undifferentiated broth of experience, what we wish to attend to, and "actually *ignore* most of the rest of the things before us."[47] Perchings and flight together add up to our awareness of the whole life-activity of our own life as, metaphorically, a bird.

Perception and transitive relations together add up to our life of experience. And both are cut out of the indefinitely rich flow called pure experience. Substantive "things" and their relations are not ultimately different, but arise from the same aboriginal source. "Mental content and object" are identical,[48] simply different aspects abstracted out of pure experience for practical purposes. "Subject" and "object" denote different aspects of the same primal flow. The distinction is real enough, for functional purposes, but not ultimate.

Nishida, too, stresses that at the background of any judgment "there is always an event of pure experience."[49] Indeed, pure experience is proposed to rest behind all experience, even the experience of thinking. Relations, thought, willing, feeling are all of them aspects of direct experience, and dimensions of pure experience. Nishida concludes that, "pure experience and thought are basically the same event seen from different points of view."[50] Perception, intelligence and will are all processes of our own self-expression and realization, directly experienced. In fact, "the distinction between the intelligence and the will or either from perception arises when subjectivity and objectivity are separated and when one loses the unifying state of pure experience."[51]

But direct apprehension of the "source," the aboriginal flow, is not simply available to babies and men in sleep-coma, or an heuristic limiting concept, as it was for James. Rather it is itself a directly experienced recognition of this very (pre-all-distinctions) oneness, an *intellectual* perception, "but in content it is infinitely richer and more profound."[52] By describing it as akin to intellectual intuition, differing only in richness of experienced content, Nishida apparently breaks with James, who urged that all direct experience was already post pure experience, and therefore already contained distinctions. Nishida seemingly parts with James' radical empiricism:

> If our consciousness were merely a thing of sensory characteristics, it would probably stop at a state of ordinary, intellectually perceived intuition, but an ideal spirit demands infinite unity, and this unity is given in the form of so-called intellectual intuition. Intellectual intuition, like intellectual perception, is the most unified state of the consciousness.[53]

I say that Nishida seemingly parts with James on this issue, for his stress on "intellectual" and "ideal" seems to move us away from experience, to the *a priori* and the contemplative. But even here Nishida maintains that such distinctions are artificially made after the fact. In pure and immediate experience, intellection, James' relations, perception, feeling, willing are all on the same level. Indeed, Nishida even writes of "intellectual perception" in order to emphasize the fact that the usual boundaries are inadequate.[54] He sums up by articulating clearly that "true intellectual intuition is the unifying activity itself in pure experience; it is the grasping of life...."[55] There is only one world, only experience flowing. To be sure, "intellectual intuition" sounds as though it refers to a subjective state of human rational or intellectual activity.

> But actually it is a state which has transcended subject and object, and one rather can say that the opposition of subject and object is established by this unity, and such things as inspired art will attain this realm. Also intellectual intuition does not refer to the direct perception of an abstract generality separated from actuality.[56]

Generality and individuality both are moments within pure experience, as are subject and object. All distinctions rest in pure experience, as perchings (distinctions) in the course of a life of flight. Thought itself is a system, "and at the base of a system there must be an intuition of unity."[57] It follows that the ground of all systems and of all unities is pure experience. The true self is precisely this unifying intuition.[58] Intuition transcends the will, intelligence (thought), emotion, perception—but is the basis of them all.

Nishida calls this awareness "religious" and defines it as "the apprehension of that profound unity which lies at the foundation of intelligence and the will, namely a kind of intellectual intuition, a deep grasp of life."[59] Logic is incapable of going "towards it," nor can human desire "move it."[60] Yet it must be present in all religion. Nishida places religion at the foundation of morality: "At the root of learning and morality there must be religion, for both of these are constructed according to it."[61] What happens to most of us, in our intellectual journey towards understanding, is that we lose touch with our connectedness with the unity given in pure experience, and retreat into the defined and purposeful realm of the intellect alone. In James' words: "The intellectual life of man consists almost wholly in his substitution of a conceptual order in which his experience originally courses."[62]

Nishida would no doubt agree. For Nishida, to be aware of pure experience is not to deny conception and the various systematizations resulting from thinking, but to ground them all in the original undifferentiated flow of pure flight. They are all perchings, and the only real error we make is to focus too fully on the perchings, the stable, fixed resting places, that we forget altogether how to fly. To keep both perspectives alive in a single consciousness, is to understand the true depths of the conscious self, for we are both capable of self awareness of ourselves as distinct from the whole, and aware of the whole as ourselves. We, too, are but temporary perchings in the cosmic flight, the cosmic flow of life.

The Identity of Self-Contradiction

Nishida's culminating understanding of things is that Aristotle's logic was incapable of accounting for either the individual in experience, or the flux of paradoxicality. Individuals are, for Aristotle, defined by means of universals, and so one can know the individual as universal, but not *qua* individual. Similarly. Aristotle's demand for non-paradoxical univocality only stripped down experience to fit the needs and limits of fixed and changeless conceptualization. Yet, for Nishida "this world of historical reality, wherein we are born, act and die, must be, when logically seen, something like the contradictory self-identity of the many and the one. I have come to this point after many years of pondering."[63]

All identity, i.e., all consciousness and objects of consciousness in the natural world, are self-contradictory unities. But two things cannot be self contradictory unless they are related by an enveloping matrix which, at the same time, unites them. For things to be in opposition implies thereby a deeper, underlying and grounding unity/system/*basho*. In Nishida's words: "To think of one thing is to distinguish it from the other. In order for the distinction to be possible, it must originally have something in common with the other."[64] To emphasize the contradiction is to plunge into the world as many; to emphasize the matrix or ground is to plunge into the world as one. The one is self contradictorily composed of the many, and the many are self contradictorily one. The world can be viewed in two directions—the double aperture—and its unity is not the unity of oneness, as the mystic would likely express it, but the unity of self-contradiction. It is *both* one and many; changing *and* unchanging; past and future in the present.

Nishida's dialectic has as its aim the preservation of the contradictory terms, yet as a unity. An individual, as an expression of the universal, negates its individuality, and yet, by negating its individuality, by becoming the universal, the universal negates itself as an individual. This is the logic of *soku*, or *soku hi*—the absolute identification of the is, and the is not. A is A; A is not-A, therefore A is A. I see the mountains. I see that there are no mountains. Therefore, I see the mountains again, but as transformed. And the transformation is that the mountains both are and are not mountains. That is their reality.

The world of contradictory self-identities, or of the "unity of opposites" as Schinzinger translates the phrase, is not some other distant world, but the actual phenomenologically experienced world in which we find ourselves. The self identity of the one points not to oneness, but to the all pervasive presence of self-contradictions. Everything is change, or impermanence, says the Buddhist, and yet it is precisely as change that persons and things are what they are.

As with Aristotle's *hypokeimenon*, there is that which endures change, but it is not as unchanging. Rather, it is that which it changes, yet changes not but remains what it is; it is many, yet is not many but one, etc. It is not that Aristotle did not know this to be so, for he is the philosopher of change who welds Parmenides and Heraclitus together, as Plato tried to do with less success.

Yet in trying to say all of this logically, Aristotle provided a logic which gave primacy to the grammatical subject, and thus to the unchanging substratum. Nishida wants to right this by placing full emphasis on the grammatical predicate, or on the underlying matrix of place out of which the subject arises, and which actually gives it its proper shape-as-contextualized. Still, it seems to me that Nishida would have been better to have spoken not of his "logic of place," but to have stressed his logic of subject *and* predicate, or of object and place. It is not exactly a logic of place, but a logic of place as the matrix or context out of which all differentiations or determinations arise, and in which they, and their mutual relationships, are grounded.

Nishida's logic of subject and predicate allows one to see exactly how the individual and the universal relate, and how they may be said to belong together inescapably. In Nishida's words, as found in a letter to a friend, we read:

> In the logic of *Basho* the correspondence must be countercorrespondence. The correspondence of the world and self, namely, of whole and one in the logic of *Basho* is linked up with the self-identity of contradiction because if we keep saying "One becomes the many, and the many becomes One" they will be forever opposed to each other.... The Absolute is what embraces both of these opposite directions as the Self identity of contradiction.[65]

The conclusion reached is that absolute nothingness, the final *basho*, is nowhere else but the place where you are. It is not something to be looked at objectively, but rather is that place where your self-consciousness and all of its objects of consciousness arise. Still, to see it objectively, i.e., to see the form of the formless, is to see the world of dialectical contradiction. The dialectical universal as the form of the ultimately formless is nothing else than the actual world of contradictory self-identity while the world and its formless base together may be said to be *absolutely contradictory and a self-identity*. It is simultaneously being and nothingness. It is transcendent of its form, yet everywhere immanent in each of its forms or instantiations.

Absolute nothingness expresses itself by means of forms in accordance with the subject/object dichotomy. Or, at least, that is how human consciousness deals with all form, all knowledge and all ordinary experience. Husserl was quite right in insisting that all knowledge and all experience is intentional. The only exception to this caveat is, for Nishida, "pure experience." Pure experience is prior to (ontologically), the subject/object split. We experience this way when we move increasingly towards the infinitely bottomless self, or when we experience the nothingness at the base of every object in the world.

In other words, when we focus on the manifold of forms of the absolutely formless, we always do so within the logical context of subject/object, *noesis/noema*. But when we look through these forms to the formless basis of them all, we realize that the forms are but expressions of the formless, which is not itself thereby caught. The formless is inescapably non-determinate, just as the self which is prior to objectification is really a no-self; it sees without itself being a seer as seen. It is prior to, or at the base of both objectivity *and* subjectivity, and itself is both of these, and neither of these. This is the paradoxical formulation of Nishida's identity of opposites, or the self-identity of absolute contradiction, or self-contradictory identity.

Self-Contradictory Identity

Translators have offered various alternative renderings of *Zettai mujunteki jikodoitsu*: the "unity of opposites,"[66] "contradictory self-identity,"[67] "self-identity of contradiction,"[68] and "identity of contradiction,"[69] and "contradictory identity."[70] What a successful translation of this phrase must communicate to the reader is (1) the paradoxicality inherent in Nishida's perspective on reality, (2) the dynamism of a philosophic perspective which in principle allows no epistemic resting place (i.e., "now I understand" must immediately give way to "and, therefore, I do not understand"), and (3) a deeper understanding of the dynamism of paradoxicality which allows the seeing of each as both different from each other, *and yet* the same as each other.

I am inclined to de-emphasize *identity* for the temptation to emphasize sameness at the expense of difference is too great. This temptation is not only to be found in Western thinkers (cf. Plato's attempt to ascertain the common form which was the intelligible reality underlying the less-intelligible sensible instances), but may be found in Eastern traditions as well (cf. the Indian assumption that multiplicity is illusory—*maya*—while Brahman, the underlying identity or oneness, is real). For Nishida, the real is no less one than it is many, no less different than it is identical. The differences must be fully retained and reaffirmed in the face of the realization of the sameness of things, and *vice versa*. Additionally, emphasis on the sameness or oneness of things tends to suggest the eternal, immutable, unchanging and static—all characteristics which Nishida is at pains to reject in his account of a reality which is (Buddhistically) impermanent, and ever in process.

The Dynamic of Paradox

Nishida's "logic of *soku hi*" (the "is" and the "is not" of a thing, or the oneness or identity of the is and is-not) can be expressed as follows: A is A, and *yet* A is not-A; therefore, A is A.[71] David Dilworth, in his

Postscript to Nishida's final essay, offers an elaborate analysis of Nishida's "paradoxical logic" which reduces to the basic predicative structure of "is *and yet* is not."

> We can alternately characterize this as the logic of the simultaneity, and bi-conditionality, of opposites without their higher synthesis. Thus "is" if, and only if, "is not," as in the *soku hi* formulation. Nāgārjuna worked out the implications of this logical operator in an exhaustive set for the Buddhist tradition. In Nāgārjuna's logic, the four positions *+1*, *-1*, *+1 and -1*, and not (+1 and -1) all return to the same basic structure of bi-conditional opposition. That is, they return to *+1 and -1* (or, -1 and +1) .... The 'and' in these various formulations is always an 'and yet' with its corresponding 'vice versa.' Nirvana and yet samsara, samsara and yet nirvana. Nirvana (+1) if, and only if, samsara (-1); samsara (-1) if, and only if, nirvana (+1).[72]

What the is *and* is not of the *soku hi* formulation protects is the dynamical tension of affirmative and negative "without synthesis."[73] The only reality which Nishida seeks to analyze, then, is the everyday world of dynamic activity, which manifests itself to ordinary consciousness as logically paradoxical. As Nakamura Hijime has emphasized, for the Japanese who is influenced by Zen thought, it is this world, the everyday world of common-sense which is *absolute*.[74] It *is* the ultimate, even though it is not known ultimately, or absolutely, or completely. "Complete knowing" is surface knowing, and it is inevitably either one-sided, or hopelessly inconclusive because paradoxical.

Kant's antimonies forever dwarf claims to know fully, while scientific discovery warns that yesterday's "proof" incessantly yields to "reformulation" in accordance with a new paradigm. More to the point, the Japanese and the Mahāyāna Buddhist recognition of the indeterminate which lies behind the determinate, necessitates the view that whatever can be said or conceptually known is not either complete or ultimate.

But it is *no less* real for that. Rather, it is but one side of, or one perspective, of reality. It is one aperture of reality-awareness, and even at that, it is an aperture of unrelenting paradox—of incessant contradictoriness. The real is, in itself (as we know it) contradictory. In order to apprehend things as they are "means to seek contradictions."[75] Through the aperture of consciousness which is the logical, conceptual, subject/object, *noetic/noematic* mode, reality appears as a contradiction, and not as a synthesis.

What made coming to this insight so arduous is the fact that Nishida had to reflect both the perspective of ordinary logic, which seeks to eliminate paradox, i.e., which takes the law of non-contradiction as its emblem (*either* a thing is, or is not) and the perspective of dialectic, which eliminates paradox and contradiction in a series of syntheses, and ultimately rests on a final synthesis of all into a single whole or oneness. What Nishida struggled for was a different perspective which could embrace both the thesis and the antithesis, the subject and the object, without suppressing either.[76] The real, phenomenal world *is* both one and many, subjective and objective, changing and unchanging. Reality is self-contradictory.

Conclusion

In *The Paradoxical Nature of Reality*, George Melhuish echoes what Heraclitus, Nishida and James seem to have discovered:

> In order to define the innate flux of things, it is necessary to state a fundamental paradox and to say that what is the same as itself is in self-modification whereby it is not the same as itself, for any *less paradoxical* operation will commit us to the acceptance of a merely static identity and this will imply that different things will not need to be in a state of change in order not to be the same.[77]

A thing both is, and yet, and at the same time is not what it is. Melhuish states emphatically that ordinary thinking only grants us half of what we need to know. We need to know that selectively, things are what they are. But we also need to know that (1) the reality of change is such that at the same time that we grasp a thing as fixed, it and we are already changing. We cannot step into the same river even once, for we and the river flow on. Of course, when we understand ourselves as flowing processes, as the Buddhist does, and we *empty* both ourself and the river of fixity gained *via* the assumption of substantiality, then we grasp as well the *other half* of things as they are. All things flow. They are not simply what they seem to be, for they are at each instant both what they are, and what they were not by virtue of change.

Additionally, (2) both individuated things, and these same individuated things now apprehended as in flux (as empty), and are further emptied by the recognition that they are selectively culled from the richer whole of experience which Nishida and James termed pure experience. All things are "lined" with nothingness. Things are not only changing. Both the individuation and the change are distinctions within a seamless web of existence. Prior to rational-linguistic selection, prior to the distinction between a particular and whatever else it is contrasted with, prior to the taken for granted distinction between subject and object, self and other, there is the universe as unselected, undifferentiated.

The double aperture of wisdom, as I will call it, is the ability to see things as individuated, to see the individuated as in continual change, and to see the changing individuals of the world as not just individuals, but as expressions of the undifferentiated whole. Just as mountains give way to the emptying annihilation of Zen enlightenment, and then are seen once again as mountains which are not mountains because they are more than just mountains, so every particular now becomes more than it was before. It is fleetingly precious, for it is already forever gone, and yet as the momentary expression of the whole, we can see through it to the undifferentiated whole of which it is, for the moment, the only expression (for us). It is what it is; it is not what it is (but has become something else, and it is everything—or better, everything is).

If we push far enough and hard enough, we see the collapse of all utterances into their opposites: existence alone needs an essence, and essence requires the freedom of mere existence–as–becoming; waves and particles, while antithetical, are together necessary ingredients in the explanation of any quantum phenomenon the *a priori* seems to be somehow experientially derived, and the *a posteriori* is already a category of purely conceptual understanding, else we could not explain why we initially attended to just this aspect or dimension of experience. No conceptual distinction has an absolute grounding, and so "any assertion of one side of a distinction over the other is, at its foundation, self-contradictory."[78]

Indeed, "any assertion or distinction only highlights one aspect of a situation and, in so doing, casts into shadows an equally important, though incompatible, aspect."[79] Concepts filter out much of the richer manifold given in immediate experience, yet it might be that *the more adequate* view is a middle one which salvages the paradoxicality of the necessary tension between the opposed contenders. The logic is a *both-and*, and not an *either–or* one.

It is also a logic of relative approximation conceptually, pointing towards the richer source, and, I think, maintaining that both dimensions need to be held, and held in tension. The nature of that tension is that one never "gets it right," for as soon as one comes down firmly, and once and for all on the side of an issue, one must return again to the indefinite no-distinction-no-thing of pure experience, in order to drink again from the richer source.

Like an artist at a favorite painting spot, one sees the vista new each time, and one could paint a thousand paintings from the same spot, each quite different from the others. One must paint, and then unpaint by looking again, and "without prejudice." It is far easier to be open in this way if one does not begin by assuming that there is a "definitive" painting to be done. It is better to capture a facet of the whole in a fresh or unique way, and to recognize it as only a facet or a portion of the scene, than to hold out for the "right" depiction which, we now see, may be logically impossible to achieve. Indeed, it is to look in the wrong direction for understanding and insight altogether.

Standing on the shoulders of Nāgārjuna, Nishida's great insight is that, while recognizing the emptiness, and therefore limitedness of all conceptual systems and their parts, nevertheless a system of philosophic understanding (1) can be truer than another because (2) it points us to, through and then beyond itself to its ground or origin, which is experienced (if not definitively then more richly) immediately or directly, and (3) which is analyzable into concepts which are, at least, more faithful to the original richness, or better approximates or represents the depths, richness, and complexity of the pure experience itself. In fact, (4) no apprehension of the immediately experienced ground (nothingness, *śūn-yatā*, *nirvana*) is complete without this fuller account of the forms-of-nothingness in the-space-time-world-of-human-conceptual-consciousness (*samsāra*).

The two are aspects of the same one, or identity. They are distinct, yet unified. They form an identity, yet they are different. This is the self-contradictoriness of the world of experience itself, as an absolute identity of self-contradiction. It is not that only pure experience is to be attended to, nor that "nothingness" or "emptiness" must be elevated to take the place of "God" or "Being." Even empt*iness* must be emptied, leaving only the *empty* and then the empty must be emptied, leaving things as relatively full and distinct. Then, one empties things, and one returns to indefinite no-thingness again, and all is empty. The process of emptying, based on the premise that all conceptualization is relativistically limited by its own necessarily arbitrary ontology, must itself be emptied by the reality of another way of knowing, *viz prajñā* by means of which a synthetic or holistic direct apprehension of reality–as–immediate–experience is afforded. These two, together, as form and as perpetually interactive process, yield as much as we can know about reality.

NOTES

1. Philip Wheelwright, *Heraclitus* (New York: Athenum, 1964), 92.
2. *Ibid.*, 91.
3. Charles H. Kahn, *The Art and Thought of Heraclitus: An Edition of the Fragments with Translation and Commentary* (Cambridge: Cambridge University Press, 1979), 21.
4. *Ibid.*, 23.
5. Charlene H. Seigfried, *Chaos and Context: A Study in William James* (Athens, Ohio: Ohio University Press, 1978), 40.
6. William James, *Essays in Radical Empiricism* (Cambridge, Mass.: Harvard University Press, 1976), 66.
7. *Ibid.*, 13.
8. Thomas R. Maitland, Jr. *The Metaphysics of William James and John Dewey* (New York: Philosophical Library, 1963), 85.
9. Nishida Kitarō, *A Study of Good*, V.H. Viglielmo, tr. (Tokyo: Printing Bureau, Japanese Government, 1960), 8.
10. *Ibid.*, 28.
11. James *Essays*, 7.
12. Edward C. Moore, *William James* (New York: Washington Square Press, Inc., 1966), 164–65.
13. William James, *Some Problems of Philosophy* (London: Longmans, Green and Co., 1948), 50.
14. James, *Essays*, 13.
15. *Ibid.*, 263.
16. James, *Problems*, 65.
17. Maitland, *The Metaphysics*, 92.
18. William James, *The Principles of Psychology* (New York: Dover Publications, Inc., 1950 first published in 1890), vol. I, 139.
19. James, *Problems*, 73.
20. *Ibid.*, 78.
21. *Ibid.*, 79.
22. *Ibid.*, 101.
23. James, *Problems*, 97.
24. *Ibid.*
25. *Ibid.*
26. *Ibid.*, 86.
27. William James, Letter to Arthur O. Lovejoy, 1909, in Ralph Barton Perry, *The Thought and Character of William James*, Vol. II (Philosophy and Psychology) (Boston: Little, Brown and Company, 1935), 596.
28. James, *Psychology*, I, 482.
29. Seigfried, *Chaos and Context*, 49.
30. *Ibid.*
31. *Ibid.*
32. *Ibid.*, 51.
33. Nishida, *Study of Good*, 7.
34. Seigfried, *Chaos and Context*, 49.
35. James, *Essays*, 46.

36. James, *Psychology*, I, 251.
37. William James, *The Varieties of Religious Experience* (New York: The Modern Library, 1902), 378.
38. *Ibid.*, 379.
39. Dilworth, "The Initial Formations," 110. Italics mine.
40. Nishida, *Study of Good*, 1.
41. James, *Essays*, 22. In a footnote on 33, James comments on the quasi-chaotic nature of experience, on the continuity of the person as body, and on the discontinuity of inter-subjective experiences, concluding that, "Round their several object nuclei, partly common and partly discrete, of the real physical world, innumerable thinkers, pursuing their several lines of physically true cogitation, trace paths that intersect one another only at discontinuous perceptual points, and the rest of the time are quite incongruent; and around all the nuclei of shared 'reality' floats the vast cloud of experiences that are wholly subjective, that are non-substitutional, that find not even an eventual ending for themselves in the perceptual world—the mere day-dreams and joys and sufferings and wishes of the individual minds. These exist *with* one another, indeed, and with the objective nuclei, but out of them it is probable that to all eternity no inter-related system of any kind will ever be made."
42. James, *Pragmatism...Truth*, 199.
43. James, *Essays*, 22.
44. James, *Psychology*, I, 243.
45. *Ibid.*, 245–46.
46. Seigfried, *Chaos and Context*, 13.
47. James, *Psychology*, I, 284.
48. James, *Pragmatism...Truth*, 246–47.
49. Nishida, *Study of Good*, 10. On p. 11 Nishida quotes from James' "The World of Pure Experience," and adds that, "Formerly it was traditionally felt that thought and pure experience were wholly differing kinds of physical activity. ...thought activity also is a kind of pure experience."
50. *Ibid.*, 17.
51. *Ibid.*, 27.
52. *Ibid.*, 31.
53. *Ibid.*, 33–4.
54. *Ibid.*, 34.
55. *Ibid.*
56. *Ibid.*
57. *Ibid*, 35.
58. *Ibid.*, 36.
59. *Ibid.*
60. *Ibid.*
61. *Ibid.*
62. James, *Problems*, 51.
63. Michiko Yusa, "'*Persona Originalis': Jinkaku' and 'Personne',"' According to the Philosophies of Nishida Kitarō and Jacques Maritain*," Ph.D. Dissertation (University of California at Santa Barbara, 1983), 223. The quoted passage is Michiko Yusa's translation from Nishida's *Collected Works*, vol. XII, 290 (1938).
64. *Ibid.*, 230. Yusa's translation of Nishida, *Collected Works*, IX, 73.

65. From a letter written by Nishida to a "colleague" and member of Nishida's "inner circle," Mutai Risaku, on Dec. 21, 1944, and translated under my direction by Tom Hino (from *Collected Works*, Vol. 19, 2nd ed., 367–368).
66. Nishida Kitarō, *Intelligibility and the Philosophy of Nothingness* (reprint), tr. by Robert Schinzinger (Westport, Conn.: Greenwood Press, Publishers, 1973), 163 ff.
67. Yusa, "'*Persona Originalis*'" 202.
68. From a letter written by Nishida to a "colleague," Matsutsuna Doi, on Sept. 6, 1943, and translated under my direction by Tom Hino (from *Collected Works*, Vol. 19, 2nd ed., 258).
69. Nishida Kitarō, "The World as Identity of Absolute Contradiction," (1939), draft *MSS* translation by David A. Dilworth.
70. David A. Dilworth, *Introduction* to Nishida's *Last Writings: Nothingness and the Religious Worldview* (Honolulu: University of Honolulu Press, 1987), 3.
71. Yusa, "'*Persona Originalis*,'" 281.
72. David A. Dilworth, *Postscript* to *Last Writings*, 130.
73. David Dilworth, *Introduction* to *Last Writings*, 46.
74. Nakamura Hajime, *Ways of Thinking of Eastern Peoples: India-China-Tibet-Japan* (Honolulu: East-West Center Press, 1964), 350 ff.
75. Robert Schinzinger, "Introduction to 'The Unity of Opposites,'" in Nishida Kitaro, *Intelligibility*, 55.
76. Nishida Kitarō, "Active Intuition" (from *Collected Works*, Vol. VIII, 1937, 541–75), tr. David A. Dilworth, draft *MSS*, 1983, 9.
77. This version of text is allegedly taken from George Melhuish, *The Paradoxical Nature of Reality* (St. Vincent's Priory, Sion Hill, Bristol: St. Vincent's Press, 1973), and it appears in Patrick Hughes and George Brecht, *Vicious Circles and Infinity: Anthology of Paradoxes* (New York: Penguin Books, 1975), 69–70. The corresponding text in Melhuish's book (29–30) is actually quite different in form, although it is substantially the same. In any case, the Hughes-Brecht version is considerably clearer.
78. T.P. Kasulis, *Zen Action/Zen Purpose* (Honolulu: The University Press of Hawaii, 1981), 21.
79. *Ibid.*, 21–2.

Contributors

Sankari Prosad Banerjee (S. P. Banerjee) is Professor of Philosophy at the University of Calcutta where his academic career has been focused, and where he also received his Ph.D. (in Arts-Philosophy) in 1966. Dr. Banerjee has been a teacher of Philosophy for more than three decades, and was the Vice-Chancellor of the University of Burdwan for more than four years. He edited *Self, Knowledge and Freedom* with Ms. Shefali Mostra (Oxford University Press, 1984). His major field of interest is the Philosophy of Man with special reference to the social and political philosophy of contemporary India. Forty of his research articles have been published in major philosophical journals, in India and abroad, and several of these have been anthologized. He is presently engaged in writing *Philosophy and Social Change: An Indian Perspective*.

Nona R. Bolin teaches Philosophy at Memphis State University, Tennessee. She received a B.A. and M.A. in Philosophy/English at Memphis State University, and another M.A. as well as her Ph.D. in Philosophy from Vanderbilt University. Areas of specialization are Recent Continental, Aesthetics, Existentialism, and the Philosophy of Religion. Her current research includes: "The Untimely Arrival of the Postmodern," an invited paper for a conference on Postmodern Religion and Philosophy, at the University of Southern Mississippi, (1989); "Recent Movements in French Thought," an invited address to the Faculty Forum on Religion and Philosophy, De La Salle College, Manila, Philippines (July 1988); and "Deconstructing Ontotheological Discourse" in *God in Language*, eds., Robert P. Scharlemann and Gilbert E. M. Ogutu, Paragon House Publishers, 1987.

Emilie Zum Brunn is Director Emeritus of Research at the Centre National de la Recherche Scientifique in Paris. After a pedagogic and political career in Lausanne, Switzerland she did research work in theology and philosophy in Paris with two doctorates (3rd cycle and doctorat d'Etat). Her chief works are: *Le Dilemme de l'Etre et du Néant chez saint Augustin* (1969, 2nd ed. 1984), Engl. translation *St. Augustine. Being and Nothingness* (Paragon, 1986). E. Zum

Brunn *et al.*: *Dieu et l'Etre* (Etudes Augustiniennes, 1978), *Celui cui est* (Cerf, 1986), *Maitre Eckhart à Paris. Une critique medievale de l'ontotheologie* (PUF, 1986); E. Zum Brunn et Alain de Libera: *Maitre Eckhart. Metaphysique du Verbe et Theologie négative.* (Beauchesne, 1984) and Japanese translation by Omori (Kokubunsha, 85); Co-editor with A. de Libera and E. Weber of *L'Oeuvre latine de Maître Eckhart.* vol. I *Comm. Genèse et Prologues* (Cerf, 1984), vol. 6 *Comm. sur le Prologue de Jean* (1989) (Text of the German Forschungsgemeinschaft, French transl. and notes); With G. Epiney Burgarde *Femmes Troubadours de Dieu* (Brepols, 1988) Engl. transl. by Sheila Hughes: *Women Mystics in Medieval Europe* (Paragon, 1989).

Robert E. Carter is Professor of Philosophy at Trent University, Peterborough, Ontario, Canada, where he is also director of an interdisciplinary M.A. Program, Methodologies for the Study of Western History and Culture. Dr. Carter is a graduate of Tufts and Harvard Universities, and of the University of Toronto where he completed his Ph.D. in 1969. The author of *Dimensions of Moral Education* (University of Toronto Press, 1984, 1986), and *The Nothingness Beyond God: An Introduction to the Philosophy of Nishida Kitarō* (Paragon House, 1989), he is also a poet. *Wolf*, a book of poems, was published in 1988 (Edwin Mellen Press), and a second book of poetry, *The Damp Woods Greening* has just been completed. Winner of the Symons Award for excellence in teaching (1987) at Trent University in Peterborough, Canada, his academic interests include Eastern Philosophy, Ethics and Value Theory, Philosophy of Education, and contemporary Hermeneutics and Deconstruction.

Daniel Charles, received his State Doctorate under Professor Mikel Dufrenne *magna cum laude*, 1977. Involved in developing interdisciplinary programs at the masters levels in music, he was the founder of the Department of Music at Paris VIII in 1969; Chairman of this Department (1969–1981); and Dean of the Faculty of Arts at the University of Paris VIII (1981–1986). During the same period, he was Head of the Program of General Aesthetics at the Sorbonne (Department of Philosophy, University of Paris IV, 1970-1980). Now a Professor of Philosophy at the University of Nice, his conversations with John Cage have appeared in French (*Pour les Oiseaux*, 1976), and have been translated into Spanish, Italian, German, Japanese and English. His other publications include *Gloses sur Caoe*, 1978; *Le Temos de la Voix*, 1978; *Musik ist los*. 1979; *Musik und Vergessen*. 1984; *Poetik der Gleichzeitigkeit*. 1987. Another book in German is forthcoming: *Zeitspielraüme*, Berlin, 1989. Editor of 3 special numbers of *La Revue d'Esthétique (Musiques nouvelles*, 1968; *Musique présente. 1983; John Cage*, 1988), he is the author of 150 articles published in various reviews, in France as well as abroad, in the fields of General Aesthetics, XXth Century Arts, and Philosophy. Current interests include the contemporary development of Hermeneutics, and the post-WW II cross-fertilization in Philosophy and the Arts, East and West.

Ewert H. Cousins is a Professor, Theology Department, Fordham University, New York. He is the author of *Global Spirituality: Toward the Meeting of Mystical Paths* (Madras: University of Madras, 1985) and *Bonaventure and the Coincidence of Opposites* (Chicago: Franciscan Herald Press, 1978). He is general editor of "World Spirituality: An Encyclopedic History of the Religious Quest, 25 vols. New York: Crossroads, 1985). He is a specialist in medieval Christian Theology and spirituality and has been active in the Dialogue of World Religions.

Brian P. Gaybba is Professor of Divinity at Rhodesia University, Grahamstown, South Africa. He has recently published *The Spirit of Love* (Chapmans, 1987) and *Aspects of the Medieval Development of Theology* (Unisa, 1988). His academic interests revolve around the history of theology as a discipline and the attempt to rethink Christianity's doctrinal heritage as well as its relations to broader humanity by using love as a key-concept. Another interest is the influence of philosophy on theology. He is a member of several academic institutions and advisory bodies.

David J. Kalupahana is former chairman of the Department of Philosophy at the University of Hawaii, where he is presently Professor of Philosophy. Able to work with both Indian and Far Eastern sources, he has broadened considerably the foundations of scholarship and the understanding of early Buddhist philosophy. His books include *Causality: The Central Philosophy of Buddhism* (University Press of Hawaii, 1975), *Buddhist Philosophy (University Press of Hawaii, 1976), Nagarjuna: The Philosophy of the Middle Way* (State University of New York Press, SUNY Series in Buddhist Studies, 1986), and *The Principles of Buddhist Psychology* (State University of New York Press, SUNY Series in Buddhist Studies, 1987).

John R. Mayer is Professor of Philosophy at Brock University, in St. Catharines, Ont. His interests lie in Comparative Philosophy; he has been Visiting Professor at IIT, Bombay, Punjab University, Chandigarh, Kyoto University, and also taught in Changchun, China. His publications include articles on the *Bhagavad Gita, Jainism, the Ramayana*, Buddhist-Christian dialogue and Neoplatonism. In addition to his teaching career, he has been active as a World Federalist, in the Peace Movement, and as a federal candidate for the New Democratic party (1984, 1988) of Canada.

Pahalawattae D. Premasiri is Associate Professor of Philosophy at the University of Peradeniya, Sri Lanka. He has Bachelor's degrees from the University of Peradeniya, Sri Lanka, the University of Cambridge, England, a Master's degree from the University of Cambridge, England and a Ph.D. from the University of Hawaii. He was Fulbright visiting professor in the Department of Philosophy and Religion, Colby College, Waterville, Maine in 1988/89. He is the author of many learned articles in the *Sri Lanka Journal of the Humanities*, published by Peradeniya University, and has contributed a chapter on the 'Ethics of the Theravada Buddhist Tradition' to the New ERA publication *World Religions and Global Ethics*, edited by S. C. Crawford (Paragon House, 1989). His principal academic interests are Comparative Philosophy, Ethics, Philosophy of Religion, Value Theory, Buddhist Philosophy and Comparative Religion.

Sōiku Shigematsu is the head priest at the Shogen-ji temple in Japan, as well as a full-time professor of English at Shizuoka University. He is the author of *A Zen Forest: Sayings of the Masters* (1981); *Sun at Midnight*, with W. S. Merwin (1985); and *A Zen Harvest* (1988). As well, as an accomplished poet he has recently won the Jerome J. Shestack Prize for poetry, presented by the *American Poetry Review*.

Krishna Sivaraman is Professor Emeritus, Department of Religion, McMaster University and is currently Professor of Hindu Studies, Concordia University, Montreal, Quebec, Canada. Editor of *Hindu Spirituality*, vols. 6 and 7, (Crossroad-Continuum Press, New York), plus numerous other books and articles. A specialist in Comparative Religion, he teaches and researches in the area of Religious Studies, Hindu Philosophy, with a specialization in South Indian Religion and philosophy.

Ninian Smart is J. F. Rowny Professor of Comparative Religions at the University of California, Santa Barbara. He was the founding Chairman of England's first major department of Religious Studies at Lancaster University, where he was also for a time academic vice-president. He gave the Gifford Lectures in Edinburgh in 1979–80, and was editorial consultant for the BBC Television series *The Long Search*. His books include *Reasons and Faiths, Doctrine and Argument in Indian Philosophy, The Phenomenon of Christianity, The Science of Religion and the Sociology of Knowledge, Concept and Empathy, A Dialogue of Religions, The Philosophy of Religion, Mao, The Religious Experience of Mankind, Worldviews* and *The World's Religions*. With others he has edited *Sacred Texts of the World, Religion and Politics in the Contemporary World* and *Nineteenth Century Religious Thought in the West*, 3 vols. He has been president of the American Society for the Study of Religion and of the British Association for the History of Religions. He has been visiting professor for a term or more at Yale, Banaras Hindu, Wisconsin-Madison, Princeton, Otago (N.Z.), Queensland, Cape Town and Harvard Universities. He was educated at S.O.A.S. and Oxford, and served three years in the British Army, in which he was a Captain in the Intelligence Corps.

Huston Smith is Thomas J. Watson Professor of Religion and Distinguished Adjunct Professor of Philosophy, Emeritus, Syracuse University; earlier appointments included Washington University in Saint Louis and fifteen years as professor of philosophy at M.I.T. Author of more than sixty articles in popular and professional journals, his six books include *The Religions of Man, Forgotten Truth*, and *Beyond the Post-Modern Mind*. His trilogy of documentary films on Hinduism, Buddhism, and Islam have all won international awards, and his discovery of the ability of certain specially trained Tibetan lamas to sing multiphonically led to a Folkways Record, "The Music of Tibet." He currently resides in Berkeley, California.

Manfred H. Vogel is professor of religion at Northwestern University, Evanston, Illinois. He is the author of *In Quest of A Theology of Budais* (University Press of America 1987) and *Feurbach's Philosophy of the Future* (Bobbs Merrill 1966). His fields of interest are the philosophy of religion, modern Jewish thought and the Jewish-Christian dialogue.

R. J. Zwi Werblowsky is Martin Buber Professor of Comparative Religion at the Hebrew University of Jerusalem where he also served as Dean of the Faculty of Humanities and Chairman of the Department of History of Jewish Thought. He has held Visiting Professorships in many countries and continents (e.g., U.S.A.:

Chicago, Harvard, Yale, Stanford; Japan: Kokugakuin, Todai, Tsukuba). From 1975–85 he was Secretary-General of the International Association for the History of Religions, and still serves as co-editor of its Journal *Numen* and from 1984–88, Vice-President of the International Council for Philosophy and the Humanistic Studies of UNESCO. He has published in the fields of East Asian religions as well as medieval Christian and Jewish mysticism. Among his books is ***Beyond Tradition and Modernity: Changing Religions in a Changing World*** (Athlone Press, London, 1976).

Index

F

M

O

P

Q

R

S

T

V

W

Y